Advance Praise

"A must-read for anyone interested in working as a coach! *Becoming a Professional Life Coach* provides an evidence-based overview of the history of coaching, along with the underlying theories, best practices, and latest advancements in the profession. This book is a comprehensive, easy-to-read guide to becoming a competent coach that is the cornerstone of our coaching program."

—**Dr. Ellen Neiley Ritter**, BCC, dean of students, Institute for Life Coach Training

"This book is solidly in the top five I have recommended to the thousands of coaches my company and I have trained. Why? Because it teaches the essence of coaching presence, mindset, and skills in such a practical and applied manner. There are lots of examples, exercises, and dialogues, and all are grounded in a foundation of behavioral science. Beyond that, it is a rich storehouse for the coach's own personal growth and development."

—**Michael Arloski**, PhD, PCC, NBC-HWC, founder and CEO, Real Balance Global Wellness

"*Becoming a Professional Life Coach* goes straight to the heart of what it takes to become a masterful coach. It blends the art and the science, the practical and the inspirational. It is a definitive text for coach training and a go-to for those engaging in their essential personal development of new capacities for 'beingness.'"

—**Fran Fisher**, Master Certified Coach, recipient of the ICF 2022 Circle of Distinction Award

"This third edition of *Becoming a Professional Life Coach* really does focus on the art and science of a whole-person approach. Patrick Williams and Diane Menendez are to be congratulated for authoring a comprehensive book on the multifaceted aspects of life coaching—from the fundamentals and basics to facilitating the client in achieving their goals and attaining personal fulfilment. Many coaches will find the techniques very useful for themselves, too!"

—**Stephen Palmer**, PhD, president of the International Society for Coaching Psychology

BECOMING A
PROFESSIONAL
LIFE COACH

BECOMING A
PROFESSIONAL
LIFE COACH

3 RD EDITION

THE ART AND SCIENCE OF A
WHOLE-PERSON APPROACH

PATRICK WILLIAMS
DIANE S. MENENDEZ

Norton Professional Books

An Imprint of W. W. Norton & Company
Celebrating a Century of Independent Publishing

For information about permission to reproduce selections from this book, write to Permissions, W. W. Norton & Company, Inc., 500 Fifth Avenue, New York, NY 10110

For information about special discounts for bulk purchases, please contact W. W. Norton Special Sales at specialsales@wwnorton.com or 800-233-4830

Manufacturing by Versa Press
Production manager: Gwen Cullen

ISBN: 978-1-324-03093-5

W. W. Norton & Company, Inc., 500 Fifth Avenue, New York, NY 10110
www.wwnorton.com

W. W. Norton & Company Ltd., 15 Carlisle Street, London W1D 3BS

1 2 3 4 5 6 7 8 9 0

We dedicate this third edition to all our teachers, mentors, coaches, and students who have been part of the evolution of the coaching profession and our continuing personal and professional evolutions as well.

CONTENTS

Acknowledgments   xi
Introduction   xiii

Part I: Coaching Fundamentals   1
Chapter 1: Listening as a Coach   3
Chapter 2: The Language of Coaching   18
Chapter 3: Coaching as a Developmental Change Process   72

Part II: Beyond the Basics   125
Chapter 4: Empowering the Client   127
Chapter 5: Stretching the Client   145
Chapter 6: Creating Momentum with the Client   165
Chapter 7: Coaching the Whole Client: Mind, Body, Emotions, Spirit   175

Part III: Coaching from the Inside Out   205
Chapter 8: The Power of Purpose   211
Chapter 9: Design Your Life   226
Chapter 10: What Gets in Your Way?   242
Chapter 11: Steering Your Life by True North   262
Chapter 12: Walk the Talk   278
Chapter 13: Play Full Out   294
Chapter 14: How Wealthy Are You?   312
Chapter 15: Mind-Set Is Causative   326
Chapter 16: Love Is All We Need   348

Appendix A: Reflections on Coaching and Post-Pandemic Global Stress   367
Appendix B: Emotions in Coaching   369
Appendix C: The Importance of Professional Coaching Competencies   375
References   376
Index   387

ACKNOWLEDGMENTS

The profession of coaching continues to evolve, impacting how people benefit from this unique relationship, in the areas of health, wealth, love, and happiness. I continue to marvel at the path of my own career and how my coaching skills have developed from the early days of the field. I am very proud of how the Institute for Life Coach Training—cocreated in 1998—continues to thrive today under the stewardship of Ellen Ritter, PhD.

To my coauthor Diane Menendez: Thanks for nurturing my original vision of this book and assisting with the content, quality, and depth of the various editions. I am the coach (and mentor and teacher) I am today because of the thousands of students and colleagues who have used my books, programs, and more in their own paths to becoming masterful coaches. This text and the readers who benefit from it are a big part of my living legacy, and a testament to the part coaching can play in improving the lives of people across the globe.

Patrick Williams
November 2022

ACKNOWLEDGMENTS

INTRODUCTION

Coaching continues to evolve as a profession that is changing the way people get help by improving their lives and their business. It is a profession that is more needed than ever, as remote learning and working becomes more prevalent, and in light of the constant change that accompanies world events. This third edition will include many changes and updated information on coaching as it is today. Our stance is still that all coaching is life coaching if you coach the person, not the problem (Reynolds, 2020). There are many specialties now in coaching that often require some special knowledge of the coach, but we don't want coaching to be purely problem solving or advice giving. New ideas, insights and revelations come to the client if we focus on who they are with the current situation, and who they want and need to become for the desired change to manifest. Coaching is a partnering conversation where clients have the opportunity to explore new thoughts and say what they might not normally express out loud, all with a committed listener (the coach). Coaching as a process is exploratory and insightful. It is a cocreative method in which the coach partners with a client who wishes to better navigate change (chosen or unchosen). All change must eventually become chosen, and coaching conversations with a trained professional coach allow for deeper exploration of any transition the client may be experiencing. These conversations help to solidify who the client is becoming and uncover what is emerging next for them.

LIFE COACHING AS AN OPERATING SYSTEM

Personal and professional coaching, which has emerged as a powerful and personalized career in the last few decades, has shifted the paradigm of how people who seek help with life transitions find a professional to partner with them in designing their desired future. No matter what kind of subspecialty a coach might have, life coaching is the basic operating system: a whole-person, client-centered approach. Coaching the client's whole life is the operating system working in the background. A client may seek creative or business coaching, leadership development, or a more balanced life, but all coaching is life coaching. Before 1990, there was little mention of coaching except in corporate culture. Mentoring and executive coaching were resources that many top managers and CEOs utilized, either informally from a colleague or formally by hiring a consultant or psychologist who became their executive coach. We later elaborate on the history of coaching but, for now, let us examine why life coaching is becoming more popular and prevalent. The International Coach Federation (ICF) was founded in 1992 but did not have a real presence until its first convention in 1996. The ICF has kept detailed archives of media coverage on coaching since the early 1990s. Two newspaper articles appeared in 1993, four in 1994 (including one from Australia), and seven in 1995. Most articles appeared in publications in the United States. Then, in 1996, a huge increase in publicity occurred, with more than 60 articles, television interviews, and radio shows on the topic of coaching. Every year since then, media coverage has increased to hundreds of articles as well as live media coverage in countries such as the United States, Europe, Australia, Canada, Japan, and Singapore. This coverage has comprised both national and local radio and television, including *Good Morning America*, *Today*, CNBC, the BBC, and other outlets around the globe. In print, the only books written about coaching before the 1990s were geared toward corporate and performance coaching. Good, solid books about life coaching and all its specialties are now becoming numerous, including some recent national bestsellers. As of this writing, there are over 50,000 certified coaches in over 150 countries who are members of the International Coach Federation. Understanding the history of coaching provides current and prospective life coaches with a framework for understanding their profession, as well as insight into future opportunities. This framework also helps life coaches place themselves squarely within the larger context of a profession that is still evolving. Casting our eyes across the diverse landscape of coaching today reveals that the profession is global, widely known, and full of specializations and diverse ways for people to access coaching.

Anyone who reads a book with this much content must be aware that to put these lessons into practical use often requires a more formal learning structure. When I created the Institute for Life Coach Training (ILCT), it was the twelfth recognized coach training program globally, and now, there are thousands.

Much of the earlier versions of this text were based on many years of our coach training and now it has evolved even further.

For a very comprehensive and scholarly history of coaching's evolution as a unique profession and the influential tributaries that flowed to it, please note Dr. Vikki Brock's *Sourcebook of Coaching History*.

THE ROOTS OF LIFE COACHING

Coaching has a unique paradigm, but it's not new in its sources, theory, and strategies. Much of the foundation of coaching goes back many decades and even centuries. The draw of pursuing life improvement, personal development, and the exploration of meaning began with early Greek society. This is reflected in Socrates's famous quote, "The unexamined life is not worth living." Since that time, we have developed many ways of examining our lives, some useful and some not; some are grounded in theory and are evidence based, while others are made up and useless. What persists, however, is that people who are not in pursuit of basic human needs such as food and shelter do begin to pay attention to higher needs such as self-actualization, fulfillment, and spiritual connection. In ancient Greece, as now, people have always had an intense desire to explore and find personal meaning. Coaching today is seen as a new phenomenon, yet its foundations can be found in modern psychology and philosophy. Coaching is a new field that borrows from and builds on theories and research from related fields that have come before it. As such, coaching is a multidisciplinary, multi-theory synthesis and application of applied behavioral change. Coach training schools today, both private and academic, must be clear about their theoretical underpinnings and the philosophy that supports what they teach. From its inception, ILCT declared that its intention was to have a content-rich, theoretically based curriculum equivalent to a graduate-level education. Because the original participant base consisted of helping professionals—therapists, counselors, psychologists, industrial-organizational practitioners, and psychiatrists—they knew that they needed to discuss participants' common and varied education, the impact of psychology and philosophy on coaching practice, and coaching's use of adult learning models. The curriculum that emerged was written by and for therapists transitioning into coaching. It has since expanded in its reach to other aligned helping professionals who have a similar educational background and a psychological orientation for achieving greater human potential.

Contributions from Psychology

So, what has the field of psychology brought to coaching, and what are the major influences? There have been four major forces in psychological theory since the emergence of psychology as a social science in 1879. These four forces are Freudian, behavioral, humanistic, and transpersonal. In recent years there have been three other forces at work, which we believe are adaptations or evolutions of the original four. Cognitive–behavioral psychology grew from a mix of the behavioral and humanistic schools. Positive psychology utilizes cognitive–behavioral approaches and repositions many of the theories that humanistic psychology emphasizes: a non-mechanistic view and a view of possibility as opposed to pathology as an essential approach to the client. Along with each revolution in psychology, a changing image of human nature has also evolved. Psychology began as the investigation of consciousness and mental functions such as sensation and perception. *Webster's New World Dictionary* defines psychology as "(a) the science dealing with the mind and with mental and emotional processes, and (b) the science of human and animal behavior." Much of the early influence on psychology came from the philosophical tradition, and early psychologists adopted the practice of introspection used by philosophers. The practice of introspection into one's desires, as well as noticing and observing behaviors, thoughts, and emotions, are core practices for increasing client awareness and are cornerstones of a whole person approach to coaching.

Introspectionists were an early force in psychology. Wilhelm Wundt in Germany and Edward Titchener in the United States were two of the early defenders of introspection as a method of understanding the workings of the human mind. But they soon realized the inadequacies of introspection in validating the young science of psychology. Consciousness and mental functioning were difficult to study objectively. Psychology was experiencing growing pains then, much as coaching is today.

Psychology's Major Theorists

What follows is a quick tour of the growth of psychology and how its major thinkers set the stage for the coaching revolution. William James was the father of American psychology. James preferred ideas to laboratory results and is best known for his writing on consciousness and his view that humans can experience higher states of consciousness. He wrote on such diverse topics as functions of the brain, perception of space, psychic and paranormal faculties, religious ecstasy, will, attention, and habit. He gradually drifted away from psychology and in his later life emphasized philosophy, changing his title at Harvard University to "professor of philosophy." Nevertheless, James had a tremendous influence on the growth of the psychology profession, and he is still widely read today. One of his most historic books, *The Varieties of Religious Experience* (James, 1902/1994), is a treatise that offers much on the topics of spirituality and transpersonal consciousness. Sigmund Freud influenced the first force in psychology, the Freudian approach. While psychology in the United States was struggling for an identity and striving for recognition by the scientific community, European psychology was being reshaped by Freud's theories. He created a stir in the medical community with his ideas and theories, and finally gained acceptance in psychiatry with the "talking cure" breakthrough—psychoanalysis. Freud brought us such terms as unconscious, id, ego, and superego, and ideas such as the unconscious, transference, countertransference, defense mechanisms, and resistance. His theories, although strongly based in pathology, allowed the pursuit of our unconscious desires and subconscious mechanisms that influenced behavior, and they soon began to gain acceptance in the United States as well.

As Freudian thought was taking shape in Europe and the United States, William James and others began to focus on measurable behavior. Many American psychologists began to combat Freudian theories as another nonverifiable, subjective pseudoscience of the mind. The time was ripe for the emergence of behaviorism as the second major force in psychology, led by B. F. Skinner and John Watson. Hundreds of years previously, Shakespeare had commented, "What a piece of work is a man!" The behaviorists took this literally and looked upon humans in the early 20th century as *Homo Mechanicus*, an object to be studied as any machine. *Homo Mechanicus* was a machine whose mind was ignored. In the 1950s, Abraham Maslow and Carl Rogers initiated the third force in psychology, humanistic psychology, which focused on the personal, ontological, and phenomenological aspects of human experience, as opposed to the mechanistic and reductionist theories of Freudianism and behaviorism. Maslow eventually posited the fourth force, transpersonal psychology, which included mind, body, and spirit. It delved into altered states of consciousness that were naturally induced by esoteric practices and drug induced by LSD (see the works of Stan Grof, Timothy Leary, and Richard Alpert, a.k.a. Baba Ram Dass) and other hallucinogens as a way to explore the transpersonal realm. This research began to open our knowledge of the human mind and expand our windows of perception and possibility. Carl Jung introduced symbolism, ancient wisdom, the spiritual archetypes, life reviews, synchronicity, transpersonal consciousness, stages of life, individuation, the shadow (both good and bad), and spiritual quests. Jung broke away from Freud in pursuing a more holistic, spiritual understanding of human motivation. He is quoted as saying, "Who looks outside dreams . . . who looks inside awakens." That is a powerful quote for coaching today. ILCT emphasizes an approach to clients that must include examining their developmental stage or orientation as part of the coach's working alliance with the client. Alfred Adler (1927/1998) worked on social connections, humans as social beings, the importance of relationships, family-of-origin themes, significance and belonging, lifestyle assessment, the big question ("What if?"), and "acting as if."

Roberto Assagioli, the father of psychosynthesis, wrote about our ability to synthesize our various aspects to function at higher levels of consciousness. He introduced such concepts as subpersonalities, wisdom of the inner self, higher self, and the observing self. Karen Horney was an early, influential feminist psychiatrist. Her key theories involved irrational beliefs, the need for security, early influences on rational-emotive theory, and modeling the goal of "self-help." She was a contemporary of Adler's and an early influence on Carl Rogers. Fritz Perls, founder of Gestalt therapy, worked with personality problems involving the inner conflict between values and behavior (desires), introducing terms such as top dog, underdog, polarity (black-and-white thinking), the empty chair technique, and awareness in the moment. Gestalt theory also valued the whole-person experience of the client, including mind, emotions, physicality, and spirituality. Perls was influenced by Kurt Lewin's change theory and his work in figure-ground perspectives. Carl Rogers developed a client-centered approach that suggested clients have the answers within them. He brought us the terms "unconditional positive regard" and "humanistic psychology." He introduced the practice of listening, reflecting, and paraphrasing and the value of silence and sacred space. Empathic listening was key to Rogers; it is also key for the profession of coaching.

Abraham Maslow introduced his hierarchy of needs and values. He reflected on being needs versus deficiency needs, the higher self, and transpersonal potential. He is considered the father of humanistic psychology and transpersonal psychology. Maslow, although often credited with the Hierarchy of Needs Pyramid, did not really create such a pyramid. That was done by management consultants in the 1960s. But Maslow's research on self-actualization and *being needs* versus *deficit needs* continues to influence coaching theory today (Kaufman, 2020). Virginia Satir was the mother of family therapy, sometimes called the "Columbus of family therapy." She believed that a healthy family life involved an open and reciprocal sharing of affection, feelings, and love. She was well known for describing family roles—such as the rescuer, the victim, and the placater—that function to constrain relationships and interactions in families. Her work was an early systemic look at relationships and one that has had a strong influence on coaching in the business context. Viktor Frankl developed logotherapy out of his personal experience during World War II. Influenced by existential philosophy and his own existential crisis, Frankl wrote *Man's Search for Meaning* while in a Nazi prison camp and later published it from notes he had made on toilet paper. He is quoted as saying that the one freedom that could not be taken from him while in prison was his mind and his freedom to think, dream, and create. Frankl introduced paradoxical intent into psychology—"what you resist persists" or "what you give energy to is what you manifest." Coaches today help their clients focus on what they want and on creating desired outcomes. Frankl is cited by coaches as an exemplar of the importance of intention as well as the necessity of finding meaning in work and life. Milton Erickson investigated hypnotherapy, as well as linguistics and the double-binding of the client. From his work we learn to focus on possibility and looking for the uncommon approach to change, including paradoxical behaviors. Erickson is the father of American hypnotherapy and, along with Gregory Bateson, an early influencer of neuro-linguistic programming (NLP) created by Richard Bandler and John Grinder and popularized by Tony Robbins. Jeffrey Zeig and Bill O'Hanlon, students of Erickson, introduced pattern interruption, the confusion technique, forced choice, assumption of the positive path, nontrance hypnosis, and unconscious competence. Reframing is another important coaching tool based in their work. We're certain that most coaches use reframing to shift a client's view of a situation. In the 1970s, solution-focused approaches emerged that emphasized less focus on the problem and instead putting energy into discovering what works. Three well-known practitioners in this arena are the late Insoo Kim Berg and her husband, the late Steve de Shazer, and Bill O'Hanlon. O'Hanlon developed solution-oriented therapy, which has now been reframed as solution-focused coaching. Berg, along with Peter Szabó, wrote *Brief Coaching for Lasting Solutions* (2005), which blends solution-focused theory and brief, short-term coaching sessions. Fernando Flores is a philosopher who took the work of J. L. Austin and John Searle on speech act theory and applied it to human interaction through conversations. By exploring how language really brings action into being, Flores inadvertently devised one of the most useful coaching tools: making requests. Flores was the early influencer of Werner Erhard and his Erhard Seminars Training (est), which later became Landmark Education and influenced Thomas Leonard's early curriculum at Coach U.

Martin Seligman promoted positive psychology as a strength-based approach to human fulfillment. Positive psychology is applied to therapy as well as coaching and education. Its consistent focus is on building and using strengths rather than weaknesses. Seligman's work is highly useful to coaches, as he focused on intense use of current academic research to back up theories. Positive psychology has evolved as an entire movement. Life coaching can be viewed as applied positive psychology. In addition to the theorists discussed here, a vast array of research into life span developmental psychology has created an understanding of developmental trajectories that can be helpful to coaches. Daniel Levinson's early work on the life development of Harvard graduates over their 50-year life span yielded great insight into men's development within that age cohort. Carol Gilligan's work on girls and women created insights into the ways women's thinking and behavior differs from men's over the life span. Robert Kegan developed theories and methods for assessing the development of levels of consciousness in human life span development. Ken Wilber's integral approaches to psychology and life built on and went beyond the transpersonal approaches. In essence, his integral psychology examines all the various therapies that exist and then plugs them into the developmental levels for which they are most appropriate. For example, Freudian psychology is most relevant to disorders that occur in early childhood (ages two to seven). Jungian psychology is best suited to existential issues of early adulthood, most of which are seldom addressed until midlife. Transpersonal therapies are best for people who have healthy ego structures but sense the absence of higher meaning in their lives. Wilber synthesized the developmental models of several leading psychologists, including Freud, Piaget, Erikson, Kohlberg, and Bandura for early development, and then added Jung, Gilligan, Aurobindo, Washburn, Kegan, Fowler, Underhill, and dozens of others to produce a developmental model that incorporates every stage from birth up to total, nondual enlightenment. These and other amazing tools that have grown out of modern psychology support coaches in helping clients change directions as desired. As research in positive psychology shows, new developments become available every day.

A hallmark of coaching is its synthesis of tools from other fields, as well as its proclivity for innovation. With current research, coaching is developing its own evidence-based theories. It has borrowed from what has gone before, just as psychologists borrowed from philosophers. As coaching grows as a profession, it is developing its own focused research base of effective strategies and tools within the unique relationship that is the coaching alliance. Our profession is strongly grounded in sound academic and scholarly theories that preceded coaching, and it will be strengthened by the validation of theories and evidence-based research as we move forward.

The Influence of Positive Psychology

In general, people have referred to psychology as a single term with the unspoken and assumed understanding that it was about pathology. Then in 1998, the term positive psychology emerged. This became newsworthy when Martin E. P. Seligman, president of the American Psychological Association (APA), formally introduced academia and the world to the term. His address to the Annual APA Conference was titled, "Building Human Strength: Psychology's Forgotten Mission." In this address he announced he had created a task force to set the groundwork for positive psychology: That is, a reoriented science that emphasizes the understanding and building of the most positive qualities of an individual: optimism, courage, work ethic, future-mindedness, interpersonal skill, the capacity for pleasure and insight, and social responsibility. It's my belief that since the end of World War II, psychology has moved too far away from its original roots, which were to make the lives of all people more fulfilling and productive, and too much toward the important, but not all-important, area of curing mental illness. With Seligman's address there was a major acknowledgment and repositioning within psychology. This shift focused on illuminating and defining the "good life." In fact, the addition of the word positive to this new initiative effectively acknowledged that in their quest to treat pathology, most practitioners in the field had overlooked a large portion of the population functioning at a healthy level but nevertheless with a strong desire to improve their life experiences.

Two years later, in their introduction to the 2000 millennial edition of the *American Psychologist*, Seligman and Mihaly Csikszentmihalyi wrote:

> We have scant knowledge of what makes life worth living. Psychology has come to understand quite a bit about how people survive and endure under conditions of adversity. But we know very little about how normal people flourish under more benign conditions. Psychology has, since World War II, become a science largely about healing. It concentrates on repairing damage within a disease model of human functioning. This almost exclusive attention to pathology neglects the fulfilled individual and the thriving community. The aim of positive psychology is to begin to catalyze a change in the focus of psychology from preoccupation only with repairing the worst things in life to also building positive qualities. The field of positive psychology at the subjective level is about valued subjective experience: well-being, contentment, and satisfaction (past), hope and optimism (future), and flow and happiness (present). At the individual level it is about positive individual traits—the capacity for love and vocation, courage, interpersonal skill, aesthetic sensibility, perseverance, forgiveness, originality, future-mindedness, spirituality, high talent, and wisdom. At the group level it is about the civic virtues and the institutions that move individuals toward better citizenship: responsibility, nurturance, altruism, civility, moderation, tolerance, and work ethic.

With Seligman's commitment to the research of positive psychology and his support to build a body of knowledge about what makes life fulfilling, psychology was beginning to return to its original meaning: the study of the spirit or soul. This dedication to scientific research strengthened what so many psychologists, psychotherapists, counselors, coaches, and people in the general public believed but had not proven, namely that individuals wanted to continuously grow, be happy, and have a fulfilling life. Seligman has a long history of doing research in psychology beginning in the 1960s. His study of what constitutes the "good life" and happiness was presented in *Authentic Happiness* (2002). He asserted that positive psychology is based on three pillars: the study of positive emotions, the study of positive traits and virtues, and the study of positive institutions. For his book, Seligman reviewed and summarized volumes of seminal research in positive psychology by Ed Diener, Chris Peterson, Lisa Aspinwall, Sandy Murray, Sonja Lyubomirsky, Thomas Joiner, George Vaillant, Barbara Fredrickson, and Mihaly Csikszentmihalyi, to name a few. Besides being abundant, many of these research studies were also cross-cultural, which added credibility and applicability to the findings. What emerged from these studies were three basic findings that predicted an increased sense of satisfaction and gratification in the lives of adults. The findings that supported increased fulfillment in life were being in a stable romantic relationship, making a living from a vocation or calling versus just having a job, and believing in something larger or greater than oneself. Interestingly, the research also showed that there was no significant correlation between wealth, health, or education and authentic happiness. As a way of researching individuals' traits, beliefs, and sense about many aspects of life, Seligman and his colleagues have created numerous surveys and questionnaires to gather data on a variety of topics related to happiness, signature strengths and well-being and have made them readily available. A sampling of these assessments, which can be found online (https://www.authentichappiness.sas.upenn.edu/), include:

- Authentic Happiness Inventory; measures overall happiness
- General Happiness scale; assesses enduring happiness
- Grit Survey; measures perseverance
- Optimism Test; measures optimism about the future
- Values in Action (VIA) Survey of Character Strengths; measures 24 character strengths
- Work–Life Questionnaire; measures work–life satisfaction
- Compassionate Love Scale; measures a person's tendency to support and understand others
- Meaning in Life Questionnaire; measures meaningfulness

These assessments provide ongoing data that add to our understanding of the factors, practices and attitudes that make life meaningful, happy, and fulfilling and therefore allow individuals to flourish. These assessments are available for anyone and provide personalized information about individual results. At the same time, each person taking an assessment becomes part of the research data pool that is informing positive psychology. Prior to Seligman's announcement of positive psychology, there was research being done on positive emotions. In the 1980s Barbara Fredrickson, then a doctoral student and now known as "the genius of the positive psychology movement," chose to study positive emotions, such as joy, happiness, gratitude, hope and love. This research demonstrated that positive emotions transform the future by bringing out the best in people and enabling individuals to build their resources. It also suggested "the capacity to experience positive emotions may be a fundamental human strength central to the study of human flourishing."

Some Differences Between Positive Psychology and Coaching

The research in positive psychology has confirmed many of the beliefs and operating principles of coaching: people want to live a fulfilling, good life; people want to utilize their strengths, skills and talents; people want to be more positive and eschew negativity; people want meaningful relationships; people want careers or work that allows them to develop; and people want to make a positive difference in the world. Still the question sometimes remains: what is different? Is the emphasis of each field the same? In his chapter in the *Handbook of Positive Psychology* (Snyder & Lopez, 2002), Seligman states, "the aim of positive psychology is to catalyze a change in psychology . . . (and) we must bring the building of strength to the forefront in the treatment and prevention of mental illness" (p. 3). Throughout this chapter he makes the case that positive psychology may prevent "many of the major emotional disorders" (p. 5) and he believes that positive psychology "will become an even more effective approach to psychotherapy" (p. 6). From this perspective the emphasis of the practice of positive psychology is on prevention and treatment, which puts it in the medical model of diagnosing and fixing something that isn't working properly. This emphasis leads to the professional or service provider being an authority and the consumer being someone that looks to the authority for answers. In coaching the emphasis is on the client as the designer and creator of his or her life.

From this perspective, the client is viewed as the expert on his or her life and is believed to be competent, capable, creative, and resourceful. At the same time, the coach is the expert on the coaching process only. This means that the coach's responsibility is to discover, clarify, and align with what the client wants to achieve, encourage client self-discovery, elicit client-generated strategies and ideas, and hold the client responsible and accountable. Through the process of coaching, clients deepen their learning, improve their performance, and enhance their quality of life. Thus, coaching is a learning and developmental model with an emphasis on creating awareness so that clients can choose outcomes that promote their growth and development while attaining what they believe are the qualities of a fulfilling life. In the positive psychology literature, authors frequently refer to what they do as "interventions." Several dictionaries define intervention as "(1) the act of intervening, interfering, or interceding with the intent of modifying the outcome; (2) when someone becomes involved in a particular situation, issue, problem, etc. to influence what happens." This means that the professionals believe they know what is right or appropriate for an individual and will step in and tell him or her what to do to change their situation. Additionally, this means that the patient (the term frequently used in the medical model) is viewed as needing directives and advice. The practitioner thus has a vested interest in the outcome. Adhering to the precepts of excellence in coaching, coaches do not make interventions because they do not offer advice. Coaches believe that clients contain all their answers within themselves and that the coach's job is the assist the client to discover those answers, gifts, talents, and strengths. The form of discovery used in coaching is based on the Socratic method. This means that coaches support and challenge their clients' thinking and actions by using deep listening, powerful questioning, and direct communication of what is being noticed and perceived so that awareness is increased. Therefore, clients are better able to make informed choices as they design the steps they will take to achieve what they want. Although some people want to minimize the differences between positive psychology's approach and coaching's approach when working with clients, these differences are important. Coaching is not psychotherapy and coaches do not perform as psychotherapists, nor do they want to. Coaching education stresses the important differences between these two fields and continuously mentors and supervises its students to stay consistently within the coaching frame. Furthermore, coaches encourage clients to get assistance from other professions when needed. In fact, the ICF's Core Competencies clearly state: "Core Competency #1: Demonstrates Ethical Guidelines and Professional Standards—(6) (The coach) maintains the distinctions between coaching, consulting, psychotherapy, and other support professions (7) (The coach) refers clients to other support professionals, as appropriate." Therefore, it is paramount to the integrity of the coaching profession and its coaches to continuously uphold the differences between the various professions so that clients can clearly choose the service that they desire and is best for them. (We thank and acknowledge our colleague, Lynn Meinke, for the context on positive psychology,) Alex Linley, a prominent researcher of positive psychology, calls it a win-win for management and employees. Who would not be attracted to a protocol and strategy, he reasons, that motivates employees to work more diligently and productively while also remaining loyal to the company because the company has improved the quality of its working conditions? In an interview he stated, "Positive psychology speaks to the important bottom lines of profit and productivity. And yet, concurrently, it also speaks to employee welfare." That is a product of a coaching approach incorporating principles of positive psychology.

THE FUTURE OF COACHING

One additional thought: We have noticed that as we gain more training and experience in working with clients, it is not so much that our skills and competencies change as that our "beingness" and our spirits as coaches reach a different level. Mastery is more about who you are than what you do or say. Research in the field of psychotherapy has repeatedly found that the relationship between the therapist and client is the most important ingredient in client success. The therapeutic approach or technique is less important than the ability of the therapist to create and maintain a strong relationship and an environment of trust and confidence. That is mastery! Where could you use some training? What new skill, technique, or personal strength would you like to master? Go for it. We all will benefit.

We are on the verge of a fundamental shift in how and why people seek helpers. We believe psychotherapy has played an important role in the lives of many clients and will still be needed in our society, especially for the seriously mentally ill. We also believe coaching will become a prevailing strategy for personal development—the most common way to learn to identify strengths and use them to overcome obstacles and challenges while pursuing possibilities. People today need connection with a mentor, coach, or guide more than ever before due to the rapid pace of change, the difficulty of sustaining relationships, and the desire to fulfill one's life purpose. We believe this is what the human potential movement of the 1970s intended. Psychological research and theory over the past few decades have contributed much to our understanding of how people change, how they adjust to life's struggles, and how they develop into self-actualized human beings. That knowledge now lends itself to this new field of life coaching, without the medical model stigma and diagnostic labeling that often comes with psychological counseling or therapy. Being able to receive coaching and have a personal coach, whether privately hired or provided by your company or community agency, is a service that we hope becomes ubiquitous and transformational to individuals and our culture. We believe that the profession of coaching will soon be bigger than psychotherapy. The public will know the distinction between therapy and coaching and will be clear on when to seek a therapist and when to seek a coach. Coaches will refer to therapists and therapists will refer to coaches. Coaching will permeate society and be available to everyone, not just executives and high-powered professionals. We expect to see a variety of specialized coaches, such as relationship coaches, parenting and family coaches, wellness and health coaches, spiritual development coaches, and career coaches. The entire profession will foster the idea of life coaching as the umbrella under which all coaching rests. Whether a client seeks specific coaching for business or job challenges, coaching for a life transition (such as a relationship change or health issues), or for pure life-design coaching, it is all life coaching. A coach may also serve as a referral source for specialty coaching as needed or requested by a client. The coaching profession is experiencing dynamic growth and change. It will no doubt continue to interact developmentally with social, economic, and political processes; draw on the knowledge base of diverse disciplines; enhance its intellectual and professional maturity; and proceed to establish itself internationally as well as in mainstream North America. If these actions represent the future of coaching, then the profession will change in ways that support viability and growth. Life coaching exists because it is helpful, and it will prosper because it can be transformational.

In the chapters that follow, we share the specific ways that coaching can bring about transformation in the lives of clients, as we have been teaching them at ILCT since 1998. As you read, you will be joining the thousands of highly trained coaches—as well as thousands of others with quality coaching education—who are now coaching all around the world.

Transformational versus Transactional Coaching

As you read and digest the Coaching from the Inside Out chapters, keep in mind that the intent is to add to the concept of whole life coaching and to encourage coaching conversations that are more transformational than transactional. In other words, we don't want to only emphasize measurable goals and outcomes with the client. Rather, we want to focus on *who* they need to be and *how* they need to change for what they want to emerge. Transformational coaching encompasses the concept of going deeper in the work with the client: coaching the person, not the problem (Reynolds, 2020). It is like snorkeling in beautiful, calm waters: when you put on your snorkel gear and look just below the surface, there is the untold beauty of a coral reef and fish of many colors and characteristics. For some, the first time they snorkel is scary. Breathing is a bit different and looking under the water's surface can be thrilling or unnerving. Going deeper in coaching is not scuba diving to eighty feet; it is only looking under the surface for what can be revealed, shared, and contextualized with the challenges or intentions that are present. In Dr. Pat's mentor coaching, he teaches skills in listening and posing evocative questions that encourage the client to go inside—to notice how they are reacting, learning, or feeling curious about what is emerging in the coaching conversation. Coaches may ask, "What are you learning as you share this challenge?" "How are you changing or how do you need to change?" "How will you be when this future state is achieved?" Transactional coaching is more formulaic and outcome focused. An example would be committing to diet and exercise changes: what did the client do and did they make progress? Or, if they are transitioning to a new job, what have they done and what else is needed to accomplish the change? Not all coaching can be transformational; however, if you go deeper with the client, you may get to the true *why* for the goals they wish to meet. Transactional coaching is more about the *doing*, while transformational coaching includes the *being* of the client.

BECOMING A
PROFESSIONAL
LIFE COACH

PART I

Coaching Fundamentals

The three chapters included in Part I, "Coaching Fundamentals," lay the groundwork for an understanding of coaching as a profession and a process of growth and change. Our working definitions are as follows.

PROFESSIONAL COACHING

The ICF defines coaching as "partnering with clients in a thought-provoking and creative process that inspires them to maximize their personal and professional potential, which is particularly important in today's uncertain and complex environment." Coaches honor the client as the expert in his or her life and work, and believe every client is creative, resourceful, and whole. Standing on this foundation, the coach's responsibility is to:

- Discover, clarify, and align with what the client wants to achieve
- Encourage client self-discovery
- Elicit client-generated solutions and strategies
- Support the client in being responsible and accountable for their desired outcomes and changes

This process helps clients dramatically improve their outlook on work and life, while improving leadership skills and unlocking potential.

LIFE COACHING AS AN OPERATING SYSTEM

Life coaching is a powerful human relationship in which trained coaches assist people to design their future rather than get over their past. It is a change process that mobilizes strengths and develops the potential of both individuals and systems of work, family, and more. This relationship is typically long term, during which coaches aid clients in creating visions and goals for all aspects of their lives, as well as multiple strategies to support achieving those goals. Coaches recognize the brilliance of clients and their personal power to discover their own solutions when provided support, accountability, and unconditional positive regard (Williams & Davis, 2007). Part I includes an in-depth discussion of "Listening as a Coach," a discussion of the language specific to coaching, and the human developmental theories that underpin the coach's understanding of clients at various stages of development. These sections offer general principles that apply to most coaching situations and approaches. If you are familiar with coaching, you are likely to reencounter basic principles. We hope that you also discover something new that will enrich your way of thinking about and practicing coaching. For us, human developmental theories have proven considerably helpful by informing the context of coaching and have become increasingly valuable in our coach training.

CHAPTER 1

LISTENING AS A COACH

Franz Kafka understood the value of paying close attention. Listening is a deceptively simple skill that is often overlooked in its power. Listening as a coach is very different from normal, everyday listening. Even when done extraordinarily well, common conversational listening lacks the intentional focus a coach brings to the conversation. A coach listens with a very different quality of attention that includes an intention to be of service, with no agenda aside from listening for "wants" to emerge. As Carl Rogers, the father of modern counseling, demonstrated, active listening, accompanied by unconditional positive regard, supports tremendous positive changes. A coach's ability to be fully present to the client, patiently listening, communicates fundamental acceptance of the client. This quality of listening and acceptance allows the client to be vulnerable in sessions. Clients seldom experience the patient listening from others that they receive from coaches. This explains why coaching can feel therapeutic, even though coaching is not therapy. Coaches often refer to this as creating a sacred, inspiring space in which the client experiences the impact of powerful listening. This space supports the client's personal unfolding. If lapses occur in the coach's ability to listen with patience and undeniable focus, or to create an inspiring space, the client's trust will erode. Lapses in being present and patiently listening can take these forms:

- Interrupting clients or speaking as soon as clients finish a sentence; allowing no space for clients to hear themselves, to feel the impact of what they have said
- Beginning to speak while clients finish the last few words of a sentence—this doesn't allow clients the choice to continue and elaborate
- Attending superficially; missing signals provided by the client's tone

of voice or body language; breaking eye contact or doodling during a face-to-face session

- Multitasking, with sounds clients hear during phone coaching
- Random or fidgety movements unrelated to clients' statements that grow out of the coach's interior thoughts or feelings

Learning to become present in the moment is important for the coach to model and emphasize. One of the gifts coaching brings is learning to be fully present during a session. Helping professionals in a wide variety of fields use listening skills as an integral aspect of their work. Those in a helping profession know how valuable it can be to simply listen and focus attention on a client. However, coaches listen in unique ways that support the goals of the coaching relationship and maximize opportunities for achieving those goals. The relationship is key. As Dr. Michael Arloski reminds us in his book *Masterful Health and Wellness Coaching* (2021) "The experience of coaching teaches about the power of relationship, of person-to-person connection because all the evidence from coaching and psychotherapy shows that this is the critical factor in determining success" (p. 115). Thousands of research studies have shown that no matter the technique or skillsets of the coach or therapist, it is the relationship that is the determining factor. Listening lays the cornerstone of coaching, just as it remains the bedrock for every human relationship. Like every professional with extensive education, training, and experience, we develop habits as listeners. Most helping professionals listen instinctively for the client's feelings, and just as instinctively they reflect, probe, and work with the client toward therapeutic change. As coaches, we listen for the client's feelings, too. However, we pay equal attention to other domains of the client's life.

> *You need not leave your room. Remain sitting at your table and listen. You need not even listen— simply wait. You need not even wait. Just learn to become quiet, and still and solitary. The world will freely offer itself to you to be unmasked. It has no choice. It will roll in ecstasy at your feet.*
>
> —Franz Kafka

THREE KINDS OF LISTENING AS A COACH

Coaches use three main forms of listening: listening to, listening for, and listening with (Whitworth et al., 1998, pp. 9, 257). (This has been updated in the latest edition of *Co-active Coaching*, but we still like the original description noted in the 1998 edition.)

Listening To (Level One Listening)

Listening to is what many people call active listening. Listen to what the client says—and does not say. Listen to the content and to what is beyond and behind the words—the story behind the story. This is the kind of listening that most of us learn readily as students, parents, and partners.

A basic skill in active listening includes knowing when and how to mirror what was heard. When mirroring, the coach repeats back to the client what he said so that he feels fully heard. Artful mirroring allows the client to hear himself. However, masterful coaches go beyond elementary mirroring. People new to mirroring sometimes make the mistake of parroting back what they heard, rather than offering a nuanced interpretation that captures the client's attention. New coaches sometimes mirror too often, interrupting the client's flow. Coaches also *listen to* by observing the client's body movements, gestures, breathing pattern, tone of voice, speech pacing, pauses, and eye movements. By paying attention to the congruence of words and nonverbal behavior, the coach can begin to sense dimensions of the experience that clients may not have brought fully into their consciousness.

Listening For (Level Two Listening)

A second kind of listening is *listening for*. Laura Whitworth describes this well: "The coach listens for clients' vision, values, commitment, and purpose in their words and demeanor" (Whitworth et al., 1998, p. 257). To *listen for* is to listen in search of something. The coach listens with a consciousness, with a purpose and focus that come from the alliance that was designed with the client. The alliance includes the client's goals and desires, which is what many coaches refer to as "the client's agenda." The coach listens to forward the client's agenda, not the coach's agenda. We sometimes call this "listening for the large life." For example, a particular client's agenda includes improving work–life balance. His coach listens for expanding the possibilities beyond just having balance, instead creating the most authentic and designed life that the client can imagine. The coach listens for the bigger picture, the richer possibilities beyond obvious improvements like reprioritizing time and focusing on time for oneself. What life can the client create so that balance would simply be a given? The coach listens as if asking, "What crucible can contain the presenting goal, providing an expanded container to support the client's unfolding?" *Listening for* may also include *listening for* the largest context that the client sees himself standing within, including how the client orients himself to spiritual possibilities and meaning, a purpose that connects him to something larger than himself. One kind of listening for that is not useful, however, is listening for "the solution." As coaches, we are not problem solvers, and so we are not the experts. People who enter professions such as coaching, counseling, and consulting are often under the impression that they need to know or are expected to know what's best for other people. Their impulse to make a difference can get confused with an inclination to impose their own values. Novice coaches, as well as coaches who have not devoted much attention to their own development and inner life, are especially prone to overlay their values onto clients. Seasoned coaches with first-hand experience of how this orientation can distort or derail a coach/client relationship are clearer about the need to release their conviction that they know what's best for a client. Coaches learn to observe their own process and let go of their investment in being the expert and having the answer. Coaching is not about listening for problems, pathologies, history, pain, and blocks—instead, it's about listening for possibilities, goals, dreams, and aspirations. It's about discovering, harnessing, and expanding on strengths and tools clients have, not about rooting out and tackling problems (which, in addition to being disempowering, is not an appropriate focus in the coaching relationship). Listening for a solution is, in fact, a block to the coaching process: It turns the client into a problem and the desired outcome into a solution. It distorts the process by superimposing an artificial agenda. The agenda might be:

- *To advise or teach something the coach is passionate about.* While coaching sometimes includes brief moments of teaching, these need to be labeled as such and used sparingly. A coach who has expertise in a domain needs to be vigilant about not listening for opportunities in this area. One such coach was passionate about nutrition and tended to insert his knowledge in coaching conversations where it didn't belong. In general, we recommend that coaches steer clients to resources when the client needs to learn something. The new coach could easily have recommended specific texts or websites to clients who needed to learn more about nutrition. He didn't serve the client by substituting teaching for coaching.

- *To find answers (often too quickly).* The coach should avoid pushing for answers. New coaches can find it difficult to detach from a client's urgency around finding pathways out of the current situation.
- *To have the coach feel successful (fulfilling the coach's needs, not the client's).* This is a definite mistake. The coach in this case is listening to her internal dialogue or her own needs, not the client's.

A metaphor we use with clients is to consider the difference between flying from Los Angeles to New York versus driving. Driving allows for adventures, unexpected insights, and meetings. Flying is more predictable and efficient. However, "flying" a client to his or her goal skips important steps and reduces the likelihood that growth will become rooted in the client's life. When we coach in the domain of work, *listening for* includes paying attention to the particular interdependence of the fundamental results of the client's work. Michael O'Brien (personal communication, April 10, 2002) describes this as "The Work Triangle" (Figure 1.1).

FIGURE 1.1
The Work Triangle

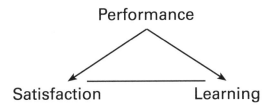

Most conversations about work focus on performance. Clients can bring this habit to coaching. Coaches listen for how the clients' satisfaction and learning grow from their work because these are critical to maintaining performance. If individuals are not learning, their performance will decline over time. If the clients' predominant experience of work is boredom or stress, both learning and performance will suffer.

Listening With (Level Three Listening)

Coaches do a third kind of listening: *listening with*. There are many ways to *listen with*. The best way we have found is to consider listening with the whole self. This includes listening with heart, listening with intuition, and listening with the body. By listening with the heart, coaches resonate with clients and notice what emotions emerge. The concept of heart-based consciousness has become even better understood with modern neuroscience research like that of J. Andrew Armour, who, in 1991, discovered that the heart has its "little brain" or "intrinsic cardiac nervous system" (Armour, 2007). This "heart brain" is composed of approximately 40,000 neurons that are similar to neurons in the brain; this means that the heart has its own nervous system, and that the heart sends more signals to the brain than vice versa.

Listening with intuition, coaches pay attention to the images, metaphors, and internal words or phrases that emerge from within as an intuitive connection. Listening with the body, coaches notice where in their body they react to what they hear or sense from the presence of the client. An everyday example occurs when people say they have a "gut feeling." That's a somatic response to a situation that lacks logical explanation. However, the coach's "gut reaction" or "intuitive hit" needs to be checked for accuracy. Often physical or intuitive reactions lead to a new understanding for both coach and client. A coach might say to the client, "I just had this sense that you may be ambivalent, and I want to check out whether that's on-target or not. You say you want to start this new business, and yet I don't sense that your energy or excitement is present or convincing as you speak about it." Sharing the intuition might lead to a shift in the coaching conversation. Skillful coaches listen and resonate with clients' words, meanings, and tones. They listen consciously to what is evoked in them by clients. They listen deeply from the heart and attend to the images, feelings, and senses that arise. These are sources of insight for both coach and client. Coaches are careful to avoid "me too" listening. We see this kind of listening every day, when one person shares a thought or feeling, and the other replies, "Gee, that happened to me, too!" That kind of listening shifts the focus away from the client's experience. However, a unique feature of the coaching relationship is the appropriate use of self-disclosure by the coach. A masterful coach differentiates between self-disclosure that enhances the client's learning and disclosure that interferes. Self-disclosure must serve one of two purposes: to increase the connection with the client or to function as a learning point. For example, a coach might say to a client that she, too, had jitters about leaving a full-time job to start a business. By coaching other clients who have started businesses, she has learned how normal that is. That disclosure enables the client to put his own jitters into perspective. For therapists becoming coaches, learning to self-disclose can be difficult. Most therapists were taught not to self-disclose with clients because it interferes with the clients' healing and shifts the relationship out of the professional role. Since coaches work with clients who are not emotionally fragile, occasional self-disclosure deepens the relationship as clients see coaches as fully human. Self-disclosure also models authenticity and transparency for the client, two capabilities that are particularly critical for those who lead others. Authenticity and transparency are also important for clients who want to take responsibility for creating their lives. Dr. Robert Terry made this link between authentic leadership and the authentic life when he wrote, "Authenticity is ubiquitous, calling us to be true to ourselves and true to the world, real in ourselves and real in the world. When authenticity is acknowledged, we admit our foibles, mistakes and protected secrets, the parts of ourselves and society that are fearful and hide in the shadows of existence" (Terry, 1993, p. 139). The great gift of coaching is that we can freely share our intuition with clients because the relationship is one of partnership. How freely we share what we hear is one of the key differences between the kind of listening we do as therapists and the kind of listening we do as coaches. Coaches need to be cautious about what psychologists understand as transference and countertransference. In simple terms, transference means that a person is unconsciously bringing their experience and feelings from another situation into a current one. Clients may bring into coaching the unconscious expectation that coaches will solve their life issues for them, thereby provoking a natural tendency that coaches may have to "rescue" or "fix" their clients. Transference can happen to coaches when conversations evoke an unconscious reaction based on something in their own life. Coaches, for example, may be listening to clients talk about the desire to have another child or live on a Caribbean island. That story might evoke in coaches their own longings, and their internal reactions can transfer to the coaching conversation. This likely interferes with powerful listening. Coaching relationships have a quality of intimacy that makes it critical for coaches to commit to reflecting on any leaks of their own "stuff." To be effective and powerful, coaches must recognize what might trigger or hook them and when it occurs, let it go.

A USEFUL LISTENING TEMPLATE

Just as maps help travelers find their way, listening templates help coaches pay attention to what can be listened for by providing a structure to guide their attention. Templates help coaches see gaps that might lend themselves as starting points for the coaching conversation.

Listening for the "Big Five"

One powerful tool the coach may use is learning to listen for the "Big Five," a coaching template drawn from work in sports psychology.[1] In early coaching sessions, the focus is on understanding the client's goals and discovering what needs to shift so the clients can create what they most want. Once clients have articulated the goals, it is time to start listening for their strengths and any potential blocks. Discovering potential blocks helps both coaches and clients identify what the clients will need to do—or become—to achieve their goal. The Big Five provides a generic listening template that helps coaches ascertain what is currently in place and what needs to be added to the clients' repertoire. The Big Five frequently guide coaches toward the specific fieldwork a client needs. In the pages that follow, the Big Five will be described in the ways that they are important to coaching: Intention and Attention, Mindset, Skills and Capabilities, Habits and Behaviors, and Energy.

Intention and Attention

Clients' focuses are the elements of their life and work that draw their attention. An ideal focus is appropriate, steady, flexible, able to be maintained, and related to goals that foster the clients' well-being. Clients may come to coaching with a fuzzy focus or unclear intention. They come to coaching with a sense that they want to do something different. They are not happy in their current situation, but they are not clear on what needs to be different or what they want to create. That is a common coaching conversation. Coaching takes stock of what's missing or desired and assists clients in gaining clar-

---

1 Dr. Pat learned many of these concepts in studying sports psychology and also in being coached in tennis, golf, and baseball, as well as in training with George Leonard, a martial arts master and teacher of "mastery in living" in the late 1970s. Dr. Pat learned to incorporate these concepts in his life and work.

ity and choice by asking evocative questions, working with clients on their vision—how they want life to be. Through powerful questions, journal exercises, and reflections, clients gain more clarity of focus and become able to move toward what they want. A metaphor we use with clients is that clarifying focus is like charting a course on a sailboat. They know they want to get there, and they have many choices about how to do so. But they can't start sailing until they know what island they want to visit. Coaching helps clients determine the destination—the coach helps the client explore various routes to get there. Knowing the routes helps. Successful sailors also adjust to various circumstances, such as wind shifts and storms. Coaches must help clients assess whether goals are feasible—whether they are appropriate and achievable for the clients at this time. One of our faculty worked with a client who wanted to open a retail store while three months pregnant with her third child. While this wasn't something the coach would have undertaken under those circumstances, the coaching conversation helped the client determine that yes, she could do this, and helped her strategize how to open the business as well as support her growing family. If your client has a goal of expanding his business, and this is his reason for seeking coaching, you will ask yourself, "Does he have a clear intention?" "Is the focus clear?" "How does he attend to that intent?" If the focus seems fuzzy, that may be a starting point for coaching. For example, he may talk about expanding but not be clear about how he would measure the expansion. Would it be the number of clients? Bottom-line revenue? New markets? New products? If he isn't clear, the coach needs to help him gain clarity about the focus for expansion—in other words, what "expansion" really means to him. If he holds his focus too generally, he will not be able to achieve his goals. It is, of course, possible to be overfocused or attentive at the risk of losing sight of what's right in front. Overfocusing hinders clients in discovering options. Being highly motivated isn't the same as being overfocused, which is like having tunnel vision. Clients can overfocus on work achievements, ignoring other aspects of their lives. Coaches support clients by illuminating a broader perspective to the clients' lives. The client who wants to expand his business may be overfocused on that goal, perhaps to an obsessive degree. This could lead to coaching conversations about work–life balance, the needs of other people in his life, and how he will maintain his health and physical well-being during the expansion. Life coaching—unlike pure business coaching—takes a whole person perspective on any client who comes for coaching.

Mindset

Coaches consider the clients' mindset by observing and listening to the clients. How do the clients interpret their experiences—negatively, seeing only problems? Positively, seeing possibilities? Is the client's mindset helpful, or is it limiting? The coaching conversations can help clients shift away from limiting beliefs and toward powerful possibilities and a more can-do attitude. Mindset and attitude are the characteristic or current mental and emotional positions from which clients view themselves, other people, events, and the world. Mindset and attitude can often be the sources of, or have significant effects on, a client's motivational patterns. For example, if clients are frequently fear driven, it is hard to move forward, even toward goals clients have set. The key factor is whether clients are aware of their mindset and attitude. Are mindset and attitude appropriate for the situation? Do they help or hinder the client reach the goal? Mindset includes the characteristic ways clients view themselves and the world. As a coach listens, over time clients will reveal mindset through:

- The ways they characteristically approach people and relationships
- The ways they define success and themselves in relation to people, events, and circumstances
- Whether they tend to see themselves as actors, participants, or victims
- How they draw conclusions about events and experiences
- How they think about their ability to create and influence
- How they evaluate the importance and value of people, situations, experiences, and results

For the client interested in expanding his business, the coach will look for whether he holds a positive attitude about the opportunity. Does he want to expand his business but describes that process pessimistically? Does he say things like, "I have a great idea but I'm not a businessman. I don't know what to do. I can't afford to hire the right people." In this case, the coach would notice that working on mind-set would be important. This client seems to have beliefs that are limiting: he is focused on what can't happen, what limits him, and what he can't afford. If this is a habitual way of thinking, he could end up inadvertently sabotaging his goal by not directing his efforts appropriately. In Chapter 15 we focus extensively on ways of noticing and working with mind-set. With corporate clients, mind-set quickly shows up when clients describe conflicts with others. Clients often focus outside themselves in conflicts, which appears as blaming others and the situation, and not noticing or claiming responsibility for their part. The coach's role is to listen and notice to what extent clients see and claim their role, and their willingness to accept accountability for taking actions to change.

Skills and Capabilities

Given the clients' goals, the key question is whether they have the necessary skills and capabilities required for success. Skills tend to be learnable and teachable and, with practice, can be mastered. Capabilities, on the other hand, can be developed but generally are not things we expect to build through teaching. An example of a capability might be a client's ability to tolerate ambiguity without rushing to action. Capabilities can be found by discovering what the client has patience for and can tolerate, or what the client has impatience for and cannot tolerate. Clients may need to develop, for example, their capacity for staying engaged when conflict occurs, instead of retreating or running away because they don't have the capability to stay calm in conflict. Coaches can help clients develop their capacities, as we describe later in Chapter 6 when we discuss assigning practices as fieldwork in coaching. First, coaches and clients identify skills and capabilities the clients have that support their goals. These are the resources the clients can draw upon. Coaching helps clients determine whether to learn needed skills, delegate, or hire someone. For example, a client starting a new business will need the basic skills to run a business such as bookkeeping, marketing, staffing, and website development. He doesn't need to be hands on with all these tasks, but he does need to identify who can assist him or provide the service. The key questions are: What are the gaps between what he currently can do or acquire and what is needed? What is the most effective way to fill these gaps? This assessment can also help the client determine whether the goal he has set is feasible within the time he wants to achieve it. Assessing skills and capabilities sometimes becomes an entry point back to examining the goal, as well as to other areas within the Big Five. For the client wanting to expand his business, you may notice skills and capabilities such as time management, networking (or the lack thereof), marketing, follow-through, and project management. Does the client complete things on time? Does he take on too many requests from others, saying yes when he really wants to say no? Can the client work satisfactorily with the level of detail required to manage the business as well as expand it? If any of these are not current capabilities, the client will need to develop them or delegate them to others. Many business owners discover that to expand their business, they need to engage more support staff or outsource personal responsibilities.

Habits and Behaviors

These are what clients do automatically—without thinking or planning. These can be habits, practices, and patterns in the physical, emotional, mental, and spiritual realms. Key questions are: "Are the clients' habits, practices, and patterns supporting them in achieving the goal? Do they need to be shifted in some way? Can they be unlearned, noticed, or developed into new patterns?" Note: This is not an invitation to judge clients. Avoid labeling the habits as bad or good. Simply discover whether they are useful—whether they support the clients in effectively attaining their goals. A common example is time management, especially if clients move into a home-based business, a romanticized notion for many people. The good news is that they are working from home. The bad news is that they are working from home. Time management as a habit becomes crucial in how they organize their work time versus play time amid the distractions from family and pets, and the temptation to go outside and goof off. Can they set the appropriate boundaries? Coaches will help clients explore their time management habits and determine whether these habits are sufficient to achieve their goals.

Clients may think they need to do all the work themselves. They may be reluctant to delegate and then get overwhelmed with administrivia. If they want to start a business, they must develop new patterns. They will need to find people who can support their business; otherwise, they risk not launching it successfully. A common goal clients set in a case like this is to gradually move from working in the business (providing direct service) to working on the business (leading, strategizing, and so on). This may be where you assess whether clients habitually overpromise and underdeliver. Clients who want to expand their business may need to have a practice of regularly contacting current and former customers, which is an accepted business strategy, sometimes describes as TOMA, *top-of-mind awareness*. Keeping the business in the forefront of the customer's mind often leads to repeat business or the willingness to buy new products or services. TOMA also creates referrals. If clients lack these habits, coaches need to reexamine skills and capabilities: what would the client need to learn to have TOMA become a new business practice? In the corporate environment, a boss might contact an employee at all hours of the evening and expect the employee to respond. Unless they have an agreement that the employee is to be "on call," the client/boss will begin to experience demotivated employees. In a case like this, the coach would explore the source of the after-hours calls. Are they occurring because the client/boss doesn't plan? Does this client make a distinction between home and work life? Does the client/boss treat situations as crises and initiate a reactive pattern, so that every crisis he experiences becomes a crisis for his people?

Energy

This factor is the clients' ability to bring forth, as needed, an appropriate amount of physical/emotional/mental/spiritual energy. Energy serves as a gateway into clients' health, motivation, commitment, and way of being in the world. Energy may be either sourced or blocked by the previous four factors. A good coach will notice regularly how clients motivate themselves and generate energy, as well as whether their physical well-being affects their energy. For example, aging, menopause, illness, and parenting or caregiving can affect energy. Even when talking by phone, coaches can sense clients' energy. It is critical for coaches to have a sense of their clients's energy from the enthusiasm they express about the goal. Are they excited about the goal? Does the energy they communicate to coaches dissipate after the coaching conversation? Can clients maintain their energy level? On the other hand, this might be the entry point for coaching: the clients' goals are valid, but they have so many energy drainers in their lives that they are unable to move forward. They simply don't have the required energy. Their intentions are great, and the prospects of growing the business are solid, but the coaches notice that they need to have more energy available consistently to make progress. Later in this book we describe how coaches can work more directly with the client's energy, working somatically and with mindsets that can foster or create obstacles to sourcing energy.

WHAT LISTENING IS NOT

Coaching is not about listening for problems, pathologies, history, pain, and psychological blocks. Instead, it's about listening for possibilities, goals, dreams, and aspirations. Coaching is about discovering, harnessing, and expanding on strengths and tools clients have, not about rooting out problems and tackling them (which, in addition to being disempowering, is not an appropriate focus in the coaching relationship).

Coaching is not about listening for solutions. This diminishes the humanness of the client by treating him or her as a problem. We distinguish possibilities from solutions and encourage coaches to listen for possibilities from the beginning. Coaches need to remain open to clients' creativity in generating solutions. Listening for solutions is a block to coaching because it distorts the process by superimposing an artificial agenda onto it. The agenda might be to find answers (often too quickly)—coaches need to not push for this and need to not be hooked into clients' urgency around coming to conclusions. Or perhaps the coach needs to feel successful. This fulfills coaches' needs, not clients' needs.

Coaching is not advising or training. Sometimes coaches do need to teach their clients something briefly to help them build a skill or capability. A coach, for example, may take 15 minutes of a coaching session to teach a stressed client how to do breath counting meditation. The coach would ask the client's permission to teach and would label the work as such. Marcia Reynolds (2020) states in *Coach the Person, not the Problem*: "Coaching the person instead of the problem can be called awareness-based coaching to differentiate from solution focused coaching. The focus of coaching is on identifying beliefs behind opinions and actions and on fears and conflicting values causing dissonance and confusion. You want the shifts to be made at the identity level instead of just trying to alter activity."

CONCLUSION

We begin this book with a focus on listening because listening creates the foundation for great coaching. One of our colleagues, Dave Ellis, believes that coaches should spend 80 percent of their time simply listening and working in a nondirective manner with what the client says. In terms of what an observer would notice, the coach would be doing any of the following (Ellis, 2006, pp. 54–56):

- Listening fully and then affirming the client. This would involve feeding back to clients what seems to be inspiring to them, which helps the clients feel affirmed as well as hear themselves. Coaches acknowledge the goals and help the clients feel heard.
- Listening fully and then feeding back clients' desires. Coaches feed back what the clients want in a way that clarifies and focuses the clients' attention. This helps clients notice the "key points" that the coaches create out of what could have been a sustained description by the clients.
- Listening fully and then asking the client to generate some new possibilities. This might involve a question such as: "What can you think of that would help you take the first steps toward this goal?"

Later in the coaching relationship, coaches may offer possibilities to clients or teach a skill on a limited basis. But early in the relationship, coaches should focus on listening and helping the clients discover what they want, what they believe, and what is possible. The coach's listening helps the client listen to himself. The coach's response as a listener clarifies the client's desires.

CHAPTER 2

THE LANGUAGE OF COACHING

THE BASIC COACHING MODEL

Our program is based on a blend of many of the theories from humanistic psychology (Maslow, Rogers, and others), the recent research in positive psychology and its strength-based approach, and the early theories of Jung, Adler, and Assagioli. We also believe, like speech-act theorists John Searle and Fernando Flores, that conversations create action. Through coaching, as narrative therapy describes, clients rewrite old stories and create new ones of their lives and possibilities.

When coaches work with clients, they simultaneously attend to three aspects of coaching: the relationship with the clients, the overall process of coaching (its goals, framework, and expectations), and the coaching conversations that occur.

In this chapter, we refer to the coaching conversation as a template for a specific type of dialogue, which has a beginning, middle, and end. Within one coaching session, several cycles of the coaching conversation may occur. Or a coaching session may focus only on the first parts of the conversation, depending on the depth. But the steps or phases will be repeated throughout each session. What makes a coaching conversation differ from a nice chat is that it has a beginning, middle, and end, which results in movement on the part of clients toward insight or action. Coaching engages clients in commitment and action of some kind.

Coaching is, above all, a conversation. A coaching relationship begins when coaches engage clients in a conversation around their visions, goals, wants, and desires. Like all good conversations, coaching requires us to listen,

I believe we can change the world if we start listening to one another again. Simple, honest, human conversation.

—Margaret J. Wheatley, *Turning to One Another*

pace the conversations, and genuinely enter a dialogue with clients. This creates what we call the sacred or inspiring space. David Bohm's work on dialogue (1996) provides a good model for coaches to follow in attending to the client.

The coaching conversation is special because clients grant coaches permission to challenge and support them. In the coaching conversation, the dialogue between coaches and clients is designed to further the clients' growth, learning, and action toward their desires and intentions. It is a creative conversation where coaches dance with clients, intuitively following their pace and style while adding to and elaborating on what unfolds in the moment. There is an agreement in place that enables the coaching conversation to occur. Without that agreement, you can have a great conversation, but it will not necessarily lead to the kind of change that coaching can facilitate. Up-to-date research in neurology that supports this idea and illuminates the process of the creative conversation between coaches and clients can be found in *Helping People Change* (Boyatzis et al., 2019). Moore and colleagues (2006) have also researched this phenomenon and written an excellent description of this process.

The magic of coaching conversations is that they would not take place within the clients' usual lives. As our friend and colleague Dave Ellis says when he teaches, coaching gives clients the opportunity to think what they've not thought, say what they've not said, dream what they've not dreamed, and create what they've not created. No two coaching conversations are alike, but there is a basic flow to the conversation that we repeat again and again. This flow is the framework for a coaching session. This chapter describes the components of a coaching conversation—its beginning, middle, and end. You can have good conversations with a lot of people, but it is not a coaching conversation until it is purposefully directed to the client's agenda and has all the components delineated here.

The coaching conversation impacts clients because it takes a whole-person approach. Tim Gallwey articulated this in his groundbreaking work, using the metaphor of the inner game, the internal world, of clients. He described three critical conversations that need to take place for clients to be successful in making a change. Each pays attention to the inner and outer world of clients. Gallwey said that coaching includes three levels of conversation: "A conversation for awareness (getting the clearest possible picture of current reality), a conversation for choice (getting the clearest possible picture of the desired future outcome), and a conversation for trust (in which the client gains greater access to internal and external resources to move from current reality to the desired future)" (2000, pp. 188–189).

Increasing clients' awareness is key because with awareness comes choice. Clients must become aware of reality—what's true and what resources are available to them. Increased choice comes when clients become aware they can respond creatively to life rather than react to it. Our normal stance as human beings is to react, particularly to challenges. When even the smallest portions of fear or anxiety arise, the human brain and nervous system react with the fight, flight, or freeze response. Increased awareness through coaching allows clients to see they always have choices available to them, including the choice to learn practices that allow them to manage their reactions. As they increase awareness, choices become more evident, allowing them to respond to life rather than react. As Candide said at the end of Voltaire's book, "We must cultivate our garden."

As clients' awareness expands to include greater choice, they learn to trust themselves and the coaching process as great support that allows them to step outside their comfort zone. Clients come to coaching because they want to make change. What holds most people back from changing is self-doubt, fear, distraction, or preoccupation. Coaching helps people focus on what they want and increases their awareness, choices, and trust in their ability to create. One only need look at Olympic athletes or people at the top of their field. Most of them would say they engage with a coach to bring out their best. There are numerous examples of high-profile athletes who make use of coaches, for both skill development and personal training.

In the description below of the flow of the coaching conversation, you'll see that the clients' awareness, choices, and trust in themselves are all intentionally engaged by coaches.

THE FLOW OF COACHING CONVERSATIONS

Clients typically hire coaches because they want to achieve or enhance something in their lives. The desired results generally fall into three areas:

- **Performance goals:** for example, improving results as a business owner, eliminating clutter, or meeting daily standards for reaching out to potential clients. These goals usually can be measured objectively, such as by examining the balance sheet of a business, measuring business processes, or tracking sales contacts.

- **Learning goals:** for example, improving public speaking, becoming a more patient parent, or learning how to meditate and do so consistently. The measurement standards for these goals may be external or internal. External measures for public speaking could come from observers' feedback. Parents might use both external and internal measures by keeping a log of daily interactions with children and rating themselves on their patience in each, as well as seeking feedback from their spouses and children.

- **Fulfillment goals:** for example, achieving work–life balance, a satisfying relationship with a spouse, or the ability to work from the heart as well as the head—a common issue for corporate leaders. The determination of whether these goals have been achieved rests with the client's sense of fulfillment. Clients can track their felt sense of fulfillment on a daily or weekly basis. They can judge subjectively whether they are feeling more fulfilled. Clients can also create measures for themselves: time at work, time with family, time for fun and so on, to provide an external source of learning for themselves. Fulfillment goals may also bring clients in tune with their life purpose. This is the central focus of Part III.

In the real world of coaching, a coach often works with the client in all three of these areas. For example, a client originally wants to improve her small business results (a performance goal), as measured by the number of sales per customer. In the process of identifying what needs to happen to create that result, the client discovers she needs to be able to contact more potential customers. To do that, she realizes she needs to become a better networker (learning goal). As she does more networking, she discovers that she is spending less time at home with her children. She sets a new goal: spend quality time with her children that is mutually enjoyable, because she deeply desires to be a caring and loving parent (fulfillment goal).

Our clients bring with them their goals and desires. They also bring the stories they tell themselves (and others) about those goals and desires—why they are attainable or not, what it will take to achieve them, and more. To paraphrase Bill O'Hanlon, a well-known speaker and author in the field of solution-oriented therapy, every human being gets "lost in storyland."

> Each of us has our own point of view about things that happen in our lives. We call these explanations stories to emphasize the fact that our points of view are not The Truth. Facts are different from stories. Facts are things we can all agree on, what we can verify with our senses. Stories involve opinions, interpretations, theories, and explanations. Facts are the "what"; stories are the "why." Most of us are caught up in the stories we believe about ourselves, other people, our relationships; we have forgotten that these stories are stories of our own doing. We are convinced that our stories contain The Truth. (O'Hanlon & Hudson, 1995, p. 19)

As you engage in coaching conversations with clients, you bring this awareness: to assist clients in getting what they want, you will be working with their stories about the goals, themselves, and what is possible. Clients may or may not recognize that their stories aren't the truth. As the coach, you will need to discover how tightly clients are bound to the idea their stories are reality. The more clients confuse stories with truth, the more difficult it will be for clients to make changes. Sometimes the first piece of work in coaching is to help clients be able to reflect on how they created and continue to create the stories, so they might rewrite them. As you read the description of the coaching conversation, refer to the transcript of a session, which follows. As we describe the structure of this conversation, we will do so from the coach's perspective because the coach is responsible for structuring the conversation. The five steps of our coaching model are presented below.

The Situation and the Desire

Step 1: Ask, "What do you want from our time together today?"
Coaching sessions usually start with a minute or two of small talk and checking in. The flow of the coaching conversation begins when the coach poses an inquiry into the client's current desires. The coach asks open ended questions—beginning with some version of "What do you want?"—to engage the client to articulate what he or she wants and clarify the meaning of that

desire. Subsequent questions will probe for more specifics. These initial questions can be about a specific situation (for example, "What do you want from your vacation?") or about the entirety of the client's life (for example, "What legacy do you want to leave?").

In either case, a powerful question engages clients in identifying more clearly what they want because, without that, clients will continue to think, act, and live no differently.

The coach's questions initiate a process of discovery and awareness for both client and coach. The coach asks questions that are designed to evoke the client's insight, inquiring into the depths of the desire, the vision the client has for what is desired, the subtleties of the situation, and why the desire is important to the client. Powerful questioning is a hallmark of life coaching and is explored later in this chapter.

Enter the Flow of the Coaching Conversation

Step 2: Listen and Clarify

Like any great conversationalist, coaches pay exquisitely close attention to what clients say, as discussed in Chapter 1. As Dave Ellis often says in his workshops, listening fully is about softness, yielding, openness, and willingness to receive. When you pay attention, your world gets bigger. The coach's ability to listen and reflect helps the client's world seem more spacious, more alive, and more vibrant.

As coaches listen and clarify, they may reframe what clients see by providing perspective and creating possibilities that mirror or build on the clients' statements.

Coaches sometimes say they coach to the gap. This means that coaches help clients identify wants and wishes and compare them to what currently exists. The gap is the difference between the two. Once the gap is identified, coaches can help clients find ways to close it.

In listening and clarifying, coaches ask questions to discover what is, what is wanted, and gaps that exist. While the intention first is to help clients clarify, coaches are examining whether they fully understand what clients are communicating. This is done by checking in with clients. Coaches summarize and ask questions that verify their understanding: "Am I understanding you fully? Do I seem to have it all? Am I hearing you clearly? What else is there for you? Is there anything I'm missing? An important point of this step is for coaches to not own or be attached to their perception of what clients are saying. Masterful coaches always check in with clients and are willing to be wrong. Good coaching is about helping clients gain clarity, not tainting the conversation by coloring what clients meant in a way that doesn't reflect their intentions. The importance of gaining this level of clarity is that, once clear, the conversation can move forward. "Okay, we're both clear about what you want. Now, what can you do about it?" The coaching can focus on creating new strategies for clients to get what they want.

Giving Honest Feedback and Observation

Step 3: Say What Is So, As You Hear It

Once coaches are clear and reflect to clients their understanding, they can add perspective by sharing what they see. This can be the point of most potency and the highest leverage for change because the coaches' perspectives shed a powerful floodlight on the story clients tell about their goals and motivations. Coaches are truth tellers, sharing the truth of the clients' situation as they see it. They bring clarity to the clients' situations by articulating what they see, from their perspective—the gaps, the opportunities, the strengths, and the possibilities—clearly, respectful, and communicated in a manner that is heard by clients as the coaches' best understanding in the moment. It is never meant to be the truth—only the coaches' perspective. It is offered as the coaches' observation of the situation. Masterful coaches do not think they know something clients do not, but they respect that power to change comes from being able to see circumstances from more than one perspective.

Coaches say what is so by sharing their perception of the truth in a way that is respectful, warm, and inviting. The coaches' language needs to be attractive and intriguing to clients, capturing their attention. Coaches share intuitions about possibilities and obstacles. Coaches share the truth about themselves, as well as about the clients. Since our coaching clients are not fragile, we do not need to withhold information from them.

One meaning of happiness is living in tune with the way things are. When coaches share what is so, they are also humbly aware that it is just one version of the way things are—their version. When coaches share what is so, clients gain another perspective on the way things are. Ideally, this produces insight—that phenomenon which occurs when a new neural link is created in the client's brain. When someone recognizes what is so, the transformation can begin. But like all new links, this insight will be fragile unless built upon deeper dialogue or through acting upon the insight. We know how fragile these links are, much like the phenomenon of having a great idea in the middle of the night. Unless we write it down, it disappears by morning.

At this point coaches often share their assessment of the situation—the coaches' take on what's going on. For example, a coach might say, "My take is that right now exercising at the health club every day is more of a 'should' than a 'want.'" The assessment might be a suggestion, from the coach's point of view, of what is keeping the gap in place. It might be a metaphor the coach offers.

Coaches assist clients in seeing the situation more fully to evoke fresh insights about both the situations and the clients in general. Ideally, these insights also shed light on factors that stagnate the situation.

Return to Focused Listening

Step 4: Listen More

Once coaches have acknowledged the reality, it is time to listen again. They may find themselves asking clarifying questions to deepen clients' ability to listen to themselves fully. A skilled coach allows the client time and space to examine what is so, to play with it, to explore it, and to discover its possibilities. Through the quality of the coaches' work during this step, they invite clients to listen to themselves, too. Giving clients the time and space to respond can create new possibilities by legitimizing the process of listening to oneself deeply and honoring what is heard.

Insight occurs when clients begin to see the situation freshly. They may reshape the story they tell themselves about what is possible. Seeing the situation in a new way will likely free them to take new action. A great and useful skill to include here is purposeful silence. Don't think you have to respond right away to a client's comments or thoughts. Ask him or her to say more and just listen and pause several seconds. Silence is powerful when used in the context of the coaching moment.

Create Accountability

Step 5: Request Purposeful Action

The action the coach may request, although a change of some kind, is not necessarily a performance goal. It could be a change in behavior, a change in a way of being, or a change in a thought pattern or mindset—any change that creates forward momentum. In this step, coaches challenge clients to do what they perhaps have wanted to do but have never had the push to try. Coaches ask for a new way; the old way has not helped clients create what they want. A request for action may sound like this: "What can you do now? What will you do as your first step?"

At this time, coaches need to assess whether clients are committed to the actions they identify. In other words, it's important to make sure clients own the action and are not doing it for the sake of their coach. Skilled coaches are aware of pacing and check in with clients to ensure the goals and actions are in line with their desired outcomes and fit with what is possible, given the rest of their life. Appropriate action combined with the clients' willingness furthers their agendas. Actions that are too big or too small may derail the clients' motivation. Coaches need to check in with clients to determine whether they own the action: Are they excited? Do they show excitement and commitment through their voice, energy, and statements? The Big Five, which we discussed in Chapter 1, is a useful method for discernment here.

Don't underestimate the importance of discernment. There are experienced clients who get pumped up by declaring they are committed to some big goal that, although in line with their life path, seems too big or too soon. When clients declare their commitment, they can be fueled by the excitement of the adrenaline rush that comes with having a big vision or a big desire. They have every intention of agreeing to something that might require too much too soon. These are situations where coaches may notice clients overpromising and underdelivering, which would be assessed in subsequent coaching sessions. In such cases, clients come back for the next session not having completed the intended actions. Coaches explore what blocked the intended actions, with an eye toward assessing whether clients have overextended themselves. Overextension might be a onetime situation, or it could be a pattern. Coaches pay attention to which of these might be the case. Clients may need to learn how to check in with themselves to assess appropriate pacing. In this or the next session, coaches would help clients begin. A coach might ask a client: "Take a moment now and check in with yourself before you finalize this commitment. Get your calendar and notice what your next week looks like. Where do you see the space, time, and energy to do what you are agreeing to? Can you write this action in your calendar? Finally, check in with your body as you imagine yourself completing this action. Do you notice any places where you are tightening? If so, what's the message for you about this commitment?"

A good rule of thumb is to have clients act in two ways: (a) ask them to take the specified action, and (b) ask them to observe themselves during the next period of time, and stay attuned to what they think, feel, and sense as they engage in taking action and practicing new habits beyond the status quo. Several things generally happen within this part of the flow:

- **You identify choices.** When the truth has been told, the story identified, and the gap between current and desired situations cleared, it's time to identify choices clients can make to close the gap. Some may be obvious; others may require the coaches' and clients' creativity to generate.
- **You examine commitment.** Since clients will choose a path, examining their commitment to act is an important aspect of the process. A conversation about what it would take to commit to a choice may be in order, as would a conversation about why a choice is or isn't attractive. Sometimes the choice is modified to increase clients' levels of commitment.
- **You identify the action(s).** Clients are about to take an action they feel some commitment to see through. The coaching conversation needs to deal with the specifics of what clients will do, when they will do it, and how they will do it. To some extent, your work is to identify the next steps clients will take to forward themselves. Leaving this step fuzzy leads to frustration for clients and coaches. As clients take action, they learn from it, particularly if coaches ask them to self-observe. This in turn leads to other possibilities and actions. This might be a place where coaches consider how clients could gather internal feedback to verify that the new action is appropriate.
- **You ensure accountability.** Accountability is the cornerstone of coaching. Clients are accountable to coaches, but at a deeper level they are

most accountable to themselves. Coaches serve clients and ask for accountability. Don't leave the session before ensuring that the *what, when,* and *how* of your clients' next steps are clear. (Sometimes it's also helpful to ask clients to consider *why* the action is important.)

THE BOTTOM LINE

In any coaching session, you may repeat this basic five-step coaching framework several times, or one basic coaching cycle may occupy the entire session. How you use the model within a session depends on the focus, length of the session, style and pace of the client, and the alliance you have created together. Sometimes you will linger within a step or recycle back to an earlier step before progressing. Generally, a session is not complete without a request for movement of some kind. That is what makes coaching uniquely able to create momentum toward the client's goals.

A TRANSCRIPT OF A COACHING SESSION

The following transcript was taken from a coaching conversation that occurred within the context of an ILCT foundational class. Dr. Pat was the coach.

COACH: So last week you said that you wanted to have a conversation about how to rediscover fun in your life. Fun is an area on the Life Balance Wheel—fun and recreation, and you want to have that be better for you.

CLIENT: Yes.

COACH: So, what do you want to be different regarding fun and recreation in your life right now?

CLIENT: Well, several years ago I had serious knee surgery and had to stop playing tennis. I noticed that ever since, I stopped being able to play tennis and have injuries in my body and don't really feel [like] the athletic person that I was, let's say, 20 years ago, that I'll choose working on my computer. I'll choose staying in the house and organizing because I like that—I'll choose other activities rather than plan something with my partner that would be fun. And because we're both professionals, we'll always say, "Oh, well, if you have work to do" or "Oh, if you have reading to do for your coaching class . . . " Fun seems to be a very low priority for me in my life right now.

COACH: Right. And yet it used to be a big important part . . . because tennis was the way you did it, right?

CLIENT: Yeah, I loved it. I had so much fun.

COACH: Well, before we talk about other options for fun in your life, tell me what was it about the tennis activity?

CLIENT: It was being outdoors in the sun, which I don't do that much anymore. And it was playing with strangers sometimes, or just meeting someone regularly, meeting new people . . . And it was the physical activity and the contact sport . . . getting better at something. Getting better, taking lessons, practicing my serve, you know, that kind of thing.

COACH: And your physical limitations now prevent tennis?

CLIENT: Yes. They prevent any kind of sport like that, any kind of repetitive sport.

COACH: Where else in your life can you imagine being outdoors, meeting new people, engaging in some meaningful activity . . . it still could be physical to the degree that it's able to be physical. . . . What comes to mind?

CLIENT: Hmmm. That's an interesting question.

COACH: What do you see in other people that you notice, "Oh, that's something to consider?" You could start making a list of things you think could be fun that meet those.

CLIENT: I think that's good, only I always come up with that the people who think they have the most fun have a sport—have something like either tennis or golf, which doesn't interest me. Or sailing, or things that don't interest me. So that's my problem. I feel like I almost must reframe fun, and I don't know how to do that.

COACH: Good, good. What I picked from your conversation were some ingredients that if being outdoors and meeting people were two parts of playing tennis, you can still have those. What you can't have is playing tennis. I don't know if you can't have that, but right now your belief is that you can't have that.

CLIENT: No, I absolutely can't ever play tennis again.

COACH: Okay . . . I'm closing my eyes a minute as I try to imagine . . . What I'm hearing is it would be very important for you to find a way for fun to be a big factor in your life again, and it wouldn't be just doing busyness to distract you from the time you used to use getting outdoors and doing something . . .

CLIENT: Right.

COACH: . . . and there are physical limitations we know about . . .

CLIENT: Right.

COACH: So who do you know in your life, either that you really know or that you see publicly, like celebrities or anybody that you know of . . . people that have physical limitations and still seem to have fun in their life? Any models that you can think of?

CLIENT: (laughing) No.

COACH: So that would be a great research project, wouldn't it?

CLIENT: Yeah.

COACH: You chuckle. Why the chuckling?

CLIENT: Well, it's funny, because I don't know anyone who would say they have fun. I mean, I heard Ann in class say she has fun with her kindergarten kids doing drawing or scribbling or something like that, and that was fun to her. And I thought that was great. I wish I had something like that, something that I could call fun.

COACH: Yes. And it sounds as if it really is a reframe of . . . shifting . . . "Damn it, my fun used to be tennis, and now I can't do it, and it's a big loss for me and I can't think of anything else to have fun with." That's what I'm hearing.

CLIENT: Yes. That's correct. You know, it might be interesting, when I see people, I could ask them what they do that they call fun.

COACH: Yeah, that's a thought—do some fun interviews with people, what we call informational interviews.

CLIENT: Yeah, what do you do for fun? Ask them that.

COACH: What do you consider fun? Because there's a myriad of activities that aren't physical that some people consider fun. They might be more mental, they might be some community activity—I'm trying to think creatively with you now. But it feels to me, my intuition tells me . . . without getting into great details, I almost need to know the degree of your physical limitations, what the current situation is.

CLIENT: Well, I have problems with my feet, problems with my toes, and so I had to have hammertoe surgery, so every time I kept playing tennis, I had to have another surgery. It was eventually about not being able to walk easily, so I stopped playing tennis. But I still have pain in the bottom of my foot, now that my foot was anatomically changed. Now I have problems in the metatarsal region, so I have pain. So I have orthotics and all that, but I don't enjoy just walking—it's not fun for me.

COACH: So you are ambulatory?

CLIENT: Yes, I can walk, I can hike, but that's not fun. I can't walk fast, I can't run, I can't jump on my toes.

COACH: A little bit of history—when did you take up tennis?

CLIENT: In my teens, when I was about 12.

COACH: And played it from then on, very voraciously?

CLIENT: Yes. And then right before I had the surgeries, I played probably singles four times a week, doubles twice a week. I played almost every day.

COACH: What did you do for fun before age 12?

CLIENT: I rode a bike and played baseball. I ran around.

COACH: Is bicycling anything that interests you now?

CLIENT: No, not anymore. I fell. (laughing) I live in the mountains now, and it's really hard to bike unless you're really strong. And where I live there's nothing flat, and it's a huge hassle going down to the ocean where everybody is crowded. So there doesn't seem to be a sport. And I think maybe one of the things I'm feeling right now is I'm feeling kind of sad . . .

COACH: Yeah I hear that . . .

CLIENT: . . .the mourning of the fact that there isn't going to be that kind of sport that I've done my whole life.

COACH: Yeah—and if sport equals fun, then that's a big limitation for you.

CLIENT: Right.

COACH: And sport isn't the only kind of fun. It just seems right now that that's the fun you lost.

CLIENT: Right.

COACH: Let's move into the future. Let's just imagine . . . I'm trying to get into your mental space here, by phone, because I really want to believe . . . I mean, I absolutely do believe, not just want to, that there is an unknown for you, of having a life of fun, because not only do you deserve it, I think there's also a unique experience that we haven't yet come upon, that would be fun for you at some time in the future. Could be next week, could be next year. So, if you had a future that had fun in it, how would you be different? Who would you become if that were part of your life?

CLIENT: I would feel more rounded. I would feel that my life was more balanced. My life feels out of balance.

COACH: Out of balance, and there's a part missing.

CLIENT: Right. So I would feel more whole. And I would feel happier, I think, because I'd be doing something that doesn't always involve my mind, or busy work that then helps me relax . . . I'd be doing something that wasn't just mind oriented or organization oriented. So that feels better, that there would be something . . .There is something—I just thought of something.

COACH: Good.

CLIENT: If I could envision a future that had fun, I think I would be involved more in drumming . . .

COACH: Ahhh, tell me more about drumming.

CLIENT: (laughing and sounding more animated) . . . because I went to this drumming circle two times, and I'm going to go this Friday night. And it's involved because you have to buy a drum, and find people to drum with if you're going to do it in a circle. But it made me have that same sense of connection to strangers, people I wouldn't normally meet.

COACH: Yeah, that's what we were looking for earlier, and that can be done outdoors.

CLIENT: It's actually done indoors, but I suppose . . .

COACH: Oh, there are drum circles that meet down by the beach on a full moon or up in the mountains.

CLIENT: (laughing)

COACH: (laughing) Trust me, you can find them if you're looking for them.

CLIENT: Right.

COACH: Well, so did you hear the energy shift in your voice and your whole body?

CLIENT: Yeah—it does excite me, that one new thing I only did twice but it did feel like it was fun.

COACH: Yeah, and we don't want to put our eggs all in one basket, but to me, it sounds like—okay, that's something to research and make a big part of your life. It's not going to replace tennis. I know that. But it is going to replace the part of you that's missing—for social connection, for laughter, for fun, for relaxation, for something that's totally away from business and work. This resonates with me as a very good alternative. What do you think?

CLIENT: Yes. The two times I did it, I really couldn't believe it.

COACH: Here's something else I know about fun, just from life experience, that I'd like you to consider. If you just follow your heart, or your intuition, in drumming, my guess is that that's going to be a door opener to other things as well. There's going to be somebody in a drumming group who does something else. Maybe they do recumbent biking, or walking with poles, or some other activity you haven't considered.

CLIENT: A recumbent bike?

COACH: Yeah, a recumbent bike . . . one that you sit low to the ground and pedals are in front of you.

CLIENT: You mean they actually have bikes like that?

COACH: Yeah, I'm buying one next week because I just test-drove six of them. I love it. I mean, I happen to have knee problems, too, and I don't like the seats on most bicycles . . . so that's something to consider. I'm just saying that things will come from being in a drumming group because everybody in that drumming group will do other things in their life for fun.

CLIENT: Right. And the thing about the drumming is that it would really help with that other aspect of my life that is very small, which has to do with the spiritual.

COACH: Ahhh . . .

CLIENT: . . . because when people get into drumming, you get into a kind of an altered state.

COACH: Yeah, I love it. It excites me. Well, I'm going to ask you this big coaching question. That's what you want in the future is for fun to come back in your life, and it sounds as if some of that can be in the immediate future with this drumming.

CLIENT: Right.

COACH: What else do you want?

CLIENT: What else do I want in my life in general?

COACH: For fun.

CLIENT: Umm . . .

COACH: I guess the question is really this: so fun becomes part of your life again. That's great. What's the bigger question? What do you really want all that to lead to—really, really, really want?

CLIENT: I want more balance in my life, and more time with my partner.

COACH: Okay. Do you begin to see how all of these are interconnected?

CLIENT: (laughing) Yeah, I see.

COACH: I mean, when you've got a gap in a big area that you've kind of put in a drawer like Peter Pan's shadow, it's like you've hidden that away.

CLIENT: Right.

COACH: And what I know about shadow work, if you will, and this is not coaching right now, it's just some pondering, from what's coming up in my mind . . . is that our shadow holds what we don't want to look at anymore, but it also holds the part of us that hasn't been expressed yet, that has greatness within what we have not yet expressed or claimed. And it sounds to me like your expression is missing that. Fun enlivens your spirit, it increases the partnership you have with your husband, it increases the benefit of that, the happiness of that, the connection.

CLIENT: Yeah, you're touching something—because some tears just formed in my eyes, and I took a big sigh, and leaned back in my chair . . . so I feel like it's interesting.

COACH: Yeah, well good, because those are just feelings. Tears are great. I consider e-motion to mean energy in motion.

CLIENT: I like that . . . what a great way to view what is happening with my feelings . . . energy is moving.

COACH: So we're touching something that connects heart and spirit?

CLIENT: Right. Exactly.

COACH: It's amazing that sometimes we say fun is just fun. It's anything but just fun. It's a demand from your soul that you have some way of getting into this human being part of you instead of just the human busy and human doing part of you. This is a great example of that. Think of what we call fun. What's the word when people play that we often use?

CLIENT: You mean recreation?

COACH: Exactly. Now look at that word in a new way.

CLIENT: Re-creation. Oh my god! (laughing) That's great.

COACH: So my invitation to you is to try to create a formula in your mind where fun equals re-creation, but put a hyphen between the "re" and the "creation." Because that's really what I sense that you're up to.

CLIENT: (laughing) Yeah, that's totally cool! I never would have thought of that.

COACH: Well, we went from tears to ecstasy there. That's pretty good. (laughing) Do you feel finished enough for this conversation?

CLIENT: Oh yeah. Thank you.

COACH: So I'm just going to end here with a coaching request that you do follow up with the drumming group and allow yourself to be open to the newness of that. Don't throw it away easily.

CLIENT: Right.

COACH: See what you can do to make it fun, and who you're going to meet, what other social contacts come from that.

CLIENT: Right.

COACH: I don't know if your partner goes with you or not. That's up to you.

CLIENT: Yes, she does.

COACH: Okay, so there's partnership time together, too. And then learn what else comes from that while you're thinking, "What I'm really doing is re-creating who I am in that newfound way."

CLIENT: That's wonderful. Thank you.

Our Comments on This Session

- A coaching conversation is a sacred and inspiring space. You need to prepare the space, be focused, ready to receive the client and to be of service. Whether in person or over the phone, limit the distractions. One of the advantages of phone coaching for the coach is that you can stand up. You may want to close your eyes, move around the room, try to sense the client, the client's world and experience. Do whatever it takes so that your coaching presence serves the client and the client's agenda. Be fully present and available.

- The transcript illustrates the coach getting the client to do the work instead of handing answers to the client. The skill of evocative questions was used frequently. The coach's assumption is that the client has the answers that are right for her, and it's just the coach's role to facilitate their emergence. The questions evoked meaningful qualities and characteristics from the past, which let the client map over to her current reality. The coach encouraged her to draw on the past for clues about what is fulfilling.

- The coach and client didn't hurry through the session, although they did work within the time allotted for this session, which was 20 to 25 minutes. This created space for the client to go deep into this issue. Silence allowed the coach to just stand shoulder to shoulder with the client, without knowing, or needing to know, where the process was leading.

- The coach believed 100 percent that the conversation with the client would lead to a shift in thinking about some possibility, and that the results were not just magical because she had the answer within— they were magical because both (client and coach) were having this conversation.
- The client felt supported because the coach was "just there with her"— she felt there was a space for her to just be, without an answer, and that felt like a very empowering space.
- Later in this chapter we focus on asking questions that provoke insight, the kinds that clients don't normally focus on. In this session, note the power of the question, "What else do you want?"
- Moving into the future shifted things toward greater wholeness— something bigger than "fun" as an activity. This session became a conversation about bigger fulfillment. This is typical of how small issues in a client's life are microcosms of the larger issues. Coaches can use a single issue as a doorway to deeper desires or into habitual patterns of thinking and behaving.
- This session shows the coach and client focused around one area on the coaching tool, the Life Balance Wheel, which we cover in Chapter 9. The coach's conviction that people have a right to incorporate fun in everyday life is a personal assumption he makes, and it illustrates the importance of examining the assumptions coaches bring to their coaching (e.g., Is fun just something for vacations? Does it have to be a big activity? How about one-minute fun breaks during the day?)
- The coach's implicit assumption is that people know on some level what is true for them and what brings them joy. Creating space for clients to get in touch with and articulate their truth opens a door to inner wisdom. Ultimately the surfacing of inner solutions and possibilities takes place.
- The coach's questions lead the client to examine all the needs previously met by playing tennis. It was more than just physical activity for her, which led her to thoughtfully consider the issue she brought to coaching in such a way that she would realize a rich alternative for tennis, one that met needs and desires that weren't immediately obvious to her. This is one reason clients often maintain the shifts they make—the obvious answers aren't the ones they come away with from coaching.

- Coaching often draws on models of various possibilities, as this session shows. If the client says, "I don't know anyone like that," the coach and client can create a research project to find people who might be models. This is a creative way of dealing with a client who lacks experience.

- The session illustrates the importance of the coach respecting and validating the emotions that arise in the process of exploring an issue. Remember that clients bring to coaching conversations the issues they feel strongly about, and there's likely to be an emotional current to the issues. The coach must allow space for this and convey respect for the information communicated by emotions—from client to coach, and more important, from the client's soul to the client's conscious self.

  > When the coach says, "And sport isn't the only kind of fun. It just seems right now that that's the fun you lost," the statement validates the client's emotions while still holding out possibilities. This is very different from a possible therapy intervention such as: "It feels to you like the end of your world," which could allow the client to sink into hopelessness. The coach's reflection acknowledges the importance of sport while opening other sources for fun. It expands the client's possibilities instead of probing the depth of the loss.

- Pointing out to the client the shift in voice, energy, and body helps the client become more aware of what enhances her aliveness and grounds insights and breakthroughs in the body. This was a phone coaching session; the coach does not have to be physically present with the client to focus attention on the body.

- The coaching in this case was effective because the coach did not put himself in the role of expert. The illustration of the recumbent bike and having knee problems let the client know that she was not isolated in her need to make decisions based on physical limitations. It normalized the client's experience, which could help the client feel less isolated and more hopeful. The coach asked the client, "What do you really, really, really want?" People who are over-achievers and over-doers often lose sight of this question and forget to ask themselves this. It breaks through a lot of *shoulds* and helps people reconnect with their center, the place from which great wisdom often emerges.

- The conversation about shadow being, in part, about the unclaimed parts of ourselves was very powerful and non-pathologizing. It was a different way to look at the shadow, which contains unrealized creative aspects of ourselves as well as hidden and sometimes less acceptable aspects.
- The word re-creation serves as a kind of touchstone for the whole session. (The client's goal was recreation, and the coach realized that this was about re-creation.) When the client can take something firmly away—a symbol, thought, or phrase—this helps ground a session and the learning that took place. The client also gets an action step, so she is clear about what's next to support follow-through.

Crucial Skills and Competencies of Coaching

In this book, we are writing to ALL coaches, beginners, and seasoned practitioners. Although we embrace the Coaching Competencies of the International Coaching Federation, we also find wisdom in competencies taught in other coaching organizations. We have listed the most prominent in Appendix C at the back of this book.

However, there are key coaching skills and competencies (behaviors) that are embraced by the coaching community at large and demonstrate the uniqueness of the coaching relationship. As you read on in this book, keep in mind these key skills that are paramount to this unique relationship.

Presence

We as coaches need to leave what's pulling or pushing in our own life out of the client–coach relationship and be present and focused on the client in our interactions.

Curiosity

This skill is the "glue" that holds all coaching together. With curiosity, we can successfully suspend judgement, avoid the need to be right, withstand the temptation to advise and direct, and create evocative questions for the client based on our curious presence.

Creating Awareness Through Evocative Questions and Inquiry

When coaching, you will not need a list of good questions to ask; nor would such a list be truly effective. While you may have learned some good questions while training, or even from your own coaching experience, having a set list of questions would be like reading the manual to your new car while driving. Good questions come from good listening . . . and they are questions for exploration, not for making a point.

Silence

I sometimes call this purposeful pausing. After a client has been asked an exploratory question, be quiet, wait, and when the client responds or states insights or new thinking, ask, "What else can you share?"

There are many more coaching skills and nuances of the relationship, and we believe many are reflected throughout this book. Your real learning will come from putting them into practice in your training and in your coaching sessions.

SETTING THE STAGE: THE FIRST COACHING CONVERSATIONS

The first coaching conversation is an opportunity for the coach to explain what coaching is and how the coach goes about it. When doing this, the coach is already modeling what coaching can offer a prospective client. That is distinct from the first conversation after the client has hired the coach, when the coach is setting the stage and creating the alliance for the coaching engagement.

We begin here with a discussion of the coaching alliance because that alliance is a distinctive feature of the relationship between coach and client that strengthens the power of the relationship between coach and client with a clear understanding of expectations and the cocreation of a partnership.

Many of the participants at ILCT have been trained as helping professionals of some kind: therapists, psychologists, counselors, teachers, human resource professionals, and so on. They know how critical a system can be when people are trying to make a change. A system can enhance people's ability to make changes, supporting the direction they want to go, or it can create obstacles that may block change. One of the essential basic systems all professional training considers is the two-person system between the professional and the client. Every training program for helping professionals spends some time focused on the therapeutic alliance. The characteristics of that alliance are explicitly designed to further the clients' therapeutic work. While coaching can be therapeutic, it is not therapy. At ILCT, we ensure that students can differentiate kinds of alliances so they can create, with clients, an appropriate coaching alliance, clearly distinguished in its scope and purpose.

An alliance is defined as an association to further the members' common interests. Common therapeutic relationship alliances differ from the coaching alliance in several notable ways:

- Many of the expectations for therapeutic alliances have been set by the codes of ethics and the licensing or governing boards of the profession, as well as the those mandated by government. Other features of the alliances grow out of the beliefs about change held by helping professionals. Consultants often also have beliefs about the alliances they create with clients. In most cases, consultants have established themselves as experts, and the resulting alliances involve the expectations that the consultants will often be directive about the course of the engagement, and assume that clients lack expertise that the consultants provide. Clients are assumed to be willing recipients of the consultants' expertise. This is also generally true of the therapeutic alliance, where the therapist is highly responsible. The therapist engages in a very specific treatment protocol, generally for a diagnosed condition. There are protocols for treating severe depression, posttraumatic stress disorder, anxiety, addiction, and other therapeutic issues. In each case, the client follows the guidance and knowledge of the helping professional. The client is generally leaning on the professional for guidance in getting back to normal. Although many people see therapists for general "problems in living" where therapists may be working in a more coach-like fashion, we are referring to clinically recognized conditions where the client is suffering and truly needs therapy. Figure 2.1 illustrates one way a coach can describe the distinctions between therapy, mentoring, consulting, and coaching to his clients.
- The coaching alliance is truly designed as a partnership in service of a particular client's goals and desires—it is co-created. In the first session after a client has committed to coaching, the coach works with the cli-

ent to design the facets of this partnership. All facets can be designed uniquely, discussed, and redesigned as needed over the course of the coaching engagement.

- The coaching alliance aims to be truly satisfying for both coach and client. Each must be challenged; each must learn. This mutuality is sometimes described as the inter-developmental aspect of coaching. Coaches expect to grow because of the work they do with clients. If they find themselves not growing and learning, they may be saying yes to clients who are not a good fit for them.

The coaches' work truly depends on the quality and kind of alliances that are created. We want to create alliances that empower clients, support their learning and development, clarify the co-created partnership, and fully embrace that partnership.

We recommend a client "welcome packet" as a starting point for a formal coaching relationship. The welcome packet is a set of handouts for the client to read and fill out that includes items like the coaching "contract" or agreement, client goals, policies, and procedures. It is a powerful tool for engaging the client in deep and long-term thinking, and it also gives much useful information to the coach.

Other things we do at a first session: If the coach asked the client as pre-work to fill out a welcome packet, the coach reviews that information with the client. The coach describes the process of life coaching, ensuring that the client understands and is prepared for the whole-life perspective the life coach takes. Coaches can also ensure that clients understand how coaching differs from therapy and consulting. This can be particularly important for clients who have been in therapy or who have used consultants, so that they understand that a true partnership is the foundation of coaching. The work of this first session is to specify and create that partnership: the coaching alliance.

Once this has been established, the coach designs the coaching alliance with the client, starting with questions like: "How would you most like to use our time together?" or "What do you most want to gain from our relationship and time together?" (Keep in mind that beneath the goal they initially express there is often a deeper desire that coaching can uncover. It's not that they are hiding it . . . they just don't yet know what it is that they really want.) The coach reviews any supporting assessments the client has available, such as the

FIGURE 2.1

Professional Distinctions

THERAPY	MENTORING	CONSULTING	COACHING
Deals mostly with a person's past and trauma, and seeks healing	Deals mostly with succession training and seeks to help one do what you do	Deals mostly with problems and seeks to provide information (expertise, strategy, structures, methodologies) to solve them	Deals mosty with a person's present and seeks to guide them into a more desirable future
Doctor–patient relationship (therapist has the answers)	Older/wiser–younger/less-experienced relationship (mentor has the answers)	Expert–person with problem relationship (consultant has the answers)	Co-creative, equal partnership (coach helps clients discover their own answers)
Assumes many emotions are a symptom of something wrong	Limited to emotional response of the mentoring parameters (succession, etc.)	Does not normally address or deal with emotions (informational only)	Assumes emotions are natural and normalizes them
The therapist diagnoses, then provides professional expertise and guidelines to give clients a path to healing	The mentor allows you to observe his/her behavior and expertise, will answer questions, and provide guidance and wisdom for the stated purpose of the mentoring	The consultant stands back, evaluates a situation, then tells you the problem and how to fix it	The coach stands with you, and helps you identify the challenges, then works with you to turn challenges into victories and holds you accountable to reach your desired goals

Life Balance Wheel (see Chapter 9), coaching session preparation worksheet, and personality or perhaps behavioral self-assessments, such as the Myers-Briggs Type Indicator, the DISC personality profile test, or the Enneagram if you are trained to deliver and interpret. During this review, coaches demonstrate partnership by asking questions that allow clients to demonstrate their level of understanding of and comfort with themselves and their own lives.

We find it useful to ask clients to think back to one or two alliances or deep relationships that have really forwarded their growth and learning. Clients explore what made these relationships so empowering and supportive. Clients may draw upon sports coaches, best friends, mentors, business relationships, or family members. Coaches listen and help clients determine what important facets from these relationships can become essential parts of the coaching alliance.

Other ways a coach works with a client to design the relationship include determining specifics such as the client's long-term goals—what we call *coaching to the large life*—and how the client's short-term desires and intentions fit into the big picture of the client's ideal life.

This alliance is reinforced in every session, sometimes in minor ways such as the small talk that can occur at the start of the session. The coach welcomes the client and engages in small talk for a few minutes, as they get to know each other. Small talk helps both coach and client become present to each other in the moment. The coach asks the client what the client most wants out of the session today and then continues to clarify and deepen the outcomes the client desires in both the short term and long term.

No matter how well the coaching alliance is designed from the outset, the alliance can break down. Sometimes this occurs because the client makes changes and wants something different from what was originally desired. Even if the coach frequently checks in with the client, sometimes there can be breakdowns. The signs that the alliance is at risk include:

- The client forgets appointments, is chronically late, or is unprepared for appointments.
- The client has lost interest, or the coach has lost interest.
- The coach or client has personal difficulties that are impacting effectiveness. For example, the coach may be managing the health problems of an aging parent and has become the parent's caretaker. Initially this can create potential distractions. Other situations may include divorce or recalcitrant teenagers. We tell our clients, "Life happens between calls." And as life happens, the coaching alliance needs to be adjusted or renegotiated.

The coach needs to watch for these signs and pay attention to any physical or emotional reactions that indicate a shift. Behaviors, body symptoms, and language—both the coach's and the client's—are all potential indicators.

Renegotiating the alliance may be as simple as moving from one coaching session per week to one every two weeks, allowing the client more time and focus. A coach could ask the client, at this stage, "Might this be a good time for us to redefine our relationship? What would be most helpful to you right now?"

As in any relationship, clients can be reluctant to end the relationship completely. So, if the coach asks, the client may agree that less frequent sessions or maintenance calls once per month would be most beneficial. Dr. Pat has a client he has been coaching for six years. In the last two years, that person has simply asked to pay for one 15-minute check-in call per month. The client sends a summary of what has occurred for her during the month. Then she checks in and, during the course of the session, gets a chance to put into words what she is thinking and feeling about that month's life and work. It is as if the client experiences this as a "wake-up call" where she becomes fully present to her life through the process of putting it into words with her coach. Speaking out loud to another person her successes and her intentions is all she needs to return to self-coaching.

Another sign that the coaching alliance may be vulnerable is if coaches become focused on themselves and their performance, or their agenda, while they coach or are planning for coaching with the client. Coaches may not be aware of this, falling prey to what the psychological literature calls self-deception. One sign this is happening is when a coach begins to see clients as standing in less than their full humanity. To the coach, the client begins to be seen as a vehicle, an obstacle, or an instrument. For example, coaches may see clients as a vehicle for gaining similar clients in that particular business. If this happens, coaches will have some part of their attention focused on that future possibility, and not on the current clients' goals, results, and relationships. Diane asks most of her business executive clients to read *Leadership and Self-Deception* (Arbinger Institute, 2010), a small book with a powerful message. She has found that executives are particularly prone to putting people "in the box," as this book calls the situation when a person's own self-interests or fears unconsciously affect the relationship and alliance with another person. Psychological research on self-deception is becoming more common and is perhaps one of the most useful sources for coaches today on common pitfalls.

Designing the coaching alliance begins with the first communication the coach has with the client. Whether the coach's communication is an e-mail, a note on the back of a business card, a voice mail, or an initial phone call, the coach sets the stage for the coaching and creates the alliance from the start of that first contact. Some clients say they begin to understand the nature of the coaching alliance by reading the coach's website, which establishes the coach's SAT (style, approach, and tone).

First contacts with clients come in several different varieties: (a) calls from clients who are committed to coaching and want to determine whether the coach is the right coach for them; (b) contacts with people whom the coach has just met and who have expressed curiosity about what the coach does; and (c) calls from people who don't know much about coaching and want to find out more to figure out whether coaching fits their needs right now. Each of these situations requires a positive initial contact and flexibility from the coach to adjust the conversation to the client's focus for the call.

Coaching Conversations: The Initial Contact Call

The phone rings. The coach picks it up and—surprise! —a prospective client is on the phone. She knows that she wants to hire a coach and has some goals in mind. She discovered the coach when a friend of hers mentioned he had hired the coach to improve his work–life balance. The prospective client starts to tell the coach what she is looking for, and then the coach looks at the clock and realizes he has a coaching appointment with another client in 20 minutes. What will the coach do? What will the coach say·to the prospective client?

When coaches first begin their business, they often feel a sense of urgency that can manifest in two ways. First, when prospective clients call, coaches feel they must do the initial screening and turn clients into a paying engagement immediately. It is as if coaches don't feel they can tolerate any delay should the clients change their mind. Second, coaches often agree to coach anyone who comes along to gain experience, competence, and confidence. Although this impulse is common and perhaps understandable, we believe that coaches and clients benefit when they can be prepared and intentional about initial calls. We recommend designing a structure for this initial interview because clients and coaches should ideally assess the fit of the prospective alliance. Setting up a planned initial screening call during which the coach and client have at least 30 minutes to determine, without feeling rushed, whether they fit as partners, is critical. This call has several purposes:

- Coaches discover whether the clients' aspirations and goals are ones they can get behind and support, whether they fall within the coaches' targeted coaching niche, and whether the fit feels good.
- Clients can ask questions about the coaches' style and to assess personal fit from their standpoint.

- Clients hear themselves talk about their goals and desires for coaching, which can be illuminating and valuable, even if they don't end up working together.
- Coaches discover what kind of partnership clients expect, want, and need from coaches, and the coaches share their general expectations of clients. (If the two go forward and agree to work together, coaches will explore this in more depth during the first initial session.) This first official session is usually longer than subsequent calls and covers the client agreement, policies, procedures, and goals for the coaching relationship. We recommend this first session be at least 90 minutes, with the second half being the start of the actual coaching.

Other areas to examine regarding a comfortable fit include the following: payment capability, hours and times available, agreement about the method and frequency of coaching (face-to-face versus phone, weekly versus biweekly), whether the clients fit the coaches' ideal or minimal coaching profile, the coaches' interest in the goals or process, whether there is something the coaches will learn through this experience that will benefit them, and so on.

Through this dialogue, coaches begin to design the coaching alliance. The coaches' conduct during the calls conveys a wealth of information about their style and proficiency: What are the coaches' ratios of questions asked versus information provided? How well do the coaches listen? Do clients have a sense that the coaches get them and their situations? These are coaches' first opportunities to model in the moment what a coaching conversation is like. Coaches need to focus on the elements of the coaching conversation, as described earlier in this chapter, even in these initial interviews.

If the client has caught the coach at a bad time, the coach must not give in to urgency and feel obligated to discuss the possibility of working together at that moment. The coach needs to be confident enough in the value she or he offers to schedule the call at an appropriate time when full attention can be given, and the coach can demonstrate the spaciousness that coaching brings into the client's life.

The Living Brochure

The coach's intention is to discover the client's initial coaching goals as well as other long-term possibilities and to enroll the client as just that—a client.

Robert Alderman (1997) was one of the first people we know of who used the term "living brochure" to describe a conversation between a coach and a potential client.

The living brochure is an enrollment conversation. It was first labeled "living brochure" because the conversation takes the place of a printed brochure the coach would hand to a prospective client. Coaching is essentially a language-based series of conversations., coupled with insight, sensing, and connection. This is one of the reasons most coaches do not depend on standardized written promotional materials other than what appears on a website or is customized for specific clients for business development. Expensive brochures and collateral materials do not demonstrate the power of coaching. Coaching is relationship based, so the power is in conversation, not in the materials. Clients hire their coaches based more on who the coach is and how the client experiences the coach than on marketing materials. New coaches often believe they can't begin coaching without promotional materials and a website. We believe this mind-set grows out of a sense of insecurity, not out of any reality. What needs to come first is the conversation. Instead of getting ready to get busy, get busy having coaching conversations.

Essentially, the screening interview conversation takes place using insight provoking questions that the coach asks the potential client in a conversational manner. When Robert Alderman initially described this conversation to coaching colleagues, he stressed that the coach's intention is to help the client experience firsthand the value of coaches and coaching conversations. Value, of course, is assessed through the eyes of the client. The coach's intention is to be of value. The structure described below is one format for creating potential value through a first conversation.

In the coaching profession, it is common to refer to this as an enrollment conversation. We prefer to call this a conversation for exploration and discovery, which emphasizes the value of this conversation and the alliance that is beginning even during this one call. The exploration and discovery are real and of value, whether the client enrolls or doesn't. There are many kinds of conversations, identified by their purpose. If the value of the conversation for exploration is apparent to the client, all that is needed at the end of the call is for the coach to ask the client if the client is ready to get started.

Sherry Lowry, one of the original trainers of the ILCT faculty, articulated this well. She recommends that the coach use this conversation to set the stage for creating the most ideal client the coach would like to have in her practice. Don't simply see it as an enrollment conversation. It is most effective when the potential client has indicated an interest in the coach's work, so there is a reason why the coach and potential client are having the conversation—it is not just idle chatter to pass the time. The conversation may be face to face or on the phone or video conference. It may have been initiated by e-mail and then taken to the next step. This conversation is intended as a verbal exchange (as opposed to written) because what the coach says and does depends on the potential client's real-time responses. *It is an active demonstration of the coach's flexibility and ability to dance with the client.*

The coach's goal during the conversation for discovery is to create a sense of synergistic partnership. If this type of alliance can be created during the conversation, the match is probably harmonious enough to build a successful coaching alliance.

Below is an example of how Sherry conducts the conversation for discovery. An important note: This isn't a script. Stay focused on outcome, keeping in mind that the coach's goal is to understand more about the potential client's values, desires, intentions, behaviors, attitudes, passions, frustrations, and difficulties.

As the conversation progresses, the coach needs to reassess the outcome. For example, if early in the conversation the coach perceives that he or she is not the right coach for that client, the coach's outcome shifts. The new outcome becomes to determine whether the client is coachable at this time, and to learn enough about the potential client to make a knowledgeable referral (or at least to make a pertinent suggestion, such as recommending a book or workshop that may be a valuable resource).

If the coach determines that the caller isn't a potential client, the coach abandons the conversation for exploration and instead asks questions that lead to a referral to another coach or to clarity about what the client's next best step might be. For example, the coach may hear the client's desires and intentions, and realize that the client's life situation—for example, going through a divorce or handling a rebellious child—may need a referral to a therapist prior to coaching. Or the client may be coachable but doesn't fit the profile of the kinds of clients this coach works with. The coach does the most appropriate thing before ending the call, including potentially explaining the coach's thinking behind any recommendation. It is acceptable for a coach to say, "I don't think I'm the best coach for you," even while acknowledge the client's intentions and desires. The coach would then give the caller the name and contact information of two or three other coaches likely to be more suitable or refer the caller to the ICF coach referral location at www.coachingfederation.org.

The point: The coach focuses on being of service and a resource to this person. Our experiences show that clients greatly appreciate this and may show up in the coach's life at some future point. They may become a client in the future or refer other clients to this coach. Through the conversation for discovery, the client has learned the kinds of clients and situations this coach best works with.

Here is an example of the conversation for exploration and discovery in action.

Step 1: Start with an Ice Breaker

People love to talk about themselves. Encourage this process. Once the coach hears more about the person, the coach will have a sense of how to proceed and will have some language to use. Ask questions like: "Describe yourself in terms of how you see yourself" or "Tell me something about how you came to this point in your life to make this contact with a coach."

Step 2: Get to the Important Issues

Find out early if potential clients have some important issues they want to bring to coaching and whether they are willing and able to uphold their own interest in a coaching partnership. (This is work as well as pleasure!) Ask questions like: "What are three things you'd like to change in your life within thirty days, starting at this moment?" or "If you could add three things of vital importance to your life, beginning this month, what would they be?"

Step 3: Discover Personal Boundary Issues

Get to questions that will uncover issues around boundaries, integrity, needs, wants, and values. Ask questions like, "Do you feel as though you run your job/business, or are there many times when it's running you?"

Step 4: Ask "Ouch" Questions

These are questions that identify sore spots, tender topics, and "pinches" the client is experiencing. Ask questions such as: "Are there any places in your life where you feel incomplete, where something is unfinished, and that needs to be addressed?" "Where in your life are you feeling burdened and carrying a heavy weight of responsibility?" "Do any of these places need to be shifted or cleaned up?" A corollary question might be: "Is there an area where you would like to become significantly more responsible for something than you are now, and you are disappointed in the lack of responsibility you have?" The goal here is to discover any unfinished business or difficult areas that the client would normally not discuss or associate with the context of his or her goals. A client whose father died the previous month, for example, might need time to grieve before beginning coaching—or not. But if the coach is aware of this, the coach can acknowledge that it could have an impact on the client's energy and attention.

Coaching may assist with these areas, and a proper referral may be suggested. Coaches can work with clients who want to take more responsibility for their children's learning and well-being, or to improve their relationships with their children. Diane worked with an executive who wanted to be more available to his teenage children. He discovered through the conversation for discovery that it was a source of a deep sense of loss for him that he had been unavailable to attend soccer games and tournaments when his children were younger, because of the extent of his travel. Through working with Diane, he turned his loss and disappointment into an intention to realign his time and commitments. Without asking an ouch question, this issue might never have been addressed.

Step 5: Plant the Seed of Self-Care

Part of creating value in the conversation is to plant the seed that doing something for oneself is a beneficial and worthwhile pursuit. For example, ask a question such as, "What kinds of things do you do for yourself when you need time alone?"

Step 6: Discuss Mutual Commitment

It's important to convey the importance of mutual commitment in the coach–client relationship. Say something like, "There is a mutual commitment we both make when we engage in coaching. If this works out for us, are you prepared to?" This can be, "Are you prepared to set aside time, energy, and space to fulfill your intentions?" Make these requests relevant to the coach's practice and the client's process.

It is useful to ask for a non-binding commitment to work together for 90 days. The coach may say something like, "After 90 days, we can then decide to go forward or determine that we've accomplished what we set out to do. In the meantime, I'll ask you to try on new ways of doing things and looking at your life. Sometimes these may ask you to stretch. For each of these options, I'll ask if you're willing to take on something new for possibly a week, a month, or longer. Would you be comfortable committing to exploring this process with me?"

Some coaches ask for a commitment and discuss the financials from Step 7 at the conclusion to the conversation for discovery. This takes more time, but it allows for fuller discovery of whether there's a match. It is necessary to discuss this as part of making a living as a coach. A major mistake new coaches make is to be reluctant to ask for commitment and to discuss fees and procedures.

Step 7: Get to the Financials

One part of creating perceived value is engaging in a conversation about the professional fee. The coach begins this step by feeding back to the client three changes or intentions the client has stated during this conversation. The coach can ask, "Do you agree that it would be valuable for you to attain these changes? Is it worth it for you to engage a coach to help you?" Then the coach explains fees and options. Most coaches have several different options for working with clients. Fees depend upon the length of sessions, the frequency of sessions, whether coaching is to occur primarily by phone or primarily in-person, the availability of the coach between sessions, and other factors.

Step 8: Focus the Client's Attention on Values

Highlight the choices clients would make if financial constraints didn't exist. Ask questions like: "If you became independently wealthy, what would you do with your life?" "If you knew success was guaranteed or that failure was highly remote, how would you be living differently?" These questions get to inherent values that may be outside the clients' awareness due to a belief that those options are impractical or impossible. These questions allow clients space to reflect on what they really value and what they really want.

For example, a client may say, "If money weren't a problem, I'd live on a Caribbean Island and own a coffee shop, like the little one I saw on the island of Saint John last year." Even though that might be a fantasy, what it points to is that the client may want more simplicity, a less rushed pace, and a life of more relaxation. Coaching can help the client surface and realize that intention, even if the fantasy doesn't become a reality. Either way, encouraging the client to take an island vacation couldn't hurt. Or the client may have articulated exactly what he or she wants for the future.

Step 9: Process Check

If the coach has decided the person would be a good fit, this step establishes whether the client is ready to sign on or is in the process of deciding about coaching. A good fit means that the client fits the coach's desired client profile or niche and the coach can fully get behind the client and his or her intentions. Ask something like, "At this point you seem like the kind of client I love to work with. I want to check in with you. Do you think your intentions can get realized through working with me? Are you ready to get started?" Or "When you imagine the life you want, how do you see yourself starting your day?" Follow that up with a "barometer question" such as, "Can you tell me how you are thinking about coaching and its value from our conversation so far?" The coach might then ask whether the potential client has any questions or whether there's anything the coach can clarify or expand on. And by the way, this check in is valuable in every coaching appointment to clarify if the client is finding the time helpful, insightful, and useful, or if something different is needed in the moment.

Step 10: Testing

This builds on Step 6, where the coach focused on mutual commitment. By Step 10, the coach will have a sense of what can be asked of this person in the coaching relationship. Ask questions to check out commitment more fully, such as: "Would you be willing to try new options, even if they are unfamiliar and very different from how you work and live every day?" Or "Would you be willing to partner with me in discovering your habitual patterns, assessing whether they are beneficial or need realigning, and seeing what new options you might create?"

Step 11: Create Awareness

This step stretches the potential client's thinking about what is possible—the life the client may not be living and the potential that coaching can unleash. "What big opportunities are out there for you personally or in your business that you are not yet taking advantage of?" "What hidden gift or talent might you have that deserves a more prominent place in your life?"

This step, along with Step 10, can open new possibilities and awareness for the client. It also lets the coach discover the client's mind-set: how the client habitually attends to possibilities and the obstacles that stand in their way. This is discussed as part of the Big Five and in Chapter 1.

Step 12: Discover What Is Working

With the recent research from the field of positive psychology, we know that the best coaching conversations are rooted in the client's strengths. In this step, the coach focuses on the client's strengths and joys. The coach asks questions like: "What kinds of things make you happy—make your heart dance?" "When do you catch yourself smiling?" "When was the last time you laughed? Is this a regular occurrence or a luxury?" Coaches also ask about how other people view the client: "What would others say you do well?" "What do you bring into their lives?"

Coaches often concern themselves with quality of life and are sensitive to the possibility of an Achilles heel issue. If clients say they haven't laughed or smiled in quite a while and that is the norm, it might be appropriate to ask, "How long has it been since you have experienced joy and fulfillment?" Asking this question might elicit an emotional reaction from the client and help to determine underlying issues. This question also allows the coach to model compassion and willingness to uncover and normalize emotions in a client's experience.

Step 13: Educate About Coaching

Find out how much clients know about coaching. Many clients have read articles about coaching and have some understanding of it. Ask, "Have you read articles about coaching?" Determine whether you need to provide clients with articles or refer them to your website or others to learn more about the profession of coaching and how it works. This can be particularly important if clients are only familiar with coaching in the business environment, which can in some cases be focused solely on correcting performance deficits.

Step 14: Make a Declaration

Coaches do not often tell potential clients how much they would like to work with them. It has been reported by many clients that even when they interview coaches, few ever say, "I'd enjoy working with you. I'd love to be your coach." If this person is someone you want to coach, find a comfortable way to tell the potential client. If the potential client says something like, "I need more time" or "Let me think about it," you can ask, "Are there more questions you'd like to ask now to help you clarify your decision?" or "Would you prefer to contact me when you're ready?"

This is the natural point in the conversation for the potential client to decide if this works. If the potential client is very hesitant or has a low tolerance for risk, or if the potential client has financial considerations, you have many ways to work with these situations. Make a nonbinding agreement, for example. Be prepared to address considerations in a completely constructive way. People rarely make good coaching clients if they need to be talked into it.

Step 15: Clarify Issues

You want to be clear that potential clients understand the commitment and concept of coaching. Here's a chance to correct any misconceptions—to clarify that a coach is not a guru or a taskmaster but a partner, a guiding mentor/coach, and so on. Ask: "Can you describe what you think my role as coach and your role as client will be?"

You want to listen carefully to clients' expectations. If they seem ready for coaching and you seem to be the right coach for them, move to Step 16. You may need to negotiate with clients their readiness to start and their expectations of you. If you don't seem to be a good fit for them, you may want to refer them to another coach who would be.

Step 16: Make an Offer

Suggest, in specific terms, the next step. "Our next step is to schedule a first session where we review our welcome packet and the agreement and reaffirm and clarify your intentions and goals for the next 90 days. Can we begin that work on the date of . . . at . . . time?" Or "My repeat client appointments are on Tuesdays and Wednesdays. Is a morning or evening time better for you? Generally, I reserve a block of time in the afternoon for my personal affairs, but from time to time I can schedule at other times or during weekends or evenings. With 24 hours' notice, there is no charge for rescheduling. After all, we both know life happens."

USING STRUCTURES

There's a truism that safety comes with consistency: what we can count on comforts us. Paradoxically, it also provides adequate space for people to make radical changes. The structures coaches use support clients in taking responsibility for their life and the coaching work. In coaching, we use consistency in the relationship and in session structure to create a large space in which the client is given free rein to experiment and explore without worrying about a safety net.

Two tools that give structure—the welcome packet and the coaching session preparation worksheet—expedite the initial work and set clear expectations for the overall engagement as well as for ongoing sessions.

The Welcome Packet

The coach's intention for a first paying session with the client is to accomplish the following:

- Review the logistics, policies, and procedures; create rapport and a beginning framework for the coaching alliance
- Begin to develop the client's long-term intentions and vision, as well as short-term goals
- Model the coaching conversation and the coaching alliance in action

The welcome packet is discussed more fully in *Therapist as Life Coach* (Williams & Davis, 2007), which offers examples of a welcome packet for new clients—something most coaches have available for email as well as in-person distribution. This packet may include additional forms, articles, and readings the coach finds relevant for a specific client. We suggest that at this time you send only what you will use during the first month: assessments, exploratory questions, policies, procedures, and the client agreement. We sometimes ask the client, "Are you a paper person? How are you at dealing with forms?" This lets us know whether to send the whole packet at one time or send individual pieces just in time for their use.

We believe it is important for the client to have to do some self-reflection as part of completing the welcome packet because reflection will be required during the coaching engagement. Without reflection, the client will simply repeat habitual patterns of thinking, feeling, and acting. Also, requiring the client to prepare will be something the coach will expect for each session. Client preparation is one of the ways that the partnership between coach and client is ensured. An unprepared client tends to foist responsibility for the session onto the coach. The welcome packet is crucial for laying the groundwork for the long-term relationship. Coaches frequently refer to the client's detailed responses for engaging conversations about original goals and intentions, which may be a resource for identifying new intentions and necessary course corrections.

The welcome packet performs two functions: (a) it introduces clients to the coach's policies and practices and (b) it provides clients with information about the work you will be doing together.

To design a good welcome packet, coaches need to clarify their intentions for using it. Some coaches get their packets to clients via e-mail. Others choose to put the welcome packet and other information into a notebook and mail it to clients. The welcome packet can even be sent a few pages at a time in the first month of coaching, as not to overwhelm the client with paperwork. Ask the client what is preferred and adapt accordingly.

The Coaching Session Preparation Worksheet

Most coaches also ask clients to prepare in advance of phone sessions. Many use coaching session preparation worksheets, which are faxed or emailed to the coach before the phone sessions. These are commonly one-page forms that help keep the coach and client focused on what the client wants from each session. Coaches keep completed forms as a resource for documenting their clients' progress and accomplishments. We like to ask clients, as part of the coaching session preparation worksheets, to record successes and highlights of the time between sessions, as well as opportunities and challenges. We also ask them to identify priorities for the sessions. These will become part of the session agenda.

Great Questions for the Discovery Conversation, Welcome Packet, and First Sessions

We discuss "powerful questions" as a coaching skill in more depth later in this chapter. However, questions that are evocative and stimulating to the client are essential to a client beginning to experience coaching as a unique and powerful conversation. Without powerful questions, the coaching conversation can fail to inspire. What follows is a list of a few powerful questions that can be used in a variety of contexts but are particularly useful in engaging the client in the beginning. The coach may want to use them for a living brochure, include them in the welcome packet for the client to think about in preparation for the first session, or ask them during the early sessions. Many of these questions are "edgy"—they'll stretch both the coach and the client.

- What gives you energy?
- What makes you feel discouraged?
- What strength, skill, or gift do you wish to use more fully?
- What do you most want from coaching?
- What are three changes you could make right now that would move you closer to your desired outcome?
- How do you get in your own way?
- Where do you find yourself feeling cautious or careful about making changes in your life?
- How will you assess the value of our work together?
- How can I best coach you? (What would not be helpful?)
- When do you waste time and energy?
- How do you like to learn?
- What three things do you really want to accomplish in the next 60 to 90 days?
- How might I recognize when you have something difficult to express to me?

The First Coaching Session

Set aside a minimum of an hour for the first session. The coach has several major goals for this first session:

- **Clarify expectations**. Clarify the nature of the partnership and discover what will make the coaching valuable from the client's perspective. True value lies in how the client attributes value to the coaching, not in how the coach perceives value. Discuss requests and expectations you have of each other and the processes you will use for the coaching (face-to-face, prep sheets, e-mail in between, and so on). Review how to use the coaching session preparation worksheet.

- **Discover intentions and desires.** You will already have asked questions that provide insight into the client. Ask more about things that interest you about the client, listen well, and draw forth the client's aspirations, desires, and wishes through evocative questions.
- **Begin work on the client's goals.** The welcome packet should contain worksheets where the client lists goals. Use these to clarify and expand the understanding of goals and their importance in the client's life, then set a timeline. Most coaches review and clarify information on goals by time frame: 30-day goals, 90-day goals, and longer-term goals.
- **Coach the client's being and life.** The client will discover rapidly that he or she needs ample energy to accomplish goals. Taking time to focus on energy drainers can be useful. If the welcome packet includes a form asking the client to list things that drain his or her energy, you can review this during the first session. This information provides insights into the client's current life and obstacles. You can directly help clear some of the deck by identifying ways the client can eliminate or reduce energy drainers.
- **Model how it is to be an authentic human being**. Listen fully from the heart. (A first session should be about 80 percent listening.) Allow for periods of silence—"the fertile void." Pave the way for the basic coaching conversation. The coach's authenticity is paramount to the coaching relationship because, like it or not, your authenticity is a model for clients' movement toward increasing authenticity in their lives. Many of their workplaces—like much of their lives—support inauthenticity rather than authenticity because the workplace is under the illusion that authenticity brings about conflict and gets in the way of achieving results. In coaching, authenticity encourages people to show up as who they really are—warts and all—and to create results that flow from their authentic desires, strengths, and uniqueness.

Preparing for Coaching Sessions

Coaches need to have practices for becoming present, focused, and centered to bring their best self to each coaching session and maintain the spaciousness needed for great coaching. Coaching by telephone requires discipline to avoid getting distracted by one's environment. Even though the client cannot see the distraction, the client will sense it and the session will be negatively impacted.

A good practice is to build in at least 10 minutes between coaching sessions and do the following before each session:

- Clear the desk of materials not relevant to the session and eliminate distractions.
- Center yourself: quiet your mind, meditate for a few minutes, and breathe.
- Hold the client in your consciousness and review materials and notes from the last session.

At the end of the session, allow enough time to provide solid closure. Set the next appointment, summarize commitments (yours and the client's), and close comfortably without feeling rushed to the next appointment. The tone on which the coach wraps up the session will stay with the client, so be sure to end in a manner that reflects your commitment to the client.

Personal Ecology: Working with Energy Drainers

Energy drainers are those things one is tolerating, ignoring, or putting up with that are draining. They can be mental clutter or physical clutter, but when handled they allow the client to reclaim lost energy. Giving an early coaching focus to energy drainers is a wise strategy. You can even begin to address this issue during a complimentary session. Ask clients to prepare a list of energy drainers and send them to you in advance. This will prepare clients for the session and give them some immediate success in areas of life that could block them from attaining the success they seek. The advantages of dealing with energy drainers are illustrated in the following excerpt from a holiday newsletter by Phil Humbert (2001), a longtime coach and author of a personal success newsletter.

> Mary and I spent most of today cleaning out closets. It wasn't supposed to be that way, but we were giving a table and chairs to a charity and started thinking about what else we ought to give.
>
> We ended up taking six blankets and assorted towels and linens to a local shelter, a large box of books to the public library, and several boxes of housewares, clothes, and assorted odds and ends (along with the table) to charity.

My point? Well, along with feeling virtuous and bragging about how "generous" we are, there is something much larger going on here.

If success is about efficiency (and it partly is), then anything that clutters up the coach's life, or adds friction, or distracts the coach, or gets in the coach's way, undermines the success. That's what the concept of "tolerations" is all about. When we tolerate a few frustrations—a few nuisances and annoyances that sap our energy and reduce our concentration—soon the impact on our effectiveness becomes significant. Don't do that to yourself!

As I look at closets that are the neatest they have been in years, my life is richer tonight. As I look at a dining room that will be more useful and more inviting, I know our meals will be more pleasant, which may reduce stress and improve digestion, communication, diet, nutrition . . . and the list goes on. All from giving away things that have cluttered our home and our lives.

Your Personal Eco-System consists of the immediate environment—your home and the people and things around you—and that environment either supports you in achieving your most important priorities, or it slows you down. Your home, office, car, friends, and loved ones function as a system to either support you or slow you down.

I think of a highly efficient environment as being a Personal Support System, while highly inefficient environments not only create friction and hold us back, but at some point, they can become toxic and can kill our dreams—even kill our sense of ambition and hope.

This holiday season, along with the parties and year-end celebrations, take time to clean out your personal ecosystem. Clean up the nest. Clean up any misunderstandings or personal hurts. Clean out the closets, both literally and figuratively. It will enrich you with an immediate sense of well-being and will allow you to perform at a higher level with greater focus and clarity in the months to come. And isn't that what success is about?

If the first coaching session and the welcome packet are well designed, coaches and clients will have learned a great deal about who the clients really are, as well as the clients' intentions and any ways they block themselves. These pieces of information alone can provide major value to the client. We recommend that coaches keep each client's welcome packet easily available. Coaches can use it to do a three or six-month review, looking back at the client's original intentions in detail. Unless the coach prefers a paper-less office, a useful practice is to create a file folder for each client. Staple the welcome packet to the inside left panel of the folder. Keep coaching session preparation worksheets and coaching notes to the right, with the newest one on top. This gives coaches the opportunity to rapidly review critical information and bring back issues the clients may have taken off their radar screen, perhaps because they were superseded by crises or by pressing issues. In essence, the coach can return the client to focus on enduring intentions and desires by referring to the welcome packet information.

Transparent Language, Powerful Questions, and Purposeful Inquiry

As we have said, coaching takes place during conversations we have with clients. A coaching conversation differs from an everyday conversation because the coach uses language intentionally and powerfully. Our language—words, rhythms, timing, nuances, metaphors, stories, and tones—becomes the most potent resource the coach has in working with the client. Unlike the usual conversational rhythms, the coaching conversation is aimed at creating insight for the client, new ways of thinking, and new connections between ideas or possibilities.

If you listen to a coaching conversation, the language of coaching sounds simple. Simple, yes—easy, no. It is deceptively simple. The coach's language encourages depth of thinking and self-reflection. Its intention is to be direct and transparent so that the client's thinking, language, and processes are highlighted. The coach's language is free of unspoken judgments and assumptions. [See David Grove's work on transparent questions as summarized in Tompkins & Lawley (1997).]

New coaches sometimes go astray by believing that questionnaires, forms, articles, and models are essential to great coaching. They are not, although they can serve as confidence-building props for the new coach. In fact, the language you use with the client—the questions you ask—will be the most powerful resource you bring to your practice. It is through your language that much of your presence is communicated.

Powerful and Evocative Questions

Stuart Wells (1998) wrote that strategic thinking is critical to the future. He offered three key questions that every leader must ask repeatedly:

- What seems to be happening?
- What possibilities do we face?
- What are we going to do about it?

These questions mirror the questions asked throughout the coaching process. The coach's primary tool is the use of provocative questions that reach deep inside the client and generate insight, allowing the client access to new possibilities.

How skillfully and successfully you navigate the basic coaching conversation depends on your ability to ask questions that form the foundation of coaching—they guide and focus the client's thinking. A coach's questions need to go well beyond the pedestrian; they need to be powerful in their ability to catalyze the client's thinking and behavior.

Powerful questions have the uncanny power to focus attention, change the way a client feels, and prompt the client to make choices and take actions not previously considered because they were outside his or her awareness. Jerry Hirshberg (1998) noted that powerful questions "are often disarmingly simple and are particularly effective in jarring 'The Known' loose from its all-too-familiar moorings, the thick, dead underbrush of old associations and assumptions, allowing for fresh light on a subject, and the potential for the growth of new ideas." We know from studies in neurobiology that the human mind cannot resist answering a question. The common experiment of asking someone not to think of a white elephant illustrates how the mind responds to suggestions. Questions work the same way. Ask the client a question, and the client will begin to search for an answer.

Helping professionals are familiar with the power of a great question. Steve de Shazer, one of the founders of solution focused brief therapy, was known all over the world for one single question he invented. His simple—but profoundly provocative—"Miracle Question" is used by thousands of therapists (and coaches) every day: What if, overnight, a miracle occurred, and you woke up tomorrow morning and the problem was solved? What would be the first thing you would notice? (de Shazer & Lipchik, 1984).

Like the Miracle Question, powerful questions serve the client in three ways:

- They draw out the client's hidden or untapped potential.
- They focus the client on high-leverage points for change.
- They speak to the client's creative powers and resources to generate new options.

Questions serve many purposes in coaching. Questions can open an area and expand, or they can probe and intensify a focus. As guides for the client's attention, they can be used to:

- Encourage, support, or validate
- Initiate, uncover, or surface issues
- Draw out and discover what is not apparent, or clarify what has been surfaced
- Generate new possibilities
- Respectfully challenge thinking, behavior, and limitations
- Identify assumptions

We sometimes ask new coaches to watch a few of Peter Falk's *Columbo* episodes, where his ability to ask an apparently stupid question is actually a wise and skillful way of focusing attention on what is missing or occurring that has yet to become transparent. Therapists reading this book might be familiar with the questions Milton Erickson asked, which were designed to cause creative confusion for the client and to create an opening beyond the client's present awareness and habitual ways of thinking. For example: "Do you think you will begin to change this Tuesday, or will you wait to begin next week?" This kind of question implies that change will happen, focusing the client's attention on when it will take place.

Erickson also used questions to interrupt habitual patterns. We have used questions this way, requesting that clients ask themselves during every hour of their workday, "Right now, how am I being the leader I want to be?" A question like this forces the client's attention onto reflecting on the previous hour, something the client otherwise might not do. The reflection creates awareness and insight from which can emerge choice-driven change.

A good practice for coaches is to tape their end of a coaching conversation to review the questions they asked. This practice lets coaches assess whether they are limiting their questions and whether their questions actually land powerfully on the clients' ears. When a client says, "That's a good question," the coach knows the question is likely to generate insight.

INQUIRY: A SPECIAL KIND OF PROVOCATIVE QUESTION

A particular type of powerful question is the inquiry. Many spiritual traditions use inquiry practices as ways of developing self-awareness and self-understanding. An inquiry is a question that a person holds in mind continuously and contemplates over a specific period. When a coach requests that the client do an inquiry, the client will live with the inquiry question daily until the next session. This is a great example of the famous passage by poet Rainer Maria Rilke (1929/1992):

> Live your questions now. And perhaps even without knowing it, you will live along some distant day into your answers.

Inquiries are questions that encourage clients to reflect deeply. Because they live with the question over a period of time, they find many ways of answering it. The principle of inquiry is that the human mind can't not answer a question. When we put the right question in front of us, we open avenues for exploration and answers that would previously not have revealed themselves.

Readers may be familiar with how journaling and silent retreats may help us outrun habitual ways of judging and certainty and create an opening for internal dialogue. This is the principle of inquiry at work. It is powerful and life changing. These are questions that don't have easy answers. Socrates made these famous through the Socratic inquiry process he used with his students. He would walk with them past the town gate, asking difficult and penetrating questions about virtue, peace, ethics, and so on. In life coaching, that is exactly what we want to do. We want to ask questions that challenge clients to think, aspire, and act beyond their current status quo.

In the field of coaching, inquiry can radically deepen and expand the way clients experience their capabilities and assets, as well as their ability to process how and what they notice. Two main purposes of inquiry are to generate self-awareness and to encourage clients to increase awareness of their beliefs, behaviors, and life to create more choices and responsibility.

Coaches model for clients the ability and willingness to be "in the inquiry," that is, be comfortable with open questions, and emphasize curiosity and discovery. Like our clients, sometimes we just want to know. Yet because coaching is a learning model, we serve our clients in significant ways when we stay willing to not know.

Coach Marilee Adams made a useful distinction. She said there are two mind-sets from which questions develop: the judger mind-set and the learner mind-set (see Figure 2.2). Judgers focus on problems, noting what is wrong, assessing issues of control, making assumptions, and attempting to be right. If coaches come from the judger mind-set, they will not be effective. Learners, in contrast, focus on what is right (about themselves, the other person, and the situation), what the choices are, what can be learned, and what they are responsible for. The learner mind-set is the mind-set of the coach. The coach's stance is to be willing to be "in the inquiry" instead of "in the answer." Adams's book, *Change Your Questions, Change Your Life* (Adams, 2009), contains examples of insightful questions and the changes they produced in specific cases (see more at www.InquiryInstitute.com).

Many business leaders commonly come from the judger mind-set, constantly looking for closure and drawing conclusions. Malcolm Gladwell (2005) illuminated how this works in the human mind and body. *Blink* focuses on the value of the judgment mind-set and its risks. As Gladwell showed, judgments are often made within a fraction of a second. For thousands of years, this has served humans well. It has allowed us to make snap decisions about safety issues and to take appropriate action.

Habitual quick judgments can be helpful or can hinder clients. Inquiry is a method coaches use to ask clients to examine their mostly unconscious patterns of judging, in the service of creating a new way of being that will allow them access to a greater fund of internal and external wisdom.

Accountability Questions

Coaching brings movement in clients' lives in part because it creates accountability on the part of the clients—to coaches, and even more importantly to themselves. At the end of each coaching session, coach and client should be able to answer these questions:

- What will you do?
- By when?
- How will you know you have been successful?
- How will I or others recognize success?

Some clients, particularly those in the business world, have become victims of their habitual tendencies toward accountability. They overuse accountability, driving themselves to accomplish tasks at the expense of self-reflection on the worth of the tasks and assessment of whether the actions lead to desired outcomes.

Staying Close to the Client's Language

The chapter has focused extensively on the ways coaches use questions, an essential part of the coaching conversation. When coaches hear the term powerful questioning, they frequently put pressure on themselves to make every question they ask a powerful question. In fact, the simplest questions can have a powerful effect on clients. Coaches often don't know whether their questions will be powerful until they ask them, and the clients respond. Powerful questions, as we think of them, are not guru questions, coming from a place of demonstrating the coach's expertise or superiority.

As an antidote to the tendency of new coaches to overfocus on having every question be powerful, coaches can explore the brilliance of very simple questions that stay very close to the clients' language. Many ILCT students come from a helping profession background, so they are familiar with trends in this profession such as working with narratives and with language and its assumptions. We ask ILCT students to explore therapist David Grove's work on transparent questions, through reading the online article, *Less Is More: The Art of Clean Language* (Tompkins & Lawley, 1997).

The authors, students of Grove, summarized how Grove's focus on clean language creates the opportunity for clients to fully self-observe. Grove's questions enable clients to experience their own patterns of thinking, feeling, and responding in "real time." As a result, transformations occur. Grove is probably best known for Clean Language, a questioning model for working with the metaphoric and symbolic domain of experience. Less well known are his later innovations such as Clean Space and Emergent Knowledge. What unites all Grovian processes is the notion of working 'cleanly.' The clean language website (www.cleanlanguage.co.uk) contains several examples showing how closely clients' words are reflected in active listening responses. Grove teaches therapists, but his lessons apply equally to those who use mirroring reflecting back to the clients so that the clients can learn. In Grove's view, the coach's words ideally reflect what the clients say, adding little, but tracking so closely that the clients truly hear themselves.

We're calling this use of language "transparent" because it does not clutter the lens of clients as they do their work. The coach uses as few words as possible, so clients have more time and space to think, work, and express themselves.

Transparent language doesn't add to what clients say, rather, it closely tracks and reflects clients' language, allowing them to see more clearly who they are, what they want, and where they will go.

A client might say, for example, "I've felt very stuck about my job for a long time. I'm trapped in this job, and I have no way out of these golden handcuffs." A coach could ask a question such as, "What resources of courage and determination would you need to leave?" This could be a useful and powerful question for the client. However, Grove's work suggests that the coach is adding a new lens and filter, that of courage and determination, adding to the client's current construct of the situation. The coach is not working transparently because the coach is focusing the client's attention on the option of leaving the situation or mustering up the resources to do so.

This might be a useful approach. On the other hand, it shifts the client's focus to what could or should be done. Another alternative for the coach is to track very closely the client's own language and stay within the current frame of the client's thinking. The following is an example of ways the coach can ask questions and remain transparent with the client:

CLIENT: "I've felt very stuck about my job for a long time. I'm trapped in this job, and I have no way out of these golden handcuffs."
COACH: "What kind of stuck is this for you?"
   or
COACH: "What is your experience of being stuck in your job for a long time?"
   or
COACH: "What is your experience of being stuck and feeling trapped with no way out of the handcuffs?"

Each of these questions asks the client to elaborate on the current experience of the situation. To use a phrase from Gestalt psychology, these questions ask the client to work with the figure-ground of the situation. The figure is what he or she is most attending to—it has arisen out of the ground of all that could need attention in this situation. In the excerpt above, the coach's question asks the client to focus more and more attention on his or her own experience of being stuck. The coach's questions ask the client to gather more information about the current situation—what is true now—before moving to a course of action that will shift things. The coach's questions invite the client to examine his or her thoughts, then experiences—sensations, awareness, emotions, and so on. This richer view of what is happening now—a richer figure in the language of Gestalt—facilitates an understanding on the part of the coach and client of what will facilitate a shift to a more satisfactory situation for the client. With more richness and texture in the client's awareness, several new directions may emerge. The client may discover that being stuck somehow yields a payoff. Or the deep exploration of feeling stuck may invigorate and energize toward doing something different.

The second choice for the coach, still working transparently, could be to explore the client's desired situation. Once the current situation has been explored, the coach might ask, "What would happen if you could find a way out of the handcuffs?"

In essence, transparency means staying within the context and language used by the client—not adding different metaphors, a new framework, or a different context to what the client says. Many coaches surprise themselves when they tape their part of a coaching session and discover just how much they add: information, assumptions, directions. Coaches need to ask, "Have I stayed close to the clients' language and given it enough time so they have a full, rich sense of their situation?" Coaches need to restrain themselves from adding too soon, even if their intention is to add consciously, intentionally, usefully, and respectfully. Coaches need to maintain appropriate boundaries—working transparently and cleanly communicates respect for clients' boundaries and ability to understand and create.

Questions form a major vehicle for moving the coaching conversation along. But when a question contains an assumption, clients can absorb that assumption without realizing its impact. Every assumption establishes a framework that creates some choices and obscures those outside the framework.

A better vehicle may be for coaches to directly state what they are thinking—to share the assumption directly. A coach might say something like, "I'm aware of how powerful the term 'handcuffs' is as you speak it. I'm aware that handcuffs call up the term jailed to me in a very visceral way." We believe that coaches need to experience the power of not adding anything and develop confidence in the power of simply tracking and reflecting before starting to voice assumptions, however overtly. We believe we owe it to clients to be responsible about what we add and how we shape thinking—theirs and ours—through our questions, assumptions, and framework.

USE OF METAPHORS IN COACHING CONVERSATIONS

We also utilize and explore the use of metaphor in coaching. Metaphors create powerful images and invite energetic and emotional awareness. They can draw forth imagination, unlock creativity and stimulate resourcefulness.

Andrew Ortony, a researcher in learning and cognition, made a radical statement some years ago: Metaphors are necessary, not just nice (1975/2001, p. 29).

A metaphor can be viewed as simply one person's description of something as "like" something else. In George Lakoff and Mark Johnson's mind-expanding book, *Metaphors We Live By*, they say: "The essence of metaphor is understanding and experiencing one kind of thing in terms of another" (1980/ 2003, p. 5).

When one acknowledges that most of our thought processes go beyond our conscious understanding, metaphors give a unique perspective into how we think about, feel, and experience our world. Consider this: the tangible world around us is made up of billions and billions of constantly moving atoms and lots of empty space in between. What we see is our own internal perception—colors, shapes, patterns. Isn't it all just a metaphor for the real thing? Perhaps metaphors are the closest we ever get to the "true" experience of reality.

Carl Jung explains the importance of the unconscious mind in his book, *Man and His Symbols* (1964 /1969a). At some point of perception, we reach the edge of certainty beyond which conscious knowledge cannot pass. The unconscious, however, has taken note of all events and experiences, and will store this information in forms and symbols that may be somewhat obscure. Jung was convinced that by analyzing those symbols that appear through connecting with our unconscious, we have access to a much wider and more comprehensive understanding of ourselves, our relationships, and the wider world around us. Our use of metaphors in everyday language is one such "key" to deciphering our unconscious wisdom.

Metaphors Give the Coach Insight

As a tool for coaching, clients' analogies and metaphors give you a window into their unique perception of their situation and goals. When clients tell you they can "see light at the end of the tunnel," that is what they are experiencing. There is light for them, and they are experiencing themselves as if in a tunnel. They will unconsciously "know" much more about their situation from this metaphoric viewpoint. They are very likely to know in which direction the light is, how far away it is, and where it comes from. They will know about the structure of the tunnel, how it feels and looks, how narrow the passage is, and where they are in relation to the tunnel.

When coaching conversations become stale and in need of a shift in energy, we find that listening for a metaphor in a client's language can lead to exploration by simply asking him or her to describe it and give it life. Encourage the client to see how the metaphor transforms. This is an elegant way to create an atmosphere of shifting thought and outcome without an abundance of dialogue, instead letting the metaphor represent the shift wanted or needed. There are 3 basic ways to utilize metaphors in coaching conversations:

1. Listen for a metaphor that the client shares. Our language is full of metaphors. Your client might say they feel stuck, or lost in the woods, or some other image. As a coach, you might ask, "What kind of stuck is that stuck?" or "Tell me more about stuck." After some exploration, the coaching might generate ideas for changing the metaphor. What needs to happen?

2. Create a metaphor by asking the client: "When you think of this issue/ challenge, it is like what? Notice the question does not say "what is that

like?" Instead, the phase *it is like what* almost always elicits a metaphor to work with.

3. Offer a metaphor that comes from your intuition. Say to the client: "Susan, I have an image that comes to me as you describe your challenge. May I share it?" Then, if they agree (most always), state the metaphor or symbol that you sense and see where it takes the client.

CHAPTER 3

COACHING AS A DEVELOPMENTAL CHANGE PROCESS

In our training, we often begin a discussion of the developmental change process by quoting the poem "Wild Geese," by Mary Oliver (1986). The poem is a meditation on a flock of wild geese heading home, and the poet's elaboration on the deep connection humans have to one another and their world. The poem's perspective is one that appeals to many people in midlife and after.

Oliver is a deeply spiritual poet whose writing, primarily drawn from her observations in nature, has gained broad appeal during the past several decades as more people search for meaning and purpose beyond their current boundaries. A winner of the Pulitzer Prize and National Book Award for Poetry, Oliver writes poetry and essays that emphasize the great connectedness of human beings with all others and the universe. The longing for such deep connectedness—to other human beings and to something universal—draws clients to the powerful process of coaching, particularly in midlife. When such people work with life coaches, their journey often takes them in new directions.

Life coaches support clients in the search and in walking the new path toward desired change. They do so by bringing multiple perspectives to the client's work. They remain fully appreciative of the unique gifts and strengths of each individual client. At the same time, they can see how the client's work fits within the context of how humans generally develop over the course of a life span.

Before we go further, let's examine the case of a client whose profile and situation are best viewed from the lens of developmental issues.

CASE STUDY: GEORGE

George, 52, is a successful chiropractor who built his business from the ground up and whose reputation for sensitive and caring work keeps him very, very busy.

Change is the law of life, and those who look only to the past or the present are certain to miss the future.

—John F. Kennedy

He lives in the same city in the Northeastern United States where he grew up. George comes to you because he feels tremendously disenchanted with his work. As a young man, he hoped to become a veterinarian, and his first love has always been animals. He has ridden horses all his life and currently owns one, which he doesn't get to ride frequently enough. He has also dreamed of owning land where he can raise llamas. He is tremendously gifted with his hands, can sculpt and create, and plays several stringed instruments well. However, he has little time for practice, sculpting, or playing. George became a chiropractor because he was urged to do so by his parents. His father was a chiropractor, and his older brother is also a chiropractor. To George, both seem to be contented in the field. He wonders sometimes why he is not and tells himself that he should be. Yet that doesn't bring him contentment.

George has been frustrated with his chiropractic practice for some time. He becomes easily irritated with patients these days, which never used to happen. He is upset with himself because of these feelings. He knows that any irritated or angry energy he gives off can interfere with the patient's healing processes. He acknowledges that he is aware he has always liked animals better than people—he has a great sense of connection with and compassion for them. He becomes impatient when people complain during a chiropractic session. He tells you the story of one patient who greatly annoys him. She is 75, tremendously anxious, and a victim of a traffic accident. She comes in twice weekly, talks incessantly through the sessions, and chronically complains about everyone. Uncharacteristically, last week, he told her, "Just shut up and let me work!"

For the past several years, George has lacked energy and motivation, which disturbs him. He wonders whether this has anything to do with getting older. George has been happily married for 20 years, is active in his church, and has twin sons who are seniors in high school. George's wife, Joanne, is 45 and in the last stages of completing her doctorate in social psychology. After teaching elementary school when they were first married, Joanne quit to take care of the children. When the boys were in junior high, she returned to school.

She is excited that she will be completing her degree and can turn to university teaching.

Discussion

Consider these questions as you focus on the case of George:

- What stands out about George's situation?
- What are the first questions you want to ask George?
- What emotions arise as you read about George?
- What do you empathize with most about George and his situation?
- What do you feel most distant from or impatient with about George's situation?
- If George were 35 or 65, how might you approach coaching him differently?

We use these questions to prompt students to think about their planned approach as well as their internal reactions. Keep in mind as a coach that you won't read a synopsis; you gain this information through conversations with the client. As those conversations occur, any of these questions and many others may prompt you to respond in a coachlike manner. However, coaching questions can only grow out of the ways that coaches understand human beings, including whether they understand stages of development and archetypal patterns that are representative of humans around the world.

When coaches are ignorant of human developmental issues, they miss great opportunities for zeroing in on what may be a source of the client's drive toward change. They may unfortunately join the clients in avoiding the clients' real work. We use the following theories to help coaches understand some widely accepted theories of human development. When coupled with James Prochaska's theory of readiness for change, coaches can understand where most effectively to enter the client's landscape of living.

Prochaska's research-based work initially emerged from the field of addiction counseling. It sought to establish a theory and strategy for how a counselor's behavior and style could be best matched to the stage of the client's readiness for change. We believe Prochaska's theory applies as well to coaching clients, even though coaching is not a treatment application. A common coaching example is given below, using Prochaska's stages. A part of the clients' goals for coaching is to improve their health and begin an exercise routine. Prochaska and colleagues (1994) identified six well-defined change stages clients move through, though often not linearly. An important thing to consider is that coaches may be working with clients who are not yet ready for action. The coaches' role is to assist the clients to get ready for action.

Prochaska's Six Stages

Stage 1: Pre-Contemplation

In this stage, clients are not yet considering making a change. Clients are unaware of the need for a change or their current patterns or behaviors. If coaches see that the clients seem to be at the pre-contemplation stage, the clients are not ready to make big changes. That may be in line with where they are developmentally as human beings. When coaching clients at this stage, the initial exploration and assessment phases of coaching can be critical.

Clients who want to improve their health are already beyond this stage. It is not as if precontemplaters cannot think of a solution; it is that they don't identify a problem. The clients above have already identified a problem and have reframed it as a goal: to improve their health and begin an exercise routine. Coaches are unlikely to find clients at the pre-contemplation stage, unless perhaps they have been sent to coaching by their employer for a problem they have not identified themselves. Sometimes, however, clients come to a coach for one reason and something else emerges. In this case, the clients may be at the pre-contemplation stage around a particular issue.

It is important for coaches using Prochaska's stage model to recognize that the stage is related to the specific area: a client may be at several different stages for several different goals, which requires flexibility from the coach. The client might go to the doctor and discover his cholesterol is high, blood pressure is high, and the doctor recommends he focus on his health. When the client gets to you, you may focus on work issues or improving his fulfillment in relationships to facilitate an improvement in his health. Here, the client has received assessment data from his doctor. Sometimes assessment data is received from the coach, as in 360-degree feedback assessments in corporations. These assessments, also called full-circle feedback, are surveys that colleagues, bosses, and sometimes others (like clients or customers) fill out on a person's strengths and weaknesses. In either case, one of the coaching strategies for moving a client from pre-contemplation to the second stage, contemplation, is the use of assessment data. A coach would be looking here to see if the client is accepting the information or denying that there is a problem he can choose to address.

Stage 2: Contemplation

Clients in this stage are considering making a change and may find themselves quite ambivalent or unsure of how to proceed. They can endlessly weigh the pros and cons but not actually decide on an action. The question, "Is it worth making a change?" may be one they are unconsciously asking themselves.

The coach can assist clients in this stage to examine how the current situation and their habits, behaviors, and patterns work for and against them. For the client who wants to improve health and initiate exercise, the coach might ask, "What first steps have you thought of?" "What kind of exercise do you most enjoy?" "What will you have if you don't make any changes?" "What are the pros and cons of initiating a regular exercise program?" Clients may be busy executives who travel quite often and feel pressed for time. If so, the coach's role might be to help clients examine the consequences of allowing work to overtake their time and schedule to the detriment of their health. In addition, the coach helps the clients explore their motivation to change versus their motivation to maintain status quo.

Diane uses Barry Johnson's (1992) polarity management model to help clients who get stuck weighing the pros and cons of two sides of an issue. While we won't discuss this here, the model asks clients to map out the pros and cons of two poles of an issue—in this case exercise program or no exercise program—and to identify the positive and negative aspects of each. The coach works with the client to create ways of avoiding downsides and securing as much of the upsides of each pole as possible. The coach is an ally who helps clients find the pathway for moving forward.

Stage 3: Preparation

In this stage, the client is preparing to change and gathering information, assembling resources, checking out possibilities, and so on. This is where the accountability coaching brings can be paramount. The coach can also help the client discover resources and identify what else is needed.

Helping the client move from contemplation to preparation can be a significant accomplishment. The client begins to overcome the inertia that characterized the contemplation stage where the action was simply thinking about action. Coaches sometimes feel they have failed when their client doesn't jump into action. The preparation stage is critical. The coach's work is effective if the client seeking health, for example, begins researching local resources for health clubs, trainers, classes, and so on. This is movement—though sometimes the coach who is unfamiliar with Prochaska's stages doesn't see it that way. Coaching with Prochaska's model in mind, the coach maintains the patience to allow the client to move through each stage, knowing the client's ultimate success will be better ensured if each stage is addressed fully according to the client's needs.

Stage 4: Action

This is the classic stage where clients actually take action, practice new behavior and try new things. The coach's role is to ensure that the clients' action is congruent with who they are. Clients have been empowered by the initial three stages to identify how they create action steps. The ideas for action haven't come from the coach's preconceptions or advice. The actions have resulted from the co-creative process of coaching.

A client's action may be hiring a personal trainer, buying a piece of exercise equipment and using it, or setting up a regular workout schedule.

Stage 5: Maintenance

In this stage, the clients have maintained the chosen actions long enough to have created new habits and integrated them into their lives. This usually indicates that new habits are being installed. Coaching currently continues to acknowledge and endorse the change. Often clients may have not been successful at maintaining change in the past. The coach's alliance with clients increases the likelihood of success: clients finally have an ally. If clients slip back to old habits or circumstances change, the coach helps them reset their goals or recalibrate their actions.

Just as in car maintenance, occasional tune-ups and adjustments are needed so the current situation can be addressed. Clients sometimes believe they can consistently maintain actions over time, no matter what. Yet life brings changes. A client may develop a health issue that requires he change his preferred way of exercise. This can be more difficult than expected. Or a new child in the family requires realignment of the parents' use of their time.

Stage 6: Termination

Prochaska used this term because it reflected the fact that the client no longer needed a programmatic approach to changing a specific behavior. The new behavior has become a natural part of the person's life, and it happens without much thought. For the clients above, the exercise program has simply become a part of what they do each week—a new habit, perhaps even a joyful one.

Stage 6 may not mean an ending of the coaching per se. It may simply mean that coaching will no longer focus on a particular goal—the need to focus has terminated, so to speak. Some clients may feel they have gotten where they wanted to go. The coach helps clients distinguish between terminating coaching for life and recognizing when ongoing maintenance coaching or coaching for new issues will be beneficial.

These steps are not linear—they are spiral. It is important to keep in mind that change is a process, not an event. On any desired change the client may cycle through these stages in a nonlinear fashion. Coaches commonly see the following scenario: Clients may say, for example, they commit to taking action by the next session. Yet when they appear for the session, they have moved back from the action stage to contemplation. The coach's role is to support the clients' movement through the cycle and to accept the clients where they are now.

VIEWS ON HUMAN LIFE AND CHANGE: PSYCHOLOGY, PHILOSOPHY, AND HUMAN DEVELOPMENT

Our introductory chapter includes a broad overview of the history and evolution of life coaching from its psychological origins. The roots of coaching run deep into the ground of psychological change theories and practices. Like all other psychological practices, coaching is a process concerned fundamentally with change: change in the client's external life, changes in observable results, and changes in the client's subjective experience of himself, others, and the world. All too often, media articles about coaching focus only on coaching's action orientation, to the detriment of the profession. They miss a critical aspect of great coaching: the coach's intention is to build the long-term capacity of the client.

Having the client take action is only one aspect of the client's change process—often the most observable and quantifiable aspect, but not necessarily the richest, most enduring, and most satisfying outcome of coaching. Coaching is not simply quick-fix, results-oriented work. Yes, coaching does produce performance changes and short-term results. However, the benefits of coaching accrue because clients build their capacity and create greater capabilities for the long term—for life. This is transformational coaching.

Coaching's great gift remains that coaches focus on clients' learning and development as well as on achieving desires. James Flaherty (1998) stressed the need for the coach to focus on long-term client capability building.

What Coaches Look for Is What They Find

We all know that once we decide to buy a car and determine what kind, suddenly we notice that the world is full of that particular make and model. If we have decided to consider a sports car, for example, we begin to notice how many ride alongside us. That is the consequence of expanded awareness. Something we were formerly unconscious of becomes very prominent, or becomes a figure, as Gestalt psychology calls it, that emerges from the ground.

When we were in training to become mental health professionals, we learned a set of assumptions, theories, techniques, and behaviors that became part of our repertoire as helping professionals. Like other helping professionals, we studied more than one school of therapy and adopted what works from several different approaches. As *The Family Therapy Networker* (1998) reported, the most common way therapists describe themselves, when asked what "school of therapy" they practice, was "eclectic." We think the same eclectic approach needs to be true for coaches. Coaching should never begin to appear overly reliant on techniques or be limited by a single theoretical approach. This is an important lesson for new coaches. Masterful coaching takes all the lessons, techniques, and theories, integrating them into a personal flow so that the coaching becomes transparent. This process is analogous to what happens when learning to drive a car. When teenagers learn to drive, they are overly observant of the pressure on the gas pedal, the turn signals, the nuances of driving a car for the first time, including all the rules and regulations of the road. By the time they become proficient drivers, driving becomes a set of automatic habits. They no longer think of the techniques and details—they simply drive.

As Albert Einstein is believed to have said, "Theory is extremely useful, because your theory determines what you can see." For coaches who come from a therapy background, much of what they have learned as therapists can be useful to their coaching practice. Whatever field coaches come from, they need to consciously examine the mindsets and assumptions they hold as part of their professional development to date—about the client, about what is necessary to bring about change, about the value of digging around in the past, and so on. Lawyers who become coaches may have internalized a set of assumptions about the need to offer advice, ask probing questions, and never ask a question they don't know the answer to. To become successful as coaches, lawyers need to consciously examine and adapt their style of relating to clients, maintaining what is consistent with the coaching alliance and relationship, and discarding what does not fit. The challenge for each coach is to sort out what is useful from what is likely to be detrimental—or at the very least what will slow down the change process for the client.

In the past several years, some schools of therapy have begun to look more and more like coaching. Solution-focused therapy (SFT), for example, uses a set of questions to focus the client's attention and awareness on what works. Therapists trained in SFT possess a valuable set of tools they can use as coaches. Life coaches also know there are limitations to transferring tools that were designed for therapeutic applications.

For example, the Miracle Question used in SFT transfers very effectively to many coaching situations. Asking the question, "If a miracle occurred overnight and you had the change you wanted, what would be the first thing you would notice?" directs the clients' attention specifically to what they desire. Asking this question of George the chiropractor might move him out of his lethargy and disenchantment to consider the possibilities available to him.

When you boil rice, know that the water is your own life.

—Zen saying

However, there are limits. For example, in many trainings including SFT, helping professionals encourage clients to create actions based on what worked in the past. The assumption is that what worked in the past will also work effectively now. Perhaps it will. However, that assumption discounts a developmental perspective. In fact, taking an action that worked before may discourage the clients' development, although it may allow them to achieve a short-term goal.

KEN WILBER'S FOUR QUADRANTS OF CHANGE

ILCT encourages a more integral and developmental perspective (Wilber, 2000). We believe that partial and piecemeal approaches to complex situations are likely to be ineffective in the long term. Whether coaches are addressing individual and personal issues of meaning and transformation—as in the case of George—complex business problems, or large-scale global issues like war, hunger, disease, and education, clients are likely to benefit from seeking approaches that grow from more comprehensive, holistic, systemic, and integrated perspectives. As you review the development models, keep a current client's desires and situation in mind. Or use your own current situation—your transition to becoming a coach and developing your coaching business—as the situation to analyze. Coaches can source comprehensive perspectives by using models and approaches such as those described in Figure 3.1.

Any situation a client brings to a coach has multiple facets available within it, each of which provides a lens and each of which can limit. Consider the four domains of coaching described by Wilber and illustrated in Figure 3.1.

Quadrant 1 is the interior/individual aspect of change—the "I" domain, as Wilber describes it. This is the interior reality of clients, including their thoughts, feelings, beliefs, and yearnings. In this quadrant, people focus on what only they can know, from the inside. This is the realm of subjective experience that is only fully known by the clients, living their unique lives. Sometimes what is in this domain may be hard for the client to articulate, as putting language to it requires the client be able to see himself as "object," so to speak. A client may come to a coach for Quadrant 1 work out of a desire for inner development. The client and coach gain access to this domain when the client engages in self-observation. Over time, self-observation reveals patterns of feeling, thinking, and response. This quadrant is a key determinant of change; people make changes only when they believe and feel that change is possible and have the resources necessary to accomplish the changes.

Most coaches find themselves naturally asking questions and working with

FIGURE 3.1

The Client and the Context (adapted from Wilber 2000)

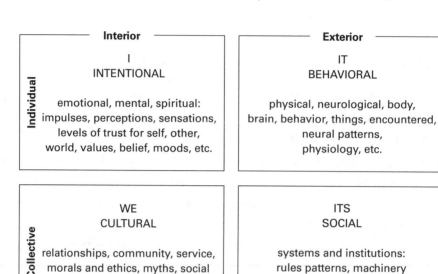

the client using a Quadrant 1 approach. They spend most of their time here. Sometimes that approach is sufficient, but it is also limited.

As a coach works with George, she will naturally pay attention to Quadrant 1 issues: his lethargy, his sense of boredom and irritation, his shame at how discontented he is, and his anger at his own frustration. Quadrant 2 has to do with the exterior-individual aspects of change—the "it" domain as Wilber describes it. This quadrant includes what can be observed about the individual from the outside.

Quadrant 2 gets a great deal of attention from executive coaches and world-class athletes. Executive coaches work with this domain when they observe clients leading meetings and notice patterns of language. This quadrant is where life coaches pay attention to developing individual behaviors and supporting the physical ingredients that spark motivation and congruent action. Nutrition, exercise, and posture are all components of this quadrant. In this quadrant, the client may have some blind spots as by definition what can be seen is exterior to the client. This perspective can only be known through feedback, observing oneself in a mirror or on a video, or listening to a recording of one's voice.

A coach working with George in this quadrant might notice that when George describes his work as a chiropractor, his body hunches over and his chest seems to collapse. It appears to the coach that George's voice becomes shriller, and the coach notices how frequently George sighs and then falls silent. The coach observes these factors and can choose to feed them back to George. If the coach asks something like, "How do you feel when you sigh?" George will report from Quadrant 1, the quadrant where only he can be aware of how he feels because the evidence relates to his interior thoughts and feelings. The coach can instead observe from Quadrant 2, which can lead into a Quadrant 1 inquiry. George may not be aware of his physical responses. As the coach shares his or her observations, George can become more fully aware of his physical responses and how they link to his moods and emotions. He can then notice how he feels in this body position. This will help him become aware of the times he holds that position, how he feels, and how he behaves as a consequence.

Quadrant 3 deals with the interior-collective aspects of change—the "we" domain. This is the domain of culture and family history. It is the interior, often hidden territory of shared assumptions, collective projections, and images and associations that direct what happens when people come together. This is the domain of myth, story, unwritten rules, and cultural beliefs. This domain includes the practices, roles, rituals, stories, and meanings that determine per-ceptions of possibilities within specific groups. This is the domain of shared history and shared visions. These perceptions and visions create themselves through conversation and dialogue, through what is said and what is left unsaid and subject to interpretation. Coaches and therapists know how strongly this quadrant can impact the client's Quadrants 1 and 2, as seen when a client's family background has a defined set of expectations for roles—for what it means to be a man, a woman, and a parent.

A difficulty for many clients is that the interior-collective domain is one of internalized values and mores. This quadrant represents the clients' internaliza-tion of values as reflected in their social systems (work, church, family, culture, neighborhood, country of origin, national identity) and the deeper meanings of symbols, purposes, vision, and values. These values are not necessarily reflected in overt messages inherent in their social web but are more the subtle messages encoded in day-to-day interactions. How clients' "I" domains mesh with their "we" domains is a rich area of exploration in coaching.

George's coach could work with him in Quadrant 3 by asking him to identify what he learned from his family and upbringing about work, about changing jobs and roles, and about a man's role. George's family heritage is German. His coach could ask him what that means to him and to his family—what that heritage assumes and perhaps does not discuss about work, family, roles, and so on.

Getting this cultural conditioning out into the open would help George notice what in his background and current relationships supports him in making changes and what blocks him. Coaches can expand their impact by asking questions from this quadrant. This is particularly important when doing cross cultural coaching. A Hispanic woman working in a U.S.-based corporate environment may have different perspectives and conversational practices than many of her colleagues. A company that has offices around the globe needs to teach its managers to inquire about Quadrant 3 issues and be aware of its effect on human change, not limiting themselves to a superficial understanding of employee behavior and values.

Important to remember is that each generation has its own cultural heritage; three clients might all have been born in the United States but if they come from different generations their experiences will differ greatly. Their mind-sets or worldviews will be, at least in part, created from key events that formed early impressions. Members of a generation are linked together by the similar events they experienced during their formative years. For example, the Baby Boomer generation cohort in the United States shared memories of the murders of President John F. Kennedy and Dr. Martin Luther King Jr., as well as political action producing change. Generation X had the common experiencing of watching parents get laid off from long-term jobs and experienced a high frequency of divorced parents. These shared experiences create some shared alignment in values, attitudes, and beliefs, like a social character distinctive of that cohort. Generation X became highly entrepreneurial and has emphasized family and personal life over work and employment. Because these experiences and their meanings are constructed through socialization, they are likely to remain relatively stable throughout the lifetime. Still, if the client's meaning-making enlarges, the way the client makes meaning of the events may also enlarge through the years.

Quadrant 4 is the exterior-collective aspects of change—the "its" domain. It is the quadrant of systems and institutions, including social systems, family systems, and work relationships observed from a systemic perspective, in other words, observed from the outside of the client. (The cultural impact on the client is the province of Quadrant 3.) This domain, like Quadrant 2, is concerned with observable, tangible, and measurable aspects of reality. Quadrant 4 reminds coaches that system design determines performance, and that if we want the system to perform at a substantially higher level, we must design for it.

To avoid confusing Quadrant 3 (the "we"), and Quadrant 4 (the "its"), think of culture as the internal, introjected, and historical impact of the clients' cultural heritage, views, and ethics on them as individuals. Quadrant 3 is concerned with the unspoken aspects of culture, whereas Quadrant 4 is concerned with the observable interactions, structures, and rules of relationships. Often this quadrant is exemplified by policies explained in print, as in an organization's orientation training or policies manual.

A key point for coaches is that all of these quadrants are connected to or related to one another, though the client may not immediately recognize or give voice to the connection. Change or development of one quadrant is inextricably bound to the others. Each quadrant affects the rest, and each is powerful. Clients may find themselves more powerful in one or the other of the domains. Sometimes becoming aware or more powerful in a neglected domain forms the focus of the coaching. Ignoring any domain can lead to haphazard or incomplete results.

George's coach might work with Quadrant 4 through asking George to examine the social groups he is a part of. The coach might ask, "Where in your life do you have social groups you are a part of—a church, community club, professional group, or family system?" George would list and identify these. Then the coach could turn to Quadrant 1, asking George, "How fulfilling is each of these groups for you right now?" The coach might also work in this quadrant by asking George to examine his environments, noting the arrangements of spaces, furniture, and so on, and then identifying how he interacts with his environment because of the way it is organized. He could also look at the records George keeps on his calendar. How does he systematically use his available time? Each of these is a potential avenue for changes that has the potential to yield greater satisfaction.

LEVELS OF DEVELOPMENT OF THE ADULT CONSCIOUSNESS

Psychologist R. D. Laing (1983) wrote about the dilemmas that adults face over the course of their development at any given time. "The range of what we think and do is limited by what we fail to notice. And because we fail to notice that we fail to notice, there is little we can do to change; until we notice how failing to notice shapes our thoughts and deeds."

Adult learning maps the general development of the ways that, according to Robert Kegan, "we make meaning; how we defend, and ultimately transform, our meaning-making systems" (Bachkirova, 2009, p. 10). Kegan goes on to say that when he and other developmental researchers speak of "transformations," they describe transformations in the ways adults make meaning, what they take as "object," or outside themselves, and what they are still "subject" to and cannot see as separate from themselves. When adults are subject, they do not see themselves as constructors of their viewpoints. They simply accept something is. "It has to do with what people can see and what they can't yet see," Kegan notes, "the thoughts and feelings we have and the thoughts and feelings that 'have us;' what agenda we are driving and what agenda is driving us" (Bachkirova, 2009, p. 11). Only when a client can see something as *object* is that something available to be worked on in coaching; when the client is so close to something they cannot see it as object, then coaching is working on the client (subject). This reminds us of the famous aphorism, "We don't know who discovered water, but we know it wasn't fish." For the fish, the water is subject; to someone outside the fishbowl, both the water and the fish are object. All developmental theorists share the sense that meaning-making capacities develop over time as adults increase their capacities to take independent perspectives, include more complexity in those perspectives, see and use authority in increasingly complex ways, and discover many shades of gray when earlier there was only black or white. Given the complexity of our global society and increasingly interdependent nations, people and institutions, understanding adult developmental stages that map complex perspectives and clear ambiguity and confusion is highly beneficial to coaches.

If we think of this existence of the individual as a larger or smaller room, it appears evident that most people learn to know only a corner of their room, a place by the window, a strip of floor on which they walk up and down.

—Rainer Maria Rilke

Returning to our case study, George the chiropractor is at a point where he has discovered how his failure to notice has shaped his career choices. The good news is that we are in an era where we understand a great deal about the promise of adult development and that adult meaning-making capacities develop throughout life. It used to be thought that adult development generally hit a plateau and declined after midlife. What we believe now is that there are stages or phases of adult development. Real transformation is possible long into adulthood. A time of disappointment like George is experiencing may be evidence that he is moving toward a more complex way of meaning making that may signal a transformation to another development level.

In early phases of adult growth, often until the 20s and 30s, the person is fully engaged in a society and a group and takes in ideas from those sources as his or her own. Consider teenagers as a primary example, for whom the beliefs, practices, and norms of the group are taken in as if they are swallowed whole. At this stage in his life, George may have made his decision to become a chiropractor instead of following his dream.

At a later stage of adult development, the person may begin to examine beliefs and values, bringing forward personal ideas about the future. Sometimes this is described as someone beginning to "author" his or her own life. With this comes the ability to take responsibility for one's choices. George may be finding himself at this stage of development.

As development continues, the person may become increasingly comfortable with uncertainty and begin to co-create with others.

Dr. Clare Graves, founder of what is now known as Spiral Dynamics, described human development as a never-ending quest:

> At each stage of human existence, the adult man is off on his quest of his holy grail, the way of life he seeks by which to live. At his first level he is on a quest for automatic psychological satisfaction. At the second level he seeks a safe mode of living, and this is followed in turn by a search for heroic status, for power and glory, by a search for ultimate peace; a search for material pleasure, a search for affectionate relations, a search for respect of self, and a search for peace in an incomprehensible world. And, when he finds he will not find that peace, he will be off on his ninth level quest. As he sets off on each quest, he believes he will find the answer to his existence. Yet, much to his surprise and much to his dismay, he finds at every stage that the solution to existence is not the solution he has come to find. Every stage he reaches leaves him disconcerted and perplexed. It is simply that as he solves one set of human problems, he finds a new set in their place. The quest he finds is never ending. (Graves, C. W., n.d.)

Much has been written about this field, particularly from an academic researcher point of view. In the past few years, adult developmental viewpoints have begun to move into mainstream thought in the field of coaching.

What we want to do here is describe basic principles of adult development that are germane to your work as a coach of adults, particularly if your clients work in organizations. Two sets of principles that are common to all developmental theories can be described as:

- Adult development proceeds through a succession of developmental stages. That means that a stage emerges at a regular point in sequence, not randomly.
- Adult developmental stages are hierarchical. That is, later stages enable more complex perspective taking. At each stage, the adult maintains the ability to hold the perspectives of earlier stages; it is as if the process "transcends and includes" earlier stages, incorporating them into a new way of meaning making and perspective taking.
- Adult development generally does not regress, though adults under stress can show more behaviors and styles associated with earlier stages, since those continue to be available to him or her.

Currently well-known adult developmental theorists include longtime Harvard University researcher and educator Robert Kegan, William Joiner, Susanne Cook-Greuter, and William Torbert. Joiner has focused his work on adult development within the business and organizational setting and is the coauthor of *Leadership Agility* (Joiner & Josephs, 2006). He created an online 360-degree feedback tool that assesses leaders' levels of consciousness, which he describes as agility. Cook-Greuter (2004) extended the research of her mentor Jane Loevinger (1998) and has created a self-assessment tool based on sentence stem completion that can be used by all adults. Torbert et al. (2004) developed a means of collaborative learning—action inquiry—that over time can create richer developmental perspectives for its practitioners, who are primarily leaders focused on large system change. Each writer has named adult development stages somewhat uniquely.

Why is their work important to coaches? Without learning, there is no coaching. Coaching as a discipline depends on fostering the client's ability to learn and grow. When the goals and desires of the client are a fit with their adult developmental level, coaching can be effective. When there is a mismatch, coaching may not succeed. This is one of the reasons clients who are referred for workplace coaching by their manager or organization may not be successful in making change.

We believe there are two kinds of learning that occur in adulthood. The first and easiest to observe is informational learning. Informational learning occurs when an adult increases their knowledge on a particular subject, perhaps developing greater and greater mastery until he or she becomes an expert. A client may return to graduate school for an advanced degree, adding to his or her informational learning. Or an executive assistant masters a new skill, embedding video in a slide presentation. Developmental learning theorists describe this as lateral or horizontal growth, where learning is additive at the current level of development.

The second kind of learning is based on the ability to internalize greater complexity and literally create a new form of understanding. This is *transformational learning*, which comes from a change in the form of how an adult knows, resulting in an altered, often bigger perspective. Developmental psychologists describe this as vertical or transformational learning, as if the adult has ascended to a new height and is able to see more broadly and richly. As Cook-Greuter writes, vertical development "refers to how we learn to see the world through new eyes, how we change our interpretations of experience and how we transform our views of reality. It describes increases in what we are aware of, or what we can pay attention to, and therefore what we can influence and integrate" (2004).

An example: As a young adult, George was at the socialized level of development. Embedded in the views of his family and social group, he chose a profession based on their wants and desires for him. His parents' desire for him to be a chiropractor might have competed with other desires he had for himself. But the internal conflict he felt—torn between others' desires and his own—was painful. He resolved it by choosing the path favored by his family.

An essential principle of adult developmental psychology is that movement from developmental stage to developmental stage is really about transformation. It does not happen all at once. Transformation may take years to unfold. Without practice in new ways of thinking and behaving, shifts from stage to stage do not happen (Kegan, 1983).

When shifts occur, they are always associated with the emergence of significant new capability. People seldom regress permanently to a previous level, although they can regress temporarily under stress or trauma. Their new order of consciousness transcends the limits of the old order and is better matched to the demands of the world the client now inhabits. It simply works better. Kegan's two early books, *The Evolving Self* (1982) and *In Over Our Heads* (1994) emerged from extensive research Kegan performed to understand the internal experience of development, which he later described as a kind of "existential cognitive-developmental psychology" (2009, p. 13) that has stayed the focus of his research and writing. When stress or crisis occurs, the client may temporarily seem to move backward, but normally the recovery will be rapid. If clients revisit issues, they consider them through new levels of complexity. The trajectory forward has been set.

Developmental psychologists' theories focus on changes in the way people differentiate between their sense of self and their environment. In this sense, development is a lifelong process of differentiation and integration. Human beings are pulled toward both autonomy and inclusion, and the various ways we work with the tensions between autonomy and inclusion are somewhat predictable. What is important, however, is that not all adults develop through all possible stages. Some stop developing at a particular stage and remain comfortably within it for the balance of their lives. Age is not a predictor of developmental level.

Developmental stages are sequential and hierarchical; each stage incorporates and builds on the learning of the prior stages, incorporating earlier stages into a broader meaning-making system. We can describe stages as earlier and later because later stages include and transcend earlier stages.

The Egocentric Self

Between the moment a child is born and the end of adolescence, an egocentric self (also called the impulsive or opportunist stage) evolves. During these early stages, the self consists of needs, interests, wishes, impulses, and perceptions, but lacks a shared reality with others. During this stage, young people lack true empathy because they cannot imagine the feelings of others. Others are instrumental: people who meet their wishes, desires, and needs. Young people relate to the "other" to get needs met because they don't yet know how to make another person's needs a priority.

Adolescence is a stage when adolescents learn how to pursue their wants and needs within a larger system of competing needs. It is a difficult time because they are learning to accept that the world does not revolve around them—they need to give up their egocentric agenda to take up membership in society.

Research suggests that 15 percent of adults do not fully make the transition beyond the egocentric self. These people can be self-centered and controlling, or they can tend to play out the victim or rebel roles. Coaching is often not a helpful strategy for opportunists.[2] The challenge of coaching someone at this level is that the client is aware of what he experiences or thinks directly but does not have a perspective on his own interior psychological functioning — what he thinks or knows simply is. This makes it difficult to think abstractly as opposed to concretely.

THE THREE CONVENTIONAL STAGES OF DEVELOPMENT: DIPLOMAT, EXPERT, OR ACHIEVER

Research has shown that most adults leave behind the self-centeredness of adolescence to function as effective adults. This takes place during three conventional stages of development. Kegan calls this the socialized or interpersonal self: the diplomat, the expert, or the achiever. Consequently, your coaching clients are most likely to come from one of these three stages.

The Diplomat or Conformist

In this, the earliest stage in the conventional tier, people take a role in society and identify themselves by that role. The new structure of the self can be articulated as "I am my role." At this stage, the self is made secure and valuable by belonging to and succeeding within prescribed, socially accepted roles, such as parents, educated professionals, and members of a social group. At this stage, people are preoccupied with fitting into a group, being liked, and not making waves. The diplomat is all about belonging to a group and creating affiliations. Consequently, a fundamental value for the diplomat is loyalty. Diplomats may prefer to associate with or hire only those who share something with them—a college history, a preference for a sports team, and so

---

2 In the long-running HBO television series, *The Sopranos*, viewers saw a mafia group, intensely opportunistic men bound together by the rules of an opportunist-conformist "family" order. In its first season the series showed the family's leader, Tony, struggling with depression. One way of viewing Tony's dilemma is that he is in transition developmentally. He seeks out therapy, knowing this course of action would be disapproved of by his men.

on. This may be seen as creating something of a "tribe." Since the diplomat's power comes from the connection to the group, diplomats want to avoid conflict. They value friendly and conflict-free relationships and may have a shared sense of values and code of conduct they follow unconsciously. At the diplomat level, adults easily fall into a way of thinking that is about "us" versus "them," or "insiders" versus "outsiders." Loyalty is a primary and core value; disloyalty is cause for dismissal and loss of privilege and is greatly feared.

As coaches, we find this stage limited by the discrepancy between people's own awareness of themselves and their actions and what they actually do, what they are good at, and to what extent others accept them. At this stage, people are unaware of how their goals and behaviors are predetermined by others or by the culture; they are essentially defined from the outside in, but if asked they would say they define their own life. They have an illusion of autonomy, as if they have truly authored their own life. Yet that is not so.

Clients at this stage do not yet see the extent to which they are directed by cultural conditioning—the expectations and rules voiced by significant others and institutions in their life. In this stage of development, clients are not yet free to follow the song of their heart. They may hear the heart song and ignore it, dismiss it as impossible, or struggle with how to respond to it. Most often, fear gets in the way of moving toward it.

When clients at this stage serve as leaders, they often function like benevolent parents, maintaining the social conditioning yet caring deeply about the people around them. Looked at through the eyes of Robert Kegan, diplomats are "in over their heads" in trying to meet the challenges of today's leaders and organizations. They work in a very short time frame, of weeks to several months, and therefore do not hold planning or strategic points of view. They find it difficult to develop an independent perspective, and rely heavily on beliefs, advice and evidence offered by others.

If you coach a diplomat, you are likely to work with the client on how conflict is or is not surfaced and managed. The client may have difficulty managing anger because it jeopardizes relationships; when anger is directed toward him or her, the client feels ostracized. Diplomats may have difficulty feeling anger; instead, sadness or a sense of incompleteness occurs. The distancing and isolating function of anger is something to be feared.

Coaches working with diplomats may explore naming and understanding the variety of emotions that humans feel, also examining where in their bodies emotions emerge. (See Chapter 7 on emotional intelligence and working with the emotions in coaching.) Diplomats may benefit from examining the classic distinctions between aggressiveness, passiveness, and assertiveness. Discovering that assertiveness means acting in a way that respects both parties' rights, the diplomat may begin to hold a more complex view of relationships where conflict does not mean the termination of relationship. Exploring conflict styles can also be useful, helping the diplomat understand that no style is best in and of itself and all have a place.[3]

Assessing the Developmental Stage of a Client

Most coaches will not be—and need not be—experts in the Subject Object Interview (SOI) or Maturity Assessment Profile (MAP) methodology to be effective coaches for leaders and other clients within organizational contexts. For those who coach leaders and primarily work with organizational clients, however, it is helpful to begin listening for the developmental stage of the client. In recent work, Jennifer Garvey Berger writes of her experience with the SOI as a researcher to work in service of coaching.

In a small research study of 15 leadership clients, J. G. Berger and P. W. B. Atkins (2009) used the SOI methodology developed by Kegan to examine its application for coaching. The methodology of the SOI is to put forward initial topical suggestions that focus on somewhat challenging situations, then follow the lead of the client as his or her thinking develops. The interviewer's role is primarily to continue to probe the client's thinking to identify his or her developmental level by having the client and interviewer follow the meaning-making to what Berger called "the edge" (Berger & Atkins, 2009). While the sample size was small, one interesting finding calls out to leadership coaches: "We were surprised at how strong the connection was between self-authorship and a kind of self-esteem and self-confidence as a leader . . . There is some anecdotal evidence that leaders making sense of the world with a fully operating socialized mind experience some pain" (Berger & Atkins, 2009, p. 30). This makes a great deal of intuitive sense, given the demands of leadership in today's organizations. It suggests that the fit of one's development level to the demands of the role is highly important to one's well-being and one's success in that role.

---

3 Based on communication with Barbara Braham.

In a similar vein, William Torbert speculated in his book *Action Inquiry* (2004) the minimum level of adult development needed to be successful in leading organizations was that of the "achiever." This supports Berger's finding that self-esteem and self-confidence for leaders below the level of self-authorship is vulnerable.

Berger recently published a fuller exploration of the ways she uses adult development level as a guide to coaching leaders in *Changing on the Job: Developing Leaders for a Complex World* (2012). She introduces methods to assist coaches in listening for the structure of the client's thinking as opposed to listening primarily for the content. The structure illuminates the development level, which she calls "form of mind." A potential window into the client's development level opens when the coach follows examples of recent experiences that carry an emotional charge for the client: (a) a story of something mostly positive, like a success; (b) a story of something where emotions seem mostly negative, as in a loss, failure, or story of anger; and (c) a story where ambivalence is a key emotion—a decision the client is struggling to make, for example. The coach's strategy is to stay curious and to begin to probe the client's story appropriately, asking questions tied to the "emotional valence" of the story. She offers several suggested questions as probes:

> Once the coach begins to probe the event, the challenge is to stay with the example and continue to use the probe to develop the new information or thought that the client brings forward. The coach will be essentially asking the same question repeatedly using it to delve deeper into the answers the client offers at each level of the question. (Berger, 2012)

Berger offers an insightful example of a person who is frustrated in the current job but cannot decide whether not to leave:

COACH PROBE 1: What would be the worst thing about making the wrong decision here?

CLIENT RESPONSE: If I make the wrong decision, I might be getting my career off course in a way I'll later regret.

Notice as the coach continues to ask the same question to illuminate the information that comes forward, the client's developmental level becomes more apparent:

COACH PROBE 2: What would be the worst thing about getting your career off-course?

CLIENT RESPONSE: The worst thing about getting off-course would be the sense that I had screwed up rather than reaching my full potential.

COACH PROBE 3: What would be the worst thing about screwing up and not reaching your full potential?

CLIENT RESPONSE: The worst thing would be that I live out my values through my work and if I misjudged the situation, it would mean that I was less able to make a difference in the way that I thought I should. It would mean that I had in some way been a failure and had not contributed to the world as much as I should have.

If the coach decided to use the probe another time, it might sound something like this:

COACH PROBE 4: What would be the worst thing about being less able to make a difference and not contributing to the world as much as you should have?

Berger's practice is to ask the question three times and then determine whether to ask it again or look inside the third answer and examine in a more focused way how the answers may reflect each of the forms of mind. In Table 3.1, we offer slightly adapted questions from those that Berger offers, from the point of view of a coach examining the client's developmental level. The questions are designed to test the coach's hypothesis of the client's particular development levels, using Kegan's levels of development.

For coaches interested in exploring more deeply what it can be like to live and coach at various stages, make Berger's book a priority for your own development.

The Independent Self or Expert/Technician

Transitioning to an independent self is the major transition of adult life. To make this transition, people must accept that following their own path often means disappointing others, risking failure, and/or contradicting the norms that link them to society and that make the socialized self worthwhile and valuable. The self, for the first time, develops an identity that has relationships with other people but is not defined by them.

"Experts" are often specialists, technicians who have accumulated experience or knowledge that lets them stand out and have a unique, respected role. Experts value being right and often believe they should have all the answers. It is often particularly difficult for an expert to go from independent contributor to manager. As a coach, you may be called in to help with this difficult transition (i.e., from researcher/bench scientist to manager of a group of scientists). Experts can be perfectionists; they have internally held sets of rules about how things should go, processes that work, and how people should act. They are often highly independent and find it difficult to set and keep priorities. They can be micromanagers, wanting those who report directly to them to do a task just as they would. Experts tend to have a relatively short time frame they work in, though longer than that of diplomats; they find it difficult to plan for large projects and time horizons, something that the next stage, "achiever," usually finds much easier to accomplish.

You can assist experts in stretching their time horizons, if they are willing, by using exercises like the leadership timeline, or inviting them to read biographies of historical figures. Understand that looking backward through time can increase the client's capability of looking forward. One of our coaching successes was with an expert engineer who liked to read military history. He was challenged by his manager to better forecast work and think more strategically, both challenges to someone at the expert level. We invited him to "write his story," seeing himself and his project as if a part of leadership history, incorporating lessons from the other figures he read about. This helped him focus on what he might envision as a successful project. He also was able to extrapolate the ways he wanted to be seen as a leader and the mistakes he didn't want to make. Coaching helped him begin to transition to the achiever stage of development. Don't be misled by the educational level of your clients in terms of assessing their adult development level. Look at their behavior and ask them about the ways they make meaning.

Listening to the expert, you are likely to sense resistance to others' ideas, particularly if the idea challenges the expert's way of thinking or perceived role. Experts are advocates for specific courses of action and can irritate their colleagues a great deal. Expert-to-expert conflicts abound in work life. Coaching the expert, you may hear a "yes, but . . ." when offering an idea or thought. Experts find it difficult to include ideas into a larger frame as opposed to rejecting them. Consequently, in organizations they are often seen as difficult to manage, and not collaborative.

TABLE 3.1

Probing Questions for Emotional Charges

EMOTIONAL CHARGE	SAMPLE PROBING QUESTIONS
Positive	What is the best thing for you about this decision?
	What are you most pleased about?
Negative	What is the hardest thing about this decision?
	What are you most worried about or afraid of?
Ambivalent	What is the most important part of this decision?
	What would be the worst thing about making the wrong decision?

Useful coaching strategies for experts include enriching their understanding of the ways people differ. The DISC assessment and Myers-Briggs Type Indicator can be useful because they illustrate useful preferences. Experts benefit from understanding that adjusting how they challenge others can be helpful. They can become engaged in developing mastery in the interpersonal domain, viewing it as another arena in which to develop expertise.

Coaches can gently challenge the expert's desire to be right, asking, "Do you want to be right, or do you want to be effective?" Help them set priorities and manage their own and others' time, particularly if the expert is managing other people. For the expert who tends to be a perfectionist, coaches can help the expert sort out where it is really valuable to be perfect, and where 80 percent will do. Draw on contexts where perfection is not possible to achieve, as in parenting. Family life can be a source of inspiration for experts.

Experts tend to value the rational and intellectual at the expense of the emotional. To work with the somatic or emotional components of coaching, be sure to provide a compelling rationale that is aligned with the expert's sense of what is accurate and right.

The Achiever Conscientious Self

The last of the conventional roles, the achiever, or the self-authorizing mind according to Kegan, generally finds it easy to succeed at work, whether in entrepreneurial roles or within large enterprises. Achievers are driven to action and focused on accomplishments and are able to set plans and priorities.

They are highly oriented toward success and sometimes find it impossible to relax when there are still things on their to do list. As the term self-authorizing suggests, achievers are able to create for themselves a perspective and point of view that may be different from those around them; this does not bother them as it would conformists. Achievers are the first level of development at which real reflection can begin. Achievers are capable of realizing they are the creators of their own stories and can rewrite them if they want to create something else.

Coaching an achiever, you get a sense of the client being driven quickly to act, not always consciously choosing action. This can be one of the downsides of the achiever mindset. Commonly multitasking, the achiever might relentlessly check emails and text at times when this jeopardizes other relationships. Achievers value feedback and learning that are oriented toward their goals and careers. At their best they bring energy and optimism to their work. They value all kinds of data and can be excellent problem solvers, particularly when analysis and classic problem-solving work effectively for a project's success. Listen to the achiever and you are likely to hear a "yes, and . . ." along with talk of goals, plans, and tasks to be done. Many achievers say their work brings them energy, and so they sometimes need to slow down or take time off. One achiever hospital administrator we worked with at age 40 told us that he just didn't need vacations, and so he seldom took them. Walking around his facility, a 650-bed city-based hospital, the image came to us that he was like the mayor of a small, bustling city. Asked to develop strategy, moving away from the project focus of his former roles, he finally agreed to take some time away from work to develop a vision and set strategy. Away from work he was able to let the busy task environments of the facility go, allowing himself to set his own pace.

Achievers can develop useful coaching skills that support success, adding insightful questioning skills to their repertoire so they can become developers of people as well as leaders in problem solving. Achievers often want to develop others, seeing the link between learning and feedback for themselves to that of supporting learning and feedback for others. Achievers are also very capable of understanding that developing others adds to their success; they do not find developing others a threat, as the expert may.

At the achiever stage, clients may begin to focus diligently on self-development as well as the development of others. They become keenly aware of what is authentic and what is inauthentic in their lives. Action becomes an authentic expression of an emerging sense of inner purpose. As clients begin to see and experience the power, creativity, freedom, and satisfaction of living from a true, authentic center, they also value those traits in others. They may become impatient with what they regard as deception, and they become defensive when chaos threatens the order and structure of the self they have created. Self-expression and cooperation become new organizing principles.

Because of their focus on development, coaches will have many clients who are either at the achiever level or are working to move from expert to achiever. Achievers flourish as leaders within organizations and as entrepreneurs. The energy and optimism they bring to work extends to their commitment to coaching and personal development.

Useful coaching strategies with the achiever include 360-degree feedback instruments to help them see their progress toward specific skills and competencies in the eyes of others. Help them explore work–life balance issues. Achievers often find it difficult to stop the action and reflect to identify patterns; they are caught up in the press of action and greatly benefit from brief strategies for reflecting.

When coaching the achiever, consider encouraging frequent reflection through a tool like the leadership log for clients whose goals are work-related. Once the client has set a goal, his or her task is to keep a daily log to reflect on the day's events, very briefly recording three to five bullet points or phrases each day that highlight their successes, quandaries, questions, setbacks, and the emotions or thoughts the event engendered. The client brings this log or journal to the coaching sessions. Keeping a leadership log can seem daunting. Help the client recognize that frequent reflection is the goal, but missing a day is not failure. You can create interest in this activity by linking it to the achiever's drive for self-development and learning. A doorway to the value of this reflection can be the activity that follows, the leadership timeline, used at a very early session.

The leadership timeline is a written reflective activity.[4] The goal is for the coachee to identify key life events that have contributed to their leadership style

---

4 We originally encountered this exercise at a Linkage "Coaching Organizational Leaders" workshop, though timelines are a staple of reflective journal keeping in many genres.

and choices, by reflecting on their life from birth to current time. The timeline preparation process for the coachee is as follows:

1. The client lists 12 to 20 "positive" events that have affected their leadership, noting the event and the thoughts and feelings generated at the time. (Note: events may have occurred over a period of time.)
2. The client lists 12 to 20 "negative" events that have affected their leadership, again noting the event and the thoughts it generated.
3. The client places a sheet of paper horizontally, drawing a line midway through it to represent the span of years. At the left is "birth," at the right is "current time." Above this line indicates "positive" events; under the line indicates "negative" events.
4. Clients place the individual events in order on this timeline, indicating by positioning whether the event was positive (above the line) or negative (below the line). Connect the events with a line, thus illustrating patterns.

This activity takes one to two hours of preparation time. When you meet with the client, ask the client to walk you through the timeline, sharing each event, the thoughts and emotions it generated, and its impact on the client's leadership. The coach's role is to listen and probe respectfully, helping the client articulate and identify the meaning of each event.

The leadership timeline exercise is a means of helping the client see himself through time, identifying patterns in what may have only seemed like random events. While our example timeline focuses on leadership, the exercise can be adapted to other roles: parenting, entrepreneurship, spiritual life, and so on. Any area on the client's Life Balance Wheel may be appropriate for a timeline exercise, which can illustrate how early experiences affect the self in many ways. Although this process opens up many possibilities, clients may also experience pain as they look back on who and what they were at earlier stages.

The leadership timeline is an appropriate activity for a client at the achiever stage, as the challenge of this stage is to create a differentiated internal self. This is the first developmental level where clients can be truly self-reflective about their roles, norms, and self-concept. As Kegan explained, the challenge of development in adulthood is to adequately differentiate, creating an individual self that can reflect and choose values and behaviors, and also stand apart from the self and view oneself as "object." Achievers are able to step apart from themselves and examine their assumptions and where they emerged. You can use activities like the ladder of inference as an aid to reflection (see Figure 3.2).

LADDER OF INFERENCE ACTIVITY

This coaching activity is useful for clients in reflecting on challenging situations, or in comparing successful situations with those that were not. It uses the achiever's ability to step back from their thoughts (rather than "my thoughts are myself"). It is particularly useful for clients who are highly intuitive and who seem to draw conclusions rapidly, often confounding and confusing their colleagues. (The common refrain may be, "You are putting two and two together and making five.")

Chris Argyris first put forward the construct of the ladder of inference, which was popularized in Peter Senge's *The Fifth Discipline: The Art and Practice of the Learning Organization* (1990), introducing this concept to a wide business audience. The ladder of inference visually describes the thinking process that leads human beings, usually unconsciously, to go from an event or a fact to a decision or action. The thinking stages can be seen as rungs on a ladder and are shown in Figure 3.2. At the bottom of the ladder are events and facts. From that rung, the client experiences and interprets events and facts based on beliefs and prior experience. The client quickly interprets the meaning of the event or experience by applying existing assumptions, often unconsciously, and then drawing conclusions based on the interpreted facts and assumptions. Our conclusions, repeated over time, then establish our beliefs, and we take actions that seem appropriate because they are based on what we believe. Our beliefs tend to affect what we can see—how we select from reality—and can lead us to ignore some things altogether.

Using the ladder of inference, the coach works with the client to examine experiences and events and reconstruct his or her reasoning process. Used around conflict situations, the tool helps a client examine where others may have climbed a different ladder, though all had the same experience or were in the same meeting. The ladder can assist the client to draw better conclusions, or to calmly challenge other people's conclusions through inquiry into what they observed, assumed, and believed.

Generally, meetings in the workplace become dominated by the conclusions of those around the table, particularly when more senior leaders are present. A useful activity is to help the client reconstruct reasoning by working back down the ladder, tracing the facts, assumptions and conclusions. As the client analyzes each step, he may need to adjust his reasoning, altering an assumption or extending the data selected. Work backward down the ladder, from examining the course of action to examining the validity of the conclusions and assumptions that preceded it. Help the client identify rungs he tends to skip, such as making assumptions too readily, selecting only part of the data, or preferring to notice emotions of people versus their words.

As the client explains the reasoning, he is likely to gain insight into his own reasoning processes and also where his differs from those of a colleague.

It is critically important to be aware of is your own biases, assumptions, frame of reference, and mental models—and how they affect or limit opportunities. This tool helps one become more fully aware.

Specifically, this exercise is designed to help one recognize implicit assumptions and unconscious biases that may direct one's behavior—even the application of strengths without one realizing it.

The ladder of inference tool provides a way for us to take a fresh look at how our thinking and assumptions can limit us even when we are fully in command of our strengths. The assumptions we make, consciously or unconsciously, limit options and opportunities we recognize as available to us. Our assumptions reduce our options, taking any number of rich, potential possibilities out of play. This narrowed field of options substantially scales back the number of conclusions left to be drawn—and we may not even recognize what mental models or assumptions were driving this process all along. The challenge is to fully unleash our strengths by becoming aware of the thought processes that govern how and when we apply them.

The recognition of how our mental models or assumptions can undermine our effectiveness is emphasized by Peter Senge, MIT professor and author of many books on learning organizations. Senge contends it is vitally important for a leader to uncover his or her own mental models, and those of others. He suggests that a leader's effectiveness and ability to achieve results are often undermined by the leader's own mistaken assumptions:

- My beliefs are the truth.
- The truth is obvious.
- My beliefs are based on real data.
- The data I select are the real data.

FIGURE 3.2

Event: Observable Data:

Our beliefs simply reflect our perceptions of the truth, which can be quite different than truth itself. Moreover, because it is based on my perceptions, my "truth" as I understand it may be quite different from yours, which is based on your perceptions. Research shows that the data that we attend to are most often those that reaffirm what we already believe; conflicting information or data that dispute what we believe are often dismissed, overlooked, or ignored. Data we select are just that—selective. They are a subset of the real data, chosen for their ability to reinforce our perceptions. All of this points to a very personal, subjective definition of "truth." This is exactly why substantial differences in perception come about, and why we tend to get even more entrenched in our selective perceptions.

Each of us can imagine how differently the same object or issue can be seen in various contexts. A good example is the Native American story of how a tree limb in the path during the day becomes a snake in the path at night. Our assumptions and conclusions are dramatically influenced by perception and in this case, context.

This is better expressed by Yoram Wind and Colin Crook, who state, "The ways we make sense of our world are determined to a larger extent by our internal mind and to a lesser extent by the external world." We create mental models to make sense of the world in a highly efficient manner. But the world changes rapidly—we neglect to update our mental models to stay current with reality.

One such example is the terrorist attacks of September 11, 2001. We were among many in the United States who had difficulty that morning recognizing the attacks as terrorism because our understanding of a hijacking didn't compute with what we saw on the news. Until that day, most of us thought of a hijacking as an incident where villains hold a pilot hostage, demand a huge sum of cash and protection, and divert the plane to some obscure airport. The passengers on the third plane, which crashed in Pennsylvania instead of its intended target in Washington, D.C., were able to update their mental models quickly enough to recognize that a model of hijacking was in play. The aircraft was being used as a highly fueled explosive device aimed at a densely populated target. Because they were not constrained by old mental models, passengers on the third flight kept that plane from reaching its intended target. Had the people on the third plane been too closely committed to their (outdated) mental models, the loss of life could have been even greater. When we act on old, outdated mental models, we preclude opportunities to create a new, different, even better and more effective solution.

This is the essence of how mental models work. They are useful and powerful, but can become outdated, inaccurate, or unduly biased by one's personal, subjective perception of what is real.[5] To be fully effective as leaders, especially in coaching others, we must recognize how and when our mental models,

---

5 Later in this book we focus on coaching for diversity. It is useful to notice that many of the stereotypes of generations, races, and ages are based in mental models. For clients who have been the recipients of bias and stereotype, their work may be to update their mental models of "the other."

biases, and assumptions are limiting. We must especially recognize how they keep us from seeing opportunities and potential, including the untapped potential in those we coach. The ladder of inference provides a useful tool for each of us to use in challenging our mental models, biases, and assumptions, to ensure they are useful, current, and accurate.

The image of the ladder of inference shows how quickly people tend to climb up the common mental pathway of increasing abstractness, which often leads to misguided beliefs and actions. It is a metaphor that shows how rapidly we can leap to knee-jerk conclusions with little information and without conscious awareness, as if rapidly climbing a ladder in our minds. It is worth noting that this process happens automatically, without thinking about or questioning whether the way we are processing information is accurate or valid.

As with real ladders, the ladder of inference starts at the bottom; at the rung, we begin to impose our biases, starting with selective attention to details to affirm what we already believe. We continue to impose our belief systems and add biases and interpretations as we climb higher, such that personal perceptions, assumptions, and mental models increasingly skew the conclusions.

Consider the following simplistic example: A team is crowded into a conference room for a meeting. Activity fills the room as people heatedly discuss the project at hand, shifting in their seats, shuffling papers, motioning to charts on the walls. In the midst of the activity, the team leader notices a young man yawn. The young man is new to the team; we know little about him. Within a second, the team leader is making assumptions based on limited and selective perceptions: he interprets the yawn as boredom and goes on to assume that the young man cares little about the project. The leader may generalize the belief about his lack of interest to other young people his age and decide not to include him in focused discussions of weightier issues. That conclusion was likely reached without any conscious thought by the team leader; it probably occurred without consideration of alternate explanations. Perhaps the yawn could have been a physiological response to the need for more oxygen in the closed, stuffy conference room. Have you had a similar experience?

AN EXERCISE FOR COACHES AND LEADER CLIENTS: PREPARING FOR A MEETING

During your next meeting, try to capture what you can of your thought process.

Before the meeting, write down:

- With whom you're meeting and your general perception of that person.
- The issue at hand and the purpose of the meeting.
- What you would like to get out of this meeting.
- What you think the other person's motive is and what he or she wants to get out of it.
- Your expectations for how the meeting will start, flow, and end (the final result).

During the meeting, write down:

- How the meeting started off—who initiated it, what was said.
- Direct quotes from the person you are meeting with.
- Assumptions or inferences you are making about what was said or why.
- Conclusions you are tempted to draw based on how the meeting goes.

After the meeting, consider the following:

- Did anything about this person's behavior during the meeting surprise you? Did he or she behave in a way that was out of character for what you have come to expect, or did his or her behavior reinforce the opinion of you already held?
- How might your behavior have affected the approach or reaction of others?
- How might your tone of voice, language, and posture have been interpreted?
- How quickly did you move up the ladder of inference in making assumptions or drawing conclusions during the course of the meeting?

- Might the conversation have taken a different turn if your perceptions or assumptions had been different?
- Was the end result affected by your assumptions, inferences, and conclusions?

Using Figure 3.2 as a tool, try applying the ladder of inference in situations where your interaction with the other person is not usually effective. Consider your assumptions and inferences before you go into the meeting. Assume your primary perceptions of that person are wrong and approach him or her in a completely different way than you normally would. Throughout the conversation, resist temptation to revert to your usual perceptions; keep approaching him or her in the new way.

Listed next are other examples of the ladder of inference. These examples illustrate how one or two behaviors can lead us to draw broad—possibly inaccurate—conclusions about others. (Start at the bottom rung.)

Example 1

7. I'm going to avoid Joe because I can't trust him.
6. People who have such little consideration for others can't be trusted.
5. He thinks he's better than everybody else.
4. Joe has no respect for others.
3. Joe knew exactly when the meeting started. He deliberately came in late.
2. Joe was the only one who arrived late.
1. The meeting was scheduled for 9 a.m. and Joe came in at 9:30 a.m. He didn't say why.

Example 2

7. I'm going to go around Ann on issues of any importance so she can't slow us down.
6. They shouldn't saddle productive teams with people who can't keep up.
5. Ann will never be promoted. I don't want her on my team; she makes us look bad.
4. She's in over her head.
3. Ann clearly isn't organized enough to get here on time.
2. Ann is usually late in the mornings, and she blames it on childcare issues.

1. The meeting was scheduled for 9 a.m. and Ann came in at 9:30 a.m. She didn't say why.

REFLECTIVE QUESTIONS FOR CLIENTS BASED ON THE LADDER OF INFERENCE

1. Identify a time when you reached a very quick conclusion about someone. Perhaps it was a first impression that turned out to be completely inaccurate. If you had persisted with that inaccurate perception, what would you have missed out on?
2. What might you be missing out on now, when you persist with perceptions you formed long ago about the people who report to you, or your colleagues? For the next week, focus on noting changes in others that you may have failed to see. What do you notice?
3. The next time you need to generate solutions, consider the ladder of inference. Challenge your own thinking, and the group's, to uncover assumptions or inferences that might be limiting the ability to recognize viable possibilities. Using a new set of assumptions, generate new conclusions and possibilities.

POST-CONVENTIONAL ADULT DEVELOPMENT

Inter-Individual, Catalyst, Pluralist/Strategist

Although development beyond the conventional stages is comparatively infrequent in the overall population, people who seek coaching may be more representative of the post-conventional levels of development than the general population. Robert Kegan estimates that only about 1 percent of adults reach post-conventional stages. However, another 14 percent are in transition to post-conventional stages, an experience that can be confusing and put the person at odds with family, work, and organizations.

At post-conventional stages, the inner self-definition shifts from "I am a whole and complete self that coordinates with other whole and complete selves" to an internal realization that, in fact, "I am not whole and complete." Rather, "I am many selves." Clients may begin to recognize there are parts of themselves they have ignored and not developed. Their work, particularly at midlife, may be to reexamine choices they have made, to explore doors they have not yet opened, and to reconstruct the narrative of who they are.

At the post conventional stages, the self seems multifaceted, a vast tapestry of personal systems. The client has a sense of expansiveness—but that vastness is not of the self but rather of the context in which the self operates. At this stage, clients understand the systems and groups that have shaped them and of which they are a part. They see and understand systems and their complexity and are capable of visioning strategically across a much longer period of time. They can seek information that causes them to make changes in behavior and are capable of constructive yet negative self-judgments. They can stand apart from themselves and view themselves without attachment to past constructions, seeing themselves as "object," much like a character in a novel or movie.

Clients at this stage no longer need to pretend to be whole and complete and can bring compassion and curiosity to their development and interaction with unacknowledged aspects of themselves. They can hold the whole complexity of personality—the good and the bad, the light and the dark, the hard and the soft. They see this inner complexity without flinching or needing to engage in some strenuous self-improvement regime. Better still, they see others this way—as complex multidimensional beings. They also see the world this way—as a dynamic interplay of forces. Seeing the self as a rich ecology of discord and harmony opens them to the richness and complexity of the workplace and the world.

Some adult developmental theorists believe that post-conventional leaders are needed to meet the challenges of our times, where agility in setting strategy, responding to new customers and stakeholders, and building relationships may determine future success. When achievers make the transition to post-conventional levels of development, however, they find themselves in new and challenging territory. They may find the drive and action orientation of the achievers around them to be frenetic and want to move away from environments where achievers dominate. They are capable of focus on the present moment, able to work with paradoxes and polarities, and comfortable with the gray areas in between black and white ways of seeing. They are in tune with systems thinking—including the complexity of themselves composed of body, mind, emotions and spirit. Pluralists who have built their careers inside organizations may be drawn to moving outside them, defining themselves independently yet relating to organizations. A common move for pluralists is from internal organizational employee to consulting or entrepreneurial work that keeps them connected to larger systems yet not controlled by them. The pluralist's ability to examine assumptions and take multiple perspectives can lead to success in roles like that of mediator; the pluralist is likely to recognize that each person makes meaning for themselves through the stories they tell, through their own ladders of inference.

Coaches for pluralists may find clients eager and ready for the inside-out work in Part III of this book. In particular, the work on life purpose may resonate with the pluralist's readiness to create a new story with personal meaning. They may also value opportunities to pursue meditation practice, yoga, or other spiritual disciplines perhaps outside of the traditional spiritual base of their youth.

Meditation

For clients new to meditation, the work of Martin Boroson can be a humorous and serious look at the value and practice of meditation. Boroson's method (and book) *One Moment Meditation: Stillness for People on the Go* (2009) seems ideal for simplifying the practice of meditation, beginning with a practice that takes just one minute. We have used his work with many clients; they find it refreshing to introduce a reflective meditation practice into their workplaces. There are many books and simple meditation techniques easily found online today.

The Sacred Self and the Magician

Research suggests that spiritual practices such as meditation and contemplative prayer accelerate one from the diplomat to the pluralist stage. The later stage, called by Kegan the sacred self, seldom, if ever, develops without a long-term spiritual practice. Up to this point, the self has been largely seen as located within the body–mind.

At the stage of the sacred self, an incredible shift takes place: the client realizes that "I am not the body, nor the mind." A client at this stage identifies with the soul—a soul in communion with the divine. The client realizes that the integral self, with all its rich nuances, is useful for acting in the world. It is functional—a useful tool of the spirit. At this stage, the client experiences the world as unified, as one. This oneness is a literal experience of oneness with life itself. This is the birthplace of universal compassion.

You are unlikely to find many coaching clients at this level unless you are a well-known spiritual practitioner or work with members of a spiritual community. Clients at this level generally focus on sustaining their work with a spiritual teacher rather than a coach.

For examples of individuals likely to be at post-conventional developmental stages, we look to leaders like Nelson Mandela. Mandela's long imprisonment and then leadership of South Africa were remarkable. Yet it was his capacity to understand the unifying powerful of forgiveness that suggests his post-conventional, perhaps even magician stage of development. When many leaders would have looked to punishment or chastisement in response to South Africa's long suppression of non-whites, Mandela held reconciliation events where forgiveness was the theme and unification in postapartheid South Africa the intention.

Fr. Richard Rohr writes from a Unitive consciousness as well as a deeply Catholic base. He is a globally recognized ecumenical teacher bearing witness to the universal awakening within Christian mysticism and the Perennial Tradition. He is a Franciscan priest of the New Mexico province and founder of the Center for Action and Contemplation (CAC) in Albuquerque, New Mexico. Rohr's teaching is grounded in what he describes as an "alternative orthodoxy"—practices of contemplation and self-emptying. His ministry expresses itself in radical compassion, particularly for the socially marginalized. We first encountered Rohr many years ago through his workshops on the Enneagram of Personality and spiritual development, where his brilliance and humility made him an extraordinary messenger of the Enneagram tradition. The mission of his institute testifies to the power of his Unitive consciousness: to produce compassionate and powerfully learned individuals who will work for positive change in the world based on awareness of our common union with God and all beings.

Following the Jesuit tradition of simplicity and belief in the oneness of people, including the primacy of work for the poor and suffering, Pope Francis also articulates the principles of nonjudgment that come from the Unitive consciousness. Asked about his views on gay marriage, he responded unlike any other pope before him, saying, "Who am I to judge?" This emphasis on unity and not duality, acceptance and not judgment, is the kind of message that springs from the highest level of adult consciousness development.

THE CASE OF GEORGE THE CHIROPRACTOR: TRANSITIONING STAGES

George is likely to be between adult development levels. Trained in the expert model, he was likely an expert developmentally during his early chiropractic career. Now, he struggles with some of the dilemmas of the late-stage achiever. His coach sees him struggling with authenticity and hears him speak that word frequently during sessions. His coach sees him beginning to want a more comprehensive spiritual life than his traditional German Catholic religious focus has given him. He wrestles with the distinction between spiritual understanding and interconnection and the "religious dogma," which is how he describes the tradition of his religious upbringing. (Notice that using the quadrant model, the dogma occurs in Quadrants 3 and 4, whereas his personal experience of its impact is a Quadrant 1 issue; an understanding of this may guide the coach's questions.)

In *Action Inquiry*, Torbert et al. (2004) described cases of leaders at various developmental levels and the results of their attempts at organizational change efforts. They believed that a leader must be at least at the strategist level to successfully undertake a complex change effort. His work makes fascinating reading for coaches who practice within corporations undertaking systemic changes.

In this developmental model, George might be moving from the achiever level to the pluralist/individualist level. He has placed a high value on achieving results and building his business. At an earlier stage, his excellence as a chiropractor may have been indicative of the expert stage. Now he seems to be in transition to an individualist focus, where he sees himself as part of a system and feels dissatisfaction when he looks at the entirety of his life.

We encourage coaches to explore their own development level. This may come through taking the assessment tool developed by Susanne Cook-Greuter, or through attending one of Bill Joiner's "Leadership Agility" workshops. Barbara Braham, a longtime executive coach, and colleague of Cook-Greuter, offers coaches the opportunity to take the MAP Assessment as well as a workshop on using adult development level in coaching.

Recall the ancient Greek admonition to "know thyself." Many believe that coaches need to be a good fit for the development level of their clients: being levels below or above might make for ineffective coaching relationships. A pluralist coach of an expert, for example, may find it challenging to meet the "right or wrong" mind-set of the client well enough to journey through change. An achiever coach may find it difficult to understand the reflective tendencies and indecision of the pluralist client.

Coach's Question for Reflection

Take a moment to consider your experience as a coach. With which clients have you been most successful? With which clients have you been disappointed? Identify the development levels of each of these groups. Is there a common theme that suggests the common concerns of a particular level of development of clients you may work best with?

WHY ADULT DEVELOPMENT MATTERS

In 2010, Robert Kegan participated as a lead of the first master class offered by the Institute of Professional Coaching at Harvard. As part of that class, he offered an amazingly simple distillation of what subject-object theory and consciousness offer to coaches. There he distilled key principles from each level of consciousness that apply to our work as coaches:

- At the conventional levels of diplomat and earlier, the client is "subject" to his other tribe: the client's values, ideals and roles are created from the family, tribe, or culture. The client makes up his "disposition, needs and preferences."
- At the expert or achiever levels, self-determination emerges. What makes the client is a belief that "I am autonomous, self-authoring, self-regulating; I want to find my true self." The client makes up his values, ideals, and roles and is not defined by others.
- At the post-conventional levels, the client is continually self-transforming and evolving. The client makes up his form of self. The client is one of multiple selves at any point in time based on the context—"I make up my autonomous self-authoring and self-regulating self."

Kegan believes that coaches are already vested in fostering constructing development. They do this by using empathy and deep listening, fostering self-motivation for change, coaching the expansion of consciousness, and dealing with apparent paradoxes that arise on the journey of change. Kegan believes the following techniques foster constructive development (Kegan et al., 2010):

- Exploration and amplification of personal values, dreams, and visions.
- Fostering of self-motivation and intrinsic motivation.
- Inquiry and reflections foster self-discovery and insight—creating awareness of what clients are owned by.
- Intuitive dance of relational flow expands client's sense of self in the moment.
- Coaching process and client achievement over time fosters and anchors outgrowth of old thinking, feeling, and behaving.

During his class, Kegan reiterated the importance of the coach's empathy to supporting the client's consciousness development. He believes it critical for coach and client to understand and appreciate levels of consciousness without judgment. While people at a lower level do not have the capacity to make meaning at a higher level, it is critical to work to connect—without judging— the client's level of meaning making. Only then is there an opportunity for the client to take small steps to expand meaning-making capacity and perspective.

Kegan made the following suggestions for coaching the expansion of consciousness:

- Create optimal conditions for expansion, including empathy, positivity, and courage, to support experiments with new ways of making meaning.
- Assist the client to find and pursue their passions; this is a motivational driver of desire for a higher level of consciousness.
- Raise the client's awareness of what the client is "subject to"—what is "inside the box," what is the client's narrative or story about why things are.
- Find small steps to experiment with the client making his or her beliefs instead of being made by them. This is getting out of the box.
- Help the client harvest the insights and reinforce steps taken toward greater objectivity and self-authoring.

In their book, *Immunity to Change*, Kegan and his colleague Lisa Lahey have developed a tool called the immunity to change map. This creates opportunities for the coach and client to identify how what the client is subject to might be blocking change from occurring.

The process seems deceptively simple and consists of having the client complete a four-column worksheet (see Figure 3.3), consisting of these columns[6]:

1. Improvement goal: What the client needs to do differently.
2. Behaviors that go against the goal
3. Explanation for the behaviors in 2: these are the hidden competing commitments really driving the behaviors.
4. Big assumptions: beliefs, fears, what the client is subject to that are holding the situation stuck.

Jessie Sholl (2011) has written an excellent blog entry including client examples of the immunity to change map. Read her article for a complete explanation of this excellent coaching tool. While adult levels of development are not consciously called out in Sholl's article, they are implicit in the tool for those who know Kegan's work.

The map is an excellent resource for life coaches and others who work with leaders. Completing the tool creates a good deal of introspection—energy emerges when the client discovers that the block to achieving the goal is not a lack of will but comes from a competing commitment.

Midlife and Its Changes

No matter what stage of development a client is at, midlife seems to be a time of transition and change. As Kathleen A. Brehony (1997) wrote, "nothing less is being asked of us than that we question all of the beliefs that seemed to hold true during the first half of our lives." This is the common experience of people moving into the pluralist stage of adult development, and it is also commonly experienced midlife.

Frederic Hudson, an early pioneer in adult learning and coaching (Hudson, 1999; Hudson & McLean, 2000), proposed a cycle of change that recurs

---

6 This worksheet is available at https://extension.harvard.edu/wp-content/uploads/sites/8/2021/03/ext_immunity_map_0.pdf.

FIGURE 3.3

Immunity Map Worksheet

SOURCE: WORKSHEET COURTESY OF ROBERT KEGAN AND LISA LAHEY. © MINDS AT WORK; WWW.MINDSATWORK.COM

Immunity Map Worksheet

Find the full article, "How to Overcome Immunity to Change," in the May 2011 archives at experiencelife.com.

Improvement Goal	Behaviors That Go Against My Goal	Hidden Competing Commitments	Big Assumptions
What I'd need to do differently:		Worry Box:	
		Competing Commitments:	

Choose a goal that would make a big difference, one you truly want to achieve. Ask yourself (or imagine asking a group of people who know you well): *What is the single most powerful change I could I make to improve my life (or work performance, relationship, finances, etc.)?*

Next, specify what concrete behaviors are necessary to achieve this goal. Frame them as positive statements (for example, "delegate more" vs. "stop doing all the work myself").

Ask yourself (or an imagined observer): *What's the thing you do, or don't do, that most gets in the way of your goal?*

Take stock of the things you do instead of the behaviors that could create positive change.

You don't need to explain or understand your obstructionist behaviors. Just notice them and write them down. Define your actions, not your feelings.

Your fears go into a "worry box" at the top of this column. They can point you to your competing commitments, which you list below the worry box.

When you write down your hidden commitments, you are now able to see across the three columns how you have one foot on the gas pedal (column 1) and one foot on the brake pedal (column 3). This is the immune system "protecting" you from feared, undesireable outcomes.

Big assumptions, says Lahey, "are the beliefs and internalized truths we hold about how the world works, how we work, and how people respond to us. They are assumptions that make each hidden commitment feel necessary."

Look for assumptions that anchor and inform your specific hidden commitments. Notice how your assumptions lead to the very behaviors that undermine, rather than support, your goal.

throughout the course of an adult's life. (See www.hudsoninstitute.com for a fuller explanation.)

Hudson proposed four phases to this cycle, which recur throughout an adult's life. He called the cycles "life chapters."

Phase 1: Go For It

This is the beginning, essentially the positive part of a life chapter, when clients seek to live their dream and take actions toward fully living it and maintaining the success and well-being they experience. In Phase 1, clients feel as if they are "on purpose." Life just seems to be working.

George probably felt like this when he first started his practice, and perhaps also when he first got married, as these phases can apply to any aspect of life. Many professionals rejuvenate themselves and return to Phase 1 through learning. They go to seminars and learn new ways to work with clients. Examining George's history, his coach realizes that George took seminars frequently, upgrading his skills and chiropractic office tools, which he reported brought him a burst of energy. Now, he has begun to study acupuncture. Before he came to coaching, he thought that new pursuit might return him to an energetic and satisfied place. He is surprised that it hasn't, although he is still interested in acupuncture.

FIGURE 3.4

The Cycle of Renewal

SOURCE: HUDSON INSTITUTE OF COACHING

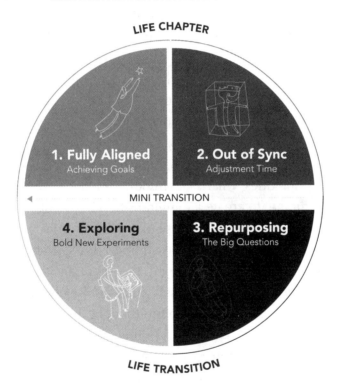

LIFE CHAPTER

1. **Fully Aligned**
Achieving Goals

2. **Out of Sync**
Adjustment Time

MINI TRANSITION

4. **Exploring**
Bold New Experiments

3. **Repurposing**
The Big Questions

LIFE TRANSITION

Phase 2: The Doldrums

This phase is a "downtime" when there is a sense of general malaise and decline. In this phase clients are unhappy with the situation but not certain about what to do. Generally, clients hang on to what was good in Phase 1, hoping it will return if they just work harder. The doldrums are meant to serve as a wake-up call, an invitation to restructure or reinvent life so it works again.

George has clearly been in the doldrums. Sometimes the doldrums can be purposeful. Clients may not get stuck in their reactions to the doldrums if they realize a little "cocooning" is needed, which is the next phase, and they engage in reflection upon their choices.

However, the doldrums may also be a manifestation of burnout—or rust out, as some career coaches describe it. People are tired and ready for something new. They continue to do what they know and to experience dissatisfaction.

The Mini Transition

One way out of the doldrums is to make a mini transition. This includes correcting and improving the chapters the clients are in by taking a shortcut across the cycle of renewal, by sorting out what works from what doesn't and creating a personal plan. According to Hudson and McLean (2000), clients keep the main themes, roles, and characters of their chapters, but make some significant changes as well—perhaps geographic location, job, career, or relationship. The mini transition renews the clients' chapter, bringing resilience, hope, and challenge. Clients return to Phase 1 with renewed energy to continue their life chapter. For George, a mini transition might involve bringing in a business partner so that he wouldn't be working alone.

This category includes what is commonly called a midlife crisis, with people often attempting to create a mini transition by changing spouses. Others add something to their life: a vacation home, a boat, or an adventure vacation that takes them out of the known and adds stimulation to their life. Done with full consciousness and thought, the mini transition is very healthy. Choosing a mini transition unconsciously and impulsively leads to unhealthy choices, such as quitting a job with no forethought, having an affair, or making an expensive purchase that is outside the client's budget. These radical behavior shifts are done without consideration or reflection, which is different from what George might do: donating a month or two of his time to do chiropractic work as a volunteer in a developing country. Doctors Without Borders is an example of an opportunity for a medical practitioner to experience a mini transition.

Phase 3: Cocooning

Cocooning is the phase where human beings imitate butterflies and enter a chrysalis to transform. This is a detachment from a chapter that wasn't working and the beginning of a major life transition. In cocooning, the client takes an emotional "time-out" to heal, reflect, and discover new directions for life, eventually leading to renewal and revitalization. Cocooning nurtures and nourishes the soul, giving birth to a new script and the beginning of a new story for the next chapter of life.

Clients cocoon in several ways. Some take an extended period of time off, such as a sabbatical, to reflect and discover. Others build cocooning time into their regular schedule. Clients may cocoon, for example, by going on a month-long silent retreat or by building in half-day retreats to their weekdays. A person could even have a special room for cocooning more briefly: a place for meditating, reflecting, journaling, exploring in the silence, and coming out rejuvenated.

George might choose to cocoon by taking off one day each week, going into nature and reflecting on his needs and desires at this stage of life. The coach can help George by partnering with him to build inquiry questions and disciplines that will enable him to explore deeply, making the best use of his cocooning time each week.

Phase 4: Getting Ready

This phase is a time for experimenting, training, and networking, resulting in a launching of the client's next chapter. Clients test the possible paths ahead that will allow them to live their purpose and values. At that point, they write the script for the next chapter of life and plunge into it. They have arrived at Phase 1 again.

Coaching can be crucial for clients in Phase 4 to help develop their ideas beyond abstract and into fruition—making the changes they want to make. George may determine, through his cocooning reflections, that he wants to bring in several junior chiropractors, fresh out of school, for mentoring then managing his business, ideally serving more clients. Ultimately, he will be able to sell the business. In the interim, he may choose to take a month-long acupuncture training session in China and a course in nutrition. He will be able to add these to the business offerings and will be the provider of these services within the business.

MAKING THE SHIFT

Taking a developmental, cyclical, and integral perspective on the client's life and goals marks the holistic activity of life coaching. How coaches have been trained, as well as the style and focus of their current profession, will be partial determinants of how they make the transition from their current profession to coaching.

Transition always requires both a holding on and a letting go. Generally, this needs to occur before something new can be embraced. Like a child receiving presents on a holiday, new things cannot be added when arms are already full.

All people who successfully make transitions clarify and engage in both holding on and letting go. Clients like George must consider what to hold on to and what to let go of, as do professionals moving into coaching.

An in-depth awareness is required for coaches who plan to continue practicing their current profession as well as beginning to coach. The Institute for Life Coach Training (which Dr. Pat founded in 1998) asks participants to determine which skills are readily transferable from their current work to coaching, which are not, and which shifts they will need to make—for example, shifting "therapist habits and mindsets" to "coach habits and mindsets."

Many therapists become very aware at this time how deeply ingrained their habits of thinking and behaving as a therapist have become. They may habitually move to ask clients about their feelings first. They may avoid challenging clients because their habit is to see clients as fragile and in need of extensive support to make changes. They may not hold clients accountable. These are all habits therapists will need to change in their coaching.

How long does it take to change a habit? Estimates range from 21 days to 60 repetitions, depending on the frequency with which the person engages in the habit. Regardless of the time span, the question remains: How can this coach develop the habits needed to become a great coach? What shifts will this coach need to make? We describe these new habits as shifts because if therapists, for example, continue to do therapy, they must shift back and forth between these two sets of assumptions, behaviors, attitudes, and skills. Coaches must be flexible to ensure they use the right habits in the right settings. This can be enabled through changes in the environment. If therapists conduct face-to-face coaching in the same office they do therapy, they may want to change chairs when they coach so they coach from the chair their therapy patients usually occupy. This will provide a new perspective, which can help them use different habits and practices than they habitually use when seated in their therapist chair. Because body and mind are so intimately connected, this shift of body can assist in the shift of mind.

Exercise 3.1 is useful in examining the shift from therapist to coach. You can use it to brainstorm what you may want and need to release, discontinue, continue, start, or enhance. To begin this process, we have written some examples from earlier coach training classes:

EXERCISE 3.1

Shifting from Therapist (or Other Helping Professional) to Coach
Read the samples that follow, which are suggestions we've gleaned from other helping professionals transitioning to coaching, then add your own.

CONTINUE DOING

1. Great listening from the heart.

_____

2. Use my intuition.

_____

3. Look at the client's life within systems.

_____

4. Use reframing.

_____

5.

_____

6.

_____

7.

_____

8.

_____

START DOING

1. More self-disclosure.

_____

2. Ask for payment in advance.

_____

3. Set fees according to what I'm worth.

_____

4. Call myself a coach, and believe it!

_____

5.

_____

6.

_____

7.

_____

8.

_____

LET GO, DO LESS OF/STOP

1. Go for feelings as the main route to change.

_____

2. Feel as though I must be the expert.

_____

3. Believe I'm dependent on insurance reimbursement.

_____

4. Always put the client's needs first.

_____

5. Think of clients as in need of change, as "patients."

_____

6.

_____

7.

_____

8.

_____

If you as a reader are in transition, we suggest you complete this fieldwork to help you apply the work from this chapter.

- Identify the two major actions you must take to make the shift from your current profession to coaching. Work with a coach or partner to identify an action plan. You will need to identify supports and resources for each of the shifts you want to make. Take at least one action this week to develop a new habit to use as coach.
- Self-observe this week how you are within your relationships with others, your relationship with yourself, and your relationship with what is larger than you. Maintain your attention and focus each day. What does this suggest about your level or stage of development?

PART II

Beyond the Basics

This section builds on the fundamentals of coaching introduced in the first three chapters. Primarily it emphasizes specific skills and ways of viewing oneself that a coach uses with clients within sessions.

In Chapter 4, "Empowering the Client," we introduce six types of conversation that can occur within the context of coaching, as well as seven specific skills that create an empowering conversation.

Chapter 5, "Stretching the Client," introduces the 10 steps of the coaching continuum in addition to three specific skills for challenging clients to stretch.

Chapter 6, "Creating Momentum with the Client," includes five strategies and common practices for creating and maintaining coaching momentum.

Chapter 7, "Coaching the Whole Client: Mind, Body, Emotions, Spirit," includes strategies and practices for engaging the client in exploring how cognitive, language, emotional, and somatic practices intertwine to support transformational shifts for the client.

Together, Parts I and II provide the platform for a coach to work with the client on the "Coaching from the Inside Out" processes described in Part III.

CHAPTER 4

EMPOWERING THE CLIENT

When Jackie Robinson was signed by Brooklyn Dodgers General Manager Branch Rickey in 1945, he became the first African American to play Major League Baseball. But "Number 42" became the target of considerable racist hatred and death threats. Rickey had warned Robinson that things would be tough, and he should learn to turn the other cheek. Prior to one game, however, Jackie received a telephone call that brought him to his tipping point. He was so devastated he could not concentrate on the game and struck out with the bases loaded. During another inning he made a fielding error. The crowd's obscenities escalated. This is very well expressed visually and dramatically in the film *42* (dir. Brian Helgeland, 2013).

Pee Wee Reese, a white shortstop from Kentucky and Jackie's teammate, called a time out. Reese put his arm around Robinson and is reported to have said, "Jackie, let me tell you something. I believe in you. You are the greatest ballplayer I have ever seen. You can do it. I know that. And I know something else: one of these days you are going into the Hall of Fame. So, hold your head up high and play ball like only you can do it." Robinson was uplifted by these sentiments and went on to deliver the game winning hit for his team.

Many years later when he was inducted into the Baseball Hall of Fame, Robinson recalled that day on the field with Pee Wee as a turning point, a moment when Pee Wee gave him hope when all hope was gone.

Pee Wee Reese, a great natural coach, intuitively knew that a few well-timed words of encouragement could change the course of an event or a life—even the course of history.

Empowerment is a word that is overused—often incorrectly. Some talk about empowerment as though it is something coaches do for clients. No one empowers anyone else. Clients must be the ones who discover, claim, and boldly stand by their own power. What coaches do is to create a climate that encourages clients to be powerful. Coaches can ask questions that point clients' attention toward sources of potency. Coaches can help clients identify blocks to their recognition of internal power and wisdom, and assist them to explore ways to overcome those obstacles. We often use the analogy of boulders and a whitewater rafting trip: You will definitely meet boulders on the rafting trip. You will either go around them in a controlled manner or hit them head on, followed by bouncing off, turning around, and moving on down the river. Obstacles are like boulders in the river. You cannot always avoid them—the key is not to get stuck.

We believe this way of thinking is behind Robert Hargrove's definition of masterful coaching. In his book by the same name, he says masterful coaching is about "empowering people to create a future they truly desire, based on unearthing what they passionately care about . . . to create their lives based on what is deeply purposeful to them" (1995, p. 20).

As coaches, we hold the intention that clients feel empowered to take action in every sphere of their lives. Clients sometimes do not like to see themselves as "powerful," possibly because they have had bad associations with power. A common distinction coaches make is between power and force. Power comes from the inside and does not have to be forceful. It just is. Claiming personal power does not mean clients become an aggressive, forceful energy. It simply means clients recognize and claim the unique power they already possess to shape their lives. Coaches assist clients in having full access to resources that may be lying dormant or the manifestations of which may be currently invisible. This invisible resource is the positive aspect of what Carl Jung calls the shadow archetype of our personality. People often assume that the shadow holds only the darker and more destructive aspect of the self, but it also hides unrealized strengths, gifts, and abilities. Coaches help clients claim these. Often what may be in the clients' shadow simply needs to be brought out into the open. We're not looking for deep, dark, personal secrets . . . only those that when illuminated grant new energy to the client and their life. Remember Wendy in Peter Pan? Wendy helped Peter reclaim his shadow as part of himself and sewed it back on for him.

We judge the effectiveness of our coaching sessions by gauging the level of the clients' motivations by the end of them. Generally, clients end sessions feeling more capable, competent, empowered, clear, and passionate, as well as better able to take action. The result of a coaching session is usually positive because we work with skill, wisdom, and humor while holding in our focus the clients' highest good. That is, our entire focus and intention are on their empowerment. We know as coaches that coaching is essentially about insight, learning, and choosing to act. These three empower the clients to feel naturally generative and empowered.

WHEN DO COACHES USE EMPOWERING SKILLS?

Clients tap into their creativity—the ability to see other possibilities for action and life—to make changes. The major obstacles that prevent clients from achieving their potential come from within: the inner critics, gremlins, and internal voices that challenge the clients' belief in themselves. Shakti Gawain puts this elegantly in *Meditations*:

> As adults, the major block to our creativity is our inner critic, that part of us that internally criticizes what we do. We have standards of perfection incorporated from the world around us, ways that we think things should be done. We have a critic within who criticizes us when we are not doing things the way the critic feels they should be done. For most of us, this inner critic is what stops us from taking the kinds of risks that need to be taken. (1997, p. 62)

Julia Cameron makes an eloquent statement about how, when courage and creativity are released, energy builds and creates its own momentum.

> It is when we fire the arrow of desire, when we start a project, that we trigger the support for our dream. We are what sets things in motion; people and events resonate toward our fiery resolve. Energy attracts energy. Our arrow is the speeding pickup truck that attracts summer dogs to chase it down the road. We generate the energy and excitement. Then others will give chase. Build it and they will come. Creative energy is energy. When we are worrying about creating instead of actually creating, we are wasting our creative energy. When we are vacillating, we are letting air out of our tires. Our pickup is not speeding down the road and may never even get out of the driveway. Our project goes flat. Does this mean we should race off wildly? No, but it does mean that once we have a heart's desire, we should act on it. It is

that action, that moving out on faith, that moves mountains and careers. (2003, p. 20)

When coaches focus on heightening clients' awareness of their potency and choices, their motivation rises, creating energy and momentum to sustain their work.

In general, coaching enhances clients' ability to recognize, embrace, and use their key strengths. Knowing and using signature strengths is one of the ways clients create lives of authentic happiness and true fulfillment. We refer here to strengths as described by Martin Seligman (2002). Calling specific attention to strengths, gifts, and choices assists clients at all phases of their work. While coaching is not therapy, it boosts clients' self-esteem and confidence (as well as their toolbox of strategies) to identify and acknowledge specific strengths.

Coaches focus on empowering the clients when:

- An obstacle has been encountered and clients are discouraged.
- Clients discount a resource or skill that has potential to enhance current effectiveness or aid in achieving a goal or desire.
- Clients label as a weakness something the coach sees as a strength.
- The goal seems temporarily unattainable, or clients are blocked in seeing a pathway toward it.
- Clients have forgotten their vision and need to be reminded of possibilities.
- No one in the clients' lives believes they can attain what is desired.
- Clients need an advocate, in which case coaches model how to become effective advocates.
- The clients' inner voice is predominantly discouraging or negative. Empowerment counters the inner voice with a strong compassionate message—the voice of the coaches.

SELECTING THE RIGHT TYPE OF CONVERSATION AND THE RIGHT SKILLS

The coach's intentions fulfill themselves using skillful conversation and seven empowering skills. The conversation type and the skill must work together to create a platform for empowerment.

The Case of the Dentist

As you read the material below about the types of conversations and skills, consider the applicability of each one to this case: a dentist in search of a career change.

You have a new client, a dentist who has been in practice for 10 years. His goal is to build his business and make it more profitable so he can sell it and retire in 10 or 15 years. You discover that he is living for the future when he will no longer be working. When you ask him about his work, he tells the truth more deeply. He is bored with dentistry and would love to do something else. But his wife is scared to death of the prospect of this type of change, especially if it jeopardizes their current comfortable lifestyle. Their two sons, ages seven and eight, both go to private schools, and his wife does not currently work outside the home, although she volunteers for several charitable causes. Both are active in their church.

You learn the dentist has always had an interest in music and the arts, and during his early college years he wanted to be a sculptor. However, he pursued dentistry because he is talented with his hands, and his father had a dental practice. While his father was alive, your client enjoyed the practice, as well as the relationship and comradeship with his father. When his father died five years ago and he began a solo practice, dentistry lost its appeal. He is discouraged about reigniting his interest in dentistry, although he has a passing interest in dental surgery. He likes to mentor others and has considered adding several dentists to his practice who are fresh out of dental school.

Your client has had a lot of fun creating a website for his practice and wonders whether he would enjoy being a Web designer or the owner of a design shop. He loves to mentor people and is lonely and dissatisfied in a solo practice. He is clear that his wife and his sons come first, though, and does not want to jeopardize their family harmony or security.

Six Types of Conversations

Ellis (2006, pp. 52–55) describes six types of conversations we use every day. As you read these descriptions, consider the value of each in the case of the dentist, as well as your coaching practice.

Sharing

When you share, you communicate the essence of who you are, what you think, and how you currently feel. This is a quick but heartfelt snapshot of yourself that you provide in a few minutes. Sharing might sound like this:

> Life's tough these days. I've been having problems with my boss, and my teenage daughter is rebellious. I wish I had more time to deal with these problems. I'm worried about my health. My doctor said that I need to come in for three difficult tests, and I'm scared. I love being active, and I don't want anything to get in the way of that. I really enjoyed the trip I recently took to San Francisco. We had a great time visiting friends and exploring the city. In general, life has been such a celebration. I just received a $3,000 raise and am really surprised. I feel so pleased that my hard work has been recognized. Now I'm starting to think about what to do with the extra money.

One way to be a powerful life coach is to demonstrate sharing yourself and in so doing, ask for sharing—speaking deeply, authentically, and comprehensively about where you are in the present moment. You and your client can learn to converse soulfully from the depths of your beings about who you both are in this moment. This is a sacred way to be with each other, a rare and precious experience.

Many people find sharing difficult at first. When someone asks, "How are you?" many people give a brief, superficial reply, "Just fine, thanks." Other people habitually go into a long report full of unrelated details. Both responses can conceal who we really are in the moment.

When we share, we do not always have to reveal deep, dark secrets, nor is the release of emotion always necessary. The main idea is to reveal an authentic and personal experience to the listener. This kind of conversation is deeply felt, soulful, sincere, candid, and direct. When a person speaks truthfully, candidly, deeply, and briefly with another person, the two individuals can create a symbiotic universe. Powerful sharing moves us deeply and alters subsequent conversations. Sharing unloads clients' burdens so they can become present and mindful to what they want to create now.

As a life coach, you can model this kind of speaking and request it from clients. You can start sessions by asking clients to share. If they respond instead with their agenda for the session, you can describe sharing in more detail, demonstrate it, and again ask them to share.

The most powerful thing you can bring to someone's sharing is full, committed, and heartfelt listening. This might be as challenging for you as authentic sharing is for the client. When people share, coaches are often tempted to give advice, launch a discussion, or expand on their comments by relating an experience of their own. Do not do this. Your job is to postpone a personal response and simply receive what the client shares.

We can even do others a favor when we ask them to receive in this way: "Please don't give me any advice about this. You don't have to make any suggestions or do any problem solving. I just want you to listen. Just witness. I just want to share."

Here is a powerful role the coach can play by just being a witness: someone who observes and creates a safe container for the client to share. Witnessing in this sense is a neutral and supportive role. Human beings on many important occasions ask others to witness their experience as a way to honor it: we ask people to come to weddings and funerals as a way of witnessing experiences and honoring their place in the human life cycle.

ASK YOURSELF:
Would you use this kind of conversation with the dentist? How would it be empowering (or disempowering) to him?

Debriefing

Debriefing is different from sharing. While sharing is about who someone is in the moment, debriefing is a description of what someone has been doing since the last session. When clients debrief, they give a detailed report. Like a newspaper article, debriefing relates the breaking events and answers the who, what, where, when, and how questions.

Sharing offers a taste of how someone is in the moment; debriefing serves up the potentially long list of what they have done and felt since you last met. In the process of sharing this information, clients feel refreshed and focused. Debriefing helps clients:

- Learn from their recent history by talking about what worked and what did not. With that insight, they are more likely to repeat what does work. The U.S. Army has put this into regular practice with After Action Reviews, where frontline troops and officers review details of recent incidents in the field.

- Forgive mistakes, celebrate successes, and release the past. Debriefing can include all of these elements.
- Set goals. As clients review the last few days, they might realize what they want to change.

Encourage clients to debrief regularly with a variety of people in a variety of ways. Clients can debrief with other significant people in their lives. They can debrief in private by writing in a journal, speaking into a tape recorder, or simply talking out loud to themselves. You can suggest your clients commit to this new behavior and monitor how often they debrief on their own.

Bring debriefing into your coaching and into your life. Reflect on what has occurred and what you have learned. It is a habit worth acquiring.

ASK YOURSELF:

Would you use this kind of conversation with the dentist? How would it be empowering (or disempowering) to him?

Clearing

Another form of conversation with a unique purpose is clearing. When clients clear, they release feelings. Sometimes that release is called venting, like relieving pressure before something explodes. Clearing is pure, emotional release where the clients' aim is to speak about a topic until they "get it off their chest."

Where sharing tends to be brief, clearing may be brief or lengthy, depending upon the clients' personal style, as well as the intensity of their response and the importance of the event. Unlike debriefing, clearing does not result in a detailed review of recent events in the clients' lives. When clearing, clients can focus on a single event and their emotional response to it.

Clearing is a powerful form of conversation that you can facilitate in a variety of ways. Coaching is not a therapy session, so the purpose of clearing is not catharsis. You may simply ask, "Is there anything you need to clear in order to move into today's session? Is there anything left over from the meeting you just left?" Clearing can occur in just a minute or two. The client speaks it, you hear it, and the two of you are ready to move on. Clearing could be simply a sentence or two where clients put into words their frustration with a meeting they just left. You create space for the clients to express and release whatever needs clearing. This, too, is a form of witnessing.

ASK YOURSELF:
Would you use this kind of conversation with the dentist? How would it be empowering (or disempowering) to him?

Given that the dentist describes his wife as reluctant to entertain change, it is likely that he may have no place in his life where clearing is supported. Coaching conversations may provide that place.

Discussion and Debate

Discussion and debate are probably the dominant forms of conversation in our society—in large groups, in small groups, and even in pairs. The political landscape is largely a landscape of discussion and debate with little ability to reconcile polarities or positions. These two ways of communicating occur when people express views and opinions. Both can promote learning, which takes place when we approach a subject from a variety of angles. If our intention is to learn, we come away with a point of view larger than what any one person originally brought to the conversation.

Discussion and debate work when people share the conversation and when space is created for everyone's brilliance. To recognize this shared space, it is necessary to give everyone equal time to speak.

Discussion and debate generally do not form a substantial part of the coaching process. Instead, coaching relies more on what David Bohm (1996) described in his extensive work on dialogue. Bohm contrasted discussion with dialogue through the root meanings of each word. Discussion, which is like the root of percussion, contains a sense of beating against something. Dialogue, on the other hand, comes from the root word for "flowing through." This is often how it works in coaching. By allowing for silences, listening, and intuition, something flows through the conversation that is larger or deeper than each individual alone brings. Even Socrates's method of inquiry was to create discussion and debate, but for the purpose of deeper thinking about common human striving. Socrates was recognized as the teacher, however, so his relationship with those he taught was not a coaching alliance. We recommend that coaches focus on dialogue, as we have said above, because dialogue is consistent with the coaching alliance.

In a coaching framework, the purpose of discussion and debate is never to focus on right or wrong, only to create deeper thinking through dialogue. Sometimes clients like to debate, and you can participate in this form of communication in a playful way. There may be occasions when a client wants your opinion or wants to debate a particular topic. This kind of communication should not focus on forcing your opinion on the client. Stay light and playful. By not expressing a point of view or not taking a stand on a particular issue, you convey your open-mindedness and can bring a fresh perspective to the conversation. You also demonstrate that it is okay not to have a point of view and that there is no need to adopt one immediately.

ASK YOURSELF:

Would you use this kind of conversation with the dentist? How would it be empowering (or disempowering) to him?

Teaching

Another way we can be in conversation with each other is through teaching. Teaching occurs when somebody says, "I know something that you may not know, and I would like to share it with you." When others want to learn from this person, they often listen intently, take notes, search to understand, and ask questions until they are clear. Sometimes in a teaching environment, debate and discussion occur; in an unusual teaching environment, even sharing may occur.

We recommend coaches be cautious with teaching. It is tempting to become the source of wisdom for a client, but it can undermine partnership. Still, some clients may need to learn exactly what the coach can teach rapidly. In small doses, teaching can be very effective.

In the case of the dentist, you might want to teach the client how to do a simple breath counting meditation as a way of centering and focusing between patients. Before you begin teaching, you might say, "It could be beneficial for you to be able to do a brief centering exercise between patients. Would you like to learn that now?" If the client accepts your invitation to learn, at that moment you have shifted into teaching. It is important to explicitly say to the client that your role has shifted. "I'm shifting into a teaching mode for a moment."

ASK YOURSELF:

Would you use this kind of conversation with the dentist? How would it be empowering (or disempowering) to him?

The Coaching Conversation

There is one more unique and distinct way that we can be in conversation with each other, and that is through coaching. This type of conversation takes place when people explore what they want in the future and choose ways to attain it—without giving or getting advice.

In the context of a coaching relationship, you do many different things with clients—exploring, problem solving, creative thinking, generating multiple options (including contradictory ones), and experimenting with new strategies and techniques. Sometimes coaching simply means listening fully and occasionally feeding back what you hear, which is a huge gift we can bring to people. Throughout this activity, the clients' purpose is to lay the ground for transformation or to generate their next new action—something that does not happen in sharing, debriefing, discussion and debate, or teaching.

ASK YOURSELF:

Would you use this kind of conversation with the dentist? How would it be empowering (or disempowering) to him?

Seven Skills for Empowering

These skills evoke the clients' best resources, allowing them to realize what they already know but may doubt, undervalue, or treat as insignificant. Keep the case of the dentist in mind as you review these skills.

1. Focusing on Strengths

Recall the Big Five model we introduced back in Chapter 1. Intention and Attention, the first of the five, asks this question: Of all the possible places to direct their attention, which do the clients choose? You also make choices as to where to direct the clients' attention. Shining the light on their strengths serves them well and counters the habitually critical climate they may inhabit.

How often in our lives are we told what we are doing right? Many clients are only minimally aware of their strengths. They may have been told that a strength is a weakness or a liability by others who do not want them to apply that strength. We all have strengths; however, most of us are more aware of our weaknesses. We hear more about our weaknesses, beginning early in our childhood, from parents, teachers, and others. Some of us even find it impossible to talk about our strengths, either because we are not aware of them or because we feel it inappropriate or even arrogant to do so.

As a coach, you want clients to recognize, articulate, and fully embrace their strengths, whether these strengths are attitudes, skills, or behaviors. You may find it helpful to begin coaching certain clients with an assessment of strengths, such as those found on www.authentichappiness.sas.upenn.edu/.

Clients come to coaching with a unique combination of strengths and weaknesses. It is important to examine these characteristics in the context of the goals they have set. Some of their weaknesses can be improved, but others may be impossible to change. For example, clients may have been diagnosed with attention deficit disorder (ADD). We know several high-level executives who learned they have this condition when their children were diagnosed with ADD. These executives are often highly creative, synthesizing and building new ideas from disparate sources. On the other hand, their ADD may bring with it a short attention span, a fidgetiness that distracts, and certain other qualities that may not be subject to change. Some executives choose to use prescription medication, but others do not, except when they must sit through long meetings. Most other factors that clients might consider weaknesses may be amenable to change, but it just may not be worth the effort for the clients to do so.

As a coach, you can best facilitate your clients' success through a combination of:

- Exploring where and how they can use their strengths.
- Exploring new behaviors and skills they can learn.
- Supporting them in making peace with weaknesses that cannot be changed or strengthened, since acceptance itself can be a powerful strength when wisely applied.

When clients are aware of their strengths and know how to best apply them, they can follow the path of least resistance in addressing a challenge or goal.

2. Acknowledging and Endorsing

No matter how strong clients may seem, all clients benefit from being acknowledged and endorsed for something they do well or a quality or a way of being they display. Effective coaches pay great attention to endorsing and acknowledging clients.

Often, clients find it difficult to hear positive acknowledgments or validating statements. If they work in organizations, they experience temporary acknowledgements where they hear they are "only as good as their last performance review," or "what have you done for me lately?" As a coach, you may find it difficult to deliver acknowledgment and validation. This may be particularly true if you did not receive much recognition from important people in your own life.

Endorsing and acknowledging are not the same as complimenting. When we compliment someone, we comment favorably on something the person has or does. A compliment expresses opinion, and by extension approval of something that is part of the clients' life. Generally, people tend to compliment others on their belongings or external features—a material possession or a new hairstyle—much more often than internal qualities.

In contrast, when we acknowledge clients, we sincerely voice our recognition of an accomplishment or a quality they have demonstrated in a particular situation. A good acknowledgment needs to be specific. It names the quality and elaborates on how it was effectively demonstrated.

In the world of politics, an endorsement is given when the endorser fully stands behind the other person. Essentially, the endorser says, "I stake my reputation on your integrity, your ability, and your intentions. I have unshakable faith in you, and I'm willing to go public with that to lend my name to your campaign." When you endorse clients, you verbalize your appreciation and recognition for who they consistently are—the essential qualities they show again and again in their life and in their work. You look beyond their actions and possessions and focus on their deeper self—the essential people they are now or are becoming.

Endorsing language can recharge clients' energy levels, in the same way as recharging a battery gives it new power. When the clients' energy level increases, they are more likely to be motivated to move into action.

3. Standing For

In organizational life, leaders are sometimes asked, "What do you stand for?" That is, what can you be counted on to be or to do because it is integral to who you are? This becomes their "leadership stand."

Less often do we experience someone else standing for us. Are you familiar with the experience of having someone advocate for your desires and ability to create the future you want? We play this role as coaches when we hold on to the clients' dreams and desires even when the clients temporarily forget who they are or what they want. We stand for the possibilities clients have said they want for themselves. In essence we are helping them stand their own ground.

Clients often feel empowered when coaches acknowledge or endorse a part of their behavior or being. We support clients' empowerment when we stand for them—their goals, desire for a more fulfilling life, and potential to create the life they want.

When you stand for clients, you remind them of their goals and power to achieve them. You advocate for them. Standing for has the power to sustain clients' energy and focus when they have temporarily lost one or both. It calls forth their latent creativity.

Standing for is an important coaching skill. As a coach, you give great support for clients' dreams and desires when you remember them, hold on to them, and believe in them. You stand for clients when you remind them of what they want, affirm that they can achieve their desires, and hold their vision and agenda for change.

4. Reframing

Human beings are essentially story-making and meaning-making beings. We have an inborn desire to connect events and draw relationships between them, creating explanations for phenomena. Reframing and perspective taking are two skills that assist clients by offering other possibilities for their current stories. Reframing is essentially putting something in a new frame, which offers a different perspective. We know how important a frame is to a piece of art. Some frames diminish the work, and others enhance it, drawing our attention to features that were not originally highlighted. (Anyone who has reframed a favorite picture knows the power of putting something into a different context; it's amazing how a new frame can give life to something we thought had lost its vitality.)

Reframing as a coaching skill is simply shifting the clients' attention to consider a new perspective or view. When you reframe, you find new language for something. You place a behavior or motivation in a new context, or frame, which causes clients to consider it differently. Reframing takes place when you draw clients' attention to the upside of something that they previously considered a liability, such as the creativity that comes with clients who are easily distracted. Rather than a weakness, it is now viewed as a strength. When you reframe as a coach, you find an authentic way to put a positive spin on an issue. The issue now appears as opportunity rather than failure, a strength rather than a weakness.

When a specific reframe works extraordinarily well, it runs the risk of becoming a cliché. This is what happened with the "reframe problem into opportunity" cliché in many business settings. When a manager shows up at a staff member's desk saying, "I have an opportunity for you," the staff member is likely to hear it as, "I have a problem for you." That is because the word "opportunity" as a reframe for a problem has been highly overused in business settings, with people wanting to avoid negative connotations around work assignments involving difficult problems.

A reframe can be powerful and compelling, and when used masterfully it retains its power. Often it does not simply because it calls attention to the person's attempt to hide a fact. It is obligatory for a coach to find unique ways to reframe when you work with clients. Do not allow a reframe to become a cliché.

Great teachers have always used reframing. In the movie *Dead Poets Society*, a prep-school poetry teacher, played by Robin Williams, uses reframing masterfully (dir. Peter Weir, 1989). He asks each student to come up to his desk and stand on it to give them a different view of things. That is often all that is needed to shift a client's block or obstacle into a positive and hopeful frame—and hence to create forward movement and effective action.

A group exercise we use is called "the behavioral junkyard." In a small group of five or six people, each participant is asked to identify a behavior they want to send to the junkyard because it has outlived its usefulness. The participant names the behavior, such as taking responsibility, or focusing on jeopardies and risks. Then, the rest of the participants brainstorm on how that behavior could be useful to them. It is an amazing experience to hear others' identifying the gifts that come from a behavior we have worn out or overused.

5. Meta-View or Perspective Taking

In strategic work for organizations, it is often said that one's ability to look forward is only as good as one's ability to look backward. That is because both offer a long-term perspective on what is occurring now. Henry and Karen Kimsey-House, Phillip Sandahl, and Laura Whitworth (2011) introduced the notion of meta-view as an extension of the coach's listening. Using meta-view, the coach takes a big-picture view of the situation, sharing with clients a statement of the big picture and providing a new perspective on the issue. In essence, perspective taking and meta-view accomplish reframing for the clients. They are specific tools for reframing. We think they are deserving of a place of their own, too. For example:

CLIENT: I've been discouraged for a long time about my work. I used to enjoy it so much. Now, after 20 years, I've lost interest in it. I just can't figure it out.

COACH: It could be that you're entering a new cycle of change and are finding yourself in what we call "the doldrums." That's a natural part of the cycles of change we all go through, particularly when we've stayed in one career for a long time, as you have.

In this example, the coach uses a teaching concept to offer a view that provides the client with a broader perspective of his experience. The coach's understanding of natural cycles of development serves as a resource for finding a useful meta-view. The client now sees the issue as common to many people at this point in life.

Coaches help clients examine situations and shift perspectives through asking them to generate multiple frames as possible answers to questions. For example, you may ask the dentist to draw a wheel diagram, with the question or issue to consider in the center. The dentist's question might be, "How can I become more fulfilled?" His task is to fill in each of the spokes of the wheel with a different way to create fulfillment. Each of the spokes may represent a specific area of his life, as in the Life Balance Wheel (see Chapter 9).

We all use perspective-taking to shift our sense of what we can choose to do, or to call up other options than those that first occur to us. When coaching executives, Diane asks clients to raise and answer the question, "What is life calling for here?" when they find themselves frustrated or irritable. Asking this perspective-shifting question can help a leader get beyond an initial reaction to access other truths and fresh ways of identifying options. Another question we use to help clients shift perspective is "What don't I know about this that could change my options here?" If clients have a role model, they might say, "What would John do in this situation?" All of these add possibilities for the client to choose from.

Shifting a client's perspective can be accomplished in many ways.

CLIENT: I intended to give myself permission to slow down today and play. Instead, I spent the day handling crises or putting out fires, one after another. Finally at the end of the day, I'd had it. Just when I thought it couldn't get worse, my computer hard drive crashed.

After you as the coach have listened and mirrored, a shift in perspective might be called for. Here are a few options. Take a moment to reflect on the changes and opportunities that each perspective offers. Then ask the client:

- How would someone you really admire respond to this situation? (For example, "What would the Dalai Lama do?")
- How would the teacher that Robin Williams portrays in *Dead Poets Society* respond to this kind of day?
- If this were a movie, who would you ask to play you?
- What will be important about this situation 10 years from now?
- How much will this matter in 100 years?
- I wonder what principles are at work here. Remember Murphy's Law: If there are two or more ways to do something, and one of those ways can result in a catastrophe, then someone will do it that way.

6. Never Make the Client Wrong

As a partner in designing the life your clients want, it is important for you to hold on to the clients' agendas—not your agenda for clients. Sometimes we can clearly see what is possible for clients or where an action is headed, but clients cannot or do not see it that way. We would love to be able to give clients the boost of our perspective. But our job is to support their agenda. By understanding this, you will never make the clients wrong.

Recall Carl Rogers's discovery of the power of *unconditional positive regard*. When clients know they can expect this attitude from their coach, they are free to experiment, knowing they are not at risk of being judged. This is one way they learn to tame the power of their self-judgments—by experiencing your freely offered regard for them.

The book *Taming Your Gremlin* (Carlson, 1983) provides a funny and insightful look into the ease with which most people have internal dialogues that are critical and harsh. If you have a self-critical client, the book provides resources and playful activities for coming to terms with this internal criticism (such as giving the gremlin a name, drawing it, and singing aloud what it says to you).

You can lead your clients by asking powerful questions, by having them engage in inquiry, and by using future pacing, but be sure to stay joined with them. Do not lead them where they cannot or do not want to go at this time. For example, if clients do not complete their assignments between calls, you can still listen. You can also explore other assignments and other methods, or simply ask if they want to refocus the original goal. All of this can be done in a direct and caring way, without adding the element of blame.

7. Possibility Thinking

We discussed earlier the importance of "coaching to the gap." When clients live with a gap between where they are now and where they want to be, they are often unable to close the gap and create fulfillment for themselves. They may have become immobile, limited by their habitual patterns of thinking and acting.

Part of a coach's job is to be a possibility thinker—to partner with clients in exploring alternatives and seeking possible solutions, new methods, strategies, or directions clients can go.

Possibility thinking offers clients an opportunity to suspend their usual reality and explore a world of potential. When they do, clients often return to the current situation and see clearly, perhaps for the first time, blocks they have been living with and ways to eliminate them. For example, clients who have been paralyzed by fear may not realize it is possible to act despite the fear and break through the fear by not surrendering to it.

If you find yourself having difficulty maintaining possibility thinking for clients, it is time to do an inquiry on yourself. The clients' dilemma may be like one you currently face, or their issues or styles may be triggering something in you. Take time for reflection and inquiry. Ask for some shadow coaching from a mentor or buddy coach. A shadow is a reflection that mirrors your own stance and actions. Shadow coaching is where you review with someone you trust what happened on a coaching call. Shadow coaching can help you discover blocks that hinder your ability to see the possibilities in clients. This is part of a reflective practice in using a mentor coach. (Some call this supervision. We believe that term is confusing and refers to skills an advanced coach would do in a mentoring agreement.) If one interprets the concept of supervision as Supra Vision, it will mean getting perspective of a more experienced coaching professional. We simply see it as a way to benefit from mentoring with a Master Coach as well as recording your own sessions for self-reflection later.

The skills covered in this chapter are tools for the coaching toolbox. They are there to choose from, to mix and match in ways that are appropriate for the situation. As you learn the techniques, do not allow these tools to own you. If you find yourself enamored of a skill, you are likely to overuse it or incorporate it in situations where it is not the most appropriate tool. Using a wide range of tools supports you in being a masterful coach.

CHAPTER 5

STRETCHING THE CLIENT

In Chapter 4 we looked at a skill called standing for clients, where the coach recalls for clients the truth of what they want for themselves and the real possibility of attaining it. Standing for is an example of a coaching skill that, in the moment, provides a clear challenge to clients' current ways of thinking.

A great dictionary definition for challenge comes from *The American Heritage Dictionary:* "To summon to action, effort or use; to stimulate." At our best as coaches, we challenge clients by using our language and ourselves to stimulate them to achieve their best and summon them to act in new ways.

Let us consider challenging and stretching and their location in the coaching continuum (Ellis, 1998).

Over time, like all helping professionals, coaches develop distinctively different styles. Some coaches may frequently direct clients' attention and focus; others primarily forward coaching through questions. Some coaches follow Carl Rogers's (1951) view that people solve their own problems when they are fully listened to and affirmed. Consider the coaching continuum below, which ranges from the least directive responses at one end, beginning with "listen fully and affirm," to the most directive practices at the other, ending with "give the answer."

THE COACHING CONTINUUM

1. Listen Fully and Affirm

This is full, heartfelt, and soulful listening with great empathy and heart. Soulful listening invites clients to bring to awareness what they know, think, sense, and feel. After a time, clients reveal their most intimate thoughts. In some spiritual practices, this is called the inquiry. You stay fully present and silent while clients speak for an extended period of time, five to 15 minutes. Then you share what you are noticing, thinking, and feeling.

2. Listen Fully and Feed Back the Problem

At this level of listening, you listen fully and soulfully for a time, affirm the clients, then feed back the issues. You briefly summarize the essence of what you hear as the focus for the clients—the key issues to coach.

3. Ask Clients to Generate a Few New Possibilities

You begin to be directive. You listen, feed back what you hear, ask questions, and specifically ask the clients to identify several new possibilities for attention and action. At this level on the coaching continuum, you might ask, "What are two possible new ways to overcome these obstacles?" Some might wonder why you would ask clients since if they knew, they wouldn't be asking for input from a coach. But it doesn't work that way. Often clients do have an idea or two but haven't been challenged to identify alternatives. Your question affirms they are likely to have some ideas to offer.

4. Ask Clients to Generate Many Possibilities

You listen, affirm, mirror, and feed back, but this time you focus on stretching clients to generate many, many possibilities. Ask for several, maybe even as many as 10 or 12 possibilities that will address their issues or concerns. If a dozen options seem too easy to generate, ask for more. The point is to act as a guide for clients and to stretch them to move outside their comfort zone. For example, let us look at a client who is working on ways to feel more fulfilled and satisfied during the workday. The coach might ask him to generate 25 or more small things he can do during the workday to create a sense of satisfaction. It would be important to have many options available in a case like this, so the client does not become habituated to just one or two. This client, for example, might put a screen saver of his children on his computer. He might incorporate stress busters at certain intervals of the day, like breathing, stretching, and walking outside. He could use a program like "Desktop Yoga" periodically. This sets the tone for out-of-the-box thinking. The important thing is to get the client to stretch beyond the obvious—beyond thoughts he generates readily.

5. Add Your Input to Clients' Lists of Possibilities

At this place in the coaching continuum, you join clients in brainstorming, adding suggestions to their list of possibilities. You and the clients brainstorm back and forth, with you adding some of your best thinking in the moment without an intention to take over for them. This adding, which is more directive, runs the risk of moving their focus to where you want it to be. The risk is that clients mistake your possibilities for suggestions or advice. You need to work hard at letting them know that these are just additions to the list—they are not necessarily better ideas than those they have generated. Your perspective as an outsider does mean you are likely to see possibilities outside the clients' blind spots or current perspective. In a sense, your possibilities may reframe or expand the clients' view of the situation. You may be of service to clients at this level if their creativity seems low or they feel stuck. Sometimes a coach needs to jump start clients' thinking, although we believe it is usually best for clients to offer the first several ideas.

6. Present at Least 10 Possibilities
(Some Contradictory for Creative Ideas)

You are more directive at this point in the continuum, placing yourself in charge of identifying and creating possibilities for clients. You may stretch clients by including possibilities that are far outside the realm of their comfort zone. You may think that presenting 10 possibilities seems like a lot, but it is important to offer contradictory possibilities so clients must choose between very different arenas of action. Be sure to make some of them practical and doable. Clients may seize upon your ideas to springboard their own creativity when you use this strategy.

For example, a client is frustrated with a female employee. At Stage 6 of the continuum, you might offer ideas like these:

- Just fire her!
- Focus on her strengths and do everything possible to turn her into a better employee.
- Pay for her to go to a training program in the area in which she needs improvement.
- Hire her a coach. Assign her a new role that enables her to develop in her weak area.

- Get her a mentor who is excellent in the area she needs to grow in.
- Ask her to shadow someone who is great in the area she needs to grow in.
- Ask her to take a vacation.
- Tell her that she has two weeks to up-level her skills or she may have to postpone her vacation.

The purpose of these seemingly contradictory suggestions is to stretch the client's thinking into the realm of all possibilities, even into the realm of the absurd. When you and the clients start laughing about the possibilities, you know you are on the right track. You have moved the conversation into a mood of lightness from which clients will have a new perspective and from which creativity can emerge.

7. Present at Least Three Possibilities

At this level you offer three possibilities of equal value. We call this level a directive action because you are essentially limiting clients' choices. Be sure that when they hear the possibilities, clients do not hear them as advice. Take time to work through the benefits and consequences of each one so clients can fully consider them.

You might wonder why Stage 6 generates 10 possibilities and this stage generates only three. Stage 6 aims to stretch clients into the realm of many possibilities. Stage 7 focuses clients' attention on choosing not between absurd options, but between doable, realistic, practical possibilities, each of which clients could choose and implement, although they may be quite different from one another. When you offer these possibilities, you must make sure they are not offered as definitive solutions.

In the case of the client frustrated with an employee, you may say, "Of all the options we've discussed, I'm aware of three possibilities that seem doable right now for you." Then do the following:

- Discuss with the employee the possibility of specific training in communication skills.
- Discuss with the employee how being assigned a mentor in communication skills would be beneficial to her, preferably someone in a different department of the company.

- Hire a coach for the employee with defined goals and outcomes mutually agreed upon between the coach, employee, and client/supervisor.

At this stage you offer the three possibilities and then invite the client's feedback. "What do you think about these? What ideas do you have that might build off these? Remember, these are just possibilities. As you hear them, what do you think?"

8. Teach a New Technique

You are directing when you are teaching. However, there are times when clients need to learn something new or request that you teach something new so they can move beyond where they are now. You might find yourself teaching a relaxation strategy, for example, a method of preparing to resolve conflict, or time management skills.

Teaching is more effective later in a coaching relationship, after rapport and trust have been built and clients have become used to the alliance as a partnership of equals. Be cautious when you find yourself teaching early on in a coaching relationship, as clients may find this easy and useful, and come to depend on it. Your alliance will be considerably different with the clients if that happens. If it is done too early in the coaching relationship, clients will be less apt to see themselves as active agents and might begin to look more often to the coach for answers. If that occurs, it takes more effort to undo or remedy that pattern. We suggest you avoid setting it up in the first place.

9. Offer an Option

This situation is even more directive because you are offering only one option for consideration. If the option is on target or acts as a reframing strategy, it can be effective in getting clients out of their current situation. Offering an outrageous option can help clients focus. It may also bring lightness into the conversation, which helps clients reframe the situation and bring more creativity to it.

For example, if a client complains about his boss, you might offer the one outrageous option: Move to another country to get away from him. The one outrageous option will likely elicit an immediate reaction from the client and will probably produce a long list of ways to act in order not to have to consider the option of moving.

10. Give Advice or Give the Answer

At this level, the most direction oriented in the coaching continuum, you are probably not coaching. Giving advice or giving the answer is more the province of consulting. If you find yourself giving advice, be sure to label it as such.

On the other hand, a very direct telling of the truth as you see it may be needed. Remember the five-step coaching model (pp. 22–26), where you say what is so. This provocative intervention can be useful when the client is trapped in confusion, resistance or fear is entrenched, the game is destructive and repetitive, or it is time to end what seems like self-destructive sabotage. These client interventions can involve phrases such as "I can't support you selling out in that way. I believe you are strong enough. You know you are strong enough. Just do it."

CLIENTS STRETCH TO MEET CHALLENGES

Masterful coaching involves times when you must challenge clients in supportive and encouraging ways rather than simply listening. Your goal is to offer a challenge that helps them stretch and grow.

Challenging is stronger than just "wanting for" or making a small request. It is straightforward, but never disrespectful. A strong request for a big change might appear to clients as a challenge.

There is a useful analogy from the sports arena about the style of delivery for challenging others. Bobby Knight, former coach of the Indiana University basketball team, often challenged his players. He was an in-your-face guy, often belligerent and loud, occasionally throwing chairs and other items. After 29 years as Indiana University's coach, Knight lost his job because he challenged disrespectfully after being warned to stop.

On the other hand, Bill Self, the highly respected men's basketball coach at the University of Kansas, demands the same amount of excellence from his players, but wisely challenges them by teaching them and building on their strengths. During a game, he rarely loses his temper or shows disrespect. When he takes a player out of the game, he doesn't do it as punishment. Instead, he often sits down next to the player and teaches or reminds him what he could do differently. The game will be going on, and Coach Self will be down on his knees in front of the player, seizing a teachable moment. Usually, the player will return to the game having been challenged to upgrade his skills.

Obviously, Coach Self is the better model for coaches. You must challenge your clients when appropriate and always do so respectfully. Experienced coaches let their clients know when they begin challenging, when they "up the stakes" because the situation calls for it.

Making a challenging request or call for evidence of progress may activate clients to make a huge shift or leap forward. This kind of challenge communicates to the clients that you are confident they can take on such a challenge. They may succeed because they begin to share your belief in their possibility and promise. Challenging clients, which takes courage, it is another way of standing for them.

As we begin to examine ways that coaches challenge their clients, consider the case of Rob:

> Several nights ago, you gave a speech on creating a fulfilling life. One of the attendees called you to inquire about coaching. He is a 33-year-old single male who works as a computer programmer. When you ask him about his coaching goals, he says he wants to lose weight and to create a financial reserve for himself. You start to work with him. During the first two calls he says the following: "I love listening to CDs, reading books, and collecting comic books." "I eat out all of the time and love food." "I'm sort of down lately; sometimes I feel anxious. Even though I have a decent job, I feel stuck." "I'm fat and pudgy, and I don't like it. I want to be trim."

ASK YOURSELF:
What do you hear from Rob that calls for using challenging skills? How might you challenge him on this first call?

MANY WAYS TO CHALLENGE

Coaches productively challenge clients in many ways. Common ways to challenge include:

- Make huge requests.
- Double the goal.

- Reduce the time to accomplish something.
- Ask clients to document and provide evidence of progress.
- Measure results and establish benchmarks.
- Ask clients to raise their standards and expectations for themselves or others.
- Ask clients to do the opposite of what they would normally.
- Ask straight questions that no one else in the client's world has the courage to ask.
- Expect a great deal from clients—perhaps more than they expect of themselves.
- Ask for fieldwork and practices to keep clients focused.
- Maintain high standards and be rigorous about examining their accomplishments and actions.
- Be patient and press clients to consider the truth, not just the first answer that may come to mind.
- Be diligent about asking clients to commit to their promises.
- Consistently help clients draw distinctions (introduced below). Encourage clients to make big shifts and to grow in perspective, approach, attitude, mind-set, patience, and so on.
- Ask clients to only live their life purpose (see Chapter 8) for a specific period of time.
- Ask clients to begin a new discipline or practice that requires reflection, such as keeping a journal or beginning a meditation practice.

SKILLS FOR CHALLENGING AND STRETCHING THE CLIENT

Use Distinctions

We began this chapter by considering the coaching continuum. Most of the time, we remain nondirective, and we use our listening, mirroring, and questioning skills to forward the action. At times, however, clients' situations will not move forward on their own because they think in a habitual way that isn't helpful or empowering. In Chapter 15, we explore more extensively this issue of how clients' mind-sets affect them and the coaching relationship. At these times, the best approach is to first offer a concise, clear statement of how you see their situation. This statement uses clean language, is direct, and is an empowering and potent way of looking at the situation. You offer a distinction that holds the key to a new way of thinking or action. If clients can incorporate this distinction, they might be able to shift the situation to a more desired outcome. Offering a distinction is part of the coaching process, not a magic bullet.

Remember that our ability to grow and develop depends on our language. It is no accident that the Bible contains a very early chapter where names are given for all the creatures of the world. The ability to name something, to put it into words, gives human beings the ability to choose, create, modify, and grow. We can only enact what we can name.

When you use distinctions, you intervene directly in your clients' learning and awareness. Your intention in using distinctions is to offer clients a chance to see something about the situation that has not been visible to them. The value of a distinction comes from the new avenues for acting it reveals, the becoming that it makes possible.

A distinction allows clients to consider making a shift in thinking and noticing. A shift is a cognitive, emotional, or behavioral movement from one state to another. The following examples of distinctions have the potential to support clients in making a shift:

- Unconscious incompetence versus conscious incompetence
- A goal versus a pipe dream
- Just being competent versus achieving mastery
- Having to be right all the time versus allowing others to be right as well

When you use distinctions, you offer clients the words to notice something that may be subtle. You may also help them articulate the distinctions. Here is an example:

CLIENT: I want my work life to go much more smoothly than it has been going recently. Everything that comes my way at work seems to be getting more and more difficult. It's an ongoing battle with my boss and my staff.

COACH: You're seeing work as if it were a battlefield. To experience something else, you need to let go of your armor. (Note: This is an assessment of the situation.)

CLIENT: Right. I am so tired of struggling.

COACH: What would it take for you to move from being in a struggle at work to making work seem easy and natural? Giving up the *going-into-battle* way you enter work means putting down your arms and armor, and making peace—with your boss, your situation, those you work with, and yourself.

Notice that the distinction the coach is offering here is "work as a battle" versus "work as peacemaking."

CLIENT: I don't know how to do that.

The coach might follow up with statements such as those below to reinforce the new distinction about how the client carries herself into work. The next step would be to find a practice and action the client could take that would begin to explore the new distinction and put it into practice. The coach might ask:

- What would be the first sign you are going into work unarmed, unarmored, and ready not for battle but for peace?
- How would you start your day?
- What would you be telling yourself as you enter the building?
- How would you prepare yourself for work as a place of peacemaking?

To use distinctions effectively, make sure your voice tone and words remain nonjudgmental. Stay unattached to whether clients seize and use the distinction. You may find initially that clients do not grasp the distinction or its power, but then return a week or so later to explore it.

ASK YOURSELF:
What distinction does Roy, the client mentioned earlier, need to learn to achieve a shift or move forward?

Use Metaphors and Analogies
Andrew Ortony, a researcher in learning and cognition, made a radical statement some years ago: "Metaphors are necessary, not just nice" (1975/2001, p. 29). He went on to show that using metaphor creates powerful, rapid learning by linking what is unfamiliar or novel with what is known.

Many coaches treat metaphors and analogies as if they were adornments, enhancements in language—like a delicious frosting on an already tasty cake. Metaphors and analogies are powerful tools for two reasons. First, a metaphor offers new perspective on an issue. Second, the perspective rapidly becomes potent because it links with preexisting thoughts, emotions, and beliefs that have already been internalized. Consequently, metaphors and analogies work quickly and naturally to change thinking because they work holistically, bypassing linear, analytic explanations and client resistance.

The use of metaphors has proven extremely powerful in many professions—mediation, therapy, consulting, and now coaching. Coaches use common metaphors to direct clients' attention to aspects of their situations and possibilities not yet considered. Below we illustrate how a coach might use the garden metaphor as well as several others in a way that draws the client's attention to other possibilities.

The situation involves a working wife discusses how difficult it is to create time for herself and any sense of balance. She says:

> I'm struggling to stay focused on my work and my relationship with my husband because the kids seem to need me so much at home. Just keeping groceries stocked and driving them back and forth to games is hard. Yet there's so much pressure on us about money now, with college coming up in just a year for the oldest.

Using the metaphor of a garden for her family situation, the coach might use the following statement:

> Imagine your family life is a garden where you are all growing. A garden is something that requires soil preparation, thought about what to plant, and then conscious, purposeful nurturing. A garden doesn't just grow by throwing seeds out there and forgetting them. All gardens have diversity—a variety of plants that contribute to the beauty of the whole design. All gardens have weeds, but you want to pull out any before they choke the plants you are nurturing. Sometimes you need to prune. So, gardening requires frequent watering, weeding, and tending. What needs tending here in your family? Where do you need to cut back or prune things to really let you and your family grow? And further, what needs fertilizing or nourishing?

Using the metaphor of a journey, the coach might use a statement like this:

A trip is different from a journey. In a trip, you have an exact route and a specific place to get. In a journey, you may have a destination, but you don't have a specific route planned. And furthermore, you are aware that things may occur that are unplanned. You may take side trips—due to weather, car trouble, or road conditions that are unexpected or unplanned. Often these side trips lead to some of the best experiences of the journey. If you begin to view your family situation as a journey for all of you, what's the vehicle you are in, and what would you like to be in? What experiences do you anticipate? How are you handling unexpected challenges, route changes, and things that take you off course? You are one of the drivers here: What changes do you need to make to get on a course that brings you satisfaction?

Using the metaphor of a game, a coach might say:

I know your kids play soccer and you like to play a lot of games together like Monopoly. Think about your situation as a game. To make the game work, you need to understand how to choose the right game and understand the rules. You can also take a time-out. Are you and your husband on the same team with the same game plan? How about you and the kids? Does anybody need to take a time-out from the play? Can the game as a family be seen as time together that brings pleasure, not a competitive race where there's a defined way of winning?

Games are a ubiquitous experience for many family trips. If you are working with someone old enough to remember road trips before Wi-Fi, they remember passing the time looking for license plates from all locations, or playing the alphabet game, where you look for road signs or advertisements that start with the letters A through Z. These are games to pass time and build relationships and experience connectedness by having fun. In today's world we know that in many families, especially in North America, trips are taken in which everyone but the driver has a personal mobile device with videos or music, and the family connection seems to be lost. The goal of the coach is to draw on positive experiences that have a universal quality and increase the client's connection to themself and others. Use a metaphor that will work positively and be matched to the client's situation.

Notice how each of the three above metaphors—a garden, a journey, and a game—illuminate different aspects of choices available to the client. One might work better than the others, depending on the client and his or her intentions. Just like a picture is worth a thousand words, a metaphor seems to shift the way a person sees the situation.

Metaphoric language is also common in the business world. Using metaphors in corporate coaching is an excellent means for highlighting aspects of the situation that can help the client think differently. Listen to the client's language for the buried metaphors the client is using, such as the following:

- We're missing a piece of the puzzle.
- We need to level the playing field.
- We need to think outside the box.
- We need to push the envelope.
- We need to get on the bus.
- We need to get in the zone.
- We need to draw a line in the sand.
- We need to stand up for ourselves.

Raise your antenna and listen to your client's metaphors, then use that as you work together. For example, your client might say, "I wish our group could think outside the box better." Ask yourself how you as a coach can work with this "box" metaphor to create a more useful way of thinking about the situation. As coaches, we are looking for metaphors that expand opportunities and widen the horizon for the client's situation. Sometimes a metaphor is off target. In business, for example, the metaphor of football can be considered exclusionary to women. Coaches may need to ensure their clients are using metaphors that work for them as well as others in their work or personal lives.

An effective metaphor in coaching needs to meet two requirements. First, the clients must be familiar enough with the metaphor to understand its application in their life. Second, the metaphor should create the intended emotional effect on clients and be carefully chosen for the situations they face.

Some metaphors work so well that we use them again and again. Clients know instinctively that when they work with coaches, they are going somewhere. Consequently, metaphors about journeys and gardens work effectively with almost all clients who consider the path they are on and the patient growth required.

The following questions can help you generate metaphors:

- What is the client's journey most like? Possibilities include a plane trip, slow walk, trek around the globe, a walk at night in dark woods, a horse-and-buggy ride, and so on. One of our journey metaphors involves imagining a road trip from California to Maine. If you're always saying, "Are we there yet?" you'll miss the Grand Canyon and all the other amazing sights, as well as all the turns along the way. The best way to get there is to be present at each leg of the journey.

- Is this a trip or a journey? Say you want to go from Denver to Portland, Oregon. You can call AAA and get a TripTik, which provides a route map, hotels to stay in, driving times, road conditions, and so on. Perhaps you will depend on Google maps on your smartphone. All the details regarding the best or quickest route to the destination are identified. Or you can take a more leisurely route, taking county roads, veering off on side streets, and seeing sights that are unexpected. This would be more of a journey where we anticipate that unexpected pleasures will be part of the experience. This can be more time consuming, but it may be more fulfilling as a journey than a faster paced trip. Dr. Pat learned the distinction between trip and journey when he went from Denver to Vancouver, Canada, choosing to avoid the interstates and taking county roads through smaller towns. The journey became as much fun as the destination.

- What kind of vehicle is the client journeying in—and is it appropriate for the trip? A client who wants to travel by spacecraft may really need to slow down and take a car ride, stopping to admire the scenery along the way.

- What kind of growth occurs in the garden where the client is working? How is the client preparing the ground, planting seeds, caring, weeding, fertilizing, watering, pruning, thinning, and sprouting back? Marge Piercy (2003) wrote a wonderful poem called "The Influence Coming into Play: The Seven of Pentacles," related to this point, which reminds us to honor the pace of things. Clients often forget this key point—that human experience and human lives often have their own pace. We can urge a baby to be born quickly, but that will not change the nine months needed for gestation.

Metaphors and analogies deepen clients' intuitive understanding of issues and encourage deep exploration. Select metaphors that match clients: create metaphors out of stories you tell, drawn from your own life.

Below are metaphors from students that express how they learn:

- Planting flowers—A seed is planted in my mind, which I nurture with water and sun in the faith that it will sprout and grow.
- Playing cards—I divide things into four categories and look for patterns across the suits until the logic and meaning emerge and I know which card to play.
- Savings account—I invest the time to accumulate data and information until there is enough interest that I can roll it over into the next idea.
- Switching on a lightbulb—it's not until the light switches on that I have an insight or an "a-ha!"
- Eating—you need to take in the basic meat and potatoes before you get to the mouthwatering dessert.
- Being a detective—it's all about uncovering facts, looking for clues, and asking the right questions until the whole mystery makes sense.
- Peeling an onion—I peel off a layer, which reveals the next layer to be peeled off. Each time, something informs me that I am getting closer to the center of the issue.
- A quest—I'm searching for that elusive something, and every step I take brings me closer to what I need to know, but I never get there . . . it's a continuous journey.
- Sculpting—you start with the raw material and shape it into a form that's pleasing to the eye.
- Wrestling—I struggle with ideas until they're pinned down and I've captured them.

Other suggestions: Listen to your clients' language and create metaphors based on the words they use. If work is like a battlefield for them, use that image as a jumping-off point for generating a series of metaphors to expand the conversation and explore the issue. Remember that you can also ask your clients to generate a metaphor for the coaching work they are doing.

ASK YOURSELF:

What metaphors would you use to describe the coaching process for clients who are stuck? What metaphor could you use with the client who is frustrated with the employee?

Make Big Requests

As we stated in the Introduction, Fernando Flores developed one of the most useful coaching tools—making requests—through his exploration of how language really brings action into being (Budd & Rothstein, 2000). Imagine an aspect of a client's life that is not working. He may expect, or at least fantasize, he'll be told what to do differently. However, a coach's job is not simply to hand over the solution, for two reasons. First, we do not know it ourselves; even if we are aware of a possible solution that has worked for others, it is not necessarily relevant to this situation. And second, even if we knew the solution, handing it to the client robs the alliance of the process of exploring the issue together. It robs the client of the learning experience of working through the steps to the solution, and it robs coaches of the opportunity for joint discovery that is an integral part of the coaching relationship.

An empowering way to engage clients in the exploration to discover a new approach to a problem is to make a request. Coaches request a very specific action or choice from clients—and most often use the word request in the statement. The request is not complete until the specific behavior or action is identified, until both client and coach understand the time expectations for when the request will be completed, and until both clearly agree on what constitutes a successful accomplishment of the request.

A request is not an invitation, although it may seem like one because clients are free to respond to it. It is also not a suggestion or a piece of advice. It does convey a sense of urgency because clients must respond to a request right away. Clients can accept it, turn it down, change it, or suggest an alternative. No matter what they do, a request leads to some action—even if it changes in the process.

Requests sound like this:

- I request you stop suffering this week. Talk to the people you need to talk to right away.
- I request that every morning this next week, you use your planner to prepare a to-do list, with each action labeled as either an A, B, or C priority, before you begin your day. Will you agree to do this?
- I'm requesting that you demonstrate how serious you are about increasing your sales by making twice as many calls to prospective clients this week as you have during the past two weeks.
- I request that you think of a way to open up to your boss and tell her how you really feel when she criticizes you publicly at work.
- What is the one big request I should make of you to get this moving? Whatever it is, that's what I'm requesting.

Clients must respond to the request. Silence is not an adequate response. Clients have three response choices: "Yes," "No," or "No, but here's what I'll do instead." When clients reject your request, explore the idea further. Requesting is a commonly used tool to elicit action steps for clients to consider. When coaches make requests, it is to further the clients' agendas. Do not become attached to the specific request you make. Clients may not agree with it, or they may create a variation. Be willing to dance with clients when you make requests. Let clients lead the dance. You join into the rhythm.

Why use requests? They clearly identify the commitments clients are willing to make. They rapidly move clients into action without undue thinking or lag time, which is particularly useful when clients tend to ruminate before taking steps. Requests encourage clients to experiment with actions they would not normally consider. They offer something else, too: the opportunity to be faced with the choice of saying yes or no. Clients may discover they have difficulty declining or reshaping a request. This creates the opportunity to explore what it means when clients feel compelled to say "yes."

Requesting is more open and fluid than suggesting. A suggestion can be interpreted as a recommendation from an expert. A request is a consideration for clients to accept or reject. The power of a request is not found in the specific action requested; it is found in the way coaches communicate confidence in the clients' ability by requesting something bigger than they might have been willing to request of themselves.

A key to skillful requesting is to make the request specific. Be clear and very targeted. Make your language as focused, accurate, and direct as a laser beam. Pause after the request to let the silence hit.

An experienced coach intuitively senses what to request of a client. The joy lies in creating the request in the moment, based on what the client presents to the coach. Beginning coaches sometimes think there is a "perfect" request that they are unable to discover. The perfect request does not exist, but the coach can be precise about the action the client should take, when and how it should be taken, and how the client will determine whether the request has been met.

SUGGESTED EXERCISE:
Write two requests you could make to a client frustrated with his employee.

Identify and Name Contradictions and Inconsistencies

Sometimes clients contradict themselves from session to session. For example, one week a client says that a balanced life, with time to attend his children's soccer games, is the top priority. He loves to see his kids in action. The following week, the client takes on a new volunteer role on a local board of directors, which will require afternoon and evening meetings every week. He speaks excitedly of his interest in the assignment and the challenge of turning around a troubled agency.

You cannot help but notice how the client's new choice will get in the way of honoring his commitment to his children. Your obligation is to point this out, so he clearly sees the inconsistency. With new clarity, he can explore the attraction of each path and what might block him from effectively accomplishing both. (Even the best coaches cannot help clients be in two places at once.)

Putting the contradiction into words might sound like this: "In our last session you were excited about your commitment to attend your daughters' soccer games this season; you told me what a high priority this was for you this year. Today, you are about to commit to a board assignment that will prevent you from consistently attending the games. What's changed?"

Inconsistencies abound in all our lives. Look for opportunities to point them out to clients when they really add value to the coaching. Over time clients can learn to detect inconsistencies themselves and become self-correcting. When inconsistencies surface, coaches spend the time to explore how they came about. Are they due to competing values? Competing desires? Or perhaps lack of time and attention to calendar issues and a realistic appraisal of the requirements of fulfilling a promise?

Common inconsistencies include:

- What clients are saying they want versus what they are doing to make it happen.
- What clients say they feel versus their nonverbal behavior, energy, and so on.
- What clients claim are their priorities versus their actions, which are more accurate indicators of their priorities.
- What clients say are their strengths and/or weaknesses versus what they are truly capable of.

ASK YOURSELF:

Identify an inconsistency or contradiction in the client (for example, the case of the father who wanted to demonstrate more commitment to his children). How would you identify this for the client?

Use the Compassionate Edge

Master coaches get faster and more powerful results because of their willingness to use the compassionate edge—to send a message to clients with laser-like truth and brevity that gets right to the heart of the matter. The compassionate edge provides a very direct challenge to clients because it is put into words and is part of the conversation.

This challenge comes from the desire to help clients avoid mediocrity, while simultaneously maintaining a compassionate and empathic stand. This combination of qualities can move clients to a deeper acknowledgment of truths and an accelerated ability to take action on their own behalf.

Mastery of the compassionate edge has benefits for coaches, too. Once you become skilled at it, you may find you will attract high-powered clients who expect the edge. They are not just learning the skills; they are high achievers who want to do what it takes to "go for the gold."

Here are some examples of the compassionate edge:

- That's good work but not nearly what you are capable of. What else can you do here?
- Tell the truth—do you really want to do this? I don't think you do.
- When are you going to be really, really honest about what you want here?
- You are complaining. Turn your complaint into a request. Who do you need to say what to?

SUGGESTED EXERCISE:
Using the compassionate edge, write a statement that you might say to the client who is frustrated with his employee.

The focus of this chapter was about maintaining a fierce commitment to the client's goals as well as compassion for his or her journey. We believe there is power in taking it to the mat with clients to overcome obstacles. The next step will be to create momentum toward new behaviors, which we discuss in the next chapter.

CHAPTER 6

CREATING MOMENTUM WITH THE CLIENT

Coaching is all about learning and action—not learning and action for its own sake but in the service of a longer-term aspiration, goal, or performance that drives the choice of action. As coaches, we want to ensure that our clients do not just reach a goal or achieve a performance, but that they maintain it. We want them to master the ability to become generative and self-correcting around their goals.

Stated another way, coaches work with clients' goals—performance, coaching focus, skills, and outcomes. This aspect of coaching focuses on what the clients want—the "what" of coaching as opposed to the "who" of coaching, which is focused on who the clients are, their way of being in the world. We also work with clients to build long-term capability and capacity so they can sustain their goals. We want them to leave the coaching experience fully able to observe their behaviors and able to correct themselves when they diverge from their goals.

THE "KNOW IN ORDER TO GROW" PRINCIPLE

Sometimes insight needs to precede learning, and powerful questions enable learning by helping clients unlock new insights. Once learning occurs, clients can choose options for action. Without insight and learning, action may just be compulsive doing. But without action, insight and learning will not help clients achieve goals. Therefore, forwarding the action is at the heart of the coaching relationship—and it is the biggest difference between coaching and traditional psychotherapy. When a coach "forwards the action," the coach helps clients move from insights into specific steps, propelling them toward their goals. Forwarding the action means that the coach's work leads to progress toward what the client wants from coaching.

Action for the sake of action, however, does not suffice. Clients hire coaches to attain goals that will offer long-term fulfillment and satisfaction. Consequently, coaches need to focus on how clients can sustain and maintain what they most want. It is not enough for clients to take action. The coaching process focuses on assisting clients sustain the results—sustain the excellence—over time. We are looking for ways to support clients to incorporate new ways of thinking and behaving into their habits and daily repertoire.

To do this, coaches keep several questions in mind:

- What new perspectives do clients need to ensure long-term success?
- What new behaviors do clients need to consistently perform to ensure long-term success? How can they practice these until they become second nature?
- What emotions or states of being do clients need to access to ensure long term success? How can clients practice accessing these until they become second nature?
- What do clients need to incorporate new thinking and behaviors into what they do naturally and habitually?

FOCUSING ON "RIGHT ACTION" THROUGH FIELDWORK

The media has focused extensively on ways clients take action when being coached. As you can see from the previous list, several kinds of actions are necessary to ensure long-term excellence and fulfillment.

Experienced coaches end each session with a summary of clearly stated actions that will forward clients' learning and growth, often described as fieldwork. Coaching conversations are not complete until clients have identified actions that lead to accountability for change. Fieldwork may include actions clients agree to take that have been discussed during the session, and it can also include requests made by coaches that hold clients on course. It is important to state here that any fieldwork is generated through collaborative discussion with clients: it is an assignment by the coaches. Coaches may make requests that, if clients agree to them, become part of fieldwork. Coaches may say, "I have an idea for some fieldwork that might be helpful to you this week." A good question to ask clients is: "What has emerged in our session today that generates some fieldwork for you between now and our next meeting?" In some sessions, fieldwork is generated throughout the entire session, particularly when clients and coaches have been working together for some time. A client should always have several agreed-upon actions to take or complete between each call. Regular fieldwork helps clients make progress by emphasizing their accountability for results and providing the satisfaction of taking steps toward their goal.

As with requests, good fieldwork is specific. Clients know exactly what to do, what completed actions will look like, and how to assess whether the actions were taken successfully. Do not overload clients with fieldwork—two or three assignments between calls are sufficient to create and sustain momentum. Initially, make the assignments small until you have a sense of their capacity for completing fieldwork successfully. Fieldwork should stretch clients, but appropriate assignments are those clients have a great likelihood of successfully completing.

The best fieldwork is likely to take into consideration all three factors that create momentum: results-oriented action, awareness observation (of self and other), and practices to create new habits.

To clarify how these three can be used with clients, imagine you are coaching this client:

The Stressed Attorney—Sharon, 35, is an unmarried attorney who wants to become a partner in her law firm. Her work environment has become more and more stressful. She works long hours, comes home very fatigued, and finds she has little energy. She seldom goes out in the evening and does not see friends. She has a church community she belongs to but has become much less active due to fatigue. She tends to overeat, especially chocolate and sweets, when she comes home. She is eating more snacks, not exercising, and finding that her situation is growing worse. She wants to work with you, her coach, on getting her eating and exercise habits in order so she can better manage her stress. You discover that this is an old habit of hers—she has managed stress in the same ways since college.

Results-oriented actions are the most obvious, readily available assignments. These are steps that directly and transparently further clients' movements, step by step, toward the goal. For the attorney, results-oriented actions might include throwing away all chocolate and sugared snacks (making her home a "snack-free zone"), buying a supply of fruit and vegetables, and taking a 15-minute walk at lunch three days a week. These actions would get the client moving in the right direction. However, they might not be sufficient to allow her to create and maintain a healthy lifestyle over the long term. To do this, she would also need to be self-aware and self-correct—to generate solutions as new issues arise.

Self-awareness observations improve clients' abilities to notice habits and patterns of sensing, feeling, thinking, and behaving. In order to grow, clients need to know themselves and their world—their thoughts and desires. Self-awareness exercises ask clients to observe self and others, and often to record these observations. A self-awareness assignment asks clients to inquire into their way of being in the world—but not to take action on the awareness.

Self-awareness observations for the attorney might include the following:

- Setting her watch to sound at 8 a.m., 10 a.m., noon, 2 p.m., and 4 p.m., each time recording what she is doing and the level of stress she is experiencing, using a scale from one (low) to five (high). She can notice when she feels the most stressed, what is happening at those times, where she is, who else is there, and what time of day it is. This exercise might also include sensing in her body whether she feels hungry before she eats.
- Identifying five specific qualities that represent her at her best; making a chart to track each of the qualities every day for a week; indicating when and where she experiences herself using each quality.
- Identifying the emotions that she regularly feels each day and the surrounding context in which they occur.
- Asking herself these questions: "In what situations and with which people do I feel most stressed in my body?" "When do I feel overwhelmed?" "When do I feel impatient?" "What gets in the way of my ability to eat healthily?" "What are my standards for healthy eating?"

Observations of others also might promote reflection during the week:

- Who do I know that eats healthily?
- What does it look like when others around me manage stress well? What are they doing differently?

In Chapter 2, inquiry was discussed as a coaching tool. Inquiries can serve as self-awareness tools. In this case, the fieldwork inquiry is designed to stimulate reflection, deep thinking, and learning around an issue that may be related to goals, life, or current issues and experiences.

ASK YOURSELF:

What are two self-awareness observations, or observations of others, from which the stressed attorney might benefit?

Practices are specific actions in which clients engage with the intent of building specific cognitive and behavioral habits. Similar to daily practice sessions to which musicians, dancers, and sports professionals commit, coaching clients also need disciplined practice times to develop ways of being and acting that will enable them to achieve goals.

To help clients build practices, coaches need to understand a client's vision of excellence. If the attorney said that excellent eating habits included eating five servings of fruits and vegetables daily and no more than three pieces of chocolate per week, this information could contribute to the clarity needed to design practices for the client. What other supporting ways of thinking, behaving, and acting would assist the client in eating healthily?

To avoid purchasing candy and junk food at the supermarket one example could be saying no and bypassing that aisle. Other examples include learning to relax and giving hourly attention to specific goals.

The following are possible practices the client can take until she develops natural habits toward her goal:

Practice 1. Schedule the maximum number of hours she will work during each of the next four weeks. When breakdowns occur in the schedule, she will cancel activities instead of adding hours. At the end of each week, she will analyze the time and keep correcting the schedule until she has maximized her hours without stress.

Practice 2. Ask her if doing one of the following each day for four weeks might help . . . or does she have ideas she would do. Carry her lunch to work; eat lunch outside when weather permits; include only vegetables, fruits, and cottage cheese in her lunch; notice and record how she feels at the end of each day.

Practice 3. Ask her to learn and practice a daily 20-minute breath meditation and/or prayer time for a minimum of five days each week for the next month. At the end of the week, note what she has learned about herself from this practice.

An excellent resource with examples of observational and practice-oriented fieldwork is Flaherty (1998). While his focus is primarily on coaching within corporations, he includes examples of working with the client's personal life as well.

ASK YOURSELF:

What are two additional practices you might offer the stressed attorney as fieldwork?

SKILLS FOR FORWARDING ACTION WITHIN COACHING SESSIONS

Five frequently used skills support coaches to forward clients' action within and during coaching sessions: accountability, contracting with clients, acting as if, stepping into the future, and creating alternative actions and choices.

ACCOUNTABILITY

The people we coach are intelligent, hardworking, and usually very successful, but they cannot do it all alone—or at least not as efficiently and effectively as they can when they partner with us.

Coaching sets a context of accountability, which includes regular contact in the form of weekly or biweekly sessions. These sessions provide clients with someone outside work and family who cares about their success and who will share in and celebrate their progress. Most of us do not have this accountability regularly in our personal and professional lives.

Accountability is a gift we give clients. Remember, if they could do it by themselves, they would have already done it. Accountability leads to sustainable results. It is the difference between paying for "training" in weekend workshops and translating those lessons into action. Countless people have taken time management seminars and then never made time to implement what they learned. Coaching can make that happen.

Successful coaching sessions end with clearly defined commitments by clients . . . actions clients commit to take before the next coaching session. One of the powers of coaching lies in accountability. Clients are fully accountable for their actions and results. At every session, the coach asks to hear about actions taken and resulting outcomes. Through accountability, clients create sustainable results over time.

ASK YOURSELF:
How would you use accountability with the stressed attorney?

Contracting with Clients

When you contract with clients, you create a verbal agreement. You establish an understanding about clients' plans to do something differently or in a new way that will move them toward their desired outcomes.

Often, this can be strengthened by contracting with clients for agreed-upon behaviors or actions for the coming week or weeks. Contracts can be verbal or in writing; both lend power to the relationship, which holds clients accountable for what they promised.

Experienced coaches often ask clients to e-mail, fax, or phone a message to report their progress on the actions agreed on in the contract. You can request feedback daily or at some agreed-upon time interval between coaching calls. Checking in like this works better with some clients than others. The best way to assess the appropriateness of regular check-ins is to ask clients what will work best for them.

ASK YOURSELF:
How would you use contracting with the stressed attorney?

Acting As If

Earlier we described powerful questions that elicit ways something could be different in the clients' present or future life.

Clients sometimes want to achieve something but feel frozen or stuck. They may be unable to move forward and reach a goal. A helpful exit from this stagnation is provided by coaching conversations that ask clients to act as if their desired change has already taken place. It helps them see who they need to become in order for their desired future to manifest. Twelve-step programs ask participants to "fake it until you make it," which is similar to *acting as if*.

An example of an "as if" strategy would be asking clients to imagine life six months into the future. Their life is more satisfactory; goals they came to coaching for are now realized. You ask clients to comment on how things are now, as if everything had occurred as they imagined. They will speak from that time six months in the future as if it is the present. You ask them to speak personally, from the "I." You follow this by asking clients to now look back and identify what actions they took to get there.

ASK YOURSELF:
How would you use acting "as if" with the stressed attorney?

Stepping Into the Future

Acting "as if" asks clients to speak from the future and then reflect on the steps and actions that got them there. Stepping into the future is a slight variation of that, where you ask clients to step into the desired future and describe it in detail: what they see, how they feel, how their environment appears, and so on. They will notice what is possible from that future view.

Remember Dr. Martin Luther King Jr.'s "I Have a Dream" speech? Most of us marvel at the compelling effect this speech had on millions of people from all different walks of life. King's speech propelled many into a desired future. King had a skill that great leaders have: the ability to paint a compelling, detailed view of the future by stepping into it and then noticing what is possible from that place.

When clients have difficulties determining forward actions, stepping into the future can be a powerful tool. It can help them "try on the future for size" by feeling what it is like to be there and looking back to see what it took to get there. Stepping into the future is a way to preview the steps, see possible snags, and develop alternatives. It also can be compelling, motivating clients to make meaningful strides toward the future that is now so vivid for them.

ASK YOURSELF:

How would you use stepping into the future with the stressed attorney?

Creating Alternative Actions and Choices

The power of a strong collaborative relationship cannot be underestimated. The level of mastery a coach brings to the coaching relationship provides a foundation for this collaboration in the following ways:

- Skillful coaches have professional mastery of core coaching competencies integrated well into their style.
- Skillful coaches have a large enough body of relevant experience—both coaching and life experience—on which to draw so that instead of being a rote recapitulation of techniques, the coaching is a fluid and unique response to the individual clients. This includes being able to zero in on relevant issues and tuning out the rest, knowing intuitively where space needs to be created in clients' lives to facilitate personal shifts.
- Coaches move between thinking and nondirected awareness, between analyzing and reflecting.
- Coaches are able to accurately assess clients' readiness to change and choose appropriate strategies, so strategies are a challenge but not so challenging that clients are overwhelmed.
- Coaches foster the flow state in clients, finding an optimal balance between one's perceived abilities and the perceived challenge at a high enough level to avoid both boredom (too much skill for the challenge) and anxiety (too much challenge for the skill). In flow, an individual is engaged in a challenging situation that requires fully engaging and stretching one's skills at a high level in response.
- Coaches can create an intuitive flow in which coaches and clients are in sync with each other and engaged in a generative dialogue.
- Coaches create a trusting relationship where clients know coaches are completely aligned with their goals, are "on their side," and are dedicated to looking through the clients' eyes and life.

In addition, coaches and clients both may have a high level of emotional intelligence and competence in creating and sustaining relationships. The experience of coaching can accentuate both skills for clients, building additional emotional and relational competency. The coaching relationship itself fosters and strengthens these attributes in clients.

Adept coaches use the skills in this chapter to co-create a variety of action plans with clients. As clients work to achieve their desired result, coaches can also point out previously undisclosed choices or alternatives for clients to consider as additional options. Together, coaches and clients discover alternative methods, choices, and strategies that neither may have been aware of individually.

In every moment, life is about choices, but in everyday life it is often difficult to recognize a full range of options. Hence, clients benefit greatly from having coaches who will see, hear, point out what is being missed, and work collaboratively with them to explore alternative methods, choices, and strategies that neither of them had previously considered.

ASK YOURSELF:
What would you do to create alternative actions and choices with the stressed attorney?

CHAPTER 7

COACHING THE WHOLE CLIENT: MIND, BODY, EMOTIONS, SPIRIT

Several centuries after he said it, the philosopher René Descartes's statement, "I think, therefore I am," is still the predominant paradigm, at least in many parts of the world. We live in a disembodied world, so to speak, where the body is reduced to a vehicle or platform for our heads (aside from times of usefulness like giving birth.) Or the body is objectified, conveyed as a sexual object or an object of shame, as when someone experiences their body as too heavy, too lean, too—well, choose the adjective. We have become gifted at denying the body as a vehicle for living, for knowing, for learning. Many of the clients you will see will treat their bodies as if they are machines—not "me," but "it." The term somatic coaching, commonly used to describe focus on the body and emotions in coaching, is based on the original Greek word *somatikos*, which means the wholeness and inclusiveness of the living, aware, embodied person.[7] Clients are invited to bring their wholeness into coaching—the living, aware and embodied client is who we coach.

Pablo Casals, the famous cellist, once said:

Each second we live is a new and unique moment of the universe, a moment that will never be again . . . And what do we teach our children? We teach them that two and two make four, and that Paris is the capital of France. When will we also teach them what they are? We should say to each of them: Do you know what you are? You are a mar-

---

7 Our intention is to provide an overview of tools we use in this area with clients. For more depth in the area of somatic coaching, see Strozzi-Heckler (2014).

vel. You are unique. In all the years that have passed, there has never been another child like you. Your legs, your arms, your clever fingers, the way you move. You may become a Shakespeare, a Michelangelo, a Beethoven. You have the capacity for anything. Yes, you are a marvel. And when you grow up, can you then harm another who is, like you, a marvel? You must work—we must all work—to make the world worthy of its children.[8]

Casals calls attention to one of the great losses of our age: that our learning institutions treat children as if logical thinking is what counts for living. Although our capacity for thinking may be what makes human being distinct from other members of the animal kingdom, it does not naturally or inevitably create the kind of fulfillment in living that is the birthright of being human. We extend Casals's thought to say our clients are "marvels"—embodied with mind, emotions, body and spirit deeply interconnected.

Life coaches take a holistic view of coaching, seeing the client's fulfillment in living as the context for the coaching. While many clients come to us prizing their intellect and rationality over their emotional, physical, and spiritual resources, their journey to full humanity may invite us to reach beyond this realm. Our clients' language, cognition, emotions, body and spiritual selves are interconnected. We see each of these as pathways, or doorways, we might enter through coaching that can invite exploration of fulfillment and fullness.

In the four decades I have been coaching executives and others, I believe all sought coaching because of life transitions—whether chosen or not chosen. Building a trusting relationship in coaching, establishing rapport and connection as early as possible, starts with my belief in the client and what they might discover through coaching. I ask questions from curiosity which often may be evocative and lead to new and deeper understandings and insights. For over 30 years, most of my coaching has been via telephone, and in-person as needed or requested. With today's improved video conferencing, a choice can be made for telephonic (nonvisual), face-to-face with video, or in-person coaching in your office or theirs.

In the world of self-help, where so-called experts are found by the thou-

---

8 Quoted at https://www.goodreads.com/author/quotes/198277.Pablo_Casals

sands, and spiritually hungry and uninformed consumers eagerly seek and gobble up unproven hyperbole accompanied by often useless advice, there is a concept that does not receive the attention that I believe it deserves: your shadow self. Initiated by Carl Jung, the shadow side of one's personality "is a primordial part of our human inheritance, which, try as we might, can never be eluded" (Jung, 1969). But the view I want you to consider is that the shadow is so much more. "The shadow," wrote Jung (1969), is "that hidden, repressed, for the most part inferior and guilt-laden personality whose ultimate ramifications reach back into the realm of our animal ancestors and so comprise the whole historical aspect of the unconscious." Also hidden in the darkness are the uniquely creative parts of who you are, which have yet to be revealed. What's in the shadow may just need some light shined on it. It is just the shadow; an archetype that is not real, a metaphor that can be transformative, rather than constraining. Instead of the popular phrase process of *elimination,* think instead of shadow work as the process of *illumination.*

In Chapters 4 through 6 we discussed coaching strategies that lean heavily on ways of working with the client involving language, thinking or perspective taking, and behavior or action. In this chapter we explore how coaches can work with body practices and emotions. We intend this chapter as a basic introduction to working with the body and emotion in coaching. At the end we refer to resources to extend your learning in these areas. We believe life coaches should be aware of the potency of these avenues for working with clients and should themselves be working with their language, thinking, body and emotions to understand how they might work with clients.

LIVING AN EMBODIED LIFE

Many coaching clients experience themselves as "having my body" as opposed to what is more real, that is, "I am my body."[9] Consequently, when they experience stress, become frightened, or go through a difficult period of

---

9 Our interest in working with the body and coaching has been developed over many years of reading and work with experts in the area. These have included "Working with the Nonverbal" with Dr. Stuart Heller (www.walkthetalk.org); Gestalt Body Work at the Gestalt Institute of Cleveland (www.gestaltcleveland.org); the Newfield Network (www.newfieldnetwork.com); Dr. Richard Strozzi-Heckler of the Strozzi Institute (www.walkingyourtalk.com); Paul Linden (http://www.being -in-movement.com/), Wendy Palmer (https://leadershipembodiment.com/) and Dylan Newcomb (http://www.uzazu.org/).

transition, they neglect the resources available to them through noticing what they feel bodily, exploring their sensations, centering and recentering, and exploring available resources regarding the nonhabitual ways they use and carry their bodies.

A basic principle of embodied living is that all of us have habitual ways of responding to life, and these include habitual ways that we hold our bodies, breathe, and move. As Stuart Heller memorably says, "How you move through space is how you move through life." Just helping clients notice how they move through space offers a vehicle for both noticing and changing how they move in our lives. Do they move quickly—walk fast, head forward, talk fast, breathe fast and high in the chest? Do they move more slowly, speaking clearly with intentional pauses, filling the space they occupy with a calm energy?

One of our clients came for work on her executive presence—we'll call her Jane. As a newly minted officer of her company, she received feedback that she seemed timid or passive in her leadership. Observing her, I noticed that she had a habitual way of carrying her body that seemed to communicate anxiety. In most humans, in the face of shock, fear or threat, an involuntary, defensive reflex often occurs, where the front of the torso contracts as a form of passive self-defense. A small and classically feminine woman, Jane may have resorted to passive defenses out of doubting her own strength or capability to defend herself more actively when challenged. However, over time this way of carrying her body had become quite habitual; the muscles that stretched her and held her upright became somewhat inhibited. She seemed to be attempting to make herself smaller, to be contracting her physical self. Of course, the energy she gave off to others also contracted, so that she seemed unavailable and frightened. Instead, she wanted to feel—and be—open, confident, responsive, and available as a leader to those who would follow her.

If you are a gardener, you can see a similar mechanism at work when you touch a garden slug and it pulls itself in, the contraction and withdrawal very apparent in such a simple creature. This defensive mechanism is initiated by the brain stem, the more primitive part of the brain that responds rapidly with fight-or-flight-or-freeze instincts. It is a more rapid instinctual response than any coming from the cerebral cortex as more conscious choices. Animals who use this defensive mechanism to escape a threat naturally and easily work off the muscular tension held in the contraction. Humans, however, with our highly developed neocortex do not seem to enter and exit these defensive patterns with the same ease as other animals. Given our ability to think, feel shame, examine our fear and rationalize our responses, we can internalize a sense of powerless or lack of control and cut ourselves off from our sources of strength. A habitual body-mind state emerges, even when it does not serve us.

In the case of Jane, she came from a family of brilliant academics and physicians. Although she was bright and had gone to select private schools, she was the least brilliant of her four siblings and often felt diminished by the teasing and competitive comparisons experienced at home. She reported that as a teenager she tended to hide in her books and music, and often around her family tried to make herself less available to teasing and family jokes. Twenty years later, experiencing both the excitement and stress of a new and promising senior role, she was feeling less than adequate to the task of leading a 100-person organization. Her habitual way of contracting herself, learned early, was easily available to protect her but was an obstacle to the kind of leadership she needed to display. By the time she came into coaching, she had read several books on leadership presence.[10] However, the journey from what she knew to how to manifest this learning in an embodied way eluded her. She understood, as Strozzi-Heckler said so well, "the way we shape ourselves will have people move toward us, away from us, against us, or be indifferent to us" (2007, p. 91). As with many clients, coaching served to support her regular practice in a new shape until this new way became comfortable and readily available to her.

Next, we offer basic ideas and practices that we used with Jane, as well as many other clients, supporting them to experience themselves as fully embodied. These allowed us to explore how shifts in the ways they embody themselves lead to shifts in other aspects—their emotions, moods, energy, ability to act, and so on.

We believe that our bodies are tremendously underutilized resources for learning and change in life and in coaching. As Daniel Siegel (2011) wrote, when we speak of intuition, we are really acknowledging the wisdom of the body:

---

10 One of the books we recommend to coaching clients is Belle Linda Halpern and Kathy Lubar's *Leadership Presence: Dramatic Techniques to Reach Out, Motivate and Inspire* (New York: Gotham Books, 2003). Their model of presence, PRES, stands for Being Present, Reaching Out, Expressiveness and Self-Knowing. Filled with specific practices, the book provides ideal resources to support coaching around presence.

Intuition can be seen as how the middle prefrontal cortex gives us access to the wisdom of the body. This region received information from throughout the interior of the body, including the viscera—such as our heart and our intestines—and uses this input to give us a "heartfelt sense" of what to do or a "gut feeling" about the right choice.

Our goals in working somatically with coaches or with coaching clients usually can be described as creating more self-awareness, more sensory awareness. Sometimes we describe this as assisting the client to become more mindful. However, for some clients "mindful" sounds highly impractical. We are cultivating the ability to observe whatever we are experiencing without judgment—simply noticing. In coaching, we want ourselves and our clients to notice body sensations, emotions, thoughts, impulses to action, interior dialogue, memories, sounds and images, and to simply witness them without judgment.

An underpinning of this work is the Gestalt point of view around contact: an essential function of the healthy human is to be able to use one's energy to connect with self and others in a healthy way. Effective contact with oneself or with another means that there is a meeting place where an exchange occurs and creates the possibility of change and growth. We can see this when two people greet each other and make eye contact in a comfortable way, acknowledging each other, connecting in an exchange of energy. Through connection and an exchange, something new may be created for each of the elements whose boundaries have come into contact. When we observe someone who does not meet the eyes of someone they are speaking to, we see someone who is maintaining a very tight personal boundary, limiting the intensity of the exchange by deflecting contact. The principle we work with in some basic exercises in increased sensory awareness is that the client's capacity to be aware and in contact with self will enable the client to be available for fuller contact with others.

In a more practical vein, we often describe our nonverbal coaching goals in one or more of the following ways:

- To bring new awareness to the mind–body connection. (Although we may not introduce this concept early on, in this way we begin to challenge the existence of any "I am only what I think" tendencies the client holds onto.) With new awareness comes more flexibility and adaptability in achieving what the client wants.

- To define and practice elements of presence and work with their importance to improve the client's ability to influence and impact others.
- To learn strategies that can be used to access new ways of being in the world. Often clients begin to sense themselves differently through somatic work.
- To be able to establish effective contact with others through experiencing contact with oneself.

TOOL: THE BODY SCAN TO INCREASE SENSORY AWARENESS

The body scan is a basic tool for developing awareness through directing attention to the body. You can find many resources describing the body scan. Our early learning came from Strozzi-Heckler (1993), who said the purpose is to focus and bring the person's attention to places in their bodies where sensations, pain, contractions or tension may be held. With attention comes energy. Simply becoming aware of the tension may create a change in or release of it, bringing more relaxation and an easier energy flow.

A body scan can be done while sitting but is easiest to teach when the person stands in a comfortable position. The goal is to notice the variety of sensations in the present moment.

Ask the client to stand with feet about shoulder distance apart, wearing comfortable shoes. Feel the feet flat on the floor. Straighten the spine, so that the pelvis is somewhat tucked in and adjust until a comfortable and balanced posture is found. Pay attention to the crown of the head, lifting it slightly so the spine slightly lengths and straightens, and shoulders and neck muscles relax. The body scan builds the capacity for inner attention.

We lead the client through a body scan with instructions like these:

- Begin by noticing your breath as it flows in and out, noticing the coolness of the air coming into your nose, the rising and falling of chest and abdomen, the warmth of the air as your breath leaves your nose.

- After four or five cycles of simply breathing and noticing, allow your awareness to slowly move throughout your body, from top to bottom.
- Bring your awareness to the crown of your head, noticing any sensations there, feeling the temperature of the air and any other sensations in your scalp.
- Move your awareness to your forehead, noticing any sensations there, then to the back of your head, face, ears, then neck. If you notice any places where muscles seem tense or sore, or where you feel tight or contracted, simply keep your attention there, noticing the tension and "breathing into that place," allowing the tension to shift or the contracted muscles to relax if that occurs. Simply notice what is there without expecting any change. Notice any temperature, warmth, coolness, or anything else that is there to observe.
- Bring your attention to where your neck and shoulders meet, to the muscles between your shoulders. Pause here and at each place in your body, simply noticing.
- Scan for sensations in your chest, shoulders, back and arms, then slowly move down through your body, finding and noticing any sensations and experiencing fully whatever is there, be it energy, lack of energy, numbness, warmth, coolness—whatever is there.
- Slowly move down, scanning your chest, waist, hips, pelvic area, thighs, knees, lower legs, ankles, feet, and toes, noticing whatever sensations are there and allowing yourself to experience them fully.
- Notice any places where you sense emotions may be present, either individual places or emotions that seem present in many places.

An alternate form of the body scan is to simultaneously scan and notice tension. If tension is noticed, contract the muscles there, tensing and releasing, until a shift occurs. Many clients find the body scan very relaxing. Clients can do a rapid scan before meetings or events where they want to have full awareness and presence. We recommend clients practice this at least once or twice daily to bring awareness to places where they habitually carry tension. We have found body scan invaluable for those of us who sit for long periods of time using computers, so that we are able to notice the habitual tension in shoulders and neck and use a tense and release scan to bring about a change before contact with others.

TOOL: THE "THINKING PATH"

Executive coach Alexander Caillet of Corentus, Inc uses a "results roadmap" tool with the coaches he teaches in the Georgetown Leadership Coaching Program. Called the Thinking Path, it graphically illustrates the importance of a holistic view in enabling clients to make changes (see https://corentus .com/the-thinking-path). The value of this approach is that a client and coach can enter anywhere on the path of the current, then elaborate the important dimensions of current and future change.

When we use this framework, we help the client appreciate the impact of their thoughts and emotions on their behavior and results. The tool enables a coach to facilitate a client's action plan to support behavioral change and success and includes emotional agility and body insights as part of that plan for change.

The elements of the framework include:

- Thoughts
- Sensations (both emotional and physical)
- Actions (specific behaviors by the client)
- Results (the observable and measurable outcomes)
- Reinforcers (the contexts, culture, policies, people, and places, in the environment external to the client that drive our thinking)

For some clients, considering the reinforcers may be new and important work to allow the client to see what needs to change for the new behaviors. Examples of reinforcers include people, values, guiding principles, organizational goals and objectives, roles and responsibilities, physical space, work processes, leadership competencies, practices and expectations, and other performance management systems.

A signal that this tool could be useful to the client is when the coaching conversations focus on habits of thinking that are limiting the client and that seem repetitive and habitual, like the following:

- My worth is really what I do—I am my work.
- If I'm not perfect, then I'm worthless.
- My success depends on me.

- I can't speak up to authority figures.
- Asking for help means I'm incompetent or not doing enough.
- There is always one right answer and I have to know it.

Work with the Thinking Path begins by asking the client to identify the results they want to achieve and comparing these with results or outcomes they are currently achieving. We invite you to practice the tool by reflecting on a situation you find challenging or upsetting, are concerned with, or feel ambivalent about how to handle. Answer based on how you are currently thinking, feeling, and acting and the results you are achieving. Choose something that is still unfinished for you. Use the following to prompt you through the results, actions, feelings, and thinking documentation:

- Results: What I'm achieving, producing, delivering is . . .
- Actions: I do . . . , act like, behave like, say, show up as . . .
- Feelings: I feel . . . , my emotions are, my mental state is, I react by, my body sensations are . . .
- Thinking: I believe, my rationale is, assumptions I'm making include, thought habits running through my mind are . . .

Once you've completed the current state, then do the same for the desired state, creating a comparative map of your experience now versus what you would like to experience. Once the map is complete, the coaching work is to identify one or two goals and actions that will support the new path and behaviors.

Another useful activity with a client is to use the template to examine a time in their history when they successfully navigated a major change. Once the change is identified, and the period over which thechange was navigated, work with the client conversationally through these questions:

1. What were the former and then post change dimensions of the path: thoughts, feelings, actions/behaviors, results?
2. How did you make changes within the four domains of the thinking path: thoughts, feeling/emotions, actions, results?
3. What were new reinforcers put in place to sustain the change?

4. How well have you sustained the change? What may still need to be put in place as reinforcers of new thoughts, feelings, actions, or behaviors?

Helping the client learn and explore what has enabled them to make positive changes is an empowering activity and one that coach and client can draw on for planned or future changes.

BEING PRESENT

A common coaching goal is for someone to move from automatically reacting to a situation to choosing his or her response, consciously and intentionally. In the case of Jane, she automatically contracted her body instead of noticing what the situation she was entering called for. Being intentional means that the client will need to be fully present to the situation.

We've found several easy and available ways to help ourselves and our clients come into the present and to let go of whatever thoughts or distractions are there. One of these is a rapid body scan. The late Doug Silsbee, a friend and colleague, as well as the author of *Presence-Based Coaching* (2008), suggests 4 steps for a quick body scan (https://presencebasedcoaching.com/wp-content/uploads/Download/PBC-Exercises-Practices/body-scan.pdf).

- Start by noticing how you are sitting or standing—what is your shape? Shift so that you let your shoulders drop, bring your back into a straight not curved stance, and allow your gaze to come up to the horizon.
- Notice your breathing; take a couple of deep breaths, paying attention to the rise and fall of your chest with each breath.
- If you are standing, notice the pressure you feel on the bottom of your feet where they meet the floor; if you are sitting, take a moment to feel the pressure on your back and bottom where the chair is holding you. Simply notice this for a moment.
- Notice any places your body seems tense and allow those places to relax.

The Presence-Based Coaching website offers several useful and practical tools for coaches and clients. We suggest you sign up to receive the series of

Six Simple Resilience Practices; by email you'll receive one excellent tip each week that you can immediately apply and practice.

BELLY BREATHING

Most of us as adults breathe shallowly, rapidly, high up in our chests. Some call this "chest breathing." Often, we wear our pants, skirts, and belts too tight around the waist, which constricts our breathing even if we find it flattering. The consequence is that we don't get as much oxygen as we really need, as we are using only a small portion of our lung capacity. One way of becoming more present is to initiate a couple of deep belly breaths. Generally, it is easy to learn to notice where your breath is coming from when you are lying down. As you begin to breathe in, begin to fill yourself like a glass, from the bottom up, breathing in from the lowest part of your belly, up through your midsection and chest, and then filling the very top of your chest. (You may experience your breath as having some catches in it or feeling halting, as your body and muscles adjust to a new way of breathing.) You can reverse the process, letting your breath out from the top of your chest, through the midsection, then releasing the air from your belly. Or make a noise and give a huge sigh of relief, letting your breath out rapidly. Repeat several times, though even once will bring you into the present.

We suggest clients use belly breathing to prepare before a stressful meeting. For one client, each doorway she entered at work was a sign to begin a belly breath, letting the breath out, but silently of course. Belly breathing can be done naturally and inconspicuously in the workplace (no huge sighs and without exaggeration) and is a tool for remaining present and focused during challenging meetings. Clients can remember to do belly breathing by resting one hand gently on the belly, and then breathing into that hand. For any difficult meeting, the client should wear a belt or waistband loose enough to allow them to take a full belly breath without experiencing constriction.

CENTERING

We frequently hear people say, "I don't feel very centered today," as a way of saying they feel pulled in a variety of directions and are unfocused or distracted. We also say "not being centered" when we find ourselves surprised or triggered into an unpleasant state. Doing a centering practice physically can be an antidote. One way to start is to experience what it feels like to be radically uncentered and try to move through space. Try this: hunch your shoulders and bring them high up and close to your ears, as if you have almost no neck. Stand up on your toes, heels off the floor. Hold your stomach in tight, push your chest out as if you are puffing up and walk around the room for a minute or two. This position represents a way of being that is dramatically off center. Your center of gravity is very high in your body, tilted forward; your breathing is shallow, and you probably have very little movement in your arms and torso. When we work with clients, we give instructions verbally and observe, if possible, how they respond to each one.

While most of us don't walk around this dramatically off center, many of us do have habitually uncentered ways of walking or holding ourselves. Some people "lead with their heads," with the head leaning forward as they walk so it is the first part of their body to arrive. Some habitually stand off balance, one hip or leg tilted so the body's balance is inhibited for hours of each day.

Once you've practiced being off center, experience what being centered can offer. Again, guide the client with verbal instructions so they fully experience the attention and guidance.

- Start by standing comfortably, feet shoulder width apart, keeping your knees soft and slightly bent, arms relaxed and hanging to your sides. Notice if you are inclined to lock your knees; if so, slightly bend them.
- Now, begin to pay attention to how your body is supporting you. Begin with your feet, feeling their contact with the floor, notice your legs bearing the weight of your upper body. Feel how your back is straight and yet flexible, not stiff. Keep your chest open and tummy soft, relaxed. Keep your eyes soft, not fixed, with an open and accepting gaze. Notice how your weight is distributed between your left and right legs; move to adjust yourself so your weight is evenly distributed. Notice how you are balanced top to bottom; adjust any place where you need to lengthen.
- Notice whether your weight is centered over your legs or whether you are leaning forward or backward.
- Adjust yourself in your body so that you are fully balanced: front to back, left to right, and top to bottom.

Center is a place we come back to after being pulled or pulling ourselves off center. So experiment with that: pull yourself up high and uncentered again, perhaps lost in your head.

Take a step back and lower yourself back into center. Bring your feet fully and firmly to the earth, legs accepting the weight of your torso, stomach relaxing, chest softening, shoulders and arms relaxed and hanging, keeping your back straight but not rigid.

Most clients report that with being centered comes a sense of aliveness, lively energy, and alertness. If the client has fully embodied being centered, they will likely feel very grounded yet flexible. From center they can choose to move flexibly in any direction, and they can return to center and recover it when shifted. Ask clients to explore how this place of centeredness compares to how they habitually carry themselves. Ask them to notice what thoughts, emotions, and images arise when centered. Where would it be useful for them to be able to experience being centered and recentering?

Silsbee created a technique using centering as an organizational resource from his Resilience series of videos. Silsbee asks the client to imagine a vertical line from the crown of the head down through the legs and into the floor, a valuable visual image. He asks, "What mood is produced in you?" and "What possibility is there that wasn't there a few minutes ago?" He had the participant make several shifts back and forth from the habitual shape to the centered shape, and notice how emotions, possibilities and moods are open and available from the centered place. The link between body experience, possibilities and emotions becomes transparent for clients in this exercise.[11]

In *Retooling on the Run,* Stuart Heller, and David Surrenda's (1995) brilliant book on nonverbal work for leaders, they offer a "centered presence" exercise. When practiced regularly, clients discover that centered presence helps cultivate sensory attention and increase flexibility in intentionally choosing a response versus reacting instinctively to events. For some reason, clients like that it begins with the cue, "find your feet." One leader who practices this says that, when events happen that could "trigger" her into an irritated or aggressive mode, she simply says to herself, "Find your feet." Feeling them, then allowing that to spread upward through her body, creates groundedness when she is challenged.

---

11 Doug Silsbee passed away in 2018, but his work is very much alive today at https://presencebasedcoaching.com/doug-silsbee-legacy/doug-silsbee

- Find your feet.
  - Feel your feet touching the floor.
  - Notice the pressure and the contact between your feet and the floor.
  - Feel the insides of your feet. Feel the muscles and bones.
  - Let the sensations grow in strength and spread throughout your body.
  - While maintaining this quality of sensation, let a new breath emerge.
- Find your hands.
  - Feel what you are presently holding or touching.
  - Notice the pressure and the contact between it and your hands.
  - Feel the insides of your hands. Feel the muscles and bones.
  - Let the sensations growth in strength and spread throughout your body.
  - While maintaining this quality of sensation, let a new breath emerge.
- Find your head.
  - Look and listen to what is going on around and within you.
  - Tune in to your senses of smell and taste.
  - Notice how your head balances on the top of the spine.
  - Let the sensations grow in strength and spread throughout your body.
  - While maintaining this quality of sensation, let a new breath emerge.
- Find your breath.
  - Inhale and exhale on purpose.
  - Focus your attention on the middle of your torso.
  - Relax and let your breath move to its own rhythm.
  - Let the sensations grow in strength and spread throughout the body.

Wendy Palmer's voice leads the audio track; the home page offers visual cues to the practice, and the app allows the user to choose an inspiring visual for the end of the practice. In addition, the app allows the user to select reminders to center, sent to their smart phones at intervals they choose. It also tracks the user's total centering practices.

In *Leadership Presence* Halpern and Lubar (2003) offer several somatic and nonverbal exercises drawn from their experience on the stage and applied to organizational work. For them, presence literally means ensuring that full attention and focus are given. Leadership presence literally means being present and available. They suggest that leaders give their full attention when someone comes into their office or space unexpectedly:

- The leader stops what they are doing right away.
- Turn to face the person and make eye contact, with your body also facing the person.
- Smile and breathe—instead of seeing the person as an interruption to a task.
- Be intentional; decide whether to speak or reschedule.
- Close the interaction when you have a genuine feeling from having connected personally with the one who entered.

The authors suggest that focusing on a task means having the internal as well as the external environment ready. Just as a leader clears the desk and arranges the environment to focus on the task, the leader can become more prepared and present by stretching, doing a body scan and centering.

The basic exercises offered here can provide a strong foundation for the coaching you do with a client that is body based. Whatever the focus of the client's work, the client's way of embodying an experience can have a significant impact. When a client wants to improve relationships, change a habit, achieve a goal, stop procrastinating—no matter what the focus—there will be an embodied presence in the current state that may not be effective for the client. Asking the client to notice his or her breathing, do a few cleansing belly breaths, conduct a body scan to identify where emotions are being held, or notice how a way of standing or sitting creates energy or diminishes it, are valuable ways to support a client's self-awareness and identify potential shifts.

NONVERBAL WORK:
EIGHT FLOWS, FOUR ELEMENTS

One of our early teachers was Stuart Heller, whose work over three decades has been to discover nonverbal and movement centered means for cultivating excellence. His premise is that the more of oneself a person brings at any time, the more authentic and influential he will be. Most people have sets of habits and mind-sets that keep them from being flexible and capable of moving in alternative directions. Using movement, nonverbal methods and practice, clients and coaches can develop the capability of bringing much more of themselves at every moment than they may ever have expected.

Heller's coauthored book, *Retooling on the Run*, is a tool we call on again and again. From a background as diverse as mathematics, operations research, hypnotherapy, and karate, Heller, who holds a doctorate in psychology, created a rich repertoire of nonverbal practices for coaches and their clients, including an online library of videos and very specific nonverbal practices for specific client needs and goals.

Heller believes that how a person moves through space is how he or she moves through life. Two core practice areas he uses with coaches and clients are the "Eight Flows" and a series of movements associated with the "Four Elements."[12] Although both are hard to describe without being experienced, they are accessible and practical. We have used them for over a decade as part of our personal practice and with clients.

The Eight Flows Practice requires about two minutes of your time. Its simplicity belies its brilliance. Because the practice requires a person to experience embodying every direction—up and down, front and back, left and right, in and out—when done over time it helps a coach or client experience where it is easy to move, and how easy it is to stay in center and to move in all directions. A client will initially enact habits when first learning the practice, we find. A client who tends to push forward in life will tend to do very large movements, particularly in the forward space, although what is being modeled is subtlety. Clients may find some flows easy and others very difficult, depending on their nonverbal habits.

Heller has a comprehensive model, the "Five Rings of Nonverbal Movement," for examining how nonverbal behavior, including stance and direction, influence mood, energy, and potential for action. He uses the four elements of ground, water, air and fire, drawn from martial arts and Chinese medicine, and has developed ways of working with subtle nonverbal distinctions that yield sig-

---

12 https://www.yumpu.com/en/document/view/52021126/the-five-rings-operating-system-walking -your-talk-home

nificant results. The client Jane had a great deal of difficulty with the nonverbal aspects associated with effective action—or fire. Her gestures and nonverbal stances in the fire domain tended to be weak; she had difficulty sustaining or using them with any level of energy. As Heller would say, her "bureaucracy of habits" worked against her. Working with the five rings system, Jane learned to practice the nonverbal of fire.[13]

HEART BREATHING BY HEART MATH

As neuroscience begins to learn more about the complexity of the human mind-heart-body system, we are learning that other organs beside the brain also have "minds." The HeartMath Institute has researched and created practices for reducing stress and improving well-being through mind–heart alignment. Their work has included providing tools and strategies to reduce test anxiety in students.[14] A practice we particularly like for centering and initiating a sense of gratitude is "Heart Breathing." The instructions that follow are adapted slightly from those on the HeartMath website (www.Heartmath.com). We used this practice with Jane as a means of reducing fearfulness and creating a sense of appreciation for those around her. After several months of practice, she reported this as a sustaining and regular practice for her, perhaps her favorite. It enabled her to prepare to give and receive feedback, no matter how challenging, and it stilled the voices (her gremlins) that wanted her to focus on herself and her performance.

1. Begin by sitting comfortably, feet planted on the floor, with your back supported and hands resting in your lap.
2. Close or soften your eyes and take several belly breaths, breathing into the count of four (one, two, three, four), holding the breath for a count of two, and breathing out to a count of four or five.
3. Continue to take deep breaths in this way, and now locate your heart in the center of your chest by placing the palm of one hand on your heart.

---

13 Heller has several other videos on YouTube and also on his website, www.walkingyourtalk.com, that demonstrate his systematic approach to change through the nonverbal. He also offers face-to-face workshops and a webinar series, accompanied by many online tools, to support nonverbal coaching work.

14 You can review the research and dozens of practices for creating heart coherence at www.HeartMath.com. Many resources are offered with no charge.

4. Continue to take deep breaths and breathe into your heart; imagine you are sending life sustaining air and oxygen into your heart as you continue to breathe.

5. As you continue to breathe into your heart, imagine a time, a place, or a person with whom you felt a deep sense of appreciation and gratitude. It could be somewhere you traveled, a favorite place, a pet, the warmth and comfort of a loved one, or some place where you felt deeply appreciated and thankful for that presence.

6. Just be in that place of appreciation and gratitude as you continue to breathe into your heart.

7. Continue for as long as you like, knowing that you can return to this place whenever you wish to.

8. When you are ready, take two more deep breaths and open your eyes slowly.

We find that Heart Breathing helps us prepare for coaching sessions in a way that evokes calm, compassion, and openness to experience and supports deep listening to the client.

COACHING, EMOTIONS, AND THE RISE OF POSITIVE PSYCHOLOGY

Emotions, the root word of which comes from *e-movere,* or to move, are critical to coaching because emotions predispose us to specific actions. A depressed person is predisposed to inaction; a joyful person is predisposed to experimenting, acting, and exploring. HeartMath also created the Inner Balance program for tracking heart coherence with a smart phone. The attachment required to activate the program can be purchased from www .HeartMath.com.) A joy filled person wants to embrace what is there. Knowing the patterns of our emotions and where they dispose us to go becomes critical to coaching for change. We sometimes describe emotions to our clients as energy in motion . . . e-motion. That is a reframe that allows feelings just to be accepted, normalized, and shifted.

Since the 1980s researchers and writers have been interested in emotions, studying them under the guise of emotional intelligence and focusing on how emotions effect thinking, decision making and relationships. Daniel Goleman has been by far the most popular writer on this topic, importantly connecting emotional intelligence to leadership success in his book *Primal Leadership* (2002). Goleman's body of emotional intelligence includes both personal and social capabilities and is strongly influenced by the context of work and organizations:

- Personal capabilities include emotional self-awareness, accurate self-assessment, self-confidence, empathy, organizational awareness, and service orientation.
- Social capabilities include self-control, trustworthiness, conscientiousness, adaptability, achievement orientation, initiative, developing others, inspirational leadership, influence, communication, catalyzing change, building bonds, teamwork, and collaboration.

When Goleman first wrote in 1995 about emotional intelligence, he verified what executive coaches had known about emotions from their work with leaders. With relief, we reviewed his core principles behind emotional intelligence:

1. Emotions influence thought, decision making and success in life (particularly organizational life) to a far greater extent than has been previously recognized.
2. All human beings are born with emotional intelligence to a greater or lesser degree, and this innate emotional intelligence can grow over time when it is supported by nurturing and developmental activities.
3. Emotional intelligence applies to the self and to others. Self-awareness is a cornerstone of emotional intelligence, and to the extent one is not self-aware, one is unlikely to be aware of others. Empathizing with others and communicating with others skillfully depend on the ability to empathize and understand others' points of view.
4. Emotional intelligence is a critical cornerstone of successful experiences working with others; it is particularly vital to those in leadership positions.

While any of the emotional intelligence dimensions may become a focus for the coach, coaches commonly work in the emotional dimension when conflict and differences emerge, generating intense emotions that can persist if the conflict goes unresolved. Books and tools like *Crucial Conversations: Tools for Talking When the Stakes Are High* (Patterson et al., 2011) provide roadmaps for having a conversation that clears the air. What the coach also needs to provide is a framework to help the client understand the source of the emotion's intensity, and some strategies for self-soothing.

Weathering a Limbic Storm

As Goleman wrote, "The emotional brain responds to an event more quickly than the thinking brain." Goleman is referring to the limbic system; its primary functions include regulation of emotions (such as anxiety, fear, and aggression), biological drives (such as eating, drinking, and sex), and the formation of long-term memories. Overall, we could say that the limbic system oversees our survival responses.[15]

The limbic system is a complex system located in the middle of the brain composed of the amygdala, hippocampus, mammillary bodies, hypothalamus, thalamus, and cingulate gyrus. Although it is not necessary to know the names and functions of each of these structures, it is important to understand they are all connected. This unique connection forms a pathway known as the Papez circuit.

Another important aspect to understand is that since many of the structures of the limbic system are part of our earliest evolutionary brain, the input is not processed verbally or rationally. The input is processed at an emotional level.

So what happens when a stimulus or strong emotion activates the Papez circuit? Let's say something in the environment frightens someone: a woman is bullied at work. This fear stimulates the limbic system, which then follows its own unique pathway or loop (Papez circuit) through the emotional brain. However, it may not end here. To the degree that she continues to reengage the emotion-provoking situation, to encounter the bullying person, more and more neurons (brain cells) will be recruited into this process. In other words, each time the person reexperiences this fear, the limbic system is restimulated, and more neurons join in causing the person's emotions to become

---

15 We are indebted to our colleague Lynn Meinke for her input on neuroscience and coaching for this explanation and for suggestions on coaching clients in the midst of a limbic storm. Much additional research in neuropsychology has emerged in the last many years and continues to influence the coaching profession.

more intense. Simultaneously, this recycling of the emotion makes it difficult to engage in rational thinking about the situation because the messages to the rational brain (cortex) have been disrupted. By now the person is probably confused, upset, or overwhelmed and perhaps sweating, shaking, crying, or raging.

The sooner this emotional engagement with the situation is stopped, the easier it is to calm the emotional brain and reduce the number of neurons involved. Since the rational brain has connections back into the emotional brain, we can often use language to begin to interrupt the cycle and calm the activities of the structures of the Papez circuit.

If a client presents in the middle of a limbic storm or gets back into it as she recounts the story of work, the coach can help the client stop this limbic storm by modeling behaviors that help. Ultimately, through the coach's modeling, the client can learn to perform these practices for herself:

1. **Be calm, centered, and empathetic.** This alone can be very comforting and stabilizing for the client. If the coach becomes rattled, upset, or entangled in the client's emotions, their emotions will heighten.

2. **State what you notice.** "You are distracted." "You're not as focused as usual." "Something has gotten hold of you emotionally." Short and simple statements are best and by making these observations you are interrupting the limbic loop. The loop will begin to slow and the ability to engage the rational brain recovers.

3. **Affirm the client's wholeness and strength.** "As big as this may seem right now, you are bigger than this situation." "This situation is just one part of your life. The rest of your life is operating better than this." "I understand that this is really frightening; you are larger than this." "You are greater than this situation." Reminding the client this situation or storm is not their whole life brings some clarity and perspective to the situation.

4. **Ask the client if he or she would like to stop this emotional chaos.** By doing this you are pointing out that the client has choices and the ability to choose.

5. **Be a resource for the client**. You can let the client know you have information about the brain that can lessen and even stop the churning if they would like to hear about it. Then, if desired, explaining the limbic

loop or emotional brain and the Papez circuit in simple terms educates the client and further calms the chaos. By providing this information you are also strengthening the client's ability to manage future situations and increasing their resiliency.

6. **Follow through with the use of good coaching skills.** Once the storm has calmed, the use of good coaching skills is imperative. As a coach, be in alignment with your client to fully appreciate the situation and the client's desired outcomes; believe wholeheartedly in your client who has strengths, skills, gifts, and talents waiting to be called into service. You can also be curious about discovering, with the client, how he or she can best approach the situation and create new ways of dealing with the challenge at hand. Focus on your basic coaching skills: listen deeply, ask thought-provoking questions, make clear and succinct statements of what you are perceiving. When you take these actions as a coach, the client can gain awareness about the situation and choose a path forward that is best for him or her.

Coaches can teach clients strategies for when they get caught up in their emotional brains while alone. As soon as a person becomes aware that the limbic loop has been triggered, it is important to do something to stop it. Some simple techniques that can be used include:

1. **Repeated words:** Try saying, "Stop, stop, stop," "Cancel, cancel, cancel," "Relax, relax, relax," or "Calm, calm, calm."

2. **Distractions:** Take a walk, take a shower, shoot hoops, run, hit a punching bag, play a video game, do a crossword puzzle, clean a closet, read a favorite book, or watch a movie. Getting the client's body and brain involved in other things can stop the chaos.

3. **Breathing:** Take some deep cleansing breaths or do some yoga breathing. Ask the client to imagine that she is bringing clear and pure energy into her being while doing the deep breathing. She can also do a body scan to see where she is tight or contracted. On the next breath, imagine sending the breath to that tight area. Watch it soften. A centering practice works well, too.

4. **Reminding:** She is greater than this one situation. Do a reality check by having the client remind herself that this event, person, or situation

is not the whole of her life, but just one small portion. This approach also keeps the client from catastrophizing or making things bigger than necessary.

5. **Gratitude:** Looking for the blessing in the situation and what she can learn from it allows her to start to manage the situation. Counting blessings is a way to focus on what is good and what is working in her life.

USING EMOTIONS IN COACHING

In the suggestions about calming emotions, as well as in our earlier discussion of the Thinking Path, we use emotions as one aspect of the client's experience that they can draw on when examining what is and in creating multidimensional change.

Using an Emotional Inventory

For clients working on emotional intelligence and self-management, it can be helpful to do a simple inventory of emotions daily. Once an hour, ask them to record the primary emotion they experienced, and what was occurring. For a client working on irritability, this proved a revelation. She discovered she was most irritable after 2 p.m. at work; as it turned out, she tended to schedule her most challenging meetings after this time. She also very likely had low blood sugar because she did not eat much for lunch.

Working with the Four Horsemen

Most clients benefit when they know a little bit about the research into emotions that derail relationships. This quotation from *Crucial Conversations* (Patterson et al., 2011) exemplifies the heart of the issue: what do people do that jeopardizes relationships?

> As people begin to feel unsafe, they start down one of two unhealthy paths. They move either to silence (withholding meaning from the pool) or to violence (trying to force meaning in the pool). Silence almost always is done as a means of avoiding potential problems, and it always restricts the flow of meaning. The three most common forms of silence are masking, avoiding, and withdrawing. Masking consists of under-

stating or selectively showing our true opinion. Sarcasm, sugarcoating, and couching are some of the more popular forms. Avoiding involves steering completely away from sensitive subjects. We talk, but without addressing the real issues. Withdrawing means pulling out of a conversation altogether. We either exit the conversation or exit the room.

John Gottmann did years of research observing couples to discover what he described as the root behaviors that create toxic relationships. He discovered four behaviors that often send relationships reeling into dysfunction, which he called "The Four Horsemen": contempt, blaming, stonewalling, and defensiveness. Clients can note behaviors that exemplify the Four Horsemen, silence (usually appearing as masking, avoiding, or withdrawing), or violence (usually appearing as controlling, labeling, or attacking). Clients benefit when they understand what they do when they display these behaviors and benefit from understanding how to recognize and limit their impact.

Studying Positive Emotions

Our clients are lucky to be living today—we know so much more about how to shift emotional states and how to generate positive emotions than we did when we began coaching in the 1980s.

One of the most prominent researchers in positive psychology is Barbara Fredrickson. At the University of Michigan, she wanted to study emotions that had not been scientifically explored. Whereas psychology had focused on negative emotions, such as anger, depression, anxiety, and fear, Fredrickson wanted to study positive emotions, such as joy, happiness, gratitude, hope, and love.

Her research resulted in her "Broaden and Build" theory of positivity. In essence, her work demonstrated that positive emotions change how the mind works, allowing individuals to widen or broaden their outlook (whereas fear and its relatives do the opposite, narrowing focus and limiting options). Positive emotions transform the future by bringing out the best in people, enabling individuals to build their resources. Fredrickson is now regarded as one of the world's leading researchers on emotional positivity.

In fact, Martin E. P. Seligman, considered to be the "father of positive psychology," has labeled Fredrickson "the genius of the positive psychology movement."

What Positive Psychology Research Tells Us[16]

An early paper published by Fredrickson reported her findings from exploring the effects of positive emotions such as joy, interest, contentment, and love. It suggests "the capacity to experience positive emotions may be a fundamental human strength central to the study of human flourishing." Fredrickson hypothesized a "Broaden and Build" theory based on the effects of experiencing positive emotions. Her research has shown that positive emotions broaden or expand an individuals' possible repertoire of actions in situations whereas negative emotions narrow or contract individuals' range of possible actions. Research also demonstrated that a positive frame, or "positivity," can transform a person's future by bringing out the best in individuals, which leads to building or expanding an individual's resources. Positive emotions also can neutralize negativity. Whereas negativity can elevate blood pressure in a heartbeat, positivity can calm it. Thus, positive emotions can act as a reset button. With this unique ability, positivity increases resiliency or the ability to deal more effectively with adversity. Keep your thoughts positive because your thoughts become your words.[17]

Keep your words positive because your words become your behavior. Keep your behavior positive because your behavior becomes your habits. Keep your habits positive because your habits become your values. Keep your values positive because your values become your destiny.

—Mahatma Gandhi

As researchers began to explore the topic of positive emotions they began to ponder, "How much positivity is enough?" Fredrickson's work has shown that a reasonable aim is to have a ratio of three "heartfelt" positive experiences to each negative experience. This formula requires positive experiences be authentic—just pasting a smile on your face or faking it does not meet

---

16 pp. 200–204 are contributed by Lynn Meinke (ILCT faculty member).

17 In 1998 Seligman, a psychologist, researcher and professor at the University of Pennsylvania, and Mihaly Csikszentmihalyi, a professor and founder of the Quality of Life Research Center at Claremont Graduate University, were working together on several projects evaluating what comprised the "good life." On the basis of their findings, Seligman and Csikszentmihalyi made a joint statement that said, "We believe that a psychology of positive human functioning will arise which achieves a scientific understanding and effective interventions to build thriving individuals, families and communities."

the test of authenticity. The ratio of one negative experience to three positive experiences is a tipping point and predicts whether people will flourish or languish.

Fredrickson identifies 10 forms of positivity: joy, gratitude, serenity, interest, hope, pride (when combined with humility this is a positive emotion), amusement (the ability to have fun and laugh), inspiration (when the ordinary is transcended and better possibilities are envisioned), awe (when one is overcome with greatness and momentarily transfixed), and love (which encompasses all of the aforementioned forms). Research also shows that everyone has a set point for positive emotions. Some people more naturally gravitate to positivity whereas others more naturally gravitate toward negativity. Because research finds that positivity is more beneficial, those with a general proclivity toward negativity may wonder if they are doomed to having a less happy and rewarding life. Fortunately, they can actively increase their positivity and reap the benefits generated by being more authentically positive.

In her 2009 book, *Positivity*, Fredrickson suggests numerous ways to increase one's positivity. These ideas include:

- "Find positive meaning in situations." What is the blessing or gift in each situation and what can be learned from the experience?
- "Savor goodness." When something pleasant happens enjoy it to its fullest.
- "Count your blessings." What good things can you be grateful for each day?
- "Kindness counts." What kind word or act can you offer in the situation you are experiencing?
- "Follow your passions." Find out what makes you come alive and do it.
- "Dream about your future." What do you want? If you were to create your best life, what would it be like?
- "Apply your strengths." Find out what your strengths are and use them often.
- "Connect with others." No person is an island. We need each other. Build relationships that support and nurture you.
- "Connect with nature." Take a walk. Watch a sunrise or sunset. Get your feet on the ground. Hug a tree. Splash in a puddle. Breathe fresh air. Get some sunshine. Fly a kite. Let nature nurture you.

- "Open your mind." Have a beginner's mind, one that is open to learning new things. Expand your thinking. Invite different perspectives.
- "Open your heart." How can you be more inclusive? What touches your being?

Developing Emotional Agility

Once a client has identified their emotional patterns through an emotional audit or questionnaire, the next task is to create agility in moving from one emotional state to another. As we wrote earlier, this can require specific strategies if the client gets caught in an "amygdala hijack," as Daniel Goleman described it.

In an article titled "Emotional Agility," published in the *Harvard Business Review,* Susan David and Christina Congleton (2013) wrote, "Effective leaders don't buy into or try to suppress their inner experiences. Instead, they approach them in a mindful, values-driven, and productive way—developing what we call emotional agility. In our complex, fast-changing knowledge economy, this ability to manage one's thoughts and feelings is essential to business success." [Susan David has since published the book *Emotional Agility* (2016).]

The article describes four practices, adapted from *Acceptance and Commitment Therapy* (Hayes et al., 2012), that most reliably broaden and build emotional agility:

- Recognize your patterns.
- Label your thoughts and emotions.
- Accept your thoughts and emotions.
- Act on your values.

Self-acceptance is key, as well as intentional and mindful practice. We believe clients should be encouraged to build a toolkit of actions that create emotional agility.

In her book, *Save Your Inner Tortoise!*, Carol Courcy (2012) describes subtle and specific ways to shift patterns of emotions. She resists labeling emotions as positive or not positive. Instead, she argues that all emotions are useful—the challenge is having them in the right degree and at the right time. Her book is a powerful tool for coaches as she offers specific insights into how to accept and make shifts in emotional states (like guilt) that some would say have outlived their usefulness. In Appendix B, Dr. Pat offers a deeper look and guidance on navigating and using emotions in coaching powerfully.

Fredrickson prefers for individuals to focus on strategies to create specific positive emotions. For example, in what appealing ways can a client build capacity for joy, gratitude, serenity, interest, hope, pride, amusement, inspiration, awe, or love? Keeping a gratitude journal is a common practice, and research shows it results in a more positive attitude when done regularly. There is even a smart phone app that creates an online daily gratitude journal, including the ability to upload pictures.

Fredrickson's website[18] contains numerous tools and assessments, based on her books, *Love 2.0* (2013), and her earlier book, *Positivity* (2009). The books describe her groundbreaking research on love—the supreme human emotion—as well as the hidden value of all positive emotions. She encourages readers to experiment with their own lives, finding ways to create more micromoments of love and positivity.

As we wrote earlier, doing an emotional audit is a powerful coaching tool. Clients can keep track of emotions on a regular basis, using the Positivity Self Test featured in Fredrickson's research. Tracking emotions and tracking the positivity ratio can help the client raise the ratio and intentionally build their best future. Read more about the Positivity Self Test or take the survey at https://www.positivityratio.com/single.php. One of Barbara's research outcomes showed the power of meditation in creating greater capacity for positive emotions. She discovered that a particular kind of meditation, Loving Kindness Meditation, formed the greatest resource for developing positive emotions. She offers loving kindness meditations for download and use on the site.

For clients interested in working with emotions, we often use questionnaires developed by Seligman and his associates that relate to happiness, signature strengths and well-being. These assessments are generally free (https://www.authentichappiness.sas.upenn.edu/) and include:

• Authentic Happiness Inventory; measures overall happiness.
• General Happiness Scale; assesses enduring happiness.

---

18 http://positivityresonance.com/index.html

- Grit Survey; measures perseverance.
- Optimism Test; measures optimism about the future.
- Values in Action (VIA) Survey of Character Strengths; measures 24 character strengths.
- Work–Life Questionnaire; measures work–life satisfaction.
- Compassionate Love Scale; measures a person's tendency to support and understand others
- Meaning in Life Questionnaire; measures meaningfulness

Clearly, positive psychology adds to our understanding of the factors, practices and attitudes that make life meaningful, happy, and fulfilling and which allows individuals to flourish.

PART III

Coaching From the Inside Out

Being a life coach is about helping clients create satisfying and fulfilling lives. Up to this point we have provided skills and strategies to support clients in discovering what authentic and happy lives look like, setting and achieving their goals, removing obstacles, and creating visions and plans.

Part III, "Coaching from the Inside Out," describes a unique set of tools and methods for coaching your clients to design their lives for fulfillment.

Part III illustrates in detail how coaches can work with clients to gain clarity about what a fulfilling life is to them. It focuses on the clients' need to reflect on and create a vision of personal fulfillment, separate from the agenda of their parents, teachers, culture, spouse, children, or anyone else, and it provides coaches with tools to assist clients in identifying blocks to living a fulfilled life and transforming those blocks.

INTRODUCTION

Since we started using the phrase "inside out" in 1998, it has become much more common in the personal and professional development arena. One of our favorite leadership books is *Leadership from the Inside Out* (Cashman, 2008)—the concept remains valid, if not unique.

To work in the human being arena demands that the coach have personal experience learning, growing, and living from the inside out. We are most often taught to live from the outside in.[19] We are not taught how to examine our own lives through the lens of fulfillment.

---

19 In our earlier chapter on adult development, we wrote the early conventional stages of adult development occur when the person internalizes the expectations of the "tribe" around him or her and acts accordingly.

Growing up, we are taught how to fit in, be a good boy or girl, fulfill our parents' expectations, and make choices that create the fewest waves. In our 20s, we get busy building a career, and sometimes those choices, too, are made to fulfill other people's purpose for us rather than our purpose for ourselves. In our 30s, most of us continue in career building and often in family building, and we are frequently too busy with both of these to take time to ask, "Am I fulfilled? Am I on the right path?" Then, in our 40s and 50s, we may find ourselves burned out or entering a midlife reexamination. This may coincide with a movement from one adult development level to the next.

In our experience, many clients hire life coaches for exactly this purpose: to reexamine earlier choices and to consider redesigning their life.

In the past several years there has also been great interest in what is often described as "purpose-driven leadership." The pursuit of personal purpose has moved into focus for leaders as well as others. Studies have found that those who have purpose in their lives are more disease resistant. The May 2014 *Harvard Business Review* published "From Purpose to Impact," a call for leaders to discover and enact their personal purpose as a beacon light for managing the complexity of today's volatile, uncertain, complex, and ambiguous (VUCA) world. If you coach people working in organizations, this article provides support for your life coaching around purpose. (Braig & Snook, 2014). The authors recommend, as we do in this book, discovering purpose through mining the highlights of your life, times when you felt on fire with purpose. They describe the value for leaders of setting a "purpose to impact plan," detailing specific actions and a roadmap for moving from purpose statement to purpose in action. Here is an example of a client whose life coaching work with purpose set her back on course:

> Dr. Pat had a client who was a lawyer in her mid-40s. She hired him ostensibly to build her legal practice and become more successful in her three-partner firm. During the third or fourth coaching call, when she was reviewing the Life Balance Wheel (see Chapter 9, p. 230) and considering life purpose questions, Dr. Pat asked her when she first noticed her passion to become a lawyer. She said, "It was always my father's dream for me. My brother is a lawyer, and my uncle is a lawyer." She ended up saying, "I never really wanted to be a lawyer." She began to

examine how her career could begin to reflect her life purpose. She did want to make a difference in people's lives and be a positive influence. But she said that she would rather be a teacher, trainer, or consultant than a lawyer, and that's what she began to explore.

The Inside Out chapters in Part III are critical to coaches as well as to clients. Coaches need to do their own work on life purpose and explore the same themes they will ask their clients to explore. Coaching is a profession that demands the coach be living a purposeful, examined life.

We ask you to do exercises in these chapters to examine your own life. These become opportunities for exercises you may want to assign to clients. At ILCT, we taught that students use their lives as a practice field for the Inside Out work. Why? Coaches need to be models for their clients. It increases the coaches' authenticity, which is key to life coaching. Coaches ask clients to probe deeply into their lives: their values, priorities, goals, and obstacles to fulfillment. Coaches must have done—and continue to do—the same work themselves.

This is your opportunity—and challenge—to focus on yourself, your life purpose, and how well your own life works for you in all dimensions. The exercises in these chapters will ask you various questions, such as: "What do you want for yourself in the future?" "What obstacles and challenges need to be addressed?" "How do you get in your own way?" "Where are your strengths?" and "How can you express your gifts more fully in your coaching and your relationships with others, yourself, and your spirit?"

The earlier sections of this book focused on particular coaching skills, strategies, and techniques. This segment focuses on you and your life—not on your skills, your clients, or your future clients. Take the time to do each exercise with intention and care. Your participation in the Inside Out process will maximize the benefits you receive from these chapters by adding richness and texture to your learning. Your participation also ensures that your whole being, not just your intellect, is involved as you read. Bringing yourself fully to this learning experience translates into bringing more of yourself to your clients.

We challenge you to commit to doing the exercises with full attention. You will learn how people use life fulfillment coaching to create fulfilling and balanced lives—by practicing it on yourself.

THE IMPORTANCE OF PARTICIPATING FULLY

Great coaches know that coaching is as much art as it is skill. They have committed themselves to fully mastering the way of being that they coach their clients to attain. They are models of what it means to fully learn, be fully effective, and create a fulfilling life.

In this respect, it is much harder to be a model coach than to be a model therapist. A therapist's commitment as a model for clients is to be functioning normally, without "dis-ease."

As a coach, on the other hand, you are committed to modeling how it is to either be living a fulfilling life or be on the path to creating that life for yourself. Your way of being is as critical to the way you coach as are your skills. This is the responsibility you carry: to model what you coach others to do and to be. Living this commitment will stretch you, which is why coaching is inter-developmental. It develops and grows both you and the client.

UNCONSCIOUS BLOCKS TO LEARNING

Eric Hoffer (1951) recognized how easy it is for us human beings to get in our own way. We fall in love with our past learning and expertise and stop growing. As experts, we expect ourselves to know it all. We act as if we are static creatures—as if doing something once or hearing something once makes it old hat and not worthy of further consideration. We resist going back to the receptivity and openness that characterized us when we were beginners. As beginners, we easily took in new data and practiced doing and thinking things that were unfamiliar. We were willing to go outside our personal comfort zone in service of learning something interesting and important. This beginner's mind, as some describe it, is essential for coaches and clients to recognize and cultivate.

Hoffer was ahead of his time. Dr. Pat's father gave him a copy of *True Believer* to read as a young teen. Dr. Pat remembers his father paraphrasing Hoffer as saying, "Our greatest pretenses are built up not to hide the evil and the ugly in us, but our emptiness. The hardest thing to hide is something that is not there."

That is why coaching requires us to be curious and work with clients to be curious about everything we believe, feel, and think we understand. Coaches strive to take nothing for granted and remain nonjudgmental and curious about their clients and about life itself. Coaching requires we become truly open, flexible learners. We require those characteristics of both ourselves and our clients. The Inside Out chapters of this book engage you in learning what is deeply personal—about your gifts and talents, your needs and desires, the blessings and challenges in your life right now. If you give yourself fully to the exercises and teachings of these chapters, you're sure to extend yourself beyond your comfort zone.

An easy way to resist this expansion is to say, "I've heard this . . . done this . . . known this . . . before!" Human neurobiology predisposes us to be habit focused. The human mind tends to want to conserve energy, so it resists thinking when automatic responses will do. We all know how this works when we find ourselves driving, having noticed nothing about the road or other drivers until we reach our destination. We are on autopilot. It works for driving and many other things. However, the tendency toward habituated action inhibits awareness and does not welcome new learning.

As you work through the Inside Out chapters, you will undoubtedly encounter things you have heard about, learned about, and perhaps even mastered previously. When this occurs, you will be faced with a choice: stay in expertness, outside the learning conversation, or see the invitation that these chapters offer as an opportunity to stretch and open yourself to the next step in your life, whatever that may be.

Educated and experienced professionals may find they have erected many barriers to learning. We see at ILCT that both our students and often their clients find it difficult to embrace the condition of being a learner. Some of the ways we can recognize this resistance to learning are:

- We find it difficult to admit we do not know how to do something or have yet to master it. We let our disappointment about our situation stop us.
- We want to be clear all the time, about everything. Consequently, we lose patience with the ambiguity and messiness—even the chaos—required for great learning to occur.
- We may live in a permanent state of judgment. We judge ourselves and our adequacy, this book and its adequacy, the book's authors and their adequacy. We find it hard to simply stop judging and start

appreciating people (ourselves included) and opportunities for what they can offer.

- We do not often grant others the authority to teach us or coach us. Instead, we tend to make them wrong and inadequate. The choice we could instead make is to see them as having a unique perspective—and allow ourselves to be the beneficiaries of their uniqueness.
- Often the need to look good (perfect, right, sensible, smart) keeps professionals reactive to life instead of responding to possibilities. Response implies choices.

ASK YOURSELF:

What are the obstacles I create that hinder a full engagement with my learning? How might they appear during the Inside Out chapters?

CHAPTER 8

THE POWER OF PURPOSE

This chapter is about life purpose: how to work with clients to discover it, maximize its usefulness, and use it in life coaching with particular clients. First, we focus on what life purpose is and how to discover life purpose. Later in the chapter we focus on how to refine a life purpose and how to use it with clients.

LIVE FROM A DEEP PLACE[20]

Rainer Maria Rilke, the 19th-century German poet, wrote to a young, aspiring poet to "live from a deep place." Only then, Rilke said, would his writing become great.

It is not easy for clients to find their deep place when their lives are cluttered and busy. It requires becoming still and quiet, focusing on beginning the work that we describe below, and making a commitment to themselves—putting themselves at the top of the to-do list. There are no slogans, no easy shortcuts. This is a process of getting to know oneself fully.

Supporting clients to find their deep place begins with discovering their life purpose. When they know their life purpose, they have access to incredible power to make choices and act.

---

20 Recognized now as the "father of positive psychology," Martin Seligman's study of what constitutes the "good life" and happiness was presented in *Authentic Happiness*. What surfaced from these studies were three basic findings that predicted an increased sense of satisfaction and gratification in the lives of adults. The findings that supported increased fulfillment were: *being in a stable romantic relationship, making a living from a vocation or calling versus just having a job,* and *believing in something larger or higher than the self.* Interestingly the research also showed that there was no significant correlation between wealth, health, or education and authentic happiness. In this context, the work you do for yourself and with your clients on the power of purpose is important and critical work toward fulfillment.

This is what worked for Terry Fox, a young man from Canada. Terry, an athlete, was stricken with cancer, lost one of his legs, and was understandably depressed about his situation. He had lost his sense of a viable future. Some months into his recovery, after being fitted with a wooden leg, Terry did the serious work of reconsidering who he was. He discovered a lively vision: that people would care enough to contribute money to find a cure for bone cancer. He found his own life purpose: he would carry the message that if communities contribute, a cure can be found. Shortly thereafter, his mission surfaced: he would run across Canada, from coast to coast, bearing personal witness to the strength of the human spirit and the need for a cure.

Terry's run across Canada was filmed and viewed by many people; however, it doesn't matter how public a client's vision, purpose, and mission become. What is important is to articulate them clearly, commit to them fully, and use them to create meaningful work and a satisfying life. This will serve them in knowing how to live, work, and be "on purpose."

LIFE PURPOSE

Each of us looks for fulfillment and authentic happiness in our own way. Sometimes the yearning for fulfillment becomes a call so loud and so intense at midlife that we cannot help but step off the path we are on and devote ourselves to the search for fulfillment. As many midlife questers discover, fulfillment often means returning to deep sources of satisfaction that we may have had glimpses of many years ago. At that earlier time, we may have lacked the courage to follow the call, or we may have allowed life's stresses and serious pursuits to cover up the glimmer of what we knew to be true.

This pattern takes place in the lives of so many because each of us has a life purpose that, we believe, has been with us since we were very young. At moments when we experienced a profound sense of being in the flow—being in the right place, at the right time, using our gifts—we are likely to be living out our life purpose. Life purpose calls us forth. It may be a calling we answer, something larger than our small selves, that deeply connects us with others, with what is larger than ourselves. Gregg Levoy (1997) eloquently illustrates how discovering one's life purpose often begins with a sense of experiencing a calling.

Bookstores are filled with information about our contemporary search for meaning. We know that life purpose has become an important focus for many:

The Purpose-Driven Life (Warren, 2002) was once the bestselling self-help book of all time. A common definition of life purpose is a calling, an overall theme for your life or intent that transcends daily activities. A quick search indicates that the word purpose means many different things to different writers. A variety of spiritual leaders and traditions say the ultimate purpose of our lives is to remember who we are and to whom we owe our lives, and to feel joy.

Ancient writers covered this topic. An ancient Tibetan text states that a life purpose is "for the benefit of self and for the benefit of others." Below are four quotations relevant to the issue of life purpose that we give to ILCT participants, asking them to reflect on what the quotes mean to them. These four seem to be particularly meaningful quotations that move students toward introspective thinking about the importance of life purpose and the variety of ways to describe it:

- "When we are motivated by goals that have deep meaning, by dreams that need completion, by pure love that needs expressing, then we truly live life" (Anderson, 1997, p. 36).
- "We can define 'purpose' in several ways. For one, when we know our purpose, we have an anchor—a device of the mind to provide some stability, to keep from tossing us to and fro, from inflicting constant seasickness on us. Or we can think of our purpose as being a master nautical chart marking shoals and rocks, sandbars and derelicts, something to guide us and keep us on course. Perhaps the most profound thing we can say about being 'on purpose' is that when that is our status, our condition, and our comfort, we find our lives have meaning, and when we are 'off purpose,' we are confused about meanings and motives" (Lynch & Kordis, 1988, p. 42).
- "The first principle of ethical power is Purpose. . . . By purpose, I mean your objective or intention—something toward which you are always striving. Purpose is something bigger. It is the picture you have of yourself—the kind of person you want to be or the kind of life you want to lead" (Blanchard & Peale, 1988, p. 44).
- "A purpose is more ongoing and gives meaning to our lives. . . . When people have a purpose in life, they enjoy everything they do more! People go on chasing goals to prove something that doesn't have to be proved: that they're already worthwhile" (Johnson, 2002, p. 23).

THE IMPORTANCE OF KNOWING LIFE PURPOSE

In industrialized countries, 21st-century culture has become obsessed with accumulating just for the sake of accumulating: information, goods, material objects, and more.

The paradoxes of our time have been summed up well by the Dalai Lama:

> We have more conveniences, but less time. We have more degrees, but less sense . . . more knowledge but less judgment. More experts, but more problems. More medicines, but less healthiness.
>
> We have been all the way to the moon and back but have trouble crossing the street to meet the new neighbor.
>
> We build more computers to hold more information that produce more copies than ever before but have less communication.
>
> We have become long on quantity, but short on quality. These are the times of fast foods but weak digestion. It is a time when there is much in the window but nothing in the room. (2002, p. 77)

As we live with these paradoxes, we have lost sight of the importance of being in life. Many people in the United States misguidedly believe that the only way to have what we want is to work hard and long. There is an alternative: be who you are first. When you focus on being, this lets you do what you want, which lets you have what you need. We need to allow ourselves to be first; the rest will follow. Discovering our life purpose focuses our attention on the essence of who we are—our be-ing.

WAYS TO DISCOVER LIFE PURPOSE

Create a Lively Vision as the Context for Life Purpose

Clients' visions are statements about the world in which they want to live. They do not need to consider the whole planet unless they want to—just their personal world of friends, community, work colleagues, the world that touches their everyday life.

We suggest using the following process to help clients create their vision.

1. List the top ten things you love to do or have always done and loved. Name several things you have consistently made part of your life,

regardless of the circumstances. Examples might include your faith or spirituality, creativity at work, heartfelt communications, ability to take action under pressure, or networking with like-minded people.

2. Identify the characteristics of the context or environment that support your list from Step 1. List the qualities of people you want and need to be around to accomplish your top 10. Draw a series of concentric circles on a blank piece of paper and write "ME" in the center circle. Each circle represents a group of people important to you. Put the names of those closest to you, who affect your life most, in the circle next to you. Then continue to draw your circles outward: family, friends, work colleagues, professional groups, and so on. In each circle, write a few words that describe the qualities this group must embody to support you in just the way you need and want.

   Then identify other resources that are essential to you: peacefulness, time in nature, other creative people, and so on. Ask yourself, "What are the essential supporting features of the world I want to live in to be at my best?"

3. Using the phrases you generated in Step 2, write one to two sentences that express your vision of the world you want to live in. This is the path of least resistance for you, the world you flourish in and want to create for yourself through purpose-full action. Crystallize the essence of your vision. For example, "My vision is that all people of the world will be able to live their lives by choice—in a way that matters to them." This vision expresses the fact that choice is essential for that person.

Examine Past Experiences to Discover Purpose

Our purpose serves us in many ways. It is our compelling reason for living. It gives meaning to our work and life. It guides our choices. Some people describe their purpose as their calling. Whatever we call it, it profoundly shapes the direction of our life.

Career counselors and coaches have known for quite some time that working with experience is a way of discovering personal strengths and patterns. Clients who want to change careers make lists of their best successes and then examine these to identify the skills and resources they have learned to use effectively. Coaches use this strategy, too, examining past experiences to uncover life purpose. The steps below draw on clients' past experiences to create a grounded sense of life purpose. This is a powerful and effective way for clients to source their life purpose because it is based on the reality of their life—what they have already experienced and what they know about themselves from many years of living—and not on what their intellect alone tells them to want.

Clients' purpose statements are unique. Whether or not they are conscious of it, they have already been living out their purpose in some way. Because of this, they can plumb their past to find their purpose. Ask your clients to consider the following exercises:

1. List a dozen or more examples of times in your life when you knew you were on purpose. That is, you had an intuitive sense of being aligned with the exact reasons why you are in the world. Some people recognize they are on purpose because they are "in the flow"—psychologist Mihaly Csikszentmihalyi (2008) has written eloquently about the satisfaction that comes when people are in a flow state. Selecting these intuitively is important because you may not be able to articulate rationally why you felt on purpose during this time. Let us give you an example: One of Diane's experiences of being on purpose occurred during a vacation to Costa Rica with her husband. She was on the side of a hill, looking out over a valley of the Osa Peninsula onto the ocean below. As she admired the view, through the valley flew what had to be at least 100 blue jeweled macaws. They swooped through the valley and alighted in the tallest trees to her left. At the time, this was the only experience she identified of this kind—the sole one that occurred outside of work, community service, or friendship. Yet, as she worked through the five exercises described here, this experience had the elements that were common to her life purpose: recognizing the universal divine in the present moment, admiring the sheer beauty of the world, and connecting the two.

   Most recently, Dr. Pat had an experience of being on purpose while in Brisbane, Australia. He was delivering the keynote address to 400 delegates in a theater-in-the-round setting at the ICF Australian conference. He felt in the flow, loving the opportunity to speak about his passion for life coaching, the profession of coaching, and the impact it can have in the world. Dr. Pat was aware he was in Australia, clear across the globe from where he lived, getting paid to be in a foreign country, speaking to people about the passion and the power of life coaching. In that moment, he was living his dream global experiences. And his youngest daughter was living in Brisbane for three months, a totally unplanned occurrence. They connected while Dr. Pat was there and remarked about the serendipitous occurrence of his keynote address where she was living.

We advise you to start your list of examples very quickly; do not stop to analyze why you choose them. The examples may be from any part of your life, even childhood. Many people have amazing childhood experiences related to purpose, perhaps because they occur prior to when analytical thought is possible. The experience makes a keen impression, and only later can the adult reflect upon why. Make sure the examples span the entirety of your life, including two or three from each decade and, if possible, more from the past five to 10 years.

2. Write briefly about each of these examples. For each of the experiences you listed, write a few bullet points, phrases, or sentences about the experience. Include what you did, where you were, what the outcome was, and how you felt. Your writing should also answer these questions:

   - What was essential to my sense of being on purpose?
   - What about this experience was richly satisfying?
   - What was of value for me?

3. Highlight key words and phrases, then copy them onto a separate page. Examine them to identify commonalities and themes. You will use these words and phrases to build your statement of purpose.

4. Draft a brief statement of your life purpose in two to four sentences using the key words and phrases of your life. Because every person has a unique purpose, no one else's statement will fit yours. How does a purpose statement sound? Here are some examples:

   - My purpose is to support and partner personally and professionally with leaders to create organizations where the human spirit thrives.
   - My purpose is to work generously and to live in service; to manifest love through connecting and caring for self and others;

and to support the development of inner wisdom and inner peace in myself, colleagues, clients, and community.
-   My purpose is to build and lead organizations that model the best practices in our industry, are profitable financially and viable long-term, and offer dedicated workers meaningful work and sustained employment.
-   The purpose of my life is to proclaim the good news that married couples live very holy lives, and that all of life is holy.
-   The purpose of my life is to create a world of love and empowerment, by loving and empowering myself and others.

Don't expect yourself to get it just right in an hour. Let your draft incubate for several days. Getting it sort of right is enough for now. Read it to others and be open to feedback.

To refine your purpose statement, read it aloud several times very slowly. Listen for the particular words that resonate—as if you and the purpose are tuning forks that resonate together when you are in sync with each other.

5. Test your purpose. A good purpose statement pulls you toward it. It engenders energy—like the wind in your sails. You know where you are headed when your purpose is clear. Does your statement clarify what you will do in your work and in your life?

    Here are some clues that you have connected with your purpose:

    -   You feel a strong connection with the purpose you have described.
    -   You have a desire to fulfill it.
    -   You feel deep pleasure when you act in concert with it.
    -   Your interests naturally gravitate toward fulfilling it.

Whatever your clients' unique life purpose, however big or small it may look to others, it is their true path—the one that gives their life meaning. When clients identify their life purpose, they have taken a powerful step toward manifesting it and creating a fulfilling life for themselves.

Encourage your clients to refine their life purpose statement until they feel an internal yes that lets them know they have captured its essence. They might also benefit from taking time to journal about how this work on life purpose has impacted them.

Refining the statement may occur over several coaching sessions or a longer period of time. It is important clients realize this statement is only for them. It is not a promotional statement and needs to speak to and inspire only them. They will never have to share it with anyone else. As the coach, your role is to help clients clarify the statement until it is succinct enough to remember and, when they speak it to themselves, it resonates. We often use this metaphor of resonating, as if the clients and the purpose statements hum like a tuning fork. On several coaching sessions, Diane has actually used a tuning fork, demonstrating how it vibrates when struck. This helps clients understand the relationship they have with their purpose statement once it has been refined.

BEING PURPOSE-FULL: WORKING WITH LIFE PURPOSE

A favorite quote about the power of life purpose comes from a well-known U.S. president, Woodrow Wilson, who said: "You are not here merely to make a living. You are here in order to enable the world to live more amply, with greater vision, with a finer spirit of hope and achievement. You are here to enrich the world, and you impoverish yourself if you forget the errand."

Wilson's quote reinforces the value of life purpose work: When our purpose, our power, and our passion intersect, we find personal fulfillment and enrich the world.

As you work with clients on life purpose, you'll find that sometimes they confuse life purpose with vision or mission.

Life purpose is our calling—the underlying reason for being that gives meaning to our life. It is the purpose an individual enacts throughout a lifetime. Spiritual traditions often describe a universal life purpose for all human beings. For example, when asked what he believed to be the meaning of life, the Dalai Lama said, "To be happy and to make others happy." Within the universal life purpose for all human beings, individuals still must find their own life purpose.

Mission is the particular way or ways we choose to fulfill our purpose at a particular point in our life. For example, individuals whose life purpose is to "honor and evoke the highest and best in myself and others" might fulfill that purpose through many kinds of work and actions over the course of their life.

Vision refers to a specific, compelling image of the future that an individual holds. Earlier in this chapter, we included an exercise for clients to consider their vision for the world in which they want to live. In Chapter 9, we'll describe an exercise for creating a vision for each of the 11 life areas.

When you work with clients, you want to assist them in distinguishing between life purpose, vision, and mission. Most clients will need to examine all three.

Ways to Work with Life Purpose

Coaches and their clients have many options for working with life purpose. We include a list of books at the end of this chapter, each of which offers suggestions for helping clients identify life purpose.

In the coach training at ILCT, we use the method drawn from career counseling that we described above. This exercise accesses clients' cognitive, intellectual, emotional, and intuitive capacities. We also use a structured way of creating life purpose that is described in *Human Being* (Ellis & Lankowitz, 1995), one of the texts in our training course.

Sometimes the clients' first reaction to sharing their purpose statement is, "Oh, it sounds so grandiose!" A rich purpose statement should, in fact, be big and inclusive, enough to compel the clients to expand. As Marianne Williamson said so eloquently, "Your playing small serves no one." A good purpose statement creates the energy to play large.

A purpose statement is a private thing, unlike a company's vision statement that hangs on the wall. It is something we use privately to create our goals and life. Make sure your clients understand that no one besides themselves and their coach ever needs to know their life purpose unless they choose to share it with others. This information usually elicits a sigh of relief.

The clients' purpose is not necessarily something they discover midlife. In fact, it has probably been with them for quite some time, though they may never have articulated it. Therefore, they will benefit from revisiting their past and working with some real experiences of being on purpose.

When we are on purpose, we live from our being, our core self. When we have lost track and are living off purpose, our life feels less fulfilling. Many clients discover that when they have chosen work or a way of life that is not fulfilling, it is because they have lost sight of their purpose. They have become a human doing instead of a human being.

Using Life Purpose with Clients

Almost all clients benefit from life purpose work if they have adequate willingness and a capacity for self-reflection. Sometimes clients need to be taught the value of reflection to benefit from life purpose work. Using inquiries with clients—powerful questions that guide their focused attention and lead to introspection—can be helpful in developing the ability to self-reflect, as can meditation practices, journaling, and many of the other tools we use as helping professionals. Some clients come to us with a strong need to reexamine life purpose. Clients may seem to have lost their way. If they were a boat, we would say they lacked a rudder and were adrift in a sea of circumstances. Clients may feel as if they are surviving, but only with a struggle, or they may be striving to achieve but do not feel much satisfaction in their accomplishments.

Sometimes in the natural cycle of life, clues emerge that suggest life purpose work may be called for:

- A client in midlife feels listless, fatigued, and disenchanted.
- The client has experienced losses—deaths, job losses, or health issues— that make the old way of living no longer possible.
- The client is overwhelmed with life and asks, "Is this the life I really want to lead?"
- The client has undergone significant life transitions—children have left, retirement is near, divorce has occurred, and so on.
- The client feels a serious mismatch between current work and/or roles and the deep desires of the self.

Earlier, in the discussion of adult development in Chapter 3, we saw that any of these clues might be signs that the client is moving from one level of development to another. Notice that these situations might also prompt a client to seek the services of a psychotherapist if clinical depression or extensive anxiety is present. Remember that life purpose work can be very therapeutic. It can be done using a coach approach either by you or by referring to a coach who specializes in life purpose coaching.

Life Purpose Work and Deep Change

In our private lives, as well as in our professional lives, getting back on purpose may require some startling changes. Living from a deep place is not easy to maintain in 21st-century life in the United States, where speed, multitasking, and constant noise make lack of depth a fact of life. Living from a deep place may require a client undergo deep change. As Robert E. Quinn, the organizational behavior and human resource management expert and consultant, wrote:

> Ultimately, deep change . . . is a spiritual process. Loss of alignment occurs when, for whatever reason, we begin to pursue the wrong end. This process begins innocently enough. In pursuing some justifiable end, we make a trade-off of some kind. We know it is wrong, but we rationalize our choice. We use the end to justify the means. As time passes, something inside us starts to wither. We are forced to live at the cognitive level, the rational, goal-seeking level. We lose our vitality and begin to work from sheer discipline. Our energy is not naturally replenished, and we experience no joy in what we do. We are experiencing slow death . . . We must recognize the lies we have been telling ourselves. We must acknowledge our own weakness, greed, insensitivity and lack of vision and courage. If we do so, we begin to understand the clear need for a course correction, and we slowly begin to reinvent our self. (1996, p. 78)

The truth is that almost any moment offers us an opportunity to live out our life purpose. By choosing work, relationships, avocations, creative pursuits, and other life elements consciously, we can find the most fulfilling ways to experience our purpose.

Life purpose work also helps clients begin to sense and live out a higher level of consciousness. In Chapter 3, you read about levels of consciousness. As you consider working with life purpose, consider the level of consciousness that clients seem to be embedded in or moving toward.

Consider the following example. What level of consciousness does Andy seem to be at? Is there a transitional stage, an urge toward transformation of consciousness at work in Andy's life? How might life purpose work be of assistance?

An Example of Life Purpose Work

Consider the case of Andy, a 38-year-old coaching client, who is a teacher and workshop leader. Andy is happily married, has two children, and is considering whether to start his own business. He has been a high school teacher and counselor during his entire career and says he finds himself "sort of itching to make a big change in my work."

Andy's Life Experiences of Being On Purpose

Andy turns in the following random list to you as fieldwork:

- Staying with my grandmother for two months after her husband of 63 years died unexpectedly.
- Being the only child in a blue-collar family to graduate from college.
- The birth of my two sons.
- Adopting two babies from China.
- Committing to completing a master's degree in counseling to enrich my work as a high school counselor.
- Working successfully as a counselor at the high school. Creating a special support group program for young unmarried fathers at the high school.
- Moving in to care for my father, a widower, for the six months before he died.

Andy's Life Purpose Themes

As Andy shares the experiences with you, you note the following words and phrases recurring time and time again throughout his stories. These become his purpose themes:

- Connecting to self, others, and the whole
- Fun, different every day
- Friends and connections
- Peace
- Creativity
- Challenges
- Persistence
- Learning
- Believing in myself and my capabilities
- Coming into my own
- In the right place, doing the right thing
- Committed, conscious, courageous

A Life Purpose Statement for Andy

The life purpose statement Andy drafted after this work was the following:

"My life purpose is to create connection between myself, my clients, and all those I contact to the universal whole of life, through joyfully living and transforming our life challenges into sources of creativity and learning."

Using Life Purpose as a Guide

The real benefit of knowing one's life purpose comes when clients use it as a guide to make choices and decisions that lead to greater, more authentic happiness and fulfillment. Life purpose work leads clients to discover new choices, as well as become clear about directions to pursue and choices to release. In later chapters we explore how clients use values and life design considerations to these ends, as well.

Helping professionals regularly encounter clients who have been living out roles, values, and commitments that were assigned to them early on by their family of origin. Clients often seek coaching because those old ways no longer work. Once they discover their individual life purpose, they may discover, with sadness or with elation, that the roles they have chosen to play and the line of work they pursued have never fit them well. This discovery often leads to a realization that they feel called to live out a different purpose—one that is uniquely their own and may have nothing to do with their family's desires or agenda.

This happened to a client who had spent 20 years working as a divorce lawyer, never feeling a sense of fulfillment from the work. When he did the life purpose work, he chose only one of his 25 on purpose examples from his legal career. Most of the examples he chose came from his church work, his volunteer work as a Big Brother, and his 10 years of service to the board of education in his township. Recognizing what these choices meant to him about his fulfillment at work, he felt deeply sad and needed to do some grief work before moving forward with his life work. He gave himself time for grieving, and then was able to articulate his life purpose in this way: "Through intuitively catalyzing people and ideas, I create understanding, awareness, and connections that enhance people's lives."

Imagine he asks you this question: "Is there any way I could live out my life purpose in my work as an attorney?" What changes might he consider that would create a better fit between his purpose and current professional role?

OTHER WRITTEN RESOURCES

As coaches, we often suggest our clients read something about life purpose. Other resources on how people have discovered and lived their purpose include:

- Carol Adrienne, *The Purpose of Your Life: Finding Your Place in the World Using Synchronicity, Intuition, and Uncommon Sense*
- Teri-E Belf and Charlotte Ward, *Simply Live It Up: Brief Solutions*
- Laurie Beth Jones, *The Path: Creating Your Mission Statement for Work and for Life*
- Barbara Braham, *Finding Your Purpose: A Guide to Personal Fulfillment*
- Stephen R. Covey, *The 7 Habits of Highly Effective People: Powerful Lessons in Personal Change*[21]
- Frederic M. Hudson and Pamela D. McLean, *Life Launch: A Passionate Guide to the Rest of Your Life*
- Richard J. Leider, *The Power of Purpose*
- Rick Warren, *The Purpose Driven Life*

---

21 Covey focuses on principles, but the intent is the same. If you offer this resource to clients, be sure they understand the difference in terminology between Covey's and what we offer here.

CHAPTER 9

DESIGN YOUR LIFE

LIVING A FULFILLED LIFE

It is no secret that countless Americans complain daily they are too busy and rushed, have lost track of friends and themselves. Many clients hire coaches because they want to find ways to make their lives more satisfying and fulfilling. At heart, they want to feel more alive. The high level of stimulation in modern industrialized societies deadens people. Writers describe this as a trance, like a hypnotic state. Bill O'Hanlon, a student of Milton Erickson, the father of American hypnosis, shared this view of life as trance with Dr. Pat in a personal conversation.

Most of us go about our lives in an unconscious or semiconscious, robot-like manner. This has its benefits: the human brain conserves energy when it does not have to think consciously about each action or choice. However, when our lives are not bringing satisfaction, the autopilot needs to be shut off. That's particularly true if clients are being driven by habitual choices and ways of coping that were developed as young children and have remained unchanged. When coping habits outlive their usefulness, adults may turn to a coach, seeking help to reshape their life. This will require them to develop new habits of thinking and behaving. This requires a personal breakthrough. Nadler and Hibino described this well: "Otherwise intelligent people take the same self-limiting thinking approaches every time without realizing they are stuck in time-worn ruts on the road to mediocrity" (1998, p. 72). Coaching clients generally clearly state they want to get beyond mediocrity. They are often less clear about the ways their habitual thinking and coping habits are limitations to moving beyond their current life choices.

In coaching we sometimes talk about life purpose and life design work being *trance-formational*. People become conscious of their unconsciousness.

We cannot always be totally conscious. Our desire is that people design their lives purposefully. We want to form new ways of being that are positive and purposeful—good new habits and daily practices, and a new way of being. These then become a new trance, like an operating system that operates in the background of their lives.

We have seen the legitimate ways that hypnosis is used to assist people in stopping smoking, losing weight, calming anxiety, and overcoming phobias and fears. In its simplest sense, hypnosis is not "watch my watch and fall into a deep trance." It is the use of language and storytelling to take people inward, so they reflect on the images and senses the language calls forth from them. Hypnotic inductions work through embedded messages. When people use hypnosis to change habits, they are given new messages that become filtered through their unconscious. These create positive habits that replace unhealthy or unwanted behaviors. So, designing a life can be trance-formational in the most positive sense. Practitioners of neurolinguistic programming would be familiar with this since much of their practice is based on Ericksonian theory and technique.

We are not saying that coaching is hypnosis. Our point is that human beings are creatures of habit who put themselves in trances all day long. Anyone who knows the effects of television or routine noise is familiar with the ways that humans semi-attend, falling into a sort of autopilot stupor. Coaching uses the principle of examining a client's everyday life habits to determine which are habitual and the assumptions that underpin them. The coach works directly with the client, exploring cognitively and emotionally ways to change habits and create more purposeful behavior that is in line with the client's desired life. As we describe in this chapter, the coach and client design a new life for the client and then craft a life that matches this design.

Oriah Mountain Dreamer's (1999) poem "The Invitation" created a stir because it speaks to this longing to feel more alive. Circulating for months on the Internet, the poem struck a chord within us and thousands of others. We learned later, at a coaching conference in Vancouver, Canada, where Oriah spoke, that her son was initially responsible for posting it online. Its impact caused people like us to spread it around the world. Ultimately, it became so popular that she wrote a book by the same name, which easily found a publisher. Her poem speaks eloquently to the need to feel alive: to inhabit our lives fully, risk, share, see beauty, and connect ourselves with a source greater than our individuality—to build our lives around a worthy core. This is in keeping with the research from positive psychology, which finds that the strongest route to authentic happiness is to use one's signature strengths in service of something greater than oneself. We encourage you to find "The Invitation" in a bookstore or online, where it is reprinted on several sites. The poem speaks to clients who are ready to consider that they are the authors and designers of their lives.

This chapter focuses on life design. Most of us did not grow up thinking we could design a life. Design a picture, maybe, or design a room, as an interior designer does. Something small, maybe—but not our lives.

What do you associate with the word design? Artistry? Craftsmanship? Architecture? Quilting? *Webster's Dictionary* offers these definitions:

- Design: to create, fashion, execute, or construct according to plan
- Devise, contrive: to conceive and plan out in the mind; to have as a purpose
- Intend: to devise for a specific function or end; to make a drawing, pattern, or sketch of; to draw the plans for

As coaches, we take the role of design very seriously. We coach our clients to become the interior designers of their lives in an integral way—body, mind, and spirit. Through our work, clients realize they can make choices about their lives. They can consciously design a way of living that will bring them deep fulfillment. Fulfillment means "a feeling of satisfaction of having achieved one's desires, or the act of consummating something" (*American Heritage Dictionary of the English Language*, 4th ed.). Coaches help clients discover what they desire and want to bring into actuality, to completion. Is anyone ever totally fulfilled? Of course not. Even the popular notion of mindfulness, represented well by Eckhart Tolle (1999), allows for the fact that mindfulness is a temporary state to which we return, hopefully more frequently than when we are unconscious of it. Generally, people experience fulfillment in the moment. Life brings new challenges and learning opportunities. What we want our coaching clients to learn is that in being more purposeful—in consciously choosing and designing their experience—they have opportunities to experience moments of fulfillment more frequently. We find that clients often choose these moments of fulfillment as the sources for their work on life purpose, described in Chapter 8. Understandably, clients want more of whatever feels fulfilling. Living purposefully and living with design allows people to be more conscious of their choices, actions, and mindset.

The basic premise of life design is that human beings can create the life of their dreams. In words sometimes attributed to Eleanor Roosevelt, "The future belongs to those who believe in the beauty of their dreams." Coaches know that this belief is necessary but not sufficient.

To create the life of our dreams, we also need to have the courage to create. As L. J. Cardinal Suenens said, "Happy are those who dream dreams and are ready to pay the price to make them come true." Cardinal Suenens's quote emphasizes the cost of courage. As coaches, we also know of the high cost of not living the life of our dreams, of not leading a fulfilling life.

Life design exercises are an excellent way to support your clients in exploring the life of their dreams. We recommend you instruct clients to give themselves several hours to complete the exercises. They will get the most out of the exercises if they take off their rose-colored glasses and are as honest as possible.

LIFE CAN WORK

Many of us need to be reminded that we create our own lives—through our intentions, beliefs, courage, and ability to link our desires with our actions. The real art of life is in balancing—living in the present with an ability to focus on the future.

Many coaches use some version of a tool called the Life Balance Wheel. It is very common, and no one seems to know its origin. We teach our students to use the Life Balance Wheel (see Figure 9.1), which we sometimes call the Coaching Mandala, referenced in *Therapist as Life Coach* (Williams & Davis, 2007). When Dr. Pat teaches it live, he asks the audience, "Why do you think we call it the Coaching Mandala?" When the participants fall into a weighty silence, Dr. Pat relates humorously, "Well, it gives it that magical, esoteric quality!"

Instructions for the Client

The hub represents the clients' core values and life purpose. Clients may have worked on this separately or may not yet have the exact language to express what belongs in the hub. Each area is interrelated in an ideal life. For each of the mandala areas, ask clients to give a score (1 to 10) and shade or color the

FIGURE 9.1

Life Balance Wheel (coaching mandala)

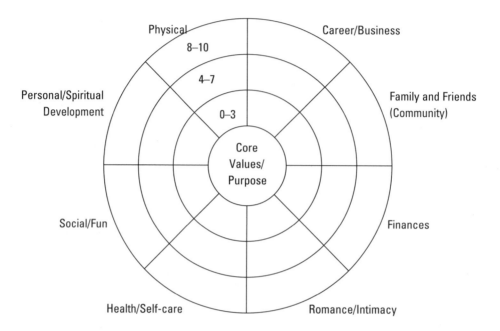

space accordingly in terms of their current level of satisfaction with this particular area right now. Use this mandala as a way to assess the current level of life satisfaction in each area. Clients may score it numerically to measure the improvement desired or use it to have a coaching conversation about gaps between where they are now and where they would like to be.

At ILCT, we recommend students use this tool early, even in the first conversation with clients, as a way to begin the conversation about gaps in their life. It allows the coach to ask, "Where do you most want coaching to focus?" Clients score their level of satisfaction in each area of the wheel, giving them a numerical comparison for the various areas of their life. This becomes a simple way to see where coaching might benefit them most. For example, coach and client might explore together what it would take to move from a 4 to a 10 in each area. In a first session, the coach and client are apt to discover many or most of the areas to be less satisfactory than the client wants. The challenge here is to help the client select several areas to start on. The client will soon see that they are all connected. This fits with our philosophy of teaching the whole person, an integrated approach to coaching. Changes in one area will inevitably impact the client's satisfaction in others. The wheel is not linear; it is just a starting point for coaching conversations.

The beauty of this tool is that it can be used in coaching check-ups at various intervals during the coaching relationship. The client might complete the Life Balance Wheel at six-month intervals, or even quarterly, to give both coach and client a current snapshot of the client's satisfaction. These snapshots can be compared to the initial scoring. We also think it important for clients to update their wheel if a change occurs that impacts an area. For example, both Dr. Pat and Diane have experienced the death of a parent and the subsequent need to become the remaining parent's caretaker. These events radically impacted satisfaction in several areas. Loss and caretaking require time and energy that must be drawn from other areas. This is just one example of how life changes require the client to reexamine satisfaction and redesign.

The Emotions of Change

Because of this natural cycle, we repeatedly experience the natural emotions of change. As we sense that loss is coming, we feel anxiety, apprehension, and worry. When loss arrives, we feel sad, angry, irritated, and frustrated. Grieving needs to be done. Along with the experience of suffering through change, we may experience stress, depression, burnout, helplessness, and even hopelessness.

Eventually hope brings a renewed energy, optimism, and enthusiasm, and happiness brings a sense of satisfaction and contentment. The Wheel of Life teaches that we cannot be happy and stay happy forever. Change is a natural part of our lives. It brings growth and is inevitably accompanied by the emotions associated with change.

We introduce clients to this classic view, part of a long human tradition, as a way of examining assumptions they hold about suffering and joy. Recognizing, experiencing fully, and accepting or surrendering to emotions help clients work through and align with the natural process of change.

We Can Turn the Wheel

The Wheel of Life is an important model for coaches because some clients initially resist doing life design work. They believe their Wheel of Life process brings them as much suffering as it does happiness. The truth for coaches is that life design work does not keep change—the turns of the wheel—at bay; it does, however, offer clients the opportunity to put their hands on the wheel and turn it at a speed that returns them more quickly to happiness. This is the possibility that conscious coaching offers. We help clients discover they can have their hands on their Wheel of Life. They can manage their lives through phases of pain so that they can navigate these times as smoothly as possible, emerging more resilient and less drained. They can fully experience loss in order to move through it. They can design their lives in the spirit of hope so that authentic happiness occurs more quickly, more easily, and more frequently.

If you have clients who are suffering greatly, you might share the medieval Wheel of Life with them. It offers a perspective on natural changes in human life. Pain in life may be inevitable. Coaches assist clients to experience and move through that pain as elegantly as possible.

USING THE CONTEMPORARY LIFE BALANCE WHEEL WITH CLIENTS

Master coaches have many ways to help clients examine and assess their lives. As we said earlier, the Life Balance Wheel is often used at an early session. There, the coach and client examine the ratings the client has assigned. Through discussion, they examine what is behind the client's ratings. This is a relatively informal and conversational process, the goal of which is to help identify early areas for the coaching focus. Other tools, like the Cycle of Renewal (Hudson & McLean, 1995), assist in determining if there is an additional cycle occurring, one that is leading the client to a need for renewal in some life area. The Cycle of Renewal and the Life Balance Wheel are both useful during times of transition. This is a major emphasis at ILCT because we recommend tools that lead to conversations about the whole of the client's life.

Sometimes clients come very reluctantly to the task of getting specific about what is and what could be. They may bring many "shoulds" with them. They can become embarrassed or ashamed about how they have been living, or barely managing, their lives up until now. We believe—and they discover in the context of the coaching relationship—that "the truth shall set you free."

We coach clients to tell the truth and to discover, perhaps for the first time, what they really want. In doing so, we use most of the strategies from Dave Ellis's "Ways to Know Yourself" (Ellis & Lankowitz, 1995, pp. 44–45):

- **Be specific**. Instead of analyzing their lives in a global manner, ask clients to focus on the details of eight to 12 areas. They often discover that some specific parts of their lives are working very well, although they may not have appreciated this fact because other parts seem powerfully lacking.
- **Collect the facts**. The satisfaction levels we ask clients to assign, from one to 10, allow for comparison and measurement. Over time, clients can track changes in their satisfaction levels, which provides them with feedback about how on track their lives are.
- **Listen to others.** Clients who are working through the life design process often share their work with significant others, asking for feedback on possible ways to close the gaps. When working with couples, each person can create a Life Balance Wheel separately. They can share their visions and create a joint vision for their life together.
- **Evaluate.** The success of life design relies on our ability as coaches to work with clients to assess how their habits, beliefs, and behaviors may need to be altered to close the gaps we have identified.

EXERCISE 9.1

The Life Design Process: Are You Thriving or Surviving?
1. Ask clients to describe their current state of life. For each of the life areas listed below (or others that are appropriate for the client), assign a satisfaction rating. Use a scale of 1–10, with 10 as high, 1 as low. Some coaches prefer scales that use 1–7, the classic Likert scale, because it has a midpoint. We suggest you use the same scale used with the Life Balance Wheel diagram so can refer to it during this exercise.

   Ten means clients are absolutely satisfied with that area of life—they are thriving in it.

   One means clients are absolutely dissatisfied with that area—they are not thriving in it. They may even be suffering.

   Clients can choose areas that they have not addressed on the Life Balance Wheel. This is their opportunity to be even more specific. For example, the Life Balance Wheel lists "Family, Friends, and Community" as a category. We encourage clients to break down that category into three or more categories. For example, if clients have children as well as other family members to consider, they may want to create additional categories, such as one for children and one for parents and/or siblings. Their level of satisfaction may be very different with their parents than with their children or siblings.

_____ Appearance

_____ Family

_____ Finances

_____ Friends and Community

_____ Fun and Play

_____ Health and Well-being

_____ Home and Environment

_____ Personal Development and Growth

_____ Primary Relationship (spouse, partner, most intimate relationship)

_____ Spirituality

_____ Work/Career

2. For each of the areas above, ask clients to write two to three bullet points indicating the key reasons for their rating. Example: "You gave a rating of 'three' for Fun and Play. Why?"

   - Working six days/week, 10 hours/day; too tired when I am finished to play with kids
   - Canoe needs repair, so we can't use it and have stopped canoeing
   - Little time to just have fun with my wife and two small children

3. Ask clients how they want to be. Ask the clients to take four sheets of paper and fold each one so it is divided into four separate areas. Write the name of one life area in each section. If the clients prefer, you may also use index cards, with the main area of focus in the middle of the card and the desired state below it. Leave space on the card so the client can record planned actions and priorities that develop later through coaching.

4. Ask clients to describe what they really want in each area of their life from Step 1—that is, what a "10" would be in each area in the next 12 to 18 months. This activity is a way of doing visioning with clients and making a vision concrete. Choose an end point far enough away so clients can use the interim to realize the vision. This becomes a working document that can be referred to and adjusted as needed.

5. Ask clients to begin the work by addressing the four life areas with the lowest scores. Treat each area separately. Clients will end up with several bulleted lists, each of which focuses on one area of life.
6. Ask clients to write a brief bulleted list—like a vision statement—that addresses each of the lowest areas, using these guidelines:

Pick a time frame—the next nine, 12, or 18 months. Make sure they set a specific time period within two years so this becomes a concrete set of goals and not simply a mental exercise.

Ask clients to focus on what fulfillment would look like and mean for them in each life area within the specific time period. A "10" means they are absolutely satisfied with the area and are thriving. Ask the clients to focus on what they really want, and to include their vision of what is possible during the time period. What kinds of fulfillment constitute a deep desire and realistic goal during this period of time? We want clients to dream big as well as identify realistic steps that will lead them there. It is not our job to judge whether it is realistic or not—that is the clients' determination. The coach's job is to stress the both-and, not either-or, in this exercise, emphasizing dreams and visions as well as the practical steps needed to attain them.

Ask clients to use present-tense verbs for the bullets or paragraph. Write as if they already have that area working just the way they want it.

Align clients' life design work with their work on life purpose. Ask them to refer to their life purpose statement (discussed in Chapter 8) as they do this work. They will ask themselves: "What would fulfillment look like in this area if I were truly living my life purpose?"

It may help clients to use visualization to imagine more vividly how this area of life would look. They can do that independently of the coach or within a coaching session if needed.

Example 1

Figure 9.2 illustrates how this life design process exercise might look. It is drawn from work Diane did in midlife. At that time, both of her parents were alive and living in Florida and she lived in the Midwest. Her parents were in their mid-to-late 70s, and her mother had recently experienced a series of small strokes, as well as two hip replacements within a four-month period. In Figure 9.2, Diane uses full sentences in the present tense (not in the future tense) and personalizes using "I."

This life design exercise uses the classic coaching strategy: identify the gap between what clients have and want. After working through Steps 1 and 2, the gap becomes vividly real. Done well, the visions they create for each area of their life will draw them forward. Your clients will have created a compelling vision of the life they most want for themselves that is achievable in nine to 18 months.

USING LIFE DESIGN WITH CLIENTS

So far, we've illustrated the key steps that constitute the clients' fieldwork, as they identify key areas, rate level of satisfaction, and then create a nine-to-18-month specific vision for fulfillment. We recommend coaches ask clients to do the fieldwork in increments, over a period of several weeks, to not become overwhelmed by the task. Clients can be overwhelmed creating specific visions for a dozen areas of life. On the other hand, many clients become inspired and can complete the visions for all areas within a week or two.

FIGURE 9.2

Sample Life Design Exercise

Work/Career	Finances/Money
Primary Relationship	**Family** 1. I consistently support my father as he cares for my mother. 2. I talk to my cousin and his wife at least once a month, and we find ways to support each other. 3. I feel an abiding sense of love for each member of my family, and gratitude that they are a part of who I am in my life. 4. I am fully connected with my sisters-in-law, and we freely share our lives, emotions, and thoughts. 5. My dad and I have found a place for him and my mom to live in Cincinnati that will meet all of our needs for the next 1 to 3 years. 6. I do this willingly and effortlessly, and feel love.

To break down the task over several coaching sessions, ask the clients to do the following, using the worksheet below (Table 9.1), which includes key items and indicators, as well as space for "How I could create it." Tell the clients:

1. Identify two or three life design areas to work on.
2. For each area, write down the three to five key bullet points that you want to have represented in that life area. These might be tangible things, relationships, people, ways of being, or ways of doing. These are either the bullet points or even more specific details drawn from the work in Step 3.

TABLE 9.1

Worksheet

LIFE DESIGN AREA 1	LIFE DESIGN AREA 2
Key Items and Indicators	Key Items and Indicators
1.	
2.	
3.	
4.	
5.	
Item 1: How I could create it	Item 1: How I could create it
a.	a.
b.	b.
c.	c.
Item 2: How I could create it	Item: How I could create it
a.	a.
b.	b.
c.	c.

Item 3: How I could create it	Item 3: How I could create it
a.	a.
b.	b.
c.	c.
Item 4: How I could create it	Item 4: How I could create it
a.	a.
b.	b.
c.	c.
Item 5: How I could create it	Item 5: How I could create it
a.	a.
b.	b.
c.	c.

3. For each of the three to five items or indicators, identify three to five ways you could choose to create it for yourself.

Ask clients to pick one of the life design areas with a gap they want to close during the next few months. Ask them to describe the gap as they see it now (Table 9.2). Then identify some first steps the clients will take to close the gap—steps they can take within the next several weeks. (Make sure clients do not overwhelm themselves by having to describe all of the steps.)

TABLE 9.2

Closing the Gap Worksheet

LIFE AREA: FAMILY

DESCRIBE THE GAP YOU WANT TO CLOSE (for example):	FIRST STEPS YOU WILL TAKE TO CLOSE THE GAP (for example):
Talk to my cousin and his wife regularly for support. Currently we speak rarely and inconsistently.	E-mail my cousin and describe what I think would be really desirable: speaking every 1–2 weeks on the phone when we can both relax and there is no crisis. Set up a time for the first of these calls.
I am fully connected with my sisters-in-law, and we freely share our lives, emotions, and thoughts. Right now we don't always get to talk when my husband calls them.	Make a specific request of my husband—that he place the calls when I am there so I can talk to his sisters after he is finished. (I know he'll say yes; I've just never asked!)
My dad and I have found a place for him and my mom to live in Cincinnati that will meet all of our needs for the next 1 to 2 years. Right now he wants to come, but there are no plans.	I will ask my dad next time we talk about his parameters for a good place: monthly costs, as well as other considerations. Then I will start researching places so that when they come up this summer we can look at some.

FREQUENTLY ASKED QUESTIONS: LIFE DESIGN

Coaches ask the following about working with the material presented thus far:

How do we integrate the life purpose work the clients do with their work in life design?

We said earlier that fulfillment in life is derived from living from one's primary values and life purpose. This is how we achieve a sense of wholeness, satisfaction, and fulfillment. Consequently, clients benefit from considering this question as they first begin to create their vision and write specific bullets: "How would this life area look in the next 18 months if you were living out your life purpose fully in this area?"

> **ASK YOURSELF:**
> *How could you coach clients to incorporate their life purpose into the work around each life area? If clients were ignoring purpose, how could you help them consider it as important?*

Does it matter whether the clients work with life purpose first?
Or can they start with life design?

There is no one way that works best with all clients. Because life design is more specific, this work can be easier for some clients, particularly for those who like concrete, actionable work. It is fine to begin here. If so, the client may need to go back to reconsider his or her life design work—once the work on life purpose is complete—to determine whether each area reflects purposefulness as well as fulfillment.

When midlife clients come for coaching and report extremely low scores on every area of a beginning Life Balance Wheel assessment, they may need to start with life purpose. Clients would be taking the most holistic and integrated view of their life in that way.

ASK YOURSELF:
Under what circumstances would you want to do life purpose work first?

Can you work with clients over a period of years with life design?

Absolutely. Because life design focuses on a specific time period, clients will need to update it periodically. As circumstances change, clients will need to change their vision for that life area. Coaches can use this material to create life design visioning retreats with clients, both individually and in groups. Many coaches do annual retreats with clients, examining current satisfaction with life areas and designing for the next year or a specific period of time. This is a rich way for coaches to stay connected to their clients. The process provides clients with new energy and perspective. We also suggest that coaches take time each year to review their own Life Balance Wheel and life design, examining and re-creating specific areas to better fulfill their life purpose.

ASK YOURSELF:
Consider the situation of a client who wants to retire in a year. You have been working with him for the past nine months. How would you use life design to assist him in planning his retirement?

CHAPTER 10

WHAT GETS IN YOUR WAY?

Once clients have identified their life purpose and compelling view of what they want for each of the important areas in their life, they are on the path to creating what they want. However, the path may not be an easy one to follow—they may encounter obstacles. Ultimately, these hinder them from living a fulfilling life.

What kinds of blocks do coaching clients typically encounter? The most common obstacles are:

- Energy drainers: psychic vampires (such as clutter) that suck the vitality out of each day.
- Unmet, and sometimes unacknowledged needs.
- Fears, which will be explored in depth in Chapter 15.

Let's begin by exploring the top two blocks—energy drainers and unmet needs—by first knowing how to identify them and then addressing them.

ENERGY DRAINERS

In Chapter 9, we presented a life design exercise in which clients rate their level of satisfaction in each area of their life and identify what would consitute full satisfaction. One strategy for creating more fulfillment is to:

- Identify obstacles, both big and small, that stand in the way of satisfaction.
- Figure out what those blocks cost the clients in terms of energy, time, and focus.
- Find ways to eliminate, minimize, or effectively manage the blocks, all of which are variations on do, delegate, delay, or dump.

This process leads clients to manage their life in a different way.

Blocks to satisfaction drain our energy—things we put with up and endure. They usually come in a variety of sizes.

Category 1: The Little Annoyances—Life's Gnats

These are the small things in life that we handle. We usually just brush them off, as we do gnats at a picnic. We ignore them, unaware that these annoyances tax our attention and energy. If they felt more like bees or even mosquitoes, we might do something about them. Mostly, we just deal with them.

Gnats are things such as messy closets and work shelves that keep us from finding things, a crowded garage, unfinished marketing brochure, car that needs a tune-up, broken lock, and dry cleaning to take in for winter storage.

Most of us tend to tolerate these until they accumulate and really bug us. Then we get so annoyed that we finally do something about them. Unfortunately, they may have grown to quite a massive size by that time. At that point, they may have moved into Category 2.

Category 2: The Big or Chronic Complaints—Life's Sufferings

These issues create tension and crowd us. We are conscious of how they diminish the quality of our life. We probably just accept them as normal because we do not know how to effectively handle them.

Sufferings might be related to long work hours as we start a new business. We cannot delegate because our staff is not well trained. Our demanding clients call us at all hours. Our child is upset and says, "You don't ever come to my soccer games, Dad!" We do not take vacations. We do not have time to talk—to share deeply—with our spouse. We have stopped exercising. Our 83-year-old forgetful mother needs more attention than we can afford.

Although gnats and sufferings are part of life, we do not have to be helpless or passive in the face of them. As the Buddha said, life is 10,000 joys and 10,000 sorrows. Every human being must expect to participate in both. In fact, the first Noble Truth of Buddhism is "to live is to suffer"—sorrow is the universal experience of mankind. This teaches us we do not need to create suffering—there will be plenty of it. The goal is to accept and embrace it, and move beyond—that is where growth occurs. Every coaching client can benefit from learning about gnats and sufferings, and doing the following exercise to gain control of, or eliminate, them, which creates more satisfaction.

Step 1: Identify your personal gnats and sufferings

List as many as you can right now. Most gnats and sufferings come in the areas of work, family, home/environment, and community. Start with these or return to your life design chart for help.

Step 2: Count the cost

Anything you tolerate has a cost. It may cost you time, inconvenience, or frustration. The cost may be your own or others' disappointments, or it may be a loss of well-being and vitality. Identify what each gnat and suffering costs you. Ask yourself whether enduring this issue and bearing the cost is worth it. The cost you are paying is probably way too high. If you want fulfillment and balance in your life, you cannot afford to give up pieces of yourself in this way.

Some people acquire energy from suffering and from enduring difficult circumstances. Feeling like a martyr energizes them—handling heavy loads, feeling oppressed, sacrificing for others. Sometimes it even makes them feel heroic to manage suffering and be miserable. There are better ways to live life including ways that are much more nourishing for both the martyrs and the people in their lives, but these ways are invisible until people stop putting energy into the gnats and sufferings and start making space for more nourishing activities.

Step 3. Do something about each gnat and suffering
if the cost is not worth it to you

There are four ways you can swat the gnats and eliminate the sufferings:

- **Find a strategy for eliminating them.** Create a plan for eliminating each one completely by handling them yourself. That might mean spending a Saturday cleaning up the garage, organizing a garage sale and discarding unsold items. For work, it could mean setting a realistic completion date for your brochure and marking it on your calendar, deciding how to delegate, then possibly hiring a graphic designer or a writer to complete your brochure.
- **Allow them to disappear on their own.** Once you decide not to have them in your life, some gnats and sufferings will just naturally disappear. They seem to realize that their time is over and just take care of

themselves without any effort on your part. These times are a great illustration of the power of intention.

- If there is no clear action that can be taken, we sometimes suggest our clients consciously park or put aside an issue to get it out of their focus—work on something else. Lacking the energy that focus brings, the issue often just disappears. This builds on the common idea that what you resist persists. Dropping resistance means the issue stops persisting.

A common example might be people who hate winter and live in Colorado. What they know is that Colorado weather is very changeable. After a few cold and blustery days, the sun comes out. They recognize that their mood changes. They realize they can intentionally recognize that "this, too, shall pass." In saying that to themselves, they accept what is—the cold weather—and focus their attention on what will be. However, if they lived in Nova Scotia, the "this, too, shall pass" strategy might not work for them. This way of thinking—surrendering to what is and anticipating what will come—is effective for things that truly are out of people's control—weather, taxes, and so on. Allowing them instead of resisting them uses the strategy of consciously choosing to delay. This is not denial. The choice is to take our focus elsewhere.

- **Neutralize them.** In order to do this, you look for a compromise—a short-term solution that will take the emotional charge out of the situation. Acknowledge that you cannot do everything at once and get real about your expectations. Establishing a realistic date for completing your brochure, for example, will take the sting out of it hanging over your head.
- **Convert them into learning opportunities or gratitude.** Some things, such as your 83-year-old mother who is in decline, may be unchangeable facts in your life. What you can change is how you respond to these situations. As discussed in a previous chapter, this situation is an opportunity to coach clients to respond (to take time to examine choices), as opposed to react with a habitual, instantaneous emotion or action. Clients in this situation, for example, might choose to think of how long their mother took care of them: she probably invested at least 16 years of her life in a nurturing, protective, and supportive relation-

ship for their growth. They might choose to be grateful for the opportunity to give something back or look for the lessons in this challenge.

A colleague, Michael O'Brien, teaches clients to ask, "What is life calling for here?" as they choose a response. Clients focus their attention on something larger than their own skin when they ask this question. It puts the situation into perspective. Clients might choose to be thankful for whatever time they have left with their parent. They might arrange as much support as they can for themselves and seek out opportunities to learn from the situation. They may need to do a life redesign to accommodate their situation.

Update your list of gnats and sufferings periodically. Revisit your list every 60 days. Add new items and eliminate those you have accomplished. Consider the areas in your life where most of these gnats and sufferings collect.

Most of us have a few areas that are especially prone to gnats and sufferings. If you find, for example, they are mostly at work, take action. Do not let new ones accumulate or multiply. One gnat attracts others, and soon you will have a swarm.

Get clear with yourself about the real costs to your vitality. How long are you willing to put up with these annoyances? Set a termination date for each of your gnats and sufferings. Put it on your calendar and become a Terminator of the things you have been tolerating. Remember Arnold Schwarzenegger's character who stopped at nothing? Use that kind of energy to handle your gnats and sufferings.

Sometimes gnats and sufferings are linked to how clients meet their needs or live their values. We will revisit the issue of gnats and sufferings in Chapter 11, which focuses on values. For the current discussion, the following worksheet on energy drainers is a useful tool to use with clients. We teach the importance of this simple tool as a way for clients to get down on paper the things that drain them of energy. This allows them to systematically begin to check drainers off the list. The magic that often happens is that when clients take care of two or three items, others tend to disappear.

Worksheet 10.1 can be an early fieldwork assignment with new clients. It can also be used to focus a sample coaching session with prospective clients. Many coaches use it to market their services. Clients complete the sheet and experience a coaching session. The conversation may be very brief—maybe just seven to 10 minutes—but they experience the coaching conversation and sees how it focuses them on what they want in life.

WORKSHEET 10.1

The Energy Drainer Worksheet

We put up with, accept, take on, and are dragged down by people and situations that we may have come to ignore in our lives rather than address proactively. Take this time to identify those things that drain your energy from positive activities. As you think of more items, add them to your list.

Energy Drainers at Work	Energy Drainers at Home
1.	1.
2.	2.
3.	3.
4.	4.
5.	5.
6.	6.
7.	7.
8.	8.
9.	9.
10.	10.
11.	11.
12.	12.
13.	13.
14.	14.

15.	15.
16.	16.
17.	17.
18.	18.
19.	19.
20.	20.

Which of these are gnats? Which of these are sufferings? Go back and mark each with a "G" or an "S" to indicate their magnitude.

Which of these can you address right away? Put a star next to two items you can do something about within the next two days.

The Energy Drainer Worksheet is a strategy to help clients be conscious of what is added to and can be taken off the Energy Drainer list. As items are removed, clients begin to experience the energy that can be reclaimed that was attached to the item, chore, or issue. Coaches can request clients make a similar list of Energy Gainers, things that impact their life in a positive way, things they love to do (Williams & Davis, 2007, pp. 38, 39). When coaches ask clients what they love to do, clients often find they do not set aside time for these activities. Clients who identify that walks in the park, listening to favorite music, spending time in nature, and going to the theater and museums are energy gainers can use the reclaimed energy to consciously put these activities in their life. Then life begins to change.

IDENTIFYING NEEDS

In most of the modern world we have collapsed any real distinctions between having needs and being needy. We say things like, "He's so needy! I just can't stand being around him." or "She's letting her neediness ruin that relationship!" How many times have we found ourselves running the other way when we heard someone described as "needy"?

The truth is, we all have needs. They are a normal and natural part of human existence. The trouble comes when we do not acknowledge they exist. When we believe it is not okay to have needs—when we are so embarrassed about our needs that we deny their existence—we drive our needs underground. There, they gain power and begin to run our life.

Maslow's Hierarchy: A Classic View of Needs

Most of us grew up afraid of being labeled needy. American psychologist Abraham Maslow proposed that every human being has a hierarchy of needs, ranging from security to self-actualization. Figure 10.1 is a recent depiction of this hierarchy.

In the years after Maslow developed his original hierarchy, several levels were added to it. Transcendence was added as the top level in 1971, and aes-

FIGURE 10.1

Maslow's Hierarchy of Needs

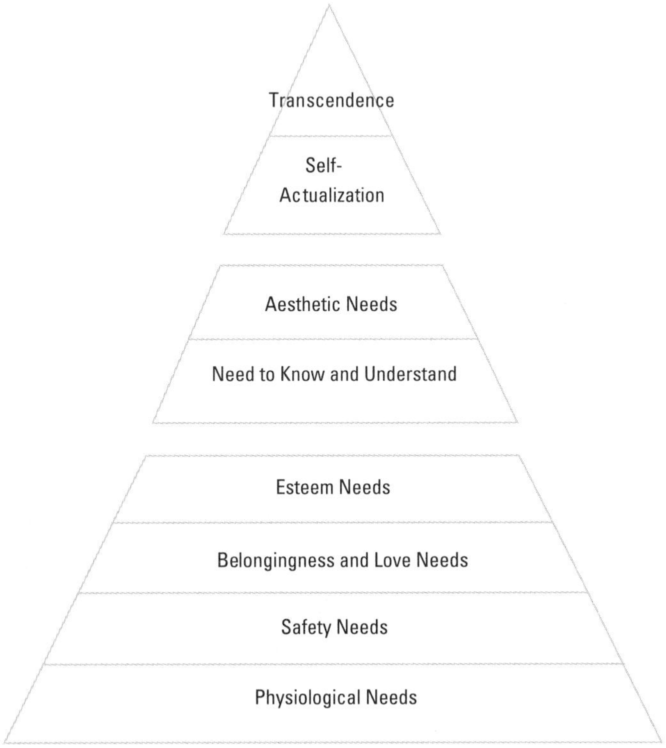

thetic needs and the need to know and understand, as precedents for self-actualization, were added in 1998.

Maslow defined aesthetic need as the need for symmetry, order, and beauty; self-actualization as the need to find self-fulfillment and realize one's potential; and transcendence as the need to help others find self-fulfillment and realize their potential.

Maslow believed that as we become more self-actualized and transcendent, we develop wisdom and automatically know what to do in a wide variety of situations. This is consistent with research on emotional intelligence, which suggests that emotional intelligence scores rise over the decades as we age.

This information should make it acceptable to have needs, but most of us learned to pretend we have it all together. We can meet all of our own needs just fine, thank you. Our popular heroes—Superman, Wonder Woman, Harry Potter, Luke Skywalker, The Avengers, and other superheroes—were the diehards of the world: they did it alone or the hard way, and did not seem to need anyone or anything.

A Coaching View of Needs

The construct of self-actualization developed by Maslow in the 1960s and 1970s is a relevant and useful contribution to coaching. Maslow's approach moved psychologists beyond the disease model when looking at how a person functions.

In 1968, Maslow redefined self-actualization as the ability of people to bring their powers together in a particularly efficient and intensively enjoyable way. He also defines it as a state in which people are more integrated and less split, living more fully in the here and now, more self-supporting, more self-accepting, more open to their experiences, more idiosyncratic, more perfectly expressive and spontaneous, more creative, more humorous, more ego-transcending, and more independent of their lower needs.

Through self-actualization, people become more capable of activating their own potential by becoming truly aware and accepting of their total person with all their gifts and concerns. Therefore, self-actualization is not an end point or destination, but rather a manner of traveling. To become more fully functioning and more fully authentic requires self-actualizing thoughts, visions, awareness, and acceptance not only of who we are but also of who we are becoming. We are not just humans being—we are also humans becoming, constantly in a state of change. To the degree to which we are aware of these changes and take responsibility for them, we are freer to become more of who we can become.

Why is Maslow's research important to coaching? Coaches work with mentally and emotionally healthy individuals; we say we work with clients' gifts, their unique creative windows to the world, and their signature strengths. Coaches partner with individuals and groups to develop greater awareness, ownership, and actualization of their gifts as they apply them to their wants, objectives, and life goals for their everyday life. In this, coaches follow the lead of Maslow and his cohorts.

Abraham Maslow was the first to study healthy persons. His model changed the way we view human beings. Maslow's research findings suggested there are basic biological needs beyond "being" needs—beyond the basic needs for survival, safety, security, love, and belonging. For example, people placed themselves in risk-taking situations not because there was something sick, he believed, but because there was something sought. He discovered that individuals had higher-order needs: the needs for self-esteem and esteem from others, as well as self-actualizing needs such as the need to seek truth, goodness, creativity, spontaneity, individuality, and beauty. Maslow also discovered that when basic needs are fulfilled, individuals move up the hierarchy. Although they constantly function at all levels of the hierarchy, their primary awareness is at one or two.

Maslow (1971) wrote a delightful chapter titled "On Low Grumbles, High Grumbles and Metagrumbles." If you listen to what people complain or grumble about, it is easy to understand at what level on the hierarchy they are functioning. People who come to a coach mainly complaining about drivers running traffic lights, concerns about whether they'll have a job the next morning, and worries about the brakes on their car working properly are functioning at a different level than people who complain about students snapping the branches off a newly planted tree on Main Street, the validity of most diet plans, whether their shoes match their clothing, or how adults are being good role models for our youth. These concerns not only shift the conscious level of personal needs, but they also suggest other differences in more fully functioning persons. Therefore, as coaches listen to a cluster of complaints, we obtain a sense of the level at which clients are primarily functioning at their stage in life. This information is relevant to our coaching work since our goal is to make a difference in our clients' lives, and we need to know where they are before we can know how best to be of service.

Maslow discovered that people who function at higher levels on the need hierarchy are more time-competent and more inner-directed. He defined time competent as the ability to live primarily and effectively in the present and to experience the past, present, and future as a continuous whole. Today is the yesterday of tomorrow. To the coach, change is always in the present and in planning for the future. If we do not live effectively in the present, we can easily become a prisoner of our past. We can become stuck in how we have been rather than focusing on how we can be. Coaches work with clients' strengths in the present to design pathways for change that are more consistent with core values and wants.

Maslow defined inner directedness as clients' abilities to rely on their internal gyroscope when making decisions. The more inner directed, the more clients live a life of responsible awareness. Being responsible is, in our language, being response-able, possessing the ability to respond and seeing oneself as the author of one's choices. When individuals develop into more responsible people, they soon discover the opposite of the cliché, "There cannot be any freedom without responsibility." They discover that the more response-able they become, the more freedom they possess. Coaches invite clients to become more proactive to discover their freedoms and gifts and make use of them to take charge of their lives. They take charge by making choices that get them what they want in life and that are consistent with the greater good of others.

Self-actualization is a lifelong developmental process that is consistent with the process and goals of coaching. Since self-actualization requires clients to work with their human needs at various levels of development, coaches need to have a working definition and principles for working with needs. These are simple but can be quite different from how other professions view needs.

Definition: Needs occur at every level of Maslow's hierarchy, and when insufficiently met they keep clients from being their best. Coaches want clients to be working toward being their best. It is not enough to be simply functioning.

Following are several principles we use when working with needs in coaching:

• Needs are situational. They can appear because something has suddenly changed, so now a need is not sufficiently met. Whenever clients are undergoing any sort of transition, new needs may appear. For example, in her 30s Diane worked in a training and development organization at AT&T with many other career minded women and men of her age. It was an environment in which she thrived. She loved the work, made friends easily, and enjoyed the vibrancy of her colleagues. People came to the organization from all over the world, which created a stimulating learning environment. Diane had never had so much fun at work. When she was offered a promotion to work in another organization, she took it. It was a small department, very quiet, where much of the work was done individually. After several months, Diane realized how important her need for affiliation was—because it was not being met. Where before the need had been met easily at work, Diane had not recognized it. At her new job, it became very visible. In her new situation, she needed to take steps to meet that need outside of work.

- When a need is insufficiently met, it drives a person. When it is sufficiently met, it goes away, drops back into the background of the client's gestalt.
- Needs are different from wants and desires; the latter are desirable but do not exert the driving force that an unmet need can create.

When we live a fulfilled life, we make friends with our needs. We do this when we:

- Acknowledge our needs—they exist; they are real.
- Identify the needs we have now.
- Discover how our needs are getting met and whether those ways nourish us.
- Find satisfying and healthy ways to meet each of our needs.

The reason we teach the importance of awareness of needs and addressing them is that, as we said earlier, needs drive our choices and possibilities. If clients are unaware of their needs, they will be unconsciously driven to satisfy them. Although they may say they want to achieve a particular goal, they will find themselves first satisfying the needs and second addressing their goals.

A second reason for addressing needs, which we learned from Thomas

Leonard, founder of Coach U, becomes clear if we look at needs metaphorically, like a green lawn that needs water in the summer. Many people who live in a dry climate install an automatic sprinkler system so the grass is watered without them having to think about it. The yard needs water regularly, but the need is automatically met and there is no scarcity. The goal for managing needs is similar: to recognize them and build an automatic system to meet them.

For example, clients might have a need for recognition. Because it sounds egotistical to them, they deny having the need. However, the need is still there, even though they are unconscious of it. They meet it in a way that is not effective for them. They appear thirsty for recognition. At work, they talk too much about small successes and appear competitive with teammates. Teammates describe them as boastful. A healthy way to meet the need for recognition might be to find alternatives, such as volunteering for a community service organization or a project they believe in. When a need is consciously acknowledged, it becomes much more possible to find healthy ways to meet it, which then can be systematized.

The following exercise, which expands on the above steps, is a good one for supporting clients in making friends with their needs. It is important for you, as the coach, not to harshly judge clients' needs. While you may not have a need for dominance, for example, clients may express their need in this way. We believe that needs drive a person's beliefs, actions, and attitudes. They may at times appear neurotic, narcissistic, or misguided. However, in coaching we have found that when explored, the needs for dominance, power, and control are underlain by original unmet needs, such as the need for acceptance, recognition, or being valued. The point for the coach is to help clients find healthy ways of fulfilling needs that are in alignment with their purpose, values, and desires for their life. Whenever possible, we want clients to build something into their life so that the need can be consistently sufficiently met. When that occurs, the need is no longer a driving force.

Step 1: Acknowledge That We Have Needs

Our needs are those things that are essential to us now in our life—essential to us doing, having, and being our best. When a need is fulfilled, we do not think much about it, much as breathable air is essential to humans but normally occurs without conscious thought or effort. Unless we are in danger of suffocation, we may not think about the breathing process. When we do not have enough clean air to breathe, our energy pours into meeting that need.

Most of us have enough air for that not to be a concern. At any given time, however, we may experience insufficiency in the areas of any of about 1,001 other needs, including the needs for achievement, intimacy, excellence, results, companionship, beauty, encouragement, allies, and mentors.

How do we recognize a need? We can often identify needs by tracking emotions. When a need is not met, we feel frustrated, fearful, disappointed, hurt, and angry. When a need is met, we feel pleased, excited, and motivated. When we track our emotions and discover patterns of difficult and charged emotions, we are on the trail of a need. This is explained in Step 2. These are opportunities to become awakened to our needs and begin seeking ways to fill them sufficiently.

An unmet need causes us to feel empty, incomplete, or less than whole. We have a nagging feeling that something is not right. In contrast, when we are not driven by needs, we have the full freedom to be ourselves.

A need can be mistaken for a desire or a want. Consumer societies such as the United States teach children and young adults not to distinguish between needs and wants. Advertising turns wants into needs to maximize sales. The way to distinguish a need is to notice if we cannot live effectively or happily without it for more than a short time (hours or days—not weeks). If that is the case, it is probably a need. In the example of Diane's work, she began to feel lonely after the first several weeks at her new job, which was an unfamiliar feeling for her as an adult. The emotion of loneliness led her to recognize her need for friendship and affiliation with other women.

Let us use the example of the need for security. If it were simply a desire for security, we would want it and perhaps even work to obtain it, but life would be okay without it. The difference between need and desire, then, is one of intensity. If we feel a sense of unease, foreboding, or discomfort with it left unfulfilled, it is probably a need.

Another indicator of a need is that we experience a feeling of relief when it is filled. If we simply desire or want security and then obtain it, we feel more of a sense of satisfaction, like having accomplished a goal.

One question coaches ask their clients is, "How would you know this need was sufficiently met in your life right now? That is, what would make the need stop being a driver of attention, behavior, or emotion?" Each of us will have particular ways to identify when a need is adequately met. We may recognize it through our thoughts, our emotions, or a physical sensation—or in all these ways. In Diane's example, she recognized that her need for affiliation was met when she no longer felt lonely for friends.

Step 2: What Are Your Five Greatest Needs Right Now?

As you create a balanced and fulfilled life, it is helpful to recognize needs you have right now. The following exercise involves creating a list of your top five needs. You may find it easy to articulate your needs.

You may already know what is causing you pain or tension. For example, you may already know that you want and need more affection from your spouse, more peace and quiet in the morning, more energy, or more evidence of business results.

Needs generally fall under one of four major categories:

1. Needs for security—safety, protection, stability, information, duty, clarity, certainty, honesty, financial security, order, authenticity, commitment to meet obligations.
2. Needs for power and influence—control, wealth, authority, management, morality, dominance, freedom, perfection, visibility, leadership, acknowledgment, praise, recognition, influence.
3. Needs for achievement or attainment—create, accomplish, achieve results, strive, perform, excel, attain calmness and peace, be busy, be responsible, succeed, contribute, be useful, be of service excellence.
4. Needs for intimacy, relationship, and connection—be listened to, needed, loved, touched, helped, included, cherished, appreciated, spiritual, connected, central to a group; to collaborate and communicate, be connected to something greater than oneself.

If you have trouble identifying your needs, that might be an indication that you do not think it acceptable to have needs. Perhaps you are ashamed of them or you have denied them for so long that you fool yourself about having them.

Write down your top 10 current needs. If it would be helpful, start with a longer list then narrow it down.

My top 10 current needs are:

1. _____

2. _____

3. _____

4. _____

5. _____

6. _____

7. _____

8. _____

9. _____

10. _____

Review your list and place an asterisk (*) by the top three. Prioritize them, if you can, with your top need identified as 1, the next need as 2, and so on.

Step 3: Discover How Your Needs Are Met and Whether Those Ways Nourish You

Reflect on the life design process in Chapter 9. In Step 1, you rated the current state of your life in many dimensions:

- Work/career
- Finances
- Family
- Friends/community
- Primary relationship
- Home/environment
- Appearance
- Health
- Personal development and growth
- Spirituality
- Fun and play

Rate your needs as they apply to dimensions of your life. For each of the 10 needs you identified above, assign a rating, from +5 to –5, as it applies to the various dimensions of your life:

+5   Need gets fully met in this dimension
 0   Need does not show up in this dimension
–5   Need does not get met at all in this dimension

Here is one client's brief list:

Need for inclusion:
Work: –3 (do not get invited to lunches)
Home: +5 (feel very included with family)
Friends: +2 (some invitations; want more)

List the ways you meet each of your needs. For example: You may try to be present at every work meeting because you want to be included. Your work may be suffering because you are spreading yourself too thin and cannot get everything done. Ask yourself: What is the exchange I am making to get this need met? Is it worth it?

Look back at the list of gnats and sufferings you created earlier in this chapter. Are any of these present because you are trying to meet another need? For example, see if you wrote, "I have too many meetings at work." If so, consider the possibility that you might stop attending half of these meetings, but that you continue to attend enough to meet your need for inclusion.

Step 4: Find Satisfying and Healthy Ways to Meet Each of Your Needs

Be scrupulous and take time when you examine your needs. Our actions are often unconscious based on what we think we want. Usually a deeper, unexpressed need is present. Becoming more aware of these underlying needs can help us make better choices and have more satisfying relationships. For example, we may seek attention when we really want acknowledgment. We may seek sexual companions when we really want intimacy. We may seek money when we really need security. We may seek answers when we really need assistance. We may seek power when the deeper need is for respect. We may seek distance when we really need freedom.

Ideally, you want to meet your needs to your full satisfaction now, and you want to do so in ways that are healthy; ways that allow you to create a fulfilled life. How to do this:

1. Examine each need and ask: How can I meet this need easily and without great effort? Is there another dimension of my life where I can meet this need more easily and fully?
2. Make a list of at least three ways you can meet each need more easily, without a high cost, and in a more satisfying way during the next two to four weeks. Then take action based on your list. Experiment until you meet your needs—until they are fulfilled. Eventually, you will be able to remove each need from your list.

Case Study: Jerry's Needs

Jerry is an entrepreneur with a significant need for achievement. He looks to work to satisfy this need, but with a new business, he has not yet received accolades for his efforts. His need drives him disproportionately. It leaks into other areas of his life. He then tries to meet his need for results at home. He bosses around his family and makes to-do lists for them. He asks to an adult sister to take care of something he could do better. His standards are very high, and she feels criticized. He overorganizes tasks to be done. He complains about a church committee that does not effectively address a problem.

Here is what he could do instead:

- At home, he could take on the job that he delegates to his sister, who simply cannot meet his standards. He could scratch the to-do lists for others and recognize that it does not help to set priorities for other people. He could work with his family to design new priorities that align with everyone's needs—or he could do tasks that are on only his agenda.
- In his community, he could take an active leadership role on his church board to have the satisfaction of short-term results. He could involve others who have influence. Together they could create and implement an action plan.

- At work, he could start a new short-term project to meet his need for achievement. The project might include upgrading his client list, asking more directly for feedback from key clients, retraining his staff, tightening up marketing, and starting a targeted marketing initiative.

Fulfilling Needs Is Critical to Clients

Clients cannot live a fulfilled and balanced life while their needs drive them. In fact, needs are like the dust on a diamond—they obscure the possibility of fully living our purpose and values.

Humans function better and live more satisfying lives when our whole life expresses our core values. Your clients will benefit from identifying and meeting needs in key arenas of their lives. When you support them through this process, you move them forward on the path toward fulfillment and balance.

Additional Suggestions to Help Identify and Work with Needs

Needs are something people usually meet by striving to gain something externally or by contrasting current life and desired life. We learn more about needs by comparing or noticing how well we manage external actions and opinions, which are usually outside our control.

For example, we may measure our need for approval by how often we are complimented or acknowledged publicly. When that happens frequently, our need for approval may sometimes be filled to capacity. At that point, it may no longer be a need. When it is filled, we may find that our self-esteem is strong enough to rearrange our life so that this particular need is no longer an issue.

Maslow once said that if a need were at least 60 percent met, it would set us free. Once this happens, we can put our energy into meeting a higher-order need. It is at this point that our values begin to draw our attention.

When our basic needs for a secure shelter, sufficient food, and a stable income are met, we may, as an example, meet our need to be more responsible by taking a time management class. That experience may lead us to develop the new habit of spending time with a calendar for 10 minutes each morning, which supports a need to be responsible. We probably would not prioritize every day with a calendar if we were unemployed, could not pay our rent, or were starving.

Needs tend to drive us until we understand how to drive and direct them. When we reach this point, we establish ways in our life to meet our needs with less effort and expense. This is one of the goals coaches have for clients: that their lives run more smoothly so they are free to focus more attention on higher-order aspects of their lives, such as values and purpose. We teach that needs and values can be directly related to each other; in other words, once a need is met, it can become a value that a person prioritizes and lives by, such as peace and tranquility. An underlying value can create a driving need. If people do not have peace and tranquility in their life, it will operate as a need, driving them. When the need is met, they can then hold it as a value, living from it rather than being driven by it. We say more about this in the next chapter on values.

CHAPTER 11

STEERING YOUR LIFE BY TRUE NORTH

ALIGNING VALUES, ACTIONS, AND HABITS

Values function like compass points. A compass needle points toward true north and acts as a consistent guide for mariners and travelers. Travelers rarely get lost if they have a working compass. Our values serve us in a similar way, guiding us in determining the direction of our life. When we align with our values, they help us make critical decisions. They also function as key indicators that we are out of integrity, which is evidenced by our frustration, anger, or feeling off-center.

What We Mean by Values

We have heard it said that one of the most important things in life is to decide what is most important.

Merriam-Webster's Collegiate Dictionary defines value as "something (as a principle or quality) intrinsically valuable or desirable." A thesaurus offers worth and quality as synonyms for the kinds of values we are considering here—those that are important to individuals.

Values are beliefs, qualities, or philosophies that are meaningful to individuals, so much so they are willing to shape their lives and actions to live by them. Values are important in coaching because clients' core values, or personal value systems, lead them to make certain judgments and decisions, which prompt actions that lead to results. By understanding clients' core values, we can predict their actions, perhaps even those outcomes.

A value or belief is a trust or conviction—a feeling, idea, or opinion—about a principle, standard, or aspect of life that is considered to be true, desirable, and inherently worthwhile.

Whether we are consciously aware of them, everyone has a number of personal values. Values can range from the commonplace and tactical—the belief in hard work, self-reliance, and punctuality—to more psychological values, such as concern for others, trust in others, and harmony of purpose.

Coaches often find it helpful to consider three kinds—or levels—of values:

- **The Superficial Shoulds**—These are relatively superficial values we hold that come primarily from things we think we should believe, do, or act in accordance with. These kinds of values, which are frequently unexamined, often have their origin in messages we "swallowed whole" from parents, teachers, our church, or some other authority, usually when we were young.
- **Chosen Values**—These are values we hold and attempt to uphold because they resonate with us personally. We have selected them as important to fulfill, and we act in accordance with them as consistently as possible.
- **Core Values**—These are the three to five critically important personal values we hold. When we are not living these consistently, we likely feel dissatisfied, depressed, embarrassed, and even ashamed. It is impossible to lead a fulfilling life that does not honor or that is out of alignment with our core values.

Values create energy toward their fulfillment through action and results. When we examine the lives of famous people, we often learn about important personal values that shaped their lives by guiding their actions and choices. These personal values propelled them to great achievement and success. For example, one famous actor was motivated by his commitment to social justice, which caused him to seek out powerful acting roles related to that value. A famous business CEO was motivated by the personal value that computers should be easy to use for the average person. Regardless of the unique personal values that guided their lives, it was ultimately their commitment to implementation that paved the way to their great success. Values, as determinants of our priorities, are the silent forces behind many of our actions and decisions. When we live according to our values, we are healthier and more satisfied. Research reveals that personal values are key to physicians' job satisfaction. A study of family physicians found that job satisfaction is highest among those who identify benevolence as a guiding principle in their lives. The researchers concluded that physicians who identify and adhere to their own personal values in their work are less vulnerable to burnout and could help raise the quality of care (Medical College of Wisconsin Health News, 2000).

Working With Values Is Critical to Great Coaching

These principles assist us in coaching clients around values:

- Values have power. The deepest and most powerful and centering force for an individual, business, or society is its values. When we coach at the level of values, outer circumstances can change 10 times faster and have much more sustained impact than if we merely try to change things on the surface.
- Values reflect the highest thoughts. An individual's personal values reflect the highest principles of mind and thought and may even be part of the spiritual domain. Values release tremendous potential for success, accomplishment, and happiness.
- A values-based life is a fulfilled life. When clients live in line with their values, it engenders a sense of well-being, self-respect, and self-esteem. When they live a life that violates their values, it can lead to confusion, frustration, and depression.
- Conscious work on values is critical. Unless or until clients consciously explore, distinguish, and clearly delineate their personal values or beliefs, it is impossible to orient and create a personal or professional life around them.
- Needs come first. Clients cannot live their values when they are driven by insufficiently satisfied needs. Addressing these needs takes precedence and eventually clears the path for clients to focus on and align with their values.

Both Dr. Pat and Diane worked with undergraduates and teachers to help them clarify their own values and bring the work into high schools. Strangely enough, outside education, the importance of values clarification seemed to wane. We believe this is one of the reasons why life coaching surfaced so strongly in the 21st century. Dr. Pat can distinctly remember being in a course at the University of West Georgia where he clarified his values. It was an affirming experience to illuminate why he had passion for what he did—and it explained the importance of aligning his actions with his values. In Diane's case, she combined her two key values, learning and supporting others, to create her first graduate program and course of study. For both of us, values have been a critical focus throughout our lives, and we consequently make values work a critical focus in ILCT training.

Even those who have experience with this realm of their life may not have done the challenging work of assessing whether their life and actions are in line with their values. Clients frequently come into coaching because they are experiencing a radical rift between their current external or internal way of being and their core values. They may not recognize that this issue is central to many of their challenges.

For example, consider clients who value family, but who are working at a job that requires long hours, which precludes spending much quality time with family members. If their work situation mandates the violation of a deeply held value, they will likely experience serious inner conflict. If clients value respect, yet their opinions and views are not listened to at work, their life conflicts with a value. The same is true of people who value health but do not make the effort to get regular exercise. These kinds of situations can cause clients considerable pain and confusion.

The superficial values (the "shoulds") clients hold may need to be challenged, developed, or worked through with coaching so clients do not use them as the basis for making critical decisions. Sometimes clients confuse other people's values with their own. They may have "inherited" values through family or other early influences that, when examined closely, do not truly belong and must be set aside. Also, the importance of values may shift as circumstances and priorities change.

Life coaching can help clients explore and give credence to their unique set of values at any point. Clients can be more self-directed and effective when they consciously choose which values have high priority—in other words, which ones they want to keep and live by as an adult. Clarity about values is particularly important when values come into conflict with one another. As clients work to redesign their life, they will make critical decisions based on the secure compass point—the true north—that a clear set of personal values provides.

Identifying Values

Coaching clients seek a life that has value—one that satisfies a deep and authentic longing for meaning. When they align their work and life with their core values, they find meaning and satisfy the longing. Once clients have addressed their basic needs, their strongest motivators, greatest sources of deep meaning, and their core values can become the primary drivers of their life.

Clients whose life and work are not aligned with their core values may be getting results but not thriving or experiencing full satisfaction. They may be bored, on the edge of burnout, or just living in a comfortable rut. Aligning their life with their core values releases two things: incredible creativity, and a sense of immense satisfaction and well-being. When these are released, their potential for success is maximized.

Core Values Are Those We Naturally Want to Act On

Core values are those qualities that have intrinsic worth for an individual. When our behavior is aligned with our most deeply held values, our actions are desirable and worthy of esteem for their own sake.

Take, for example, the value of integrity. How do you know someone has integrity? If people hold integrity as a core value, they just naturally demonstrate it—right? And you naturally recognize it? If clients hold the core value of service to others, for example, helping someone in need is an action they will naturally take because they believe it is desirable and worthy. It will feel good to clients to honor that value by acting on it and making more of their life consistent with it.

Our set of values is unique to each of us. We may not expect others to do what we do or derive the same sense of self-worth from it. The coach must suspend judgment about others' values and help clients identify and articulate them. The values then become compass points—the true north—for directing clients' life journey and choices.

Coaching around values helps clients make frequent course corrections, both big and small. This is like an airplane that is off course about 90 percent of the time, arriving at its destination through a series of course corrections, some minor and others major, due to weather, traffic, or turbulence.

It is our belief that most people look to others too much for validation and lack sufficient tools for looking within to access inner validation. They do not know how to access or articulate their values. Clients may come into coaching with a sense they are off course. Working with values gets them back on track.

We believe people naturally act in accordance with their values whenever they have the opportunity. But they can only do that when they are familiar with their values and consciously make choices based on values.

Knowing and Articulating Values

The benefit in supporting clients to know and articulate their values is so they create more opportunities to honor themselves, increase their satisfaction and sense of meaning and worth, and find fulfillment. The coaching relationship supports clients in designing their life to maximize opportunities to live values fully. Assist clients to find the language they need to describe their values in compelling terms. It is critical for clients to know what they stand for before starting to set goals around values and before working on life design.

IDENTIFYING CORE VALUES

Most of us have three to five core values that are abiding. They may have been with us since childhood. We generally trust they will continue to be our core values for many years. Identifying these core values through a variety of exercises can help clients find inspiration.

The following values exercises are those we use with clients. We recommend clients create a list of three to five items for each exercise. Then, putting all the work together, they cross out any repeated items and select the words that have the most resonance. Like a tuning fork, they will be able to feel an internal ring—like a vibration on a subtle level—when they say each of those words aloud. When they imagine living those values, the thought should bring them a great sense of satisfaction and joy. If it does not, they may be listing superficial values, what they have been told they should do, believe, or value— not their own core values. If this is the case, they need to start again. Living out a list of "shoulds" does not elicit a sense of joy and satisfaction.

You can choose from any of the following exercises with your clients. Coaches generally have preferences for which exercises work best depending on the clients. Values work is generally not done in just one session. Sometimes it is useful to give clients several exercises over several sessions as different means for identifying their values. Diane prefers to use a combination of Exercise 11.3 and Exercise 11.1, so her clients have both a cognitive and experiential path for identifying values. She finds this works well with very intellectual clients who are often guided more by what they think their values should be, given their roles or work. Dr. Pat frequently starts with Exercise 11.2 because he likes to go back to the client's formative years when values began to appear.

EXERCISE 11.1

Values Exercise 1

Identify your values from the list below, which is drawn from the work of researchers and experts in motivation. Read through the examples and circle 10 or more words to which you are drawn or add your own. Select those that are most important to you as guides for how you act or as components of a values-oriented life. Feel free to add any values of your own to this list. Then use Exercises 11.2–11.4 below to whittle your list down to three to five core values.

From reviewing various writings on values, we believe that generally values are drawn from these three major areas of our lives:

- **Experiencing**: Values that are fulfilled through what you experience, what comes to you and how you respond, acting on the world outside of you, and achieving. Examples of experiencing: discovering, questing, catalyzing, achieving mastery or excellence, teaching, entertaining, communicating, appreciating what is, playing sports, joining with others, inspiring others, leading others, showing expertise, sensing fully, participating, exploring, guiding, nurturing, being a model, dancing, experiencing pleasure, doing, and acting with speed.
- **Creating**: Values that are fulfilled through what we bring into existence through our unique selves. Examples of creating: clarifying, beautifying, innovating, ordering, creating, generating symmetry, ideas, discipline, novelty, originality, intuition, designing, playing, and architecting.
- **Being**: Values that are fulfilled through our attitudes, mind-sets, emotions, and the qualities of our character. Examples of being: integrity, joy, love, peace, truth, uniqueness, loyalty, empathy, spirituality, authenticity, godliness, flow, energy, transcendence, and unity.

EXERCISE 11.2

Values Exercise 2

Think back to the qualities you had as a child. List five to 10 qualities that were true of you between the ages of six and 12.

You have been naturally drawn toward certain things ever since you were a child. You may have been naturally creative or thoughtful, or a lover of nature or beauty. You may have been a natural helper of others or may have been drawn to things that were new or different. Or perhaps you were an experimenter or explorer. These qualities may be among your core values or may be clues to help you identify them.

Sit down and quickly list five to 10 of these qualities right now. Circle the qualities that are still a part of your life and come naturally. Include anything you would be and do if your work, time, and life supported you in fulfilling them. Also include things that people cannot stop you from doing.

EXERCISE 11.3

Values Exercise 3

Make a list of 10 to 12 times in the past two to five years when you were being and doing your absolute best. These are times when you felt you were living your best self—living your values.

(One of the exercises in Chapter 8 asks clients to make a list of times in their life when they were "on purpose." You may want to use that exercise as a jumping-off point by having clients ask, for each of those times, "What values was I displaying there?" Ask clients to write a word or two indicating the value that was being fulfilled in each example.)

EXERCISE 11.4

Values Exercise 4

Ask three people who know you well to name your values. Sometimes our values are more obvious to others than they are to us. Our values show up, no matter what. Because our values are a key driving force, they show up in the decisions we make, the work we choose, and the things that bring us pleasure (and pain when we disregard our values).

Write down what you hear from these three people. Ask questions for clarity, but mainly just listen. Do not argue with what you hear—treat it as a gift and a potential window into your true self.

LIVING YOUR VALUES

Once clients identify core values, they will benefit from exploring the extent to which they inform their life. This exploration can create "a-ha" experiences as clients make deeper connections between their core self and the ways in which their life is and is not an expression of these values. This exploration also opens the door to many coaching opportunities because it can reveal gaps between a client's actual and ideal life.

The following exercises are designed to support clients in exploring ways to live their values.

Live Your Values: Three Exercises

EXERCISE 11.5

Reflect on Your Values and Your Life for a Week
Take a week to find out to what extent you are living out your core values. Track how you are spending your time. Each time you participate in something that gives you a full sense of satisfaction, record it on your values list. At the end of the week, you hopefully will have listed six or more examples under each core value.

When you have designed your life to be aligned with your values, the possibility for fulfillment is maximized. This translates as expressing your values through choices and behaviors daily. Living your values is not a thing you save for weekends or vacations. When your life is consistently aligned with your values, you are intensely creative, and you experience immense satisfaction and well-being.

EXERCISE 11.6

Get Clear About Your Top Three to Five Values
Write them down and hang them on your bathroom mirror. Your values are the habits of your heart. You can only live your values if you are clear about

what they are and conscious of them every day. When you clearly identify your core values, you will feel an immense sense of relief at articulating what is most important to you.

EXERCISE 11.7

Pick One Goal that Allows You to Demonstrate One of Your Values
Create a goal that will allow you to measure and observe how well you demonstrate one of your core values through acting on it. Identify blocks you need to eliminate to free your energy to live the value.

Case Example

A client explored her core values of creativity and living with passion. When she looked at her life, she saw her needs for structure and detail were getting in the way of living from those two values. She set a goal of turning first to her intuition when she was making decisions. Before she analyzed her situation and put a structure in place for solving a problem, she asked herself, "What do I intuitively believe is the right answer or approach here?" She held herself accountable for doing this every time she had a business or personal problem to solve during a 30-day period. She wrote down her intuitive insights to make them concrete. Then she let herself use other analytical skills.

As a result of this process, she found that her decision making was easier and more efficient. Her solutions were more creative because she was living her values as she worked and consequently allowing herself to thrive. Her solutions were also more satisfying and more an expression of her core self. The actual solution was more in line with her deepest desires because she listened to herself at a deeper level and accessed a deeper level of knowing.

Creating New Opportunities for Living from Your Values

A key principle that coaches bring to their work with clients is: look to yourself, not to the outside world, for satisfaction—another reminder of why we call this coaching from the inside out. Not all opportunities are created equal. Sometimes current projects or clients will not allow you to fully live your core values; you will thrive when living your values, but do not do it because you expect to be rewarded by others. The reward is your thriving.

Example: An advertising client who had a core value of creativity was frustrated at work. He would create and present eight terrific ad options to his clients, yet they consistently chose the least creative option. He learned that the real joy was in the creation itself. As a result, he quit overdelivering to clients who could not appreciate this aspect of his creativity and eliminated his own disappointment in their lack of discrimination. Then he created a portfolio of all the extra jewels they did not select and used them to market outside his current client base to more creative companies.

Aligning Life and Work Goals with Core Values

Many clients bring desires for greater life balance to coaching. Often clients' core values are out of alignment in their work. It can seem difficult to align values with work if it seems their organization does not support this. This can be particularly true if clients work in a large, bureaucratic corporation. Here are some exercises to support clients in aligning their life and work goals with their core values.

EXERCISE 11.8

Goals

1. Make a list of your short-term goals for the next 60 to 90 days. Then make a list of your long-term goals for the next two to five years. Examine these lists closely. For each of the goals listed, assess whether you can really live out your core values as you meet these goals. You may need to change the goals themselves, or you may need to change your plans for attaining them.

   Say you are building a business that requires a great deal of solo work yet have a core value of being a close friend. You may need to reprioritize in order to stay connected with friends, or you might get your friends involved in your business by creating a mastermind group (Greenstreet, 2004). A mastermind group creates a synergy of energy, commitment, and creativity as group members meet to support one another in their desires and intentions. The concept was formally introduced by Napoleon Hill (1937/1966) in his timeless classic *Think and Grow Rich*. He wrote about the mastermind principle as "the coordination of knowledge and effort of two or more people who work toward a definite purpose in the spirit of harmony."

2. For each of your three to five core values, create a list of ways you can live them regularly. Brainstorm 8 to 10 ways, both small and large, that you can live out your core values daily, weekly, and monthly. These are your "values rules of the road," so to speak. It's not enough to have only a few opportunities to live out your values each month. A life that allows you to thrive is one where you live out your core values daily. When this happens, you'll see the result—your energy is higher, your creativity flows, and your work and life feel almost effortless.

3. Examine your current week. Where are each of your values being expressed? Look at your weekly calendar. Circle the places where you found you were living out a value. Find ways to increase those activities during your week. For the value of creativity, for example, you might do the following:

   - Get outside every day. Connect with nature. Notice what's around you.
   - Keep a daily journal. Write for 20 minutes every morning.
   - Keep flowers, greenery, and other living things around you.
   - Change the things around your desk so that you are stimulated by what you look at as you work. Get a fountain in the proximity of your desk.

4. Eliminate things that block you from living out of a core value. Take another look at your weekly planner. Draw a square around the activities that are "blockers" for you—activities that act as obstacles to you living your core values. You may want to delegate these or to let them go.

5. Always keep your values list in front of you. Write your values on a sticky note that you post on each day of your planner. Look for opportunities for fulfilling your values as you get calls, consider projects, and do your work. Remember: a life in which you thrive is one in which you live out of your values. Redesigning your life to make that possible brings endless rewards.

ARE VALUES DRIVEN BY PLEASURE OR PAIN?

When clients have identified their top values, they will be able to recognize their significance and ability to live through them or honor them more consciously in their daily life. In short, they can lead clients to a new perspective on what they will allow in their life from this point forward and what they will not.

Values work can also take clients to a different place with a different perspective. A key piece in this shift in perspective comes when clients ask themselves: "Is this value driven by pain or pleasure?" The odds are high that all the clients' values provide one type of benefit. Another valuable question for clients is: "Is this a value that helps me maximize pleasure and enjoyment, or does it help me avoid pain or penalty?" A value driven by pleasure tends to increase motivation and joy when living it. A value driven by avoidance of pain suggests clients are less focused in present time and are directing attention toward the future. Sometimes this means clients are living lower on the hierarchy of needs than is desirable and fulfilling. This may indicate additional work is needed so clients can explore what is being avoided.

Let us look at a concrete example with the value of wellness. One person may live this value by having a weekly or monthly massage. However, if a chronic pain condition is the motivating factor, the massage may be a pain-driven value activity that serves to alleviate or prevent pain. In contrast, if a person in great physical condition elects to have regularly scheduled massages for the sheer joy of it, massage would be a pleasure-driven value. We are not saying that pain-driven values are not important or should not be central to clients. The coach needs to look for patterns in clients' values and encourage clients to reflect on them. Values work brings to consciousness clients' values that might otherwise be out of their awareness. Once clients are conscious of them, values act as a true north point of a compass, guiding clients in a direction that makes their life journey less haphazard and more purposeful.

For each of the values clients have identified, have them ask themselves: "If I do not get to live through a pleasure-driven value for a week or month, will I feel the loss of a good experience? If I fail to live through or honor a pain-driven value, will I notice anything more than a sense of regret?"

The question to examine with clients is, "Do I want to have choice about whether my values are driven by pain or pleasure?" If they do want to have choice, they have an opportunity to implement their preference regarding the kind of values they want to make primary.

We seldom find clients with all top five values driven by pain. Asking clients to reflect on values driven by pleasure versus pain is an important way of deepening their understanding about their choices and their life.

HELPFUL HABITS

Our habits are really our values in action. When we look at our habits, we discover the attitudes and mind-sets that drive our life—our POP or personal operating program. One way to create more fulfillment is to create habits that bring health, joy, and satisfaction. On the basis of the values work in this chapter, you can encourage clients to identify three to five helpful habits (daily or weekly) they can commit to implementing in the next 10 weeks.

We ask clients to examine their daily calendar to compare the reality of how they spend their time as compared with the values they have articulated. For example, a busy executive might say he values family and personal balance. Yet his calendar shows only one evening at home eating dinner with his family, four evenings traveling out of state, and no play or exercise time. He also reports that he takes work home with him, and answers emails 20 hours of the day.

Once clients uncover their values, we ask them to begin blocking time in their calendar that reflects their values. The clients make friends with their calendar by blocking in daily self-care, date nights with their spouses, or children's sports games. There is an old law that work seems to expand to the time available. Committing a values-directed activity to a calendar is a way in which clients hold themselves accountable for acting in accordance with their values. Smart phones are modern-day conveniences that support this practice.

We suggest clients take charge of their schedules instead of being controlled by them. In the above example, the client decided to not answer work messages after 8 p.m., which allowed him to have uninterrupted time with his children and wife in the evening. While 8 p.m. sounded late to his coach, it was a radical departure from being on call 24/7 to his phone's text-messaging system. The next radical departure for this client took place when he agreed to his coach's request to leave his computer home when he went on vacation.

DEVELOPING NEW VALUES

Sometimes we find ourselves at a time in life when we desire to adopt new core values. We may be moving a value up in importance, for example. This often occurs in midlife when a value such as spirituality, which may have been important but not on the top-five list, begins to take on more importance. Values also shift when a client is emerging into a new level of consciousness (relating to Kegan's work on levels of consciousness presented in Chapter 3). At these times, certain values become more central and others peripheral.

To assist clients in developing a new value, we suggest they first go back and examine values that have been powerful and life-shaping. Ask clients to think about two to five values that have shaped their life, the specific ways in which these values have benefited them, and the ways in which they were reflected in their choices, actions, and daily habits.

Then ask the clients to review a list of values, such as those included earlier in this chapter, and to consider which one or two new values they would like to implement in their life. Ask them to create a definition for each value, as well as identify people in their life who demonstrate each value. These people can be personal acquaintances, people in the public view, or historical figures.

Once an operational definition of each new value has been created, the work can get very specific as far as the actions they might take in their life to implement each of these values. Ask the clients to be very specific, and then come up with a specific action plan (with specific events, dates, and so on) to implement each of these values in daily life. Make sure the plan has a review process to evaluate every few months. Encourage clients to make values, including new values, the cornerstone of their life, contemplating them deeply and ensuring a values-focused life.

One additional step can be useful. Living according to one's values can have both benefits and potential costs—witness the price that Gandhi and Dr. Martin Luther King Jr. paid for living out their values. Ask your clients to reflect on how some of their past life-changing decisions might be made now through the lens of values that currently have a high priority. What would the cost of these decisions be? What would be gained or lost?

We have shared in this chapter how values are crucial to our view of successful life coaching. Values work is at the heart of coaching from the inside out. It allows clients to explore the depth of change possible for them and to avoid superficial changes or simple problem solving. Clients who can articulate their values find fulfillment in the integrity of life from the inside and outside.

CHAPTER 12

WALK THE TALK

In previous "Coaching from the Inside Out" chapters, we explored life purpose and the vision of fulfillment and satisfaction in each life area. We discussed how needs and values fit with the life clients want to create. This chapter focuses on what it takes to create that life by taking actions that are aligned with the clients' vision and values. We call this alignment integrity. Clients who are serious about creating that life need to "walk their talk." In other words, they need to do what it takes to turn their vision of a fulfilling life into a reality. If they do not act on their vision, it is just a wish—a dream.

PERSONAL INTEGRITY

Several years ago, two friends experienced a life event that illustrated the essence of integrity and alignment, demonstrating what happens when these qualities are lacking. The couple bought a house and had been living in it for about three months. It was a very old house that was situated on a hill. When they bought the house, the seller gave them a packet of information from an engineering firm that had inspected the house to determine whether the foundation was firm, and the walls were in alignment. The firm said that the house had architectural integrity—in other words, that the foundation was firm, the walls were square, and the basement did not require any foundational supports.

Every room in the house was wallpapered, some with costly and expensive wallpaper that did not suit our friends' tastes. As they began to steam off the wallpaper, they discovered cracks in the walls. Almost every corner had big fissures that expanded as spring came. As the spring rains hit, two doors went out of alignment.

Despite the engineering firm's written report, the house was obviously not in good shape. When our friends contacted the seller, she refused to take responsibility for the cracks, saying she was not aware of them and had believed the engineering firm's report to be accurate.

Was this seller displaying integrity? If so, why was every room wallpapered?

Good fences make good neighbors.

Our friends investigated the situation with the engineering firm and learned that two pages from the back of the firm's report were missing. These missing pages contained an account of the existing cracks, as well as a record of the fact that the hillside had started to slip. The report recommended that another engineering survey be done in a year; otherwise, the house's structural integrity might be in jeopardy.

—Robert Frost, "Mending Wall"

Our friends learned a major lesson about integrity: both in architecture and in relationships, integrity is essential.

Sometimes we consider that taking action only counts if the gesture is grand. The small daily actions are equally critical because they create the foundation for something big to happen. Every day, we create our vision by consistently acting in ways that are aligned with our vision and our goals. If we fail to create our vision by acting in ways that are inconsistent with our vision and goals, we get off track. Small habitual actions affect integrity. As the father of one of our ILCT participants said, "Integrity is the first chapter of the book of wisdom."

To paraphrase one of our colleagues, Madelyn Griffith-Haney, someone has personal integrity when what they do, who they are, what they say, what they feel, and what they think all come from the same place.

In recent years, we have seen scandals in formerly respected U.S. companies, such as Enron, where leaders lost their integrity at work. Many people deny the implications of their actions and their impact on integrity, as did the Mayflower Madam, who said, "I ran the wrong kind of business, but I did it with integrity" (Christy, 1986). Having personal integrity means taking responsibility for the whole. As the U.S. banking collapse has shown, integrity is more difficult to restore once it has been lost.

Integrity is important enough for leadership and life to include in the models and assessments of emotional intelligence. In the 360-degree assessment, the Emotional Competence Inventory, published by the Hay Group, integrity is described as the competence titled transparency. Cynthia Cooper is a contemporary example of integrity: she stood up and reported unethical business practices at WorldCom. Sherron Watkins was the whistle blower whose integrity and courage led to the recognition of the fraudulent business practices at Enron. Both women risked their work lives to live up to their personal integrity.

PISA: A TOWER AND ITS INTEGRITY

Watching a house, a city, or a life collapse is an emotionally challenging experience. Take, for example, the Italian engineers who tried to save what is known as the Leaning Tower of Pisa. According to *Discover* magazine (Kunzig, 2000), work on the tower began Aug. 9, 1173. The builders, contractors, engineers, and architects did not plan for it to lean. The tower was designed as an upright structure and was expected to point plumb starward.

However, tilting became a problem—a sudden and immediate problem. For centuries, the 177-foot-tall Tower of Pisa has looked as though it is about to topple. The combined weight of the marble stones has pressed downward into the soft, silted soils, squeezing water from the clay and bulging into the dense sand. The tower teetered on the extreme edge of disaster for 800 years. All 32 million pounds of marble constantly verged on collapse. Its 5.3-degree tilt is startling, even shocking—a full 15 feet out of plumb.

Computer models proved that the tower was going to fall—sooner, rather than later—and a committee of engineers and scientists set about to right the tilting tourist trap. Thanks to some high-tech engineering, the tower was stabilized during the decade between 1991 and 2001. Engineers removed bits of clay from beneath the tower through long, thin pipes at a rate of a shovelful or two a day. By removing these small amounts from the right places, they were able to stabilize the tower for at least another 300 years.

Of course, it still leans a little, thereby preserving the tourist trade for the town and the surrounding region. This is by design. Bringing the tower into a perfectly upright position would kill the sale of thousands of ceramic replicas.

To correct the Pisa tilt, three important processes were inaugurated: extraction, replacement, and restraints. First, the bad soil was extracted. Then a solid foundation replaced the weak soil. Finally, steel cables were added to hug the structure to assure it would remain in place.

These same three elements apply to life coaching:

- To regain integrity, there may be things we need to extract—habits, people, work, and things to which we are attached.

- A process of replacement is needed, and a solid foundation must be built—new habits, actions aligned with life purpose, and perhaps new people and practices that will facilitate and support solid choices.
- Restraints need to be applied consistently. The steel cables that hug the tower's structure and keep its true function are analogous to the boundaries we set—the standards to which we hold ourselves accountable, the rules and guidelines by which we live, our spiritual practices and disciplines, and the ways we hold ourselves to the life design we create.

In coaching and in life, staying aligned and true to those things that are most valuable to us is important. We get off course when we are not aligned.

SIMPLE RULES FOR CREATING PERSONAL INTEGRITY

In recent years, writers have popularized the simple life rules that indigenous cultures practice that preserve the integrity of individuals and thereby the community. Coaches use these as illustrations of principles and practices that create and maintain integrity.

Don Miguel Ruiz identified four Toltec practices that he called "a guide to personal freedom" (1998). These agreements are four simple personal rules that foster integrity:

1. Be impeccable with your word.
2. Do not take anything personally. Nothing others say and do happens because of you.
3. Do not make assumptions.
4. Always do your best. Recognize that your best is going to change from moment to moment.

Joan Borysenko attributed four guiding rules for life to Angeles Arrien, who may have derived them from Shaman Pete Ketchum's work:

1. Show up.
2. Pay attention.
3. Tell the truth.
4. Don't be attached to the results (Borysenko, 1994, p. 96).

Another example of the importance of integrity comes from Rotary International's four-way test, a guide for member conduct utilized since 1932 (Rotary International, n.d.). Its simple steps may assist the coaching community not only to practice ethically but live with integrity. The four-way test provides a concise and easy reminder of the intent to live with integrity. Rotary members receive a wallet card with the test on it as a constant reminder to check their integrity.

The Four-Way Test of the Things We Say and Do, from Rotary International

1. Is it the truth?
2. Is it fair to all concerned?
3. Will it build good will and better friendships?
4. Will it be beneficial to all concerned?

Taking a stand for one's integrity can be a cornerstone of a person's leadership and reputation. Leonard Roberts took over the CEO role at Arby's at a time when this fast-food franchise chain was struggling financially. He promised his franchisees more support with their services and finances and was able to turn Arby's around. However, Arby's owner threatened to withhold bonuses for Roberts's staff and not to give promised help to Arby's franchisees, and Roberts resigned from the board in protest. He was eventually fired as CEO. He later became the CEO at Shoney's and was pushed out as head of that chain again because of a stand he took based on his values. Later he became the CEO at Tandy Corp because of his well-known reputation for integrity. "You cannot maintain your integrity 90 percent and be a leader . . . It's got to be 100 percent" (National Institute of Business Management, 2006, p. 1). We do not know whether Roberts is a Rotarian, but he certainly modeled the four-way test. Another example is investor and philanthropist Warren Buffett. In the biography *The Snowball: Warren Buffett and the Business of Life*, Alice Schroeder describes Buffett's sound advice on emphasizing personal integrity in life and business. Buffett says integrity is the most important leadership trait.

Because of the importance of integrity to coaching, coaches need many ways of asking clients to consider the alignment of their actions with their goals and visions. Here we offer some of the exercises we frequently use with clients.

EXERCISE 12.1

Personal Journal Questions

The following exercise can be useful in early explorations of integrity. Using journaling, ask clients to reflect on integrity as they currently experience it.

- What is your definition of personal integrity?
- What are the clues (physical, emotional, intellectual, spiritual) you use to notice when you are in integrity?
- What are the clues you use to notice when you are not in integrity?
- What are the two or three circumstances or situations that most frequently move you out of alignment? When your behavior does not match your words or your promises, you are out of alignment with your personal integrity.

Identify three to five places in your life where you are currently out of alignment, lacking sufficient integrity for yourself. For each one, identify the action you need to take to get back in alignment (e.g., "I committed to complete X by Y date. It is beyond that time, and I am only halfway through").

I am without integrity in . . .	What I need to do is . . .
1. _____	1. _____
2. _____	2. _____
3. _____	3. _____
4. _____	4. _____
5. _____	5. _____

Do any of these examples identify the ways you break your personal rules (see below)?

What does each one cost you? Name five personal rules you want to live by that will help you create the life you want and walk your talk (not "shoulds," but "I want tos"). What "personal rules for life" can you create that will help you live each day with integrity? What actions will align you with your five personal rules?

1. _____	1. _____
2. _____	2. _____
3. _____	3. _____
4. _____	4. _____
5. _____	5. _____

Rule	Action to take
1. _____	1. _____
2. _____	2. _____
3. _____	3. _____
4. _____	4. _____
5. _____	5. _____

EXERCISE 12.2

The Impact of Loose Ends

Many coaches and coaching articles describe the importance of eliminating clutter from clients' lives. Clutter is a distraction and an energy drainer. Integrity—a sense of wholeness—also comes from completing things, from tying up loose ends.

How many loose ends do you have in your life? List below the top 20 things, both big and small, that you need to get closure on. What is incomplete or unfinished in any area of your life—finances, home, relationships, work, and so on?

1. _____

2. _____

3. _____

4. _____

5. _____

6. _____

7. _____

8. _____

9. _____

10. _____

What do you notice about your list? Do the incomplete items seem to be concentrated in any one area? How do these gaps direct you toward the actions you need to take?

THE IMPACT OF LOOSE ENDS

Back in the 1970s, Werner Erhard popularized the phrase, "Get complete" (Erhard, 2000). He may have borrowed the idea from Fritz Perls (1969), the father of gestalt therapy, who made completing unfinished business the cornerstone of his therapeutic approach. Getting complete and finishing unfinished business are useful concepts for coaches and their clients. To achieve fulfillment, our clients may need to get complete with any number of things in their life:

- The past—by getting over it, letting it go, honoring its lessons or handling what needs to be handled.
- People—by having courageous conversations.
- Projects—by finishing them, closing them down, or setting dates for completion.

- Home—by achieving closure on where and how they want to live, by taking action or letting it go (no pining or whining).
- Work—by finishing the essential.

Coaching borrows the term incompletion from football, where an incompletion occurs when a receiver does not reach the ball. Metaphorically, clients have examples in life of incompletions, where something gets dropped and remains unfinished. In life, these loose ends operate like mental clutter: they are distracting and de-energizing. These are the things we put off and avoid finishing. They may be projects or difficult conversations—anything unfinished that stays in our awareness. Having too many incompletions keeps us hovering between what we committed to in the past, feel we should do in the present, and want to do in the future. We cannot be fully present or fully focused when incompletions immobilize us.

What actions can we take to address incompletions? As Dr. Pat often says, "Do it, delegate it, dump it, or delay it!" Stated more eloquently we have four options:

- Plan for it. Create a plan for completing it, establishing a timetable and due date, and delegating as needed.
- Let it go. Acknowledge that although we once made a commitment, we are withdrawing it. If we choose this option, we must have certain conversations (with ourselves or whoever else is involved) to officially terminate the commitment.
- Get busy and complete it now.
- Create and implement workable systems so that incompletions like this do not pile up again.

SETTING PERSONAL STANDARDS: A WORKABLE SYSTEM

A standard is a criterion by which something is judged. People set and hold standards in areas in which it is important to create consistency. Standards are an acknowledged measure of qualitative value—a criterion against which people judge behaviors, worth, or merit. Setting standards is a practice that is widely recognized and employed because it creates a benchmark for excellence that, if made public, carries authority. People commonly speak of standard reference books, like *The Merriam-Webster Dictionary*. Standards describe what is basically accepted, such as the gold standard against which we measure economic stability. Coaches encourage clients to examine and set personal standards for their behavior to ensure that choices and behaviors live up to what clients really want. In health care, quality is measured by "evidence-based best practices."

Personal standards are the principles we choose to live by—the rules we set for ourselves that we choose to obey. They are not the rules that others set for us. We hold ourselves accountable to our personal standards. They are freely chosen, unlike "shoulds." One reason people lose integrity is that they have not examined their personal standards and adjusted them to reflect current goals and desires.

This is where Exercise 12.1, Personal Journal Questions from earlier in this chapter comes into play. When we work with our personal standards and rules, we examine what we willingly hold ourselves accountable for. From time to time, we need to reexamine, update, and adjust our standards. Breakdowns in our satisfaction can be caused by standards that no longer work. Here is an example:

> In her many years of coaching, Diane did a variety of coaching and consulting work in organizations. Diversity is a strong value for her. Back in the 1980s, she set a standard of not allowing herself to participate in any conversation where someone was being stereotyped or where racism or sexism was present. That standard allowed her to disengage from the conversation.
>
> A few years later, she realized that disengaging from such a conversation was not enough—she needed to speak up. She raised her standards and expectations for herself. When she found herself in that kind of conversation, she implemented her new, higher standard by speaking up and saying, "I can't participate in this conversation and here's why," and requesting that the conversation cease.

Certain risks may be associated with the higher standards we set. If we decide not to participate in any conversations where gossip takes place, we may risk losing some friends. However, the value of setting higher standards is in preserving our integrity.

We believe that personal standards are the mechanism through which we implement our values moment by moment. When our standards are serving us and working well, they allow us to complete things and to maintain our integrity.

One way to support clients to discover and set effective personal standards is to use their list of core values (discussed in Chapter 11) and have them ask themselves, for each one: "What standard must be in place so I can live out that value, as my life is organized right now?"

EXERCISE 12.3

Values and Standards

You can use the two-column chart below with clients to help process this question. First, ask them to fill in the blanks in Column 1 with their core values. Then, for each item, ask them to identify a key standard they commit to meeting so they can be in integrity with their values, and write it in Column 2.

Column 1 I am a person who . . . (fill in values)	Column 2 And so I must choose to . . . (fill in standards)
1. _____	1. _____
2. _____	2. _____
3. _____	3. _____
4. _____	4. _____
5. _____	5. _____
6. _____	6. _____
7. _____	7. _____
8. _____	8. _____
9. _____	9. _____
10. _____	10. _____

Consider the following example. What standards would you help this client set in Column 2 so he or she can be in integrity?

Column 1
I am a person who . . .
(fill in values)

Column 2
And so I must choose to . . .
(fill in standards)

1. Respects others
2. Cares for my friends

3. Is honest
4. Maintains good finances

5. Shows love for my family

1. Listen and not interrupt
2. Initiate contact, be available, ask how I can help in difficult times
3. Tell the truth—but not brutally
4. Limit my debt; keep good records
5. Be cautious in overpromising at work, which impacts my available time and energy; when I come home from an on-site coaching session, greet my spouse with a kiss before I start work again; give each other a great hug every day—at least six seconds; write a love letter to each other monthly; when out of town, e-mail every morning and evening, sending a note of appreciation and love

Sometimes when clients work through this exercise, they find it challenging because the second column asks them to consider what they must choose. If coaches hear clients commonly saying, "I can't," clients need to recognize that saying "I can't" is fundamentally usually saying, "I choose not to." Rephrasing in this way assists clients in become more aware of personal accountability for their actions and recognizing that most things in life really come from their choices. Obviously, there are some things that clients really cannot do: a 5′4″ 50-year-old woman probably cannot train for the Women's

National Basketball Association. But she could get into a local senior basketball league if she chose to.

EXERCISE 12.4

Life Is in the Details

Coaching is, in part, about the big picture—clients' vision, values, and goals. But the big picture hinges on the small picture—the day-to-day choices and actions that either support the big picture or do not.

If you want to get real insight into a person, observe in detail how she performs the simplest, smallest activities of daily life. A person who keeps a neat closet is also likely to be well organized at work. The person who supports human rights organizations is likely to give up her seat on the bus for an elderly person. The person who exercises regularly is more likely to pay close attention to what he eats. In a way, small behaviors provide an imprint of the entire person, just as the chromosomes of a single cell provide the blueprint for an entire human.

We coach clients to reflect and become aware of their processes and choices, to develop the practice of taking time each day to observe themselves and their habits. That awareness can lead to more thoughtful choices that bring life into greater alignment with their values. Small choices add up to big results. Moment-to-moment choices are the building blocks of momentous results.

One of our favorite exercises from *Human Being* (Ellis & Lankowitz, 1996) asks the client to examine an everyday routine activity to explore how it reflects the client's values and creates or limits integrity. The following example, from a student, concerns the daily task of doing dishes:

1. My routine activity is: I let the dishes pile up in the sink after dinner and only wash them when the sink is full.
2. What this reveals about how I approach other aspects of my life is: When there is something to do that I don't enjoy doing, I don't make myself do it until I must. I let things pile up. And then I get frustrated because all of a sudden, I have a lot of time-consuming things to do that aren't fun or enjoyable.
3. Identify a simple related behavior that you can and will commit to change immediately—one that might pave the way for larger changes

in the future. I will start doing the dishes before the evening is over. And I will commit to starting in on unpleasant tasks before they pile up on me. I will also look for ways to make things like doing the dishes fun. I can play music, dance while I do them, and stop thinking about them as a chore.

EXERCISE 12.5

Making and Keeping Promises

Our commitments, including our habits, help us identify how we live our values. This is how it seems to us from the inside. Outside of us, those who know us understand us through what we say. They hear us make promises and state our intentions and commitments. What we say to others defines our core values. Consequently, we can really know ourselves by paying attention to the commitments we make and the commitments we avoid making.

Our words and our behaviors must be aligned for us to have integrity. We have two ways of going about that: we can align what we do with what we say, or we can align what we say with what we do. Alignment of words and behaviors brings with it the experience of freedom and a sense of comfort. When there are no broken promises to distract us, we live cleanly and truthfully. We have no one or nothing to avoid because of having reneged on a commitment.

If clients tend to be reluctant to make commitments, or tend to make promises and break them, you can recommend that they put into practice some of the following strategies to help them keep promises and consequently maintain integrity.

- When you make promises, make them challenging and realistic. Effective promises avoid being too extreme in either direction; they commit you to doing enough but not too much. A challenging promise asks you to stretch to your potential but does not set you up to fail.
- When you break a promise, use it as a learning opportunity. It provides feedback—results to learn from. Avoid punishing yourself unnecessarily. Take the learning and make more effective promises next time. We suggest examining the intentions behind the broken promises. Were they in your best interest? Were they in the best interest of the other persons? Was the promise the right one to make in this situation? We believe that

clients who break promises can benefit from making amends—through apologies, conversations, or other acts of contrition. Making amends is a core precept of Alcoholics Anonymous. After a member has been sober for some time and has a strong footing in the program, they are asked to survey past relationships and become willing to make amends. If nobody will be hurt by such an amend, they are encouraged to do so whether it's accepted by the person they approach or not, as part of adopting a responsible way of living.

- When others break promises to you, help them recognize the learning opportunity. Hold a courageous conversation with them, but do not harbor resentment.

- Before you commit, explore the consequences of making and keeping the promises you are considering. Try mental rehearsal. Look especially for unintended consequences. Think about the systems these promises and actions will touch and identify how these promises may precipitate other actions as reactions, both positive and potentially negative.

- Fernando Flores (Spinosa, Flores, & Dreyfus, 1997) developed a useful way of looking at commitments, called the Cycle of the Promise. It invites people working together to look at the full cycle of a promise, from the request to the agreement that fulfills the request. Flores stressed the need for clear communication and for specific times to allow for clear and honest renegotiation when any breakdown, as he called it, occurs. People who promise or who receive others' promises can expect breakdowns. This is part of life. How we handle them, on the other hand, is the measure of who we are. When you experience a breakdown that jeopardizes your commitment, talk to others early on, perhaps even when you anticipate the breakdown. This allows for renegotiation and gets you back on track.

- When you make a commitment, put it in writing on a list so that you remember it. E-mail can be helpful in this regard. If you are someone who dislikes details, developing a specific action plan for how you will accomplish the promise may be necessary to keep your commitment on track. Keep a written list of your promises for a month, like a to-do list of your major commitments. Review the promises daily and record your progress. This chart can be used to explore with your coach patterns of unanticipated breakdowns. These may require you to develop new systems or habits.

- Really big promises in human life usually are accompanied by a ceremony or ritual. Think about marriages, bar mitzvahs, and other kinds of big promises that we make to others. Often these take place in public, and we create ceremonies to honor them. Many indigenous or native cultures have ceremonies for life's promises. Consider developing a ritual or ceremony to accompany your promise. For an entrepreneur, this may, for example, be a ceremony to honor the bonuses that follow an excellent business year.

This chapter has focused on how integrity emerges from the alignment between what we say and what we do. As we have emphasized in all Coaching from the Inside Out chapters, we believe that coaches' work is to help clients connect head and heart. As someone said, the longest distance we ever go is the 12 inches between our head and our heart. Coaches become models of integrity when clients are doing this work. Both coaches and clients need to pay exquisite attention to walking their talk.

CHAPTER 13

PLAY FULL OUT

Peter Block (1999) was right when he said, "If you can't say 'no,' your 'yesses' don't mean a thing." Imagine what a waste it would be to own a beautiful piano, with all its notes, and be restricted to two octaves. Yes, you could play most melodies, but the music would not be as rich and sonorous. What a disappointment that would be to anyone who knew the full, gorgeous potential of a piano.

In coaching, we are the instruments. This is also true of our clients —their lives are their instruments. When we look at self as an instrument, our commitment becomes to live and to use ourselves as fully and richly as possible. That is what we mean by playing full out (Ellis & Lankowitz, 1995). We do not want to restrict ourselves to half of our range.

To play full out requires us to make great choices and stay conscious while doing so. It also means taking responsibility for the choices we make and have made. Through exercising our power of choice, we create the kind of life we want.

BEING AT CHOICE

Early in the development of coaching as a profession, the phrase "Be at full choice in your life" began to appear frequently in writing and teaching. In coaching, we believe that to be at full choice in our life means that (a) we examine our choices fully, (b) we are deliberate—we are choosing consciously, and (c) we are being responsive, not reactive to what is going on. When we are at choice, we are not choosing by default—avoiding a decision is not the same as choosing consciously.

Consider this question: What role does choice play in the situations where we play small versus the situations in which we play full out?

We use the word play in two ways. To play full out means that we play the game of life—or whatever we do—fully and richly. We bring our all. We play big, like the dolphin. As someone once said, the dolphin as a master of play behaves as if there is no competition, no loser, and no winner—only fun for all.

In *Tuesdays with Morrie* (Albom, 1997), the author's English professor and mentor, Morrie, played full out. He drew his philosophy from a quote sometimes attributed to Mark Twain: "Live like there's only today, love like you've never been hurt, and dance like nobody's watching." To play also means to have fun, be joyful, and take ourselves and others lightly. The Dalai Lama exhibits this kind of playfulness—a quality of lightness and joy. Even though the Chinese devastated his monastery home and practiced genocide on many of his people, he forgives them. He is light and even giggles frequently.

Sometimes the sheer demands of daily living and family responsibilities seem to rob us of the ability to play. "I have found that remembering what play is all about and making it part of our daily lives are probably the most important factors in being a fulfilled human being. The ability to play is critical not only to being happy, but also to sustaining social relationships and being a creative, innovative person," writes Stuart Brown, MD, in *Play: How It Shapes the Brain, Opens the Imagination and Invigorates the Soul* (Brown, 2009). Dr. Brown, who is the founder of the National Institute for Play, further presents his ideas in his TED video "Play Is More than Fun." Sprinkled with anecdotes demonstrating the play habits of subjects ranging from polar bears to corporate CEOs, Brown promotes play at every age while defining it thus: "Play is an absorbing, apparently purposeless activity that provides enjoyment and a suspension of self-consciousness and sense of time. It is also self-motivating and makes you want to do it again." We tend to underestimate the power of play. Imagine a world without it—not only the absence of games or sports, but also the absence of movies, arts, music, jokes, and dramatic stories. No daydreaming, no teasing, no flirting. Play is what lifts people out of the routine of the mundane and offers a means to find joy in even the little things. When we stop playing, we stop growing—and we will not experience vital aging, but death waiting.

Play at Work

It's obvious that play outside of work—through sports, games, family activities, and community functions—is essential. What is less obvious is our need to play *at* work, *as* we work. Play—as we work—can energize us, help us to see new patterns, spark curiosity, and trigger ideas and innovation. What kind of play is appropriate at work? You don't have to engage in off-site team-building games to play at work, although those are occasionally beneficial.

A playful attitude gives people the emotional distance to rally. Often the problem is not the problem; it's how we react to the problem. Play is a social lubricant that allows individuals to be close to one another. When we play, we don't put up defensive walls; we accept others as they are. We have a responsibility to play fair. When our interactions are based on a foundation of caring, we avoid hurting others. Play enables cooperative socialization and nourishes trust, empathy, caring, and sharing. Perhaps one of the biggest advantages to those with a playful mindset is that it stimulates creativity. Playfulness leads to imagination, inventiveness, and dreams—which help us think up new solutions to problems. And the important relationships in your life will be more vibrant if there is love and laughter! The story of Rose, which follows, is a reminder that playfulness and joyfulness create blessings for all.

The Story of Rose

The first day of school, our professor introduced himself and challenged us to get to know someone new. I stood up to look around when a gentle hand touched my shoulder. I turned around to find a wrinkled, little old lady beaming up at me with a smile that lit up her entire being.

She said, "Hi, handsome. My name is Rose. I'm 87 years old. Can I give you a hug?"

I laughed and enthusiastically responded, "Of course you may!" and she gave me a giant squeeze.

"Why are you in college at such a young, innocent age?" I asked. She jokingly replied, "I'm here to meet a rich husband, get married, have a couple of children, and then retire and travel."

"No, seriously," I asked. I was curious as to what motivated her to take on this challenge at her age.

"I always dreamed of having a college education, and now I'm getting one!" she told me.

After class, we walked to the student union building and shared a chocolate milkshake. We became instant friends. Every day for the next three months, we would leave class together and talk nonstop. I was always mesmerized listening to this "time machine" as she shared her wisdom and experience. Over the course of the year, Rose became a campus icon and easily made friends. She loved to dress up and reveled in the attention bestowed on her by the other students. She was living it up.

At the end of the semester, we invited Rose to speak at our football banquet. I'll never forget what she taught us. She was introduced and stepped up to the podium. As she began to deliver her prepared speech, she dropped her 3 × 5 cards on the floor. Frustrated and a little embarrassed, she leaned into the microphone and simply said, "I'm sorry I'm so jittery. I gave up beer for Lent, and this whiskey is killing me! I'll never get my speech back in order, so let me just tell you what I know."

As we laughed, she cleared her throat and began.

We do not stop playing because we are old; we grow old because we stop playing. There are only four secrets to staying young. One is being happy. Another is achieving success. You also must laugh and find humor every day. And you've got to have a dream. When you lose your dreams, you die. We have so many people walking around who are dead and don't even know it!

There is a huge difference between growing older and growing up. If you are 19 years old and lie in bed for one full year and don't do one productive thing, you will turn 20 years old. If I am 87 years old and stay in bed for a year and never do anything, I will turn 88. Anybody can grow older. That doesn't take any talent or ability. The idea is to grow up by always finding the opportunity in change.

Have no regrets. The elderly usually don't have regrets for what we did, but rather for the things we did not do. The only people who fear death are those with regrets.

She concluded her speech by courageously singing "The Rose," made famous by Bette Midler. She challenged each of us to study the lyrics and live them out in our daily lives.

At the year's end, Rose finished the college degree she had begun all those years ago. One week after graduation, Rose died peacefully in her sleep. Over 2,000 college students attended her funeral in tribute to the wonderful woman who taught, by example, it is never too late to be all you can possibly be.

Remember, growing old is mandatory, growing up is optional.

WHISTLE WHILE YOU WORK OR PLURK

Rose knew how to plurk, a term used by coach Teri-E Belf and Charlotte Ward (1997). They define plurk as "play while you work." Belf has even passed out buttons at conferences that say, "Ask me how I PLURK!" Remember how the seven dwarfs in Snow White sang "Whistle While You Work" as they marched off to work? Yes, it is possible to be playful and joyful in all we do, Belf says. How would our lives be different if we plurked instead of just worked?

Children are masters of plurking, and watching them or—better yet— participating brings out that quality in us. Coaches and other helping professionals often report that Fun and Play are two of their lowest-rated areas on the Life Balance Wheel—for coaches and clients alike. Why is this so? Perhaps it is because work has taken over many professionals' lives in a way that leaves little time for fun and play. We have become human doings instead of human beings. We also speculate that the kind of work people do has a pervasive influence on their attitudes. Psychologists, counselors, nurses, and other helping professionals often work daily with people whose situations are dire. After spending 8 to 10 hours focused on what the Buddha called the 10,000 sorrows of life, it is easy to forget the other half of the Buddha's statement: 10,000 joys.

Making time for play requires real excellence at saying no if our fun and play quota is low. Address the imbalance by examining the places in our life we say yes when saying no might be more beneficial.

PLAY AND BEING AT CHOICE BOTH REQUIRE GOOD BOUNDARIES

Every time we say yes when we want to say no, we're jeopardizing our ability to take life lightly and to play, which are the roots of resilience. When we do this, we compromise our boundaries and allow things into our life that should not be there. Those things sap our energy and zap our commitment to our priorities.

Boundaries are the borders we create around ourselves by the limits we set: limits around time, whom we let into our life, and the activities we allow to take up our attention and time. They are the imaginary lines that tell people how close they can come to us and what they can expect. Good boundaries allow us to spend our time and energy wisely. We do not waste energy on what is not good for us—people, activities, or food. Boundaries put us in charge by allowing us to consciously choose what we allow inside our life.

For example, an executive client of ours decided she would no longer take work home and do it after supper. Instead, she wanted to use that time to help her children with their homework and to simply enjoy being and playing with them. She decided she was willing to stay a half hour later at the office to be free and focused at home. Her decision not to take work home meant she was drawing a boundary around her home life, which kept work from leaking into it. Yes, it was hard. And, it was worth it.

Boundaries Create Safety and Protection

Boundaries are a fundamental tool for keeping us safe and supporting our well-being. We all learned how to set boundaries as a child—to say no to strangers, turn away people who wanted to touch us inappropriately, stay away from kids who had chicken pox or who were not good playmates. If we were parented well, we learned how to make our boundaries tight and steadfast, and to resist people who were boundary invaders. We learned how to keep ourselves safe and well.

Two-year-olds know the power of saying no. When things occur that children do not like, they will immediately scream "No!" Saying no helps children feel powerful and set limits—it is the natural foundation for independence. Saying no and establishing boundaries give us power.

So why as adults are we often afraid to say no? Probably because when we first heard our parents say "No!" to us, it meant, "Stop immediately—you have no choice!" "No" was a signal that we were either unsafe at the moment or that what we were doing, and who we were being, was unacceptable. "No" was a sign of rejection, a signal we were not okay as we were. When we were young, rejection meant being cut off from the love and caring that sustained us. We could lose everything we had.

Saying no and maintaining good boundaries are hard when we think it means giving up approval. We become afraid to say no, afraid of losing a client, being rejected, or being disliked. When we avoid saying no once, it seems like a small thing. When it becomes a habit, we are in trouble.

Keep Tight Boundaries

Whenever we say yes when we should say no, we allow someone to invade our boundaries. We interpret a request or need as a demand. We tell ourselves we have no choice about the situation because we cannot run the risk of rejection or loss.

When we say yes to the demand, we are really saying no to ourselves. For that moment, we make the other person more important than ourselves. Worse yet, when we say yes to something to which we want to say no, we cheapen our word. As Peter Block said in the quote at the start of this chapter, our ability to say yes is only as good and viable as our willingness to say no, which means that we are grounded. We know exactly the firm ground we are willing to stand on, and we are clear about what we are willing to do.

People usually respect those who are grounded and clear. If we say no gracefully and share the reasons why, for the most part we will be respected. But gaining the respect of others is not the reason why being grounded is important. Most important is that we will regain respect for ourselves.

People do not always respect others who set clear boundaries. We need to make a point of paying attention to whether people in our lives support our autonomous choices regarding what is best for us, or they want what they want and do not care how they get it. If they just want what they want, the situation is an opportunity to set a boundary and disengage. We choose to do this. It is our responsibility to recognize the people and situations that do and do not nourish us and take appropriate action. We cannot ever expect another person to be fully looking out for our best interests and take care of us—that is our job. If we do not do it, it will not get done.

Once we recognize our need for healthy boundaries and create them, we are better able to respect other people's boundaries. We have acquired a new distinction and apply it to ourselves and others. We are better equipped to recognize that everyone, not just us, has a right to boundaries.

When working with clients on issues related to boundaries, we use several metaphors that we once used with counseling clients. One common metaphor is that boundaries are like the moat around a castle. If clients want to connect with someone, they lower the drawbridge to let the person into their space. If not, they keep the drawbridge up, and the moat prevents access, just like boundaries do. When clients know they are in a safe, nurturing environment, they may choose to keep the drawbridge down, metaphorically speaking. Other metaphors we have used include: the alarm system on your house (what are your personal alarms?) or border guards who maintain the gate between countries—you need a passport to be admitted (how do you admit people into your territory?).

We work with coaching clients on boundaries from these perspectives:

- Boundaries are the limits we set around who and what we allow to get close to us. They define our safety zones, delineating what is out of bounds for us and unacceptable, and what is in bounds and acceptable.
- Boundaries define who we are and how we live. They define who we are and who we are not.
- When we have tight, strong boundaries, we attract people who have similar boundaries and consequently can maintain them well. When our boundaries are weak, we attract people who also have weak boundaries. They can show up as needy people who deplete our energy and whom we eventually tire of.

To be able to give generously, clients must have good boundaries. Recall that boundaries create freedom. Many spiritual teachings point to the truth of this—in order to give, you must be sufficiently full. One line we have heard is to compare giving as if from a pipe or a cup. Do not give like a pipe: it is open at both ends and never remains full. Give like an overflowing cup. The cup never runs out, but the overflow is available to be given to others.

Dr. Pat and Lloyd Thomas wrote in their book, *Total Life Coaching*, "When you establish healthy boundaries, you feel more secure. Your level of anxiety lowers, and you strengthen the trust you have in yourself, in others, and in the world" (Williams & Thomas, 2005, p. 55).

Clients who want to have a fulfilling life must be able to make choices freely and fully, to play full out so they do not feel the need to overprotect themselves from others or events. We believe that to fully choose and play full out, we need to have three things in place, all of which are related: (a) good boundaries, (b) high standards, which when combined and done well, help us (c) create integrity.

EXERCISES ON BOUNDARIES

Most clients need to set tighter boundaries and higher standards to give them-selves more room, freedom, and choices in order to create the life they really want to live. Playing full out means different things to different people: it can mean pursuing excellence, having a sense of urgency, taking risks, keep-ing things in perspective, working smarter instead of harder, or consciously choosing how hard to play.

Journal Inquiries

- What are one or two places in your life where you are playing small instead of playing big? What is that about?
- What are the rules you learned about work and play?

For many clients, rules about play and work are tied together. Many say, for example, that play can occur only after work is done. In a 24/7 environ-ment, where clients are continually accessible by instant messaging and cell phones, work may never end. Consequently, clients need to be vigilant in setting good boundaries to ensure that they get to play.

Play Full Out

The following exercise can be used to encourage an experience of the interplay between hard work and having fun (Ellis & Lankowitz, 1995, pp. 127–136).

To balance the interplay between working hard and playing hard, consider that playing hard requires letting go. It requires us to examine our lives, notice what we can change, and accept what we cannot. Playing, to some extent, means going with the flow. If clients can detach from the need to win and the fear of losing, they free themselves to play full out. They can compete fiercely, but in a spirit of play and flow.

Letting go and lightening up require clients to examine their roles—work, family, community, and so on—and to commit to putting their soul before their role. That is, happiness can be independent of most of what people in indus-trialized societies are attached to. We are more than our roles, behavior, bank accounts, credit cards, or possessions.

In the first part of the exercise below, clients are asked to rewrite their per-sonal equation for happiness so they can move beyond whatever their current equation is, such as defining their happiness by possessions or their role. (My happiness = my car; my happiness = being a perfect parent.) We want them to rewrite the equation as: My happiness = my happiness. We first encountered this exercise in Roberto Assagioli's book, *Psychosynthesis* (Assagioli, 1965).

EXERCISE 13.1

Journal Exercise (Disidentification)
- Write a list of those things that are important to you.
- Then write the sentences as attachments and let them go, using the following form:

I have a beautiful home, but I am not my home.
I have a Mercedes, but I am not my Mercedes.
I am married, but I am not my marriage.
I have a beautiful body, but I am not my body.
I have an overweight body, but I am not my body.
I have a great job, but I am not my job.
I have a _____ , but I am not my _____ .

Through this journal exercise, clients discover and work with limiting beliefs. They can emerge from the exercise with the awareness that they used to believe their happiness depended on their list. They learn that happiness is simply a choice. They can choose to be happy by separating from all they have. Happiness is a way of being . . . it does not depend on having.

EXERCISE 13.2

Taking a Risk: Costs and Benefits
This exercise asks clients to identify something they have been attracted to, something they would love to do but have chosen not to because they are afraid. They may fear looking foolish (for example, going to a dance when they feel they have two left feet). They may fear giving presentations to groups they do not know. They may fear wearing a particular kind of clothing even though they love the fabric and the cut. Singles may fear dating because they anticipate being rejected.

- In the prompts that follow, identify first what you would love to do. Then list the benefits and costs of choosing not to take this action. (For example, the benefits of avoiding the dance might include not feeling uncomfortable or embarrassed. The costs might include not meeting new people and being bored at home.)

> "The action I have chosen not to take is . . ."
> "The benefits of choosing not to take this action include . . ."
> "The costs of choosing not to take this action include . . ."

- How might making the choice to take this action help you to play full out?

Identify two situations or people in your life that you experience as disempowering. For each situation, identify the consequences of your feeling of disempowerment.

Situation	Why Disempowering
1. _____	1. _____
2. _____	2. _____

A good place to begin working with clients on the topic of boundaries is to have them reflect on the following questions and journal about them.

One of the ways to create more room for choice is to set clear boundaries. List three to five places in your life where you need to set better (stronger, tighter, or clearer) boundaries. Examples might include your time, health, relationships, finances, and spirit. These might be places where you need to say no to someone else so you can say yes to yourself.

1. _____	1. _____
2. _____	2. _____
3. _____	3. _____
4. _____	4. _____
5. _____	5. _____

EXERCISE 13.3

Setting a Tighter Boundary

Do the following exercise using one of the situations you listed as disempowering. When doing this exercise with clients, we have found that it works best in a live coaching session, not as a written exercise.

Step 1. Name a boundary that you now hold that you could tighten.

Step 2. What would a tighter boundary look like, and how would it function?

Step 3. Examine needs and values issues around setting this boundary.

What need is behind the old, loose boundary? In other words, what need is being met by keeping the boundary loose? What are two other ways you might meet that need? If you set a tighter boundary, would it conflict with your values or be truer to your values?

Step 4. What standard would you set for yourself to make that tighter boundary work?

Step 5. What part does this new standard play in helping you maintain your integrity?

Keeping Boundaries Tight

We recommend sharing the following guidelines with clients who are working on tighter and clearer boundaries.

- Be clear about your limits. A good rule of thumb is: Allow no one to make demands of you. Allow people to make requests of you, ask for your help, or say what they need from you. However, no one has the right to make demands of you as long as you are not causing harm or breaking the law.
- If you hear a request that makes you uncomfortable, your discomfort is likely a signal that this is an attempt to invade your boundaries. The person may not recognize this as an invasion, but you know it—your body knows it. Do not say yes under these conditions. This is a time to say no and really mean it.
- Exercise your freedom to choose. When you cannot choose to say no to others, or when you take on other people's troubles, you probably are

not free to make choices in any part of your life. Start today to exercise your choice muscles.

- Set tight boundaries and attract great people. Remember that good boundaries attract good people. Tight boundaries keep out needy and demanding people.
- Say no when you mean no.
- Be willing to hold a courageous conversation if needed to reinforce your boundaries. Often, we need to have these conversations with people who have violated one of our boundaries. The goal is to teach them to respect your boundaries. The key steps of reinforcing boundaries require you to be willing to hold several conversations to reinforce the boundary.

1. Inform them that their behavior is violating a boundary or limit of yours. Tell them it is not acceptable. It is likely that the person may not have any clue that they violated your boundary.
2. Request that they stop. Invite them to figure out alternatives forgetting their own needs met.
3. If they persist, request that they stop.
4. Terminate the relationship if the boundary violation continues. You do not need people in your life who continue to violate and disrespect your boundaries.

A PRIMER ON SAYING NO GRACEFULLY

On a day-to-day basis, most of us violate our own boundaries by saying yes when we really want to say no. We are awkward around saying no—to everyone but ourselves.

We can say no gracefully. If we are not yet seasoned practitioners of the art of the graceful no or if we're having trouble being consistent, these reminders can help:

- Saying no to trivial requests gives meaning to the things we say yes to, both for ourselves and for others who make requests of us.
- Saying no allows us to set and keep good boundaries in order to honor our commitments to ourselves and others.

• Saying no wisely creates space and time for us so we have the energy to create what we really want for ourselves.

Stephen Covey knew this well. As he said, "It is easy to say 'no' when there is a greater 'yes'" (1989, p. 156). Saying no is key to staying on track and on purpose.

Saying the Graceful "No"

Cultivating an ability to say no is not the same as becoming one of those people whose first answer to every new idea is "No." We never have to take any chances if we always say no. In contrast, we all benefit by giving ourselves the time and freedom to generate new ideas of our own and create new ways of being and doing. We support this process by saying no to others whose requests are not in our best interests right now.

Below is a bouquet of suggestions about how to say no with grace, preserving the relationship with someone who hopes we say yes. Adapt them as you see fit in working with clients. This list was developed by asking colleagues to share their experiences with saying the graceful "no."

In the material below, we have written these to you, the reader. Each of the sections presents situations where a "no" is appropriate, followed by suggestions about how to say it.

How to Say No When Someone Suggests
Something You Would Like to Consider

> RESPONSE: "This sounds like something that may be for me, and I've just committed to sticking to three other priorities right now. Will you come back in 90 days and give me another chance to look at this opportunity with you?"

This one works because it acknowledges your interest and keeps you from taking on more than you can realistically complete. If the other person is really interested, he or she will ask again. Tell the truth—you really do see an opportunity for yourself. Do not use this one when you really do not want to do what is being asked. You will just have to say no twice. Worse yet, you will have intentionally misled the other person.

How to Say No When the Timing Is Just Not Right

> RESPONSE: "I wish I could, but it's just not possible right now. Thank you for thinking of me."

Your no is based on the timing of the request. Thanking the requester really helps in this situation. Be sincere. Because you acknowledge your thanks, the person will think of you again when similar opportunities arise. You said no to this one but not to other similar requests. The requester will be back with future requests. Make sure you want that to happen before you use this strategy.

Similar variations include:

> "Thanks for thinking of me, but I don't think so right now."
> "I hate saying no to you, but I really must this time."
> "It doesn't work for me at this time."

Make sure you stop after any of these responses. Do not say more—there is no need to justify or give reasons.

If you do not have the time now but might want to say yes at some other time, say something like:

> "I'd love to help you with this, but I just don't have the time. Please let me know next time this comes up, and maybe our schedules will be a better match then."
> "I would like to help, but I'm already overcommitted. How else might I support you?"

How to Say No When You Have Other Priorities

> RESPONSE: "This year my priorities are very few and very focused. I won't be able to squeeze this one in."

Laura Berman Fortgang, a friend and colleague of ours, is adamant about saying no in the right way and sticking to her priorities. She, like other well-known published writers, gets many requests for public appearances and speaking engagements. Using her values as a compass, she modeled for Dr.

Pat the importance of priorities based on values. Shortly after her first book came out (Berman Fortgang, 1998), she appeared on Oprah. She was inundated with requests for appearances and speeches—to many of which she said no, since her priority at the time was a book tour. You will be in good company if you say a graceful no because you have other priorities. You might say:

> "This isn't a good time for me to do that. I have other commitments. I'll let you know if I can spend time on it later."
> "What a wonderful invitation, but I'm just stretched too much to accept it."

Remember that you do not have to share your priorities with the other person. We suggest, in fact, you do not. You do not want to get into a debate about whether your priorities are truly more important or valuable than what the other person is asking of you. You have a right to your priorities—without any justification.

We suggest you practice saying each of these graceful "no" lines until you become comfortable hearing yourself say them. Then, when the time comes, you will be ready to respond gracefully.

Once you have mastered the basic ways to say no, you are ready for the "black belt" skills. When you do these well, you will be a master of the graceful "no." Here are more examples of graceful and artful ways to say no that you can practice regularly.

How to Say No New York–Style

This one is a favorite, learned from a playwright in New York City who used it with actors asking for roles in his shows. It works best with people who seem to make endless demands of you with great persistence.

You say, "Gosh, I really wish I could, but it's just . . . [count silently to four] . . . impossible." [Shake your head slowly.]

That usually does it, especially if you say nothing else. If, however, they ask, "Why?" do this: Open your mouth as if starting to speak, then take a breath, and say, "Well, it's . . . [count silently to four, look down, and then say, almost under your breath] . . . just impossible. I wish I could say 'yes,' but I simply cannot." [Look up at the person at the very end and smile wanly.]

Why does this work? The requestor has nothing to argue with. You haven't lied, and he or she will fill in the blank with whatever awful thing happened to you that they would have difficulty talking about.

Remember, you do not need to give a reason why. The truth is, it usually is not their business. Often, they will not hear anything after "no" anyway. We are often just trying to justify our decision to ourselves.

How to Say No if You're Asked to Do Something That Goes Against Your Values or Values-Driven Priorities

The best option is to say no quickly. If you hesitate, even for a moment, the person making the request will believe there is a chance you will change your mind. Say no firmly. Just no—no reasons.

A next best choice is to make a sincere comment about your commitment to the results you are focused on achieving, for example:

> "I must commit all my time to my writing. It's what is most important to me right now."

Then reaffirm your commitment to the person: "Although I'm saying no to your request, I want you to know how much I value you as a colleague."

If you have time, you might spend a few minutes brainstorming with the person about other ways he or she can fill the need.

> "Sorry, I'm unable to do that."
> "I'll have to say no to that, but might I suggest we talk next week?"

In the last case, you've given the person a gift of your creativity by suggesting another way he or she might handle the need.

How to Say No When You're Asked to Do Something for Free That You Usually Charge for Doing

You may be one of those people who is asked to speak or contribute your consulting or services for free. Sometimes that may work for you. When it does not, say something like this:

> "I do pro bono work on a limited basis, and that time has already been committed for this year. Would you like to be put on the waiting list for months/years from now? I can do that."

Most people do not plan that far in advance. Consequently, they end up having to say no to your suggestion.

How to Say No When Someone Continues to Ask You Repeatedly for Free Advice

After an ongoing fee-paying relationship ends, you give away your services. If you do not want to continue to do that, you might respond with something like this:

> "I feel awkward helping you at this point because I feel I'm being unfair to my paying clients. Let's put together a list of things I can really help you with and see how we can work together."

That usually will end the "for free" requests once and for all.

EXERCISE 13.4

Where Do You Need to Say No Right Now?

Identify the places in your life where you see the need to say no. These are places where you need tighter boundaries. Identify 5 to 10 "no's" you need to say. Then, for each one, ask yourself, "What would I be willing to say yes to in this case?" If there is something you are willing to do, say it. Choose wisely—only what you are willing to do and can do gracefully, without resentment.

This chapter has focused on the connection between maintaining good boundaries and the freedom to choose that comes with them. Choosing means creating the possibility of playing full out, having fun, and creating a balanced life. Many clients come into coaching around the challenge of maintaining life balance. They will need to examine and rework boundaries in order to attain balance.

Helping professionals often think boundaries are dealt with in therapy. We have found that the most severe cases of boundary violations—situations involving abuse or trauma—do in fact usually require a therapeutic intervention. However, human beings need to reexamine and re-create their boundaries throughout their lives. Consequently, coaches need to be able to work effectively with boundaries. They also need to recognize when a client's old boundary issues may not have been dealt with sufficiently and require therapy. At those times, a referral is in order.

CHAPTER 14

HOW WEALTHY ARE YOU?

In the 1980s and 1990s in the United States, the motto was, "There's no such thing as too much." Money, time, possessions —"more is better" was the mantra. That time marked the appearance of the bumper sticker, "He who has the most toys wins."

Many coaching clients lived through that period of frantic striving and now have returned to seeking a simpler life. When we try to simplify our lives, sometimes we bump up against our unconscious beliefs about how much really is enough.

A classic definition of wealth can be helpful here. *The American Heritage Dictionary of the English Language* (4th ed.) has a multi-part definition. One definition is the state of being rich or affluent, or "all goods and resources having value in terms of exchange or use." The last definition is "a great amount, a profusion, a wealth of advice." As coaches, we work with clients to see that their wealth in life goes well beyond simply money. It extends to any area when having a great amount or a profusion of something is a source of fulfillment and satisfaction. We want clients to have a wealth of time, an abundance of joy, a profusion of friends.

In the coaching profession, coaches describe how much is enough, and we define having more than just enough as having a reserve, sometimes described as being in reserve, to emphasize that we work with the state of being, not the state of having.

PERSONAL RESERVE

Personal reserve is a bit like the gold vault at the Federal Reserve Bank in New York City, which always has a stash of currency and gold that remains unused and out of circulation. Because it is there—safe and unused—it guarantees that the rest of the nation's money can be freely circulated without worry. Money in reserve stabilizes the currency if the economy changes.

Here's another example. If you are old enough to have driven a car back in the 1960s and 1970s, you may have had the good fortune to own a Volkswagen Beetle. Instead of a gasoline gauge indicator, the Volkswagen Beetle had a component called the reserve tank. You never got caught without gas because your reserve tank held two extra gallons. You always had more than enough gas to get to the next gas station. The reserve tank in the VW Beetle kept you from worrying about running out of gas and getting stuck somewhere. It is likely that most of us who owned one were, in fact, not very wealthy in terms of how much money we had stashed away. We were probably college students or starting a first job. But the lesson of the reserve tank stayed with us.

A real sense of personal wealth comes from knowing that we always have a reserve of whatever resource we are focused on. We never need to be afraid of running out, so we can focus our attention on other things. This is another example of how Maslow's hierarchy of needs comes into play around a client's sense of fulfillment. When survival issues are addressed, clients focus on higher-order issues. The role of the coach is to work with the client to examine any scarcity mind-set that prevents the client from ever feeling a sense of abundance.

HOW MUCH IS ENOUGH?

As we stated at the beginning of this chapter, people living in nations like the United States have become confused about what is really necessary for a fulfilling life. Many never consider the personal question, "How much is enough for you?" In a consumer-driven society, the sense is that people always need to accumulate more. That sense is interrupted at times when people see disasters such as hurricanes, typhoons, fires, or floods, which show that people can lose many of their possessions and still find a gratitude for life and relationships that exceeds what they had before their losses, after serious adjustments of course.

LIVING IN A WORLD OF ABUNDANCE

Many spiritual writers would say we have available to us an abundance of everything we need in the universe, but our blindness keeps us from seeing this. Working with abundance in this way is a matter of mind-set, which is addressed in Chapter 15. People can believe in a world of abundance but not do their part to ensure that it is available to them when needed. This is one reason why abundance and availability can differ.

Many teaching stories and parables in spiritual writings emphasize that readiness and preparedness are critical. A good example is in the Bible's parable of women waiting for a bridegroom. Darkness had fallen, and some women had not prepared their oil lamps in advance. It is not enough to know where to get oil for one's lamp—we must place it in the lamp and have the wick trimmed in order to be ready to live our intentions and to open the doors to all that is available.

An example of how the world changes through abundance versus scarcity thinking is a story told by a Native American man about when he was a boy, living with his grandfather in a wooden house along the shore of a lake. In wintertime, the wind whistled through the chinks in the wood of their home. Life as the boy knew it was the grandest adventure of all time. He experienced unbounded happiness and joy in his daily living. He and his grandfather had everything they needed.

But then one day a white man entered his grandfather's home and pronounced the pair poor and in need of assistance. The storyteller stated that his young life (his whole life, really) changed in that instant. In one fell verbal swoop, abundance mentality was replaced by scarcity mentality. In that moment, the grand adventure that was his life began to feel tarnished.

Some would argue that the white man's words just introduced a note of reality and described things as they really were. We disagree. Viewing the same situation, stepping into that house on the shores of the frozen lake, we would have said that the boy and his grandfather were extraordinarily rich relative to people who own many possessions and have a lot of money in the bank or whose houses do not have any wind whistling through them.

The white man made a declaration that, from his point of view, the boy and his grandfather were poor; he did this without offering any definition of what it means to be rich. Had the boy been coached by one of us, we would have asked him to consider what he needed to have in reserve in a multitude of areas—to put his specific needs, wants, and desires within a context. Without specificity, we may always feel poor because we work without clarity and without context. To paraphrase Henry David Thoreau: The boy gathers his materials to build a bridge to the moon, and the middle-aged man uses them to build a woodshed. Both are rich. Their contexts and intentions differ. So, how much wood is enough for each of them?

We want you to work with your clients and their specific details. "The angel is in the details," we sometimes hear people say. It is critical for you and your clients to know your standards around reserve, so that you, and they, can begin to create it, one small step at a time if necessary.

GETTING IN SYNC WITH WHAT WE WANT

As adults, we may need to shift the ways we think about money and wealth—how it gets created and how it works—if those beliefs no longer serve us. If we grew up believing that we needed to struggle, work hard, suffer, and exhaust ourselves to make enough money, our beliefs need some revision. In fact, we need to discover that those beliefs may deter us from achieving what we want because exhausted, depleted human beings do not attract richness, spaciousness, and openness to their life—they attract more exhausted, depleted resources.

How does this work? Dr. Wernher von Braun, whom many consider the father of the U.S. space program, was once quoted as saying, ""One cannot be exposed to the law and order of the universe without concluding that there must be a divine intent behind it all" (Hill, 1976, p. ii).

According to the concept of the law of attraction, living things attract what they most need for their existence at any given time, based on what they communicate. How it works, very simplified, is that everything in the universe is in a constant state of movement, of vibration. The impulses communicated by this vibration draw other moving, vibrating things that match in some way the impulses that are emitted. People and other living things resonate with one another. We are all composed of electrical and cellular impulses, and we resonate with what is like our being or what our thoughts are holding. You might say that the vibrations attract similar vibrations, much as a logical person often is drawn to other logical people or an emotional person often is drawn to other emotional people. We even use language that reflects the physics of this phenomenon—we say that two people are on the same wavelength. As coaches, we can harness the law of attraction to assist clients in examining and refining their intentions.

Bob Proctor, in his book *You Were Born Rich* (Proctor, 1997), uses an acorn as a graphic example of how the law of attraction works. Like anything else that appears to be solid, an acorn (like we as human beings) is really a mass of molecules at a very high speed of vibration. Within the acorn is a patterned plan that governs the product into which it will grow. As soon as the acorn is planted, the patterned plan sets up a force and begins to attract everything that vibrates in synchronicity or harmony with it. It attracts all the necessary particles of energy from the ground, and they begin to join up and grow. As it expands, little shoots grow out of the bottom, forming roots. They begin to grow upward and eventually break through the earth. These top shoots then begin attracting molecules from the atmosphere, continuing their growth until eventually they become an oak tree.

An even simpler example is to think of two magnets. If you flip them one way, they repel each other. If you reverse them, the opposing polarities when in close proximity have a strong attraction. This is why we say some people have magnetic personalities. When we say someone is attractive, we often confuse attraction with their looks. What we really mean is that people are drawn to them.

The attraction principle works similarly in human beings. The human body is one of the most efficient electrical instruments in the entire universe. This is not new information—for many years we have been reading the electrical impulses of the brain (an electroencephalogram) and the heart (an electrocardiogram). In fact, the brain is really a vibratory instrument. Energy is palpable and is felt by us when we are in contact with it. Daniel Goleman's books, including *Emotional Intelligence* (1995) and *Primal Leadership* (2002), contain excellent, readable information about the ways in which our human neurobiology creates open loops so that we are affected by one another and by all living things. Goleman says that our emotions are as contagious to other people as a virus.

We have all heard people talk about good vibes, bad vibes, and vibrations, but most people are not aware of the connection between their vibrations and what they create in their lives. It is very common to see people with bad vibes trying very hard to get good results, while at the same time their negative vibrations draw to them all manner of negative people and situations. You know how this works and how palpable it is if you have ever walked into a room filled with a group of angry people. Even if you are facing their backs and cannot see their faces, you can clearly feel the energy of anger.

Unlike human beings, acorns do not have the ability to change their vibratory rate. Consequently, they can only grow into what they have been programmed to become—oak trees. But we have the ability to change our vibratory rate and therefore to make choices about what we are creating. We do this through what we envision, how we hold our emotions, how we choose to meditate, and how we synchronize ourselves with something larger than ourselves.

If this sounds purely metaphorical to you, solid research exists on how it works.

Meditation, prayer, and spiritual practices are ways in which we affect our thoughts and bodies, which affect the ways that our vibratory systems work. Recent research on the heart's vibrations conducted by Doc Childre's group HeartMath supports this assertion (www.heartmath.com). It turns out that a person's thoughts and visualizations affect the heart's ability to synchronize with the brain, and that when synchronization occurs, it is detectable by research and is apparent to others. This synchronization can be detected through biofeedback methods that are simple and reliable. And, of course, we notice it in the way we feel. The simple practices that HeartMath recommends can alter the synchronization of the heart and brain. HeartMath has created research and programs for schools that focus on using Heart-Math processes for character building and reducing the stress associated with math exams, as well as for teaching kids about love. Their website is located at www.HeartMath.com. One of their best research papers is called "The Appreciative Heart: The Psychophysiology of Positive Emotions and Optimal Functioning" (McCraty & Childre, 2006), which describes their research on how the heart rhythms associated with gratitude, appreciation, and prayer affect stress, health, and well-being. This and other research papers are downloadable as e-books from the HeartMath site.

HeartMath research found that even when we are not consciously communicating with others, our physiological systems interact in subtle and surprising ways. Did you know that the electromagnetic signal produced by your heart is registered in the brain waves of people around you? Or that your physiological responses sync up with your mate's during empathic interactions? The heart's electromagnetic field is believed to act as a central synchronizing signal within the body, an important carrier of emotional information, and a key mediator of energetic interactions between people.

It should be no surprise that the goal or image we plant in our mind by constantly dwelling on it is the patterned plan or nucleus that determines what we will grow into. It determines what we will attract to us and what we will repel.

In an orderly universe, nothing occurs accidentally. The images a client plants in his marvelous mind instantly set up a force that intentionally creates specific results in life. This means that we coach clients to intentionally get into harmony with what they want out of life rather than what they do not. In that way, clients draw to themselves what they need to learn to create what they want. Clients often discover that this principle appears as if it is synchronicity at work, as Carl Jung wrote about extensively. Synchronicity works because clients draw to themselves what they need at any given time. Sometimes what they need comes in the form of key experiences that create significant learning and shifts that are necessary for forward movement at a specific time in their life.

MAKING IT PRACTICAL

How can clients create more than enough of what they need so they never need to worry about running out? How can clients learn to manage themselves, so their emotions do not get in the way of creating? For most clients, the major challenge is to manage themselves around fears and anxieties. Some of these fears and anxieties are based in old learning, and others may come from television or video images, or the bombardment of political statements designed to create urgency through a sense of impending terror.

Some writers have said that babies come into the world with only two innate fears, one of which is a fear of falling. Without unnecessary fear, humans are free to create, act, and to explore. When clients come to terms with unnecessary fears, most of them come to understand that scarcity is simply a habitual way of thinking. Scarcity robs clients of the ability to feel appreciation for the abundance in many areas of their lives. When we coach clients, we focus on the importance of having a sense of abundance—a reserve or a sense of wealth—in key areas: relationship (or love), time, vision, money, career, and contribution.

Coaches can start clients in working with their reserve by asking them to consider and record their initial responses to these questions:

- How would you know you had a reserve in each of these areas—relationship/love, time, vision, money, career, and contribution?
- What structures would be in place so that you would have more than just enough and could generously give to others?

The coaching skill of visioning can be helpful to clients as they consider these questions. After identifying what would be present, ask the clients to answer the following:

- How would you behave differently?
- How would you give to others in this area?

EXERCISE 14.1

Examining Reserve
Ask the clients to complete this exercise as a fieldwork assignment. We find it best to have a strong alliance with clients already in place before doing work on reserve, as the coaches will likely find themselves challenging some of the clients' deeply held beliefs.

A reserve of time for me would be evident in this way:

How I would then give time to others:

A reserve of money for me would be evident in this way:

How I would then give money to others:

A reserve of caring or love for me would be evident in this way:

How I would then give care or love to others:

When clients return for the next coaching session, the task is to help them develop a plan for creating a reserve in one of the key areas identified in the exercise. The plan should include specific actions, and the coaches should request clients complete at least one of the actions during the time between this session and the next one. Sometimes clients discover that to create a true sense of wealth for themselves, they need to simplify. For example, they may discover that to create a wealth of time, they need to have a smaller house with a smaller yard to mow. To create a plan for this may take more than one session, and it will not be accomplished necessarily in a short time. However, taking the steps to create the plan will bring a sense of future freedom.

EXERCISE 14.2

Creating a Reserve of Time

We commonly ask clients to explore through fieldwork how they spend their time by listing typical weekly recurring activities—not responses to crises but those things they allow time for. They often need to examine work calendars, confer with a spouse, and examine children's sports schedules as well as family requirements. Once clients create the list, coaches ask them to consider each of the typical activities and identify to what extent each is consistent with or supportive of their values and commitments, or the extent to which it conflicts with their core values and commitments.

At the next coaching session, coaches work with clients to identify ways to eliminate recurring activities that are not aligned with values, or to modify the way clients do these activities to bring them more in alignment with core values and commitments.

EXERCISE 14.3

Choices versus Obligations

Clients tend to feel a stronger sense of a reserve around time when they choose how to spend it instead of investing time in obligations imposed by others. Obligations are part of human life, of course, but people often misjudge and minimize the extent to which they have control over obligations and consequently do not explore ways to create more choice in their life. Ask the clients these questions:

- Are you satisfied with the way you currently spend time?
- Are you doing what you've chosen to do?
- How much time do you spend on obligations imposed by others?
- How much alignment is there between what you want and what you do?

- What is the most important thing I can do to bring your activities in line with your values and vision?

Coach clients, using the above exercises, to make informed decisions about how they spend their time. For example, ask them to do a planning exercise that includes predictable events, errands, unexpected events, time for recreation and other self-nurturing activities, and so on. Ask them to plan time around life purpose and other priorities.

Then ask them to find a blank weekly calendar form. The task is to plan an ideal week, determining how they would spend their time during such a week, given their current job, family situation, and so on. They can include events from the previous planning exercise but will be making conscious decisions about all other unplanned available time so the week will serve as the ideal.

EXERCISE 14.4

The Meaning of Money

Clients have many deeply held beliefs about money that can interfere with their desires. As Deepak Chopra says, we call money currency (Chopra, 2005). Consequently, there should be a flow as we earn, use, and spend money. Many quoted masters describe an attitude of abundance such that if money is used wisely, it returns to us. On the other hand, hoarding is a misuse of money. Saving is good; hoarding is not.

Ask clients to complete two lists about money. First, ask them to list on one side of a page their beliefs about what money is. Then, ask them to list on the other side their beliefs about what money is not.

At the next coaching session, discuss the lists with them, looking for any patterns of thinking that sound childlike—that once may have served them well but no longer do.

For example, it might be difficult for clients to find fulfillment in life if they have any of the following beliefs:

- Money is a measure of competence.
- Money is a source of evil.
- Money solves all problems in life or cures all diseases.
- Money is a source of power and control.

- Money is an indication of one's worth.
- Money buys happiness.

Some healthy beliefs about money might include the following:

- Money affects how people and organizations come together in relationship.
- Money catalyzes people to work, take action, serve, and do things that organizations and others are willing to pay to have done.
- Money is something that some people inherit, but few are born with extensive wealth.
- Money requires management and takes a level of responsibility to manage wisely.
- Money is a primary source of unnecessary anxiety and worry in many lives.
- Money can be used to measure the value of time, energy, and contribution.
- Noticing how we spend our money can be a measure of what we value.

EXERCISE 14.5

Early Beliefs About Money

We find it useful to ask clients, as fieldwork, to write down several of their earliest memories around money. They might include the following:

- Two early memories, preferably from elementary school or earlier.
- What they learned about money from each of their parents or other family members who were prominent influences during their elementary school days.
- When they have had a sense of being wealthy. Feel free to interpret wealth as beyond just money. What was occurring in their life at that point?
- Some people believe that "money is condensed personality." If that is true, what does their relationship with money say about them?

For example, one of Diane's earliest memories took place in kindergarten. At that time, kindergarten was the first year of school, and Friday was banking day. During class, kids could bring in whatever money they wanted to bank. They received a savings passbook, and the savings contributions were recorded by the teacher in the passbook. The teacher had a student who served as the banker, making sure that the money was deposited in a metal box with a lock. Diane always volunteered to be the banker. It gave her practice in learning to count, which she had learned from her parents before kindergarten.

What this early memory meant to her is that savings were always important. No matter what, have something that you save regularly. It gives her pleasure to notice her savings.

From both of her parents, Diane learned that money came through working, and working always came before play. Diane needed to work to reprogram herself around this latter belief to create a fulfilling life for herself.

Other Exercises

From the *Human Being* text (Ellis & Lankowitz, 1995; now out of print) we use at ILCT, we assign students these exercises:

EXERCISE 14.6

Take a First Step About Money
This exercise asks clients to fill in the following sentence stems. We use it as a fieldwork exercise and then work on it during a coaching session.

> When it comes to money, I usually feel . . .
> My greatest difficulty with money right now is . . .
> One thing I do well about managing money is . . .
> To me, financial success means . . .
> What I most want to change about my relationship with money is . . .
> The career I want to have five years from now is . . .
> The things I want to be doing in my nonworking hours five years from now
>   include . . .
> The biggest change I would like to make in my life regarding money is . . .
> Managing money more effectively could help me make that change by . . .

The next part of this exercise asks clients to examine their statements and to engage in reprogramming attitudes about money.

Fallacies:

> Money is evil.
> Money is sacred.
> Money is complicated.
> Money is scarce.
> Frugality isn't fun.

Consciously choose which beliefs about money to keep and which ones to let go. Then write a new belief statement about money.

EXERCISE 14.7

Match Values and Money

This exercise asks clients to begin by monitoring what they spend. This first step can be eye-opening, as many people do not know how much they spend each day, each week, or each month.

> Write your expenses from the past month on separate cards.
> Write fundamental values on separate cards.
> Sort the cards, trying to pair each expense card with a values card.
> Assess how well your spending aligns with your values.
> Write a discovery statement ("I discovered that I . . .") and an intention statement ("I intend to . . .")

EXERCISE 14.8

The Life Balance Wheel and Money

Clients can be in reserve in areas of life beyond finances and money, coaches believe. Ask the client to refer to the Life Balance Wheel areas and to indicate in which areas they feel in reserve. The coaches can also provide clients with a list of areas to consider, such as these:

> Time
> Money
> Love

Relationships
Space
Freedom
Connections
Possibilities
Play
Quality of Life
Spirit
Energy

Then, in a coaching session, ask clients what principles or practices enable them to be in reserve in areas where they experience a reserve. Look for opportunities to apply similar practices and principles in areas where clients are not in reserve and believe they would benefit from having a sense of more than just enough in an area.

Even though this chapter is titled "How Wealthy Are You?" it is not limited to the usual sense of wealth as money. Wealth, in the larger view, is about having a sense of abundance—a ready reserve in all areas of life. A sense of wealth is unique to each individual and can be created thoughtfully in any area of a person's life.

CHAPTER 15

MIND-SET IS CAUSATIVE

The experience you have is a result of how you see . . . and how you see is a result of the experience you have. Your mind-set, beliefs, and body all work together.

As we begin to examine how coaches work with mind-set, you might take a look at a poem by Portia Nelson—"An Autobiography in Five Short Chapters" (Nelson, 1993)—and how it speaks to you about your work with clients. The poem points out, in just five stanzas, the importance and difficulty of changing how we observe, explain, create stories, take responsibility for our choices, and ultimately create new lives for ourselves.

Responses to events are mediated. In other words, when an event takes place, our responses—our behaviors—are shaped by (a) our interpretation of the event, which is a consequence of our beliefs, attitudes, and assumptions, and (b) the feelings generated by those beliefs, attitudes, and assumptions. Those beliefs, attitudes, and assumptions are the preexisting lenses we wear and look through, which determine, or at least color, our observation and interpretation of events. We discussed this earlier, offering the Ladder of Inference tool as a means of helping clients unpack their experiences.

This chapter focuses on mind-set—habitual patterns of thinking, feeling, and responding. Without calling these habits into question, clients will likely continue in a certain pattern in the absence of a big interruption or disruption. Because our memories, learning, and consciousness reside in all of our cells, we include the body in our definition of mind-set.

One of the coach's key roles is to assist clients in learning how they habitually see the world. As Peter Drucker (2003), the well-known business consultant and author, once said, "We don't know who discovered water, but we know it wasn't fish." Our own thinking—our mindset—tends to be invisible to us, as water is to the fish. The adage, we don't know what we don't know, is the basis for being unconsciously incompetent about something. Coaching helps with this and helps clients create what they want through creating conversations about possibilities. We sometimes say that coaching is a possibilities conversation, not a guarantees conversation.

Many research studies illustrate the power of mind-set, including an often-cited experiment in shooting baskets. An experimenter divided a group of basketball players into two groups. One group was to practice shooting free throws. The other group was asked to just visualize shooting free throws: to look at the basket and visualize themselves making the shot. Each person then shot a series of free throws. The not surprising conclusion, as many star athletes will tell you, is that the group that visualized made more free throws than the group that actually practiced. Why? Visualization—which is the mind-set at work—coupled with skill yields a better result. The opposite is also true. How many times have you seen an athlete choke because he was visualizing a negative result? He is afraid to miss the shot, swing the club, drop the pass. The very thing he is imagining and afraid of actually does happens. How many of you have played golf and know you can hit a nice approach shot—until you see water in front of you? Your mindset is, "Don't go in the water, don't go in the water." You repeatedly tell yourself about the water. And, of course, you are focused on the water and your ball goes right there, in exactly the place you are focused.

It is because of this fact that we say mindset is causative. To change a mindset requires two things: recognizing the need for change and being able to observe yourself and notice when you focus on things negatively.

As coaches, our main tasks are to:

- Surface clients' mind-sets and name them: "I'm operating from fear," or "You're operating from fear." In other words, the coaches support the clients to notice how they notice—the lens through which they view life.
- Build in conscious choice. Ask clients: "Does that mind-set support you in creating the future you want?"
- Have clients act on a new choice of mind-set and practice acting as if they live from that mind-set all the time.

Here is an example from a participant in an ILCT class, a man who flourished in the military and then became a counselor. He reported how he changed his mind-set. He used to have the belief, "I need to take control." In a class we were leading, we asked him to say more about that: "What's the WHY that underpins that belief?" He responded, "Because if I don't take control, we'll flounder!"

Most long-held beliefs like this are deeply ingrained because clients have thought them so many times that strong, myelinated neural pathways in their brain make it easy for the thought to run in that way: these are like brain ruts. In the case of the counselor with a background in the military, class discussion started him on a new path. With the teacher as coach, he decided that his first step was to learn to notice the pervasiveness of the mind-set of control and the places where his attention went in everyday life. He learned to consciously catch himself and lightly say, "Okay, Joe, now you're being a control freak."

Since awareness on its own is not enough, how did he change this pattern? His coach asked him to notice people who held mind-sets different from his. He noticed what those mind-sets were and asked himself what it would be like if he held them. He noticed that one thing he might say to himself is, "I could trust that the best will always happen. I don't always need to make it happen." He experimented with this new mind-set for a few weeks, religiously, and then noticed what was happening. He discovered that when he held this mind-set, "other people stepped up to the plate and made things happen, too, because he let them."

Some readers who have studied phenomenology, which was part of existential psychology during the 1960s (Rollo May, R. D. Laing, Victor Frankl, and others), call this the observing self: the ability to observe what you do as you do it. When clients access their observer self, they notice the phenomenon of their experience in the moment and then ask themselves what they can learn. The *observer self* increases clients' awareness—as if from an outside observer frame—which thereby increase choices for action.

Dr. Pat used to teach clients who were fearful of attending a family reunion, for example, to go and imagine themselves sitting outside themselves watching themselves participate as if in the show. They noticed whether the patterns played out as usual: was the usual drama going on? This third-party perspective helped them be neutral and detach from habitual emotional patterns. In the strategies from Neuro-Linguistic Programming, this is described as "third-person perspective." A first-person perspective looks at the situation from the person's own eyes. A second-person perspective experiences the situation from the perspective of another person. A third-person perspective watches both (or all) of the people, as well as the situation. From a third-person perspective, you can see yourself as well as observe; it is a further layer of detachment.

Coaches assist clients in developing their skills at observing themselves and their habitual behaviors, thoughts, and emotions. Clients need to be aware of how to gain distance from and perspective on their thoughts, feelings, and behavior, and how to step outside automatic behaviors.

Becoming aware of the observing self requires us to detach from our experience enough to notice how we see and explain to ourselves and others what occurs.

Our everyday way of observing allows us to see some things and causes us to disregard others. Consequently, our experience is shaped by the ways in which we characteristically and habitually observe, dwell in, and explain our world. Our habits of thinking, our habitual moods, our habits of using our energy, the ways we hold our bodies, and the stories we use to explain what has happened, what is happening, and what will happen—all of these habits and actions shape how we see and experience the world. They circumscribe our world and limit our possibilities.

We tend to notice only what our mind-set accepts. Depressed clients seldom notice the good things. They are too mired in the mind-set (and bodily experience) of depression to have anything else register in their awareness.

When coaches work with clients' mind-sets, they work with the greatest potential for the clients' development. Once clients have identified what they want to create, the major question becomes whether they have the mind-set—the beliefs, lenses, flow of energy, determination, and persistence—that it takes to bring their vision into reality. If they do not, your challenge as a coach is to support them in shifting their mindset and clearing the path to their self-expression and fulfillment.

HOW MINDSET IS SOURCED

When a mind-set becomes so familiar that it is habitual, we may lose sight of it as something we have adopted and mistake it for reality. When this happens, we may focus outside ourselves and say, "That's just how the world is," unaware we have choices. When this occurs, we are operating out of core beliefs that tend to be pervasive across the contexts of our experiences. Core beliefs generally dominate thinking and lead to predictable behaviors. They also limit our lives because we can only experience what our mind-set allows us to perceive and predict.

Back in Chapter 3, "Coaching as a Developmental Change Process," we introduced Kegan's levels of consciousness as one way of describing how consciousness develops. At each level, a particular mind-set is likely to dominate. Clients struggle when what they want to achieve in coaching is blocked by a mind-set that is a holdover from an earlier level of consciousness. Or they struggle when they are blocked by specific experiences that were so intense, they created brain ruts; that is, the habitual response is so wired into the clients' neural pathways that when the stimulus occurs, the neurons immediately fire in the habitual sequence. It will take many repetitions to create a new "brain trail" to replace the old one.

As clients grow, they are often in transition between levels. This is when coaches are most likely to see them struggle with issues of mindset.

For example, let us return to the case we examined in Chapter 3: George the chiropractor, who is working with you on career issues. His plans and goals primarily reflect the independent self or Expert stage (see p. 96). Perhaps he wishes to make a career change, which would move him away from a familiar 20-year career and which strays from others' expectations of him. He has not fully transitioned into the Expert stage, as evidenced by his intense fears around being judged and separated from others. These fears manifest as a lack of confidence in his ability to create a different career for himself.

George's fear is a signal that his current way of being and observing will not take him where he wants to go without addressing how he observes and interprets the situation and his choices. This is a perfect opportunity for a coach to support George's development by providing him with tools for transforming his mind-set.

What does the coach do? Some self-help writers might say, "Feel the fear and do it anyway." As life coaches, we encourage clients to first become astute observers of themselves—to observe the ways they consistently gather data, what they notice and what they ignore, how they make judgments about situations, and what data they use to make these judgments. We ask them to notice how they hold their body and, how they breathe in situations where they feel fearful. We ask them to notice their internal dialogue and to notice which aspects of the situation they take in and which they ignore.

As a coach, you work with George the chiropractor to assist him in becoming aware of his tendencies, and how to make distinctions about other possible perspectives and options. Once he has stopped to notice, can make distinctions, and can comfortably live with the fact that, "Yes, this is how I'm seeing the situation—and I recognize that there are other ways of observing it," he is ready to make a transformational shift that can be maintained.

Clients' mind-sets often show up visibly around their perceptions of their body, their health, and the ways they consider self-care. Superb self-care is critical to our clients as well as to us as coaches. Our integrity is jeopardized when we encourage self-care for clients but do not take care of ourselves. These are common areas where human beings struggle. Sometimes the issue is that the clients are holding old or outdated, unexamined beliefs about body, health, and self-care (or other areas).

Matthew Budd made a distinction that can be useful in coaching mind-set. Budd and other philosophers, including Fernando Flores, believe that human beings often confuse assessments with assertions. An assessment is "a judgment that you make about the world in the interest of taking some action" (Budd & Rothstein, 2000, p. 138). For example, Diane might say, "It's a beautiful day!" She's in Cincinnati on the first day of spring, the sun is shining after weeks of rain and cloud cover, and it is 60 degrees outside. On the other hand, Dr. Pat might not agree at all that it is a beautiful day. For Dr. Pat, who spends a lot of time in the Rocky Mountains, a "beautiful day" would be a summer day where the sun is shining through a grove of aspen trees next to a mountain stream or a beautiful day might be a winter day when the weather is snowy, the sun is out, and Dr. Pat can snowshoe through the woods. Our point here is that beauty as a quality is not in the day itself, but rather in the eyes of the person who makes the judgment about beauty using his or her particular standards for it. Assessments are not facts—they are interpretations and opinions. They may have once been informed by facts and standards, but the person who makes the assessment may no longer remember the standard.

An assertion, on the other hand, is a statement a person makes for which he or she is willing to provide evidence, and the evidence is something that can be measured—height, weight, size, event, and so on. A good assessment is grounded in assertions. The person can return to commonly agreed-upon standards for making the judgment that is the assessment.

When we coach clients around body, health, self-care, and almost any other area, what will emerge first is their assessments. Their assessments are windows into their mindset. These may have been formed very early in their lives and not adjusted. They may no longer be based in facts—assertions—but instead on some memory of being the recipient of someone's judgments or of learning how something should be. This occurs frequently with young women, who take in their culture's assessments on how much a young woman should weigh and how she should look. In the United States, this has resulted in many young women believing they are overweight without realizing that they have taken in the culture and the media's assessments as their own without consideration. So, one way of working with clients around this area is to ask them to list their beliefs about body, health, self-care, and so on, and then help them discover the sources of these beliefs. What assertions and assessments are holding the beliefs together?

ASK YOURSELF:

What is your mind-set around your body? Your health? Self-care?

USING WILBER'S FOUR QUADRANT MODEL TO MAKE DISTINCTIONS FOR OBSERVING

In Chapter 3, we introduced Ken Wilber's Four Quadrant model for identifying factors that shape the way an individual views a situation. A person is often more aware of some quadrants than others. For example, many physicians are highly skilled in the exterior-individual quadrant and much less skilled in the interior-individual quadrant. The two left-hand quadrants, the interior-individual and the interior-collective, are generally fertile places from which to ask clients to observe their way of being and observing in the world.

When the coach asks George to observe his ongoing interior dialogue, the coach is asking him to identify the running commentary his mind makes on his experience. That is an interior-individual (Quadrant 1) approach to George's experience. George might discover how pessimistic his internal dialogue is and how a common mind-set for him is "It won't work!" when considering new possibilities.

George, for example, may be ignoring how much his way of being and observing has been shaped by the cultural (interior-collective) quadrant. To examine the impact of that quadrant, we need to look at the cumulative impact of events on an individual at a particular time in history or from a particular culture. You might consider steering George to the internet to explore this issue. The caution, of course, is that searching the internet today can lead to false facts and algorithms that only feed you one side of the "news." Look for reputable sources.

FIGURE 15.1

The Client and the Context

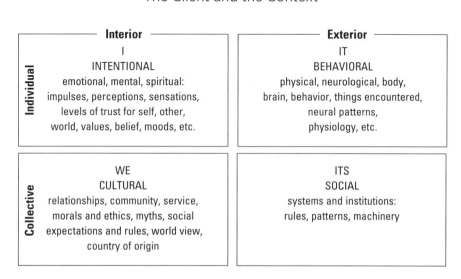

A coach might ask George to consider what a mindset list for his generation, his family, and his cultural background might include—since all these factors influence him and the fear he is experiencing. In Figure 15.1, first introduced in Chapter 3, the interior-individual quadrant is the focus of most of the work done in the helping professions, including spiritual direction. This quadrant is rich territory for coaching. If you use the Enneagram in your therapy or coaching, you could say that each of the nine Enneagram types has a pervasive mindset. The Enneagram is an ancient system of examining the preconditioned points of view of nine spiritual-psychological frameworks. Each of these frameworks has its strengths, and each one also has characteristic ways of blocking individuals from a sense of wholeness in the world.

When we work with clients to develop their abilities to self-observe, we can ask them to consider where they may be holding their beliefs too rigidly.

For the client George, it might be beneficial to invite him to think about rigidity by introducing him to the ideas of learned optimism and pessimism. You might ask him to read the article summary below, "Learned Optimism, Learned Pessimism," and then to observe which of the patterns (or a modification thereof) he is using that may be driving his career fears.

Learned Optimism, Learned Pessimism

Martin Seligman, a past president of the American Psychological Association, devoted much of his later career to researching how the observer becomes rigidified. In a lecture, Seligman linked the incidence of depression in teenagers to mind-set patterns that we can trace back to a disturbance in Wilber's Four Quadrants. Seligman's research indicated that depression is 10 times more common than it was two generations ago. In fact, the average age for the onset of depression in wealthy nations has dropped from 29.5 to 14 years old. Seligman (2003) attributed the drop to three causes:

I/We Balance: We have become rampantly individualistic, where our grandparents had larger entities with which to connect. Our grandparents had rich, comfortable spiritual furniture in which to sit—God, community, and extended families to console them. These have crumbled. Our children have threadbare spiritual furniture to sit in.

Self-esteem Movement: Thirty years ago, it was *The Little Engine That Could*, while today the emblematic books suggest feeling good about yourself no matter what you do.

Victimology: It is legion in the United States to blame others. Seligman noted some of the benefits, for example, for alcoholics who can now say they have a disease and seek treatment without thinking they are terrible people, and for the Civil Rights movement, which acknowledged the capabilities of people while stating many are victims of discrimination. Victimology disempowers people because it takes the focus away from what they can do and puts their focus on others. We know this from examples like that of Victor Frankl (1946/2006). Frankl survived Auschwitz, the World War II concentration camp, by focusing on a future he desired and using his day-to-day experience of suffering as a means of learning about human behavior. It would have been easy for him to embrace victimology: he was, in fact, an incarcerated victim of religious persecution. He did not succumb but instead took it upon himself to forgo the role of victim and play the role of a survivor. He took responsibility for his life. The major cost of victimology is the erosion of responsibility, according to Seligman.

Seligman's research on learning indicates that individuals have a pessimistic or optimistic explanatory style based on a pessimistic or optimistic way of thinking. In other words, optimistic individuals tend to see the benefits of events, have half the tendency for depression, achieve more, enjoy better physical health, sustain better interpersonal relationships, and are less realistic. Here's how they do it:

When a setback or negative experience occurs, three characteristics of an optimistic individual's thinking come into play. An optimist's explanatory style, in contrast with a pessimist's explanatory style, is to perceive and experience the event as: (a) temporary rather than permanent; (b) local (to the event) rather than pervasive; and (c) attributable to external causes. This third characteristic is worth elaborating on—the optimist makes an external attribution, crediting outside contributing circumstances, as opposed to an internal attribution, crediting the individual's actions, lack thereof, or way of being for the setback.

Conversely, when optimistic individuals have a positive experience, they see it as permanent and pervasive, and make internal attributions—the same characteristics of the pessimistic style for setbacks! The pessimistic explanatory style, when a setback or negative event occurs, is a key contributor to depression.

Not all pessimists end up in therapy. You will find many coaching clients using a pessimistic explanatory style around specific areas of their lives, such as health, body, relationships, and family. As coaches, we help by challenging their explanation—that is, raising questions that challenge and dispute their mindset. This is different from simply affirming a different way of being or behaving.

Ideally, a coach aims for assisting a client in developing flexible optimism. Seligman suggested in the same lecture, "When the cost of failure is high, use the pessimist's realism. When the cost of failure is low, use the optimist's realism. You don't want a pilot using an optimist's realism to decide whether he or she should de-ice the plane. You certainly don't want to use an optimist's realism to decide whether you should have an affair that could ruin your relationships with your family."

Optimism can be an important coaching focus. Much of the research on emotional intelligence done by Reuven Bar-On (1997) and by Daniel Goleman (2005) identifies optimism as a competency of emotional intelligence. Bar-On's self-assessment, the Emotional Quotient Inventory (or EQ-I), identifies two factors that are highly correlated with success: optimism and happiness. At ILCT, we have trained many practicing psychologists and licensed therapists, and consequently many students can readily use psychometrically valid assessments with clients. The EQ-I is particularly helpful to coaches working with client mind-set (Bar-On, 1997).

How can you use this to assist your client? Use optimism assessment tools, like the one Seligman has developed, as a stimulus for self-observation.[22]

WORKING WITH MIND-SET

In the following pages, we describe frequently used coaching methods for working with a client's mind-set or beliefs.

Disputing the Belief

A commonly used process to work with beliefs comes from rational-emotive behavioral therapy (REBT), of which one famous practitioner is Albert Ellis. The ABC framework is used to clarify the relationship between an activating event (A), our beliefs about it (B), and the cognitive–emotional or behavioral consequences of our beliefs (C).[23] While REBT was developed by a psychologist, it has been widely used in nonclinical settings, including schools. If a coach were to use this framework with the control-oriented client described above, the conversation might go like this:

A: The activating event—Joe finds himself at a church committee meeting, in charge of a major fund-raising drive for a new building. He is already heading up two other major projects for his church and is very busy at work. When the minister asks, "Who can lead this project?" Joe finds

---

22 Seligman has an optimism assessment available on his website at www.authentichappiness.sas.upenn.edu/.

23 A good site for the nonclinician is https://counsellingresource.com/therapy/types/rational-emotive/.

himself automatically thinking, "I must do it—I must be in charge of it. If I don't, we'll flounder."

B: The belief—"I must do it—I have to be in charge of it. If I don't, we'll flounder."

C: The consequences—If Joe takes on this assignment, he will probably do it well. But he will be overwhelmed and overloaded and feel irritable and somewhat victimized by the fact that nobody else seems to step up.

Once the client has surfaced the belief, the coach's task is to help Joe discover the alternatives. The coach can help him surface some evidence that contradicts this belief as a way of disputing the fact that this is the only way things can happen. The coach might ask, "What evidence do you have that this isn't always true?" Joe will probably have to stretch himself to find some examples. In this case, he reported that when he was laid up after surgery for 8 to 12 weeks, he was amazed at how his church, family, and work all seemed to do okay without him. The coach would help him identify specific examples that contradicted his belief and discuss how other people stepped in when Joe was unavailable.

The next step would be to generate alternatives through coaching. The coach might ask, "Joe, what are other things you could say to yourself in situations like these?" and would help Joe identify some new options. Joe might say, as above, "I can trust that the right thing will happen and wait for someone else to step up. Things always do work out." This is a time to have fun with the client and help him take a different perspective. We sometimes ask clients, "What would Robin Williams say or do in this situation?" to jostle them out of a fixed mindset. Generate several other alternatives with the client, asking how an objective observer might see the situation. For example, what do other people in Joe's congregation seem to be thinking?

The next step is to help Joe identify other actions he can take that grow out of this new way of thinking. For example, the coach might request that Joe wait at least three minutes before volunteering for anything, to leave room for others to step up. Joe could also nominate somebody else or mentor someone in the church. Any of these choices are based on a new mind-set. The client's task is to notice, surface, experiment, and then choose to act differently when appropriate.

The hard part, of course, is that many clients have become very successful with the mind-sets they are now trying to change. They often come to coaching because these mindsets contribute to success but not fulfillment. The coach can help clients visualize how they can be successful and fulfilled by thinking differently.

Affirmations

Many of us use affirmations to make mind-set shifts. Since we constantly affirm our beliefs and values, and demonstrate our consciousness through our thoughts, speech, writing, and other actions, affirmations provide unique opportunities for clients to literally put into words, with conviction, what they intend to hold, maintain, create, and declare. A popular tool we use with clients is asking them to buy a daybook such as Joan Borysenko's *Pocketful of Miracles* (1994), which contains a thought that is a good mind-starter for each day of the year. These small statements of inner wisdom function to affirm a positive, connected, universal mindset for clients. They are affirmations.

Affirmations are generally thought of as single sentences repeated frequently that people intend to adopt as a new way of thinking and being. Most affirmations are intention statements. Someone may affirm something and be surprised that nothing happens—at least initially. Affirmations are not designed to dispute reality. They are designed as statements of intention, to increase the likelihood that the intention will come to pass. But they are also habits of mind. If clients' minds have been repeating to themselves for 20 years that they are not good enough, it will take many repetitions of an alternative affirmation before their habits of mind change. They are creating new neurological links, and the brain will tend to want to run in the old tracks instead of the new. Someone using affirmations must keep up the practice until the new way of thinking overtakes the old.

Dr. Pat spoke with Bill O'Hanlon (personal conversation, 2001) about O'Hanlon's labeling of his brand of therapy as possibility counseling. O'Hanlon said that he doesn't like the terms negative thinking and positive thinking. Instead, he uses the rubric of possibility because possibility leads a person to a desired outcome via his or her intention. It does not guarantee that something negative or positive will not happen—it just makes the outcome more likely based on the client's desired intention. Teaching someone to think positively is not enough: there need to be actions that support the desired possibility, as well as an understanding there is no guarantee. We wonder whether it might instead be called probability counseling.

This ties in with our discussion of mind-set in that we believe in living purposefully with a designed plan for change or creation, while also understanding that life happens, and adjustments may need to be made. Sometimes the work clients do with regular affirmations succeeds. At other times, to our dismay, something seems to work against the new mind-set taking root in the clients' life.

If you and a client discover that new mind-sets are not taking root, we suggest you follow the process that Jeanie Marshall has described in "Five Types of Affirmations for Empowerment" (Marshall, n.d.). By choosing the appropriate affirmation from five possible types, you increase the likelihood of its effectiveness.

Five Types of Affirmations for Personal Development

Five categories of affirmations support you in manifesting powerful change. You may work with affirmations in every category concurrently, or you may focus on a different category each day or each week. It is important that affirmations you select resonate—they should feel natural and appropriate. To experience this resonance, you may need to change words in the ones listed here as examples, let these inspire you to create ones you prefer, or develop your own from scratch.

Popular Affirmations

Many popular affirmations are beautiful; indeed, they are quite extraordinary. However, if you do not believe them, they are useless or even counterproductive. If you say an affirmation you do not believe, saying it repeatedly will not make you believe it. The repetition can build up greater resistance to believing it. Consider this example: Sam feels powerless. He has had many experiences he can point to that justify his feelings and his belief in his own powerlessness and unworthiness. Saying "I am powerful" is less likely to erase his feelings of powerlessness than to prompt an emphatic reaction, such as, "Oh, no, I'm not!" If Sam does not deal with the resistance, he carries it with him.

An empowering process emerges by using these five categories of affirmations in a systematic way to assist you in embracing an affirmation that you desire to believe but currently do not. If you have an intention and a desire to say and believe "I am powerful," start by releasing powerlessness, open to the possibility of being powerful, affirm an intention and readiness to live in your power, claim your power, and let the idea of powerfulness integrate into your life.

Following are the five categories of affirmations described briefly, with a few examples of each type.

1. Releasing/Cleansing Affirmations

The purpose of releasing and/or cleansing affirmations is to let go of unwanted and unneeded stuff. They allow you to purify your system. These affirmations stimulate the release of toxins such as negative thoughts, repressed or suppressed emotions, old memories, negative bonds with others, dark consensus reality, and illusions of all types.

Examples:
I rescind outdated commitments to poverty, celibacy, struggle,
      silence, and unworthiness.
I release resistance.
I let go of old programs that keep me stuck in old patterns.
I let go of everything I do not want or need for my highest good.

2. Receiving/Accepting Affirmations

The purpose of receiving and/or accepting affirmations is to allow something to be. They allow us to receive goodness from the universe. They also neutralize the disproportion of energy—that is, they can reverse illness, or another imbalance. They help us shift the attention from disempowering actions such as getting or taking to more freeing concepts such as receiving, allowing, and accepting.

Examples:
I open to the gifts of the universe.
I allow abundance to flow through me.
I accept support when I need it.
Dear God, please let me know what to do in a way that I can
      understand.

I accept peace and joy in all aspects of my life.

3. Being/Intending Affirmations

The purpose of being and/or intending affirmations is to ground your purpose, especially your higher purpose. These affirmations enhance conscious awareness of your intention about something or your mission in life. These affirmations deepen your understanding of your reason for being and/or acting, either in general or in a specific situation. They can be used to enhance all actions.

Examples:
I know this is for the highest good of all concerned.
I deepen my awareness of the consciousness from which
*   actions spring.*
I live my mission.
My intention is to live free from struggle, fear, and hopelessness.
I remember.

4. Acting/Claiming Affirmations

The purpose of acting and/or claiming affirmations is to bring something into manifestation or to direct the energy of your intention to appropriate manifestation. These affirmations bring into physical being those ideas that you hold in your mind and/or heart. In addition, these affirmations help you claim your power and establish boundaries in relationships.

Examples:
I act with high intention and purposeful awareness.
I step into the world to live my mission in every word and action.
I demand my good right now.
I make every act an act of love (or freedom, mastery, or hope, etc.).
I am powerful. I am worthy. I am loveable. I am free.

5. Integrating/Embodying Affirmations

The purpose of integrating and/or embodying affirmations is to allow the energy and meaning of the affirmations to merge with your consciousness. Affirmations and ideas that do not resonate drop away. Integrating/

embodying affirmations support us in knowing more deeply—in integrating what we have learned, rather than introducing new information.

> Examples:
> *I integrate trust into every aspect of my life.*
> *I breathe love into my job, my body, and my relationships.*
> *Yes to life!*
> *Today is an opportunity for peace.*
> *I breathe in abundance, letting my whole body feel its energy.*

Affirmations as Lifestyle

As you work with intentional affirmations—written, spoken, read, chanted, meditated upon—you will make them part of your lifestyle. Affirmations are already working for (or against) you. It is your job to select the ones you want to live by. Remember, you are already using affirmations every time you think or speak. If your current affirmations are disempowering, you can intentionally change them to ones by which you choose to live.

Moods, Emotions, and the Body

Affirmations work primarily on a cognitive level. An affirmation is a new thought. Until it is repeated enough that it can develop a neurological connection in the brain, it will not become a habitual way of thinking.

Body and emotions are critical to observing and shifting mind-set, too. Using Wilber's Quadrant 1 (interior-individual), we can ask coaching clients to observe their personal pervasive moods and to compare them with the pervasive moods of Wilber's Quadrant 3 (interior collective). Imagine that George the chiropractor finds, for example, that dealing with the chronic pain and complaints of his patients creates a mind-set of irritation, despair, and resignation in the culture of his office. He and his staff feel resigned to dealing with the litany of daily complaints and feel relatively powerless to step outside the negative effect their patients have on them. George finds himself frequently feeling down, disempowered, and resigned to this way of life. He is not angry—just resigned that nothing will change.

We focus now on Quadrant 2 by asking George to observe and demonstrate how he sits when he feels resigned—how he holds his body at the office. As he reports to his coach, his reports will be from Quadrant 1 (interior-individual). He discovers that he tends to experience a great deal of tension, to hunch over, and to clench his forearms and lower legs. George is telling you that he contracts his body, making it smaller. One possibility for working with George might be to ask him to deliberately hold his body in a different way and notice whether that changes his feelings and emotions. A useful fieldwork assignment for him would be to identify how he holds his body when he is feeling open, flexible, and light, to practice holding his body that way in his office or at times when he experiences moods of resignation, and to notice what happens.

Working with the Judging Mind

Once a client begins to self-observe, many paths for working with mind-set open. Many useful practices exist for working with or moving beyond a chronic tendency toward an assessing and judging mind-set, which may block a client from feeling and experiencing life (Menendez, 2000).

Managers and professionals are paid to become highly adept at making judgments: "What's a right investment?" "What's a wrong investment?" "Who's capable and who's not?" "What's the right plan?" "Am I good enough, capable enough, worthy enough?" These thoughts fill up their mental space with plans and stories that can interfere with their ability to experience the present moment. This is mind clutter.

Chronic attachment to a judging mind has a high cost. The potential for change—the moment of choice—is always right now, in the present. When clients spend too much time judging, dwelling on the past, or imagining the future, they miss the beauty and power of the moment. Fulfillment comes when they focus on the here and now.

Clients experience joy and fulfillment when they let go of the judger and embrace the learner in themselves through the discovery of a beginner's mind. They shift in consciousness from "It isn't enough, and here's what it could be instead" toward a recognition that "What's here is just right for now."

EXERCISE 15.1

Examine the Judging Mind

A judging mind sees the world in either/or terms—in black or white. A judging mind is reactive; it asks questions such as:

What's wrong with this person, the situation, or me?
What do I need to do to stay in control?
Who is to blame; whose fault is it?
How can I win?
How can I look good?

Set a digital watch so that it sounds on the hour, every hour, between 6 a.m. and 10 p.m. When it sounds, write down the specific thoughts you were having at that moment. At the end of the week, ask how your habits of mind serve you and how they limit you.

EXERCISE 15.2

Practice Beginner's Mind

A beginner's mind sees the world with fresh eyes, allows for both/and terms and shades of gray, and responds flexibly to whatever it encounters. A beginner's mind asks questions such as:

What can be appreciated here?
What can I learn?
What are the choices?
What am I feeling and experiencing right now?

Set a digital watch so that it sounds on the hour, every hour, between 6 a.m. and 10 p.m. When it sounds, use a beginner's mind. Write down what you experience in specific terms.

EXERCISE 15.3

Breathe Consciously and Focus on the Present

Do a four-minute meditation once per hour at work. Sit in a quiet place and focus your attention on your breath. Exhale fully from the deepest place inside your being. Focus only on your breath. When distracting thoughts come, notice them, and simply return to your breathing.

EXERCISE 15.4

8-4-8 Breathing
One mindful breathing approach is to count and create a rhythm of inhale and exhale that induces relaxation. This can be done by inhaling to a count of eight, holding the breath for a count of four, and exhaling for a count of eight. Many clients find the counting focuses their attention on the present and allows them to return to whatever they are doing in a more conscious, open way.

Fear versus Trust

In its simplest form, we can identify a client's mind-set by asking whether it is based on fear or trust. In the example of the client earlier who believed he had to be in control and make things happen, his mindset can easily be tracked on the four-celled matrix (see Figure 15.2). Above the horizontal axis are cells representing beliefs that are positive, life-giving, and sustaining for most clients—in other words, beliefs based on trust. Below the horizontal axis are beliefs about insufficiency and danger that generate fear. The left columns are beliefs about the self, or "I." The right columns are beliefs about others or the world in general. Clients can use this matrix to observe how they judge

FIGURE 15.2

Belief Matrix

I am . . .
    Enough
    Worthy
    Competent
	You/Environment are . . .
	    Supportive
	    Enough
	    Abundant

I am not . . .
    Enough
    Worthy
    Competent
	You/Environment are not . . .
	    Supportive
	    Enough
	    Abundant

themselves, others, and possibilities, and track any core belief to discover whether it is rooted in fear or trust. Joe was focused outside himself—on other people and on the environment, which would not readily give him what he wanted. With a new mind-set, others started to behave differently: they supported his actions, and he easily got what he wanted.

As another example, a client says to us, "I'm really afraid to step out and start this business." That statement might have undertones concerning a belief about the self—"I am not sufficiently worthy or skilled to do this." It might have undertones concerning a belief about others and the world—"There are not enough people out there who want this product, and there is too much competition."

We can use the matrix to help clients vocalize fears. Listen to what clients say, and then place each statement in the appropriate cell(s) of the matrix. The key questions to ask are: "Is this belief helpful?" "Does it support you in creating what you want?" If not, explore together what beliefs would be more supportive, then discover what it would take for clients to begin to step into those new beliefs.

Replacing Fear with Love and Trust

When clients learn to suspend judgment, they notice how the mind tricks them into feeling anxious by focusing on the future and making judgments. Research shows that human beings naturally fear only three things: falling, high places, and tight spaces. A judging mind creates fear by focusing on "what if" and imagining a terrible future. Fear causes muscles to contract and creates chronic tension. Energy invested in contracting is energy clients could be investing in growth.

When clients acknowledge the limiting power of fear and can let go, they release themselves from tension that clamps down on their life like a vise. They open up to trusting themselves, others, and experience in general. Here are some exercises clients may find useful (Menendez, 2000):

- Examine the energy of your relationships. Who are the people around you with whom you feel most energized? Most calm? Most de-energized? What story do you tell yourself about them that is de-energizing you?
- Experience others. How skilled are you at connecting with others well? Can you be close and feel safely vulnerable? Can you maintain distance

without feeling arrogance or anxiety? Rate each of your key work and family relationships using a scale from 1 to 10 (1 = distant, 5 = optimal, 10 = merged). What is your pattern?

• Find the root. When you are feeling blocked by fear, ask yourself, "What other fears are fueling this one?" Identify a root fear, such as the fear of pain, loss or lack, abandonment/separation/ rejection, being of no value, being judged, or being meaninglessness. Root fears fuel feelings of being anxious, nervous, unsettled, and unfocused. The trick here is that our brain links habitual thoughts—one fearful thought has elaborate links to others.

• Find opportunities for love. Situations that trigger fear are opportunities for love—in other words, for relationship and connection with others. Find out who or what you need to connect with and love, because love drives out fear.

• Learn from my teachers. See every person and every situation as a teacher. Ask, "What can I learn here?"

• Cultivate gratitude. Cultivate a sense of appreciation and gratitude for everything that shows up in your life. Practice wonder, reverence, and awe daily. These are ways of expressing love. They relieve pain and connect us with joy. Each day this week, end your day by listing 10 things for which you are grateful. Do not name anything you named on previous days.

In this chapter we have focused on one of the most deceptively simple truths from ancient times: What you think determines what you believe, and what you believe influences your experience . . . and may even create your reality. This is one of the most powerful places for coaches to work.

CHAPTER 16

LOVE IS ALL WE NEED

Sigmund Freud once said that what is important in life is to love and to work. For many of us, it is easier to work well than love and be loved well. That may be because intimacy is where the greatest struggle often takes place. According to research done using the FIRO-B, a psychometric instrument that determines fundamental interpersonal relations orientation, intimacy is the area for most people with the biggest gap between what they express (i.e., what they offer to others) and what they want.

What we mean by love in this chapter is not the usual sense of love as romance or intimacy with a partner. The world's major spiritual teachers have said that there are only two real emotions: love and fear. We speak of love here in the same sense as spiritual leaders and writers: Love as an emotion is the absence of fear. Love is a potential we want to experience. Love is a state of being—a love consciousness our clients can access that allows them to be courageous, purposeful, and in harmony with their values. Love is experienced in the body as well. Experiencing love, our body feels expansive. We feel centered, grounded, energized, available, and in touch with our whole being—what some might experience as a state of bliss. This state is the opposite of fear. When we experience fear, our body contracts. Physiologically, fear causes our muscles to tighten and prepares us to flee, fight, or freeze. We know from research that states generated by fear literally cause our field of sight to narrow, giving us tunnel vision. We literally experience our world as contracted, more limited, and more threatening. Therefore, we say love is all you need. When in doubt, come back to love as a centering point.

In common understanding, love is also the act of creation. So, when clients are attempting to create in their life, love is the state that allows them to be creative. We create the feeling of love through connecting to people, to the earth, to life itself, to something larger than ourselves. Whether we realize it or not, we are always connected. When we are conscious of this connection, love can occur. One basic issue that we encounter frequently in our coaching is that clients feel isolated, particularly in industrialized cultures like that of the United States. They may feel this as loneliness. We coach them to acknowledge the connectedness they live in. Connectedness is a quality of life for all human beings, and to be unaware of our own connectedness is to be unaware of love.

Because human life is a connected life, the quality of each depends on the quality of our relationships—with family, friends, community, a higher power, and ourselves. When one or more of these relationships becomes unfulfilling, our life becomes unfulfilling.

EXPRESSIONS OF LOVE

The title of this chapter comes from a great song by the Beatles (Lennon & McCartney, 1967). You may be old enough to have heard it on the airwaves. It was easy to remember and carried a profound, timeless message. Written by John Lennon and Paul McCartney, "All You Need Is Love" repeated the title line over and over throughout the song. It addressed the listener directly as "you," reinforcing the personal message that love is an essential and powerful force for change. This is a message coaches often use with clients encouraging them to care for and appreciate others, as well as to let love in.

Sometimes love scares us because it can bring hurt. Mother Teresa tried to make sense of this for a reporter who asked her how to love without being hurt. She said, "I have found the paradox that if I love until it hurts, then there is no hurt, but only more love." Dr. Martin Luther King Jr. echoed her poetic statement of this paradox: "Darkness cannot drive out darkness; only light can do that. Hate cannot drive out hate; only love can do that."

Sometimes our role as parents requires us to love until it hurts. Especially for parents of adolescents, loving until it hurts seems like a hard road. The National Longitudinal Study of Adolescent to Adult Health found that a sense of connection at home and a sense of connection at school were the two conditions most protective of children's well-being. It was the perception of connection itself that was key, not any specific program or set of actions.

For coaches and parents of adolescents alike, Harry Palmer's definition of love offers us a hand to hold in times of frustration: "Love is an expression of the willingness to create space in which something is allowed to change" (1997, p. 18).

Some people resist intimacy and love because they seem confining—a prison of sorts. Being separate feels somehow safer. As Larry Dossey said, "We have for so long defined ourselves as separate personalities that we have fallen into the hypnotic spell of believing that separation, not unity, is the underlying reality" (2006, p. 72).

Yet those who truly love then bring that love wherever they are, bridging even extreme spaces of separation and distance. An example of this ability to transform through love was told by Frida and Kate Berrigan (2003), as they offered reflections at the funeral of their father, the Reverend Philip Berrigan. Philip Berrigan died on Dec. 6, 2002, at the age of 79. A white Catholic priest whose early ministry among African Americans opened his eyes to racism and social injustice, he later left the priesthood but never left his commitment to justice, nonviolence, and peace. He was jailed numerous times for acts of nonviolence and spent a total of 11 years in prison for these acts. As a writer, teacher, and activist, he stirred the conscience of many with his call to radical fidelity to the gospel of peace as an expression of love for all. At his funeral, his daughter said:

> Over the years, we had many occasions to visit our dad in countless prisons. We have spent time with him in all these dead spaces: spaces meant to intimidate and beat down; spaces that repel and resist children, laughter, loving and family; spaces.
>
> Some families would sit silently in the visiting rooms, some would play cards, some would fight. It seemed like those families and the loved ones they were visiting were burdened by a sense that in jail, everything was different; life does not go on as usual. You are not free to do as you please or be who you are.
>
> But our dad never seemed touched by that weight. Even in prison, even in those awful spaces, he was free. In prison, as in the outside world, his work and his life were to resist violence and oppression, to understand and try to live by God's word, to build community and help people learn to love one another.
>
> When we visited our dad in prison, we paid no heed to those spoken and unspoken rules; we filled those places with love, with family,

with stories, with laughter. He was free in prison, thereby showing us that freedom has nothing to do with where your body is, or with who holds the keys and who makes the rules. It has everything to do with where your heart is.

LEARNING TO LOVE OURSELVES

Most of us are taught early how to love others—that we should love others—but we do not learn how to love ourselves. Many have been taught that to love ourselves is wrong, even a sin. Consequently, many clients in midlife discover they do not love themselves very much at all. We believe that we need to learn to love ourselves so we have the capacity to fully love others. Think of the metaphor of a cup that, when full, has enough reserve to give to others. If all people do is empty their cup all day—through conflict, stress, and worry—and they are not having experiences that refill their cup, they have nothing left to give to others. When they arrive home, they cannot give to spouses, children, or themselves. Be aware of when your cup is empty. Consider what you can do to refill yourself.

Loving ourselves is nothing we need to feel ashamed of or embarrassed about. Loving ourselves makes us more loveable. In addition, loving ourselves teaches us how to love and care for others, which means we can love others more richly. Sometimes this is the task of coaching—to help clients recover their capacity to love. Before we can love someone else fully, we must care for ourselves.

Before we can fall in love with someone, we must fall in love with ourselves. Loving ourselves will attract people to us. People who love themselves are a delight to be around. If you have ever been around someone who lacks self-love, you know how distressing that can be. Underneath a thin veneer of adaptation to what others expect lies a pool of self-hatred. It depletes us to be around that kind of energy. Those who love themselves naturally love others and have a respect for others and their well-being. Self-love creates positive energy that attracts more positive energy.

Until we truly create a loving relationship with ourselves, other relationships will not be as fulfilling as they could be. When we do not love ourselves, we look for others to fill the void, which drains the energy from our outside relationships. When we love ourselves, we do not have to look outside to have our needs met and, therefore, we can simply enjoy the other relationships for what they are. Outside relationships do not have to compensate for what we are missing inside—they can add to it. This can make the love of others that much sweeter because it is the extra, the icing on the cake.

Self-love is the quiet inner sense people carry that tells others they are competent, valuable, and worthy of giving and receiving love. Self-love is critical for mental health and happiness, as well as the best insurance against mental distress and depression. A person with self-love can face and handle the shocks and setbacks that inevitably happen in life. Without self-love, the problems of life are more difficult. Something is always missing that can only come from within.

When clients lack self-love, they find it difficult to take care of themselves. As they learn to love themselves, their willingness and ability to care for themselves increases (Williams & Davis, 2007, pp. 176–197, Chapter 12).

LOVE IS A CHOICE

Love is a choice . . . not simply or always a rational choice, but rather the willingness to be present to others fully without pretense. We both use this and teach others to ask, "What does this statement mean to you?" Many reflect on the fact that being present—authentically present—makes exquisite sense and sounds simple. Yet it is very difficult for many of us.

If love is a choice, a key coaching question becomes, "What gets in the way of choosing love for you? What do you choose instead of love?" We ask clients to do this as a fieldwork activity, noticing over the course of a week what they choose instead of love or connection. Common examples of what people choose instead of love include self-focus, anger, judgments, expectations, being right, being busy, and worries. Once clients have identified what gets in the way of choosing love, we can then ask these questions: "How is it you choose these instead of love?" "How can you help yourself choose love instead?"

Sometimes clients need to begin a practice of some sort to begin to build their capacity to choose love. One thing we know is that many people who report feeling very fulfilled have practices associated with gratitude. Keeping a journal in which clients record at least three daily gratitudes is highly associated with increased joy and lowered incidence of depression (Seligman, 2003).

We also offer Harry Palmer's quote to clients and students as a fieldwork inquiry: "Love is an expression of the willingness to create space in which something is allowed to change." We then ask clients, "If you accepted this view of love, what would you do differently with yourself and with others this week?"

We use several exercises to help ILCT coaches and clients engage with the issue of love as a choice.

EXERCISE 16.1

The Compassion Exercise

The exercise is based on Palmer's (1997) belief that when people are honest with themselves, they will feel compassion with others. That is, people need to recognize they are not special but are simply human beings, just like other human beings. Those they are angry with are human. With this humility comes compassion for themselves as well as others. This exercise actively demonstrates the powerful role of mindset and its impact on the clients' emotions and well-being. The clients pick a specific person on which to focus for the exercise and then complete the following five steps mindfully.

Step 1. With attention on the person, repeat to yourself:
"Just like me, this person is seeking some happiness for his/her life."
Step 2. With attention on the person, repeat to yourself:
"Just like me, this person is trying to avoid suffering in his/her life."
Step 3. With attention on the person, repeat to yourself:
"Just like me, this person has known sadness, loneliness, and despair."
Step 4. With attention on the person, repeat to yourself:
"Just like me, this person is seeking to fulfill his/her needs."
Step 5. With attention on the person, repeat to yourself:
"Just like me, this person is learning about life."

We have used this exercise with clients by reading the steps to them as they focus their attention on the person. Most clients report a shift in their emotions after the exercise, which usually brings them to a sense of compassion for the other person that may have been missing earlier. We also find it brings about the sense of connection that is the foundation for love, as we have been describing.

We once tried a variation of this exercise with a client who was having difficulty justifying any time she spent on her own self-care. We asked her to identify someone she respected and cared about, whose way of treating herself she admired. We then asked her to visualize herself as that person—acting as if—and to look from that friend's eyes onto her own face, repeating the five steps. This exercise resulted in a great sense of personal peace and opened the possibility of self-care for this client.

EXERCISE 16.2

Expressing Love

We said earlier that human beings learn better how to love others than how to love themselves. Through this exercise, we ask clients to learn from themselves how they can better love themselves. These exercises are meant to be done within a coaching session when the intention is to raise clients' awareness about choices they can make.

Step 1. Ask the client, "What do you do for a person you really love? What do you do for or with that person?"

A client might say that he does things he would not do otherwise, such as scratch his wife's back without being asked or paying close attention and listening when someone talks about their day. As the coach, take good notes on the particular words the client uses.

Step 2. Ask the client, "Do you do the same for yourself?"

For the client above, the coach would say, "So you do something your wife loves without being asked. How often do you do things for yourself without others asking you or prompting you to do them?" Or "So you pay exquisite attention, really listening to that person. How often do you pay exquisite attention to yourself, really listening to yourself?"

Most clients report that they do a better job with others than they do with themselves in the specific ways they show love. That leads to the next question.

Step 3. Ask, "How can you do more of this with yourself? How can you pay more exquisite attention to yourself—really listen to yourself?"

This exercise focuses on doing—the actions that spring out of the feeling of love. It is important to identify specific actions in Step 1 to get the clients to consider what actions they can create for themselves. As coaches know, actions can shift attitudes.

EXERCISE 16.3

Expressing Care

This exercise is like Exercise 16.1 in its structure and intention. It is designed to help clients focus concretely.

Step 1. Say to the client, "Think of something—a concrete thing—that you own and really value and care about. What is it?" Then wait until the client identifies the thing.

Some client examples have included a family photograph album that goes back two generations, a piano, a Mont Blanc pen given to them as a gift, and a 1957 Chevy Corvette.

Step 2. "How do you take care of it?" Make sure the client gives specific actions here.

The client puts the photograph album in a place close to her, protected from light, to preserve it. She also says it will be the first thing she grabs if there is ever a fire or disaster.

The client dusts the piano every week, polishes it every other week, keeps its keys covered, and has it tuned regularly.

The client keeps the Mont Blanc pen in a special leather case so that it will not get scratched by other things in her purse.

The client keeps the 1957 Chevy Corvette in a garage and does not take it out when the weather is bad. He drives it carefully and has it maintained by the best mechanic he knows. He does not use it for everyday driving but reserves it for special occasions and celebrations.

Step 3. Ask the client, "How could you do similar things to take exquisite care of yourself?" Treat the client's statement as an analogy and find analogous actions by brainstorming. This can be a stretch—and a lot of fun—for both coach and client.

"So you put the photograph album in a safe place to protect it and preserve it. Are there ways you can better protect yourself and preserve yourself?" This client ended up thinking about the fact that she did nothing, really, to preserve her skin. She started a skin-care regimen.

"So you keep your piano very clean, well-covered, and polished, and you tune it regularly. Are there ways you can do those things for yourself?" This client thought the question was a stretch but realized she does not go regularly to her doctor for check-ups (i.e., "tuning"), needs to take better care of her nails and hands ("covering the keys"), and really loves massages but does not regularly get one ("polishing it").

"So you keep the pen in a special leather case so that it won't get scratched. Are there ways you need to keep yourself from being hurt needlessly?" This client realized she tended to walk and move so fast that she bumped into things and was always getting scratched or bruised. This led to a discussion about slowing down and paying attention as a way of protecting herself.

"So, you reserve your car for special occasions, keeping it out of situations that will potentially damage it and keeping its engine maintained. How can you keep yourself out of harm's way and keep your body maintained?" This client decided to have his cholesterol checked and stop taking on a particular kind of consulting gig, one that was stressful and brought him into contact with companies whose cultures were harsh and bruising. He decided that he was not reserving himself enough for things that could be celebrations. Work did not have to be so bruising.

THE POWER OF FORGIVENESS

To foster healthy self-love, we may need to forgive ourselves, just as healthy love of others requires us letting go of resentments, old angers, and unforgiven wounds. Forgiveness can be difficult to give when revenge seems more appropriate. Yet it grows out of love and can change the course of a life.

We offer a disclaimer here: Many cultures glorify forgiveness to the point where those who have experienced a grievance feel they should easily forgive. This can bring about what Janis Abrahms Spring calls cheap forgiveness (Spring, 2004). Those who engage in this behavior easily pardon others without really dealing with their own emotions and coming to terms with their own injury.

They may make excuses for others or hold themselves at fault when someone mistreats them.

Refusing to forgive is also an unhealthy approach to forgiveness. Those who refuse to forgive stew in their own hostility, rigidly cutting themselves off from connections with life. Someone who adopts this style can be easily offended and harbor grudges. Through this reactive, rigid style, the person becomes cut off from emotions other than resentment and anger.

We do not recommend coaches work with clients who are invested in either of the above two styles; in either case, it is likely that therapy is needed. But Spring's principles are useful for many coaching clients who are ready and willing to gain closure on hurtful experiences. Her work also offers two healthy options for forgiveness: acceptance, in which a person works toward a lasting inner resolution in the absence of the offender's availability or willingness to work on the issue, and true forgiveness, which is a healing process that the offender and hurt party engage in together.

In a time when many leaders are unable to say they are sorry or offer forgiveness, this story shows the power and wisdom of forgiveness:

During the American Civil War, a young man named Roswell McIntyre was drafted into the New York Cavalry. The war was not going well. Soldiers were needed so desperately that he was sent into battle with very little training.

Roswell became frightened—he panicked and ran. He was later court-martialed and condemned to be shot for desertion. McIntyre's mother appealed to President Lincoln. She pleaded that he was young and inexperienced, and that he needed a second chance.

The generals, however, urged the president to enforce discipline. Exceptions, they asserted, would undermine the discipline of an already beleaguered army.

Lincoln thought and prayed. Then he wrote a famous statement. "I have observed," he said, "that it never does a boy much good to shoot him."

He then wrote this letter in his own handwriting: "This letter will certify that Roswell McIntyre is to be readmitted into the New York Cavalry. When he serves out his required enlistment, he will be freed of any charges of desertion."

That faded letter, signed by the president, is on display in the Library of Congress. Beside it there is a note that reads, "This letter was taken from the body of Roswell McIntyre, who died at the battle of Little Five Forks, Virginia."

Given another chance, McIntyre fought until the end. (Goodier, 2002)

When we ask clients to consider this true story, they often realize that Lincoln's forgiveness changed the course of a life. They can consider where forgiveness—for themselves, for someone else—might be offered as wisely and generously as Lincoln's.

The Water Bearer, a Teaching Story

A key task of coaching is learning to love ourselves so that we are available to love others and receive love. In the teaching story below, the water bearer learns how love can turn flaws into gifts through acceptance.

A water bearer in India had two large pots, which hung on each end of a pole that he carried across his neck.

One of the pots had a crack in it, and while the other pot was perfect and always delivered a full portion of water at the end of the long walk from the stream to the master's house, the cracked pot arrived only half full.

For two years this went on daily, with the bearer delivering only one and one-half pots of water to his master's house. Of course, the perfect pot was proud of its accomplishments. But the poor, cracked pot was ashamed of its own imperfection and miserable that it was able to accomplish only half of what it had been made to do. After two years of what it perceived to be a bitter failure, it spoke to the water bearer one day by the stream.

"I am ashamed of myself, and I want to apologize to you."

"Why?" asked the bearer. "What are you ashamed of?"

"I have been able, for these past two years, to deliver only half my load because this crack in my side causes water to leak out all the way back to your master's house. Because of my flaws, you must do all of this work, and you don't get full value from your efforts," the pot said.

The water bearer felt sorry for the old, cracked pot, and in his compassion he said, "As we return to the master's house, I want you to notice the beautiful flowers along the path."

Indeed, as they went up the hill, the old, cracked pot took notice of the sun warming the beautiful wildflowers on the side of the path, and this cheered it some. But at the end of the trail, it still felt bad because it had leaked out half its load, and so again the pot apologized to the bearer for its failure.

The bearer said to the pot, "Did you notice that there were flowers only on your side of the path, but not on the other pot's side? That's because I have always known about your flaw, and I took advantage of it. I planted flower seeds on your side of the path, and every day while we walk back from the stream, you've watered them. For two years I have been able to pick these beautiful flowers to decorate my master's table. Without you being just the way you are, he would not have this beauty to grace his house."

We use this story with clients to help them recognize that each of us has our own unique flaws. We are all cracked pots. But if we will allow it, our flaws will be used to grace our own and others' tables. In the connected world we live in, nothing goes to waste. We need not be afraid of our imperfections and our flaws. If we acknowledge them, we too can be the cause of beauty. In our weakness we find our strength.

REFLECTIONS ON LOVE AND SEEING ANEW

Anthony de Mello, a Jesuit priest who grew up in India, brought the benefits of being in the present—of meditative practice—to everything he did. He writes eloquently on the relationship of love and mind-set in one of his most famous books, *Awareness* (de Mello, 1992). He states how we must let go of our need for the approval and love of others to truly love. He uses the terms drug and addiction(s) below to refer to our attachment to fitting in, gaining others' approval, and staying busy and distracted.

We encourage you to read *Awareness* because the lessons he describes here often become some part of what clients bring to coaching. They are ready to understand the distinctions between love and need, and between love and attachment.

He says, for example: "If you wish to love, you must learn to see again.

And if you wish to see, you must learn to give up your 'drug.' It's as simple as that. Give up your dependency . . . To see at last with a vision that is clear and unclouded by fear or desire. You will know what it means to love. But to come to the land of love, you must pass through the pains of death, for to love persons means to die to the need for persons, and to be utterly alone" (1992, pp. 171–173).

De Mello's reading makes an excellent fieldwork inquiry for a client who is ready to understand the paradoxical nature of love in human life. The book offers many exercises and reflections that can become a client's fieldwork on the journey to loving without neediness.

Reflections on Love for the Coach

Marilyn Gustin, a participant in a 2001–2002 ILCT training, participated in the class from which this chapter is based. She sent Dr. Pat and Diane the following eloquent piece of writing based on her personal experience of losing her husband and her subsequent thoughts about love, loving, and the place of love in coaching. We print it here with her permission.

> Our culture commonly assumes that love is a "something"—almost quantifiable—that is given by one person and received by another. We know, especially from general psychology, that love is essential to a full human life—perhaps even essential to biological survival. We almost believe it can be "poured" from one heart into another heart, like lemonade from a pitcher. We usually think that if a person does not love a child, that child is doomed to experience life as empty of love and therefore be unable to give love to others. With this assumption, we often go through life wishing for more love from others—and we seek it sometimes in very odd places.
>
> Yet the seers, sages, and saints of the major spiritual traditions do not understand love in that way. They universally say that love is our own essential nature, pure and lasting. They say that this ultimate love is the core of every human heart, that the only reason we do not experience it all the time is that it is covered up by a mountain (or a thousand veils, or a darkness—the metaphor depends on the tradition) of lesser realities. These include all our self-centered desires and aims, our focus on the senses, and the chatter of the mind.

Love, they say, is constantly available, no matter what is going on around us, no matter how life may seem to be treating us. Love just is— flowing, spontaneous, and independent. Love sustains. Love is divine; it is God. Love is never absent. It's just that we are sometimes unaware of its presence, or we misunderstand the meaning of our experience.

This truth about love has become clear for me in the process of spiritual unfolding. But it became unmistakable soon after my beloved husband died. From that time to this, at the thought of John, love springs up, full and beautiful, in my awareness. His body, his personality, all the qualities that I associated with him are gone from this earth. Early in our marriage I would have said that he loved me, that he taught me to love by giving me his own.

Now I know better: the quality of his presence, his awareness of inner love, evoked my own awareness of Inner Love. That is why it can endure now. It was always there within me—I needed only to come to recognize it and revel in it. It is still true: I need only become aware, and it is there for savoring, for resting, for delight unlimited.

Do I forget love? Yes. But not as often or as thoroughly as I used to. Is the love I experience all there is? Hardly! Love is infinite. We are pilgrims in love and pilgrims into love just as truly as we walk through air and let it fill our bodies.

These reflections are not included to demonstrate that the sages are correct in their assertion that love is our true nature and dwells equally in all. They are, rather, meant to stimulate us to ask these huge "what-if" questions:

- What if love is our true essence and it is therefore accessible to anyone and everyone?
- What if love is, in fact, always present within us and therefore always available to our perception?

Here are some thoughts in response to those questions.

- No one would be seen as helpless to discover love, because the field of inquiry would not depend on another, but rather on one's own willingness to look deep within.

- Romantic love and spousal love could be reframed as a particular expression of the essential Inner Love, thereby freeing relationships from thinking such as, "If you loved me, you would . . ." and "I want you to love me more."

- We could acknowledge that when we "feel loved" by another, what is really happening is that something in the quality of the "other's" presence stimulates our awareness of our own Inner Love. This happens, perhaps, most easily when the "other" is aware of her Inner Love. This awakens us, momentarily at least, to the reality of love in our own center.

- The experience of love is independent of circumstances; it can be accessed even in great pain. It does not require the presence of another human being—although two human beings focused on love bring immense joy to living.

- Doubts about whether one is lovable are also dispelled with the experience of inner love. In fact, the question disappears: there is Love, flowing and grand, within oneself. The experience dissolves even the question of whether I am lovable. Instead, I begin to understand that I am love.

In the modern world, a need is often felt for definitions of love. Our difficulty seems to be that English is not the best language for expressing nuances of profound subjects. It is, however, the language we have.

We use Greek (*eros, agape, philia,* for example) to try to define types of love. We easily say what love is not—for instance, what we feel about our car. Some say that love and sexual involvement are equivalent, while others disagree.

We suggest a reframing to think of love as the force or capacity that is the source of all our feelings of wonder, gratitude, beauty, affection, concern, interest, enjoyment, and fondness. As the endless capacity that makes all these experiences possible, it may well be beyond definition. Perhaps that is good!

Our society seems to believe we have confused ourselves about love, so much so that Kevin Cashman, in *Leadership from the Inside Out,* says that it's a forbidden word in business circles. It seems true that we are confused, but perhaps we have only mixed in other inner states with love and are not making the necessary distinctions. We have mixed love with attachment, for example, so that we may feel we "love her/him/it so much" that we must have it in our lives to be happy. We have mixed love with sex so that many cannot tell the difference between the two. Akin to this one is the confusion between love and infatuation.

If love is the capacity flowing beneath all our positive experiences, creating our delight in the beautiful, the lovely, the precious, then love is always present within us, revealing to our perception its many-faceted nature in infinite ways, all of them quite grand. We can call it Inner Love.

We are reminded of a story told by Rachel Naomi Remen in her book *My Grandfather's Blessings* (2000). When she was a child, her grandfather described to her eight levels of giving and their relative worth. She promised to always "do it right," meaning to give in the highest way. Her grandfather's reply was that "some things have so much goodness in them that they are worth doing any way that you can." Love is like that—so utterly good that all expressions of love, no matter how mixed or how "confused" they may be, are worth including in life. If we know this, then to touch a flower tenderly, to experience a romance, to revel in a new possession, and to dedicate oneself to the Divine may all have similar value because they all spring from that deeply inward capacity called love—that capacity which is our true nature.

As long as we imagine love to be a "something" given and received, we also feel that love is limited, that it is dependent on other people, even that it can be destroyed or come to an end. Again, the seers disagree with this. They insist that love is infinite, strong, steady, constant, dynamic, and always accessible. It does not end. It does not depend on other people or on circumstances. They say that all we need to do to uncover this immense love within ourselves is to focus deep within our being.

If all this is true, what are the implications for coaching?

- All coaches should be practitioners of some form of "entering within." The most common one is meditation, which itself has a number of forms. Just spending quiet time with a focus on the physical space of the heart can open the awareness to the great Inner Love (see below for more on this).
- If a coach is aware of her own Inner Love while she works with a client, the client will also experience his own Inner Love. From this can come safety, delight, trust, and eagerness to allow the coach to do her

best. Aware of Inner Love, the coach creates a wonderful atmosphere in which coaching can occur with ease, with insight, and with great joy, for both the coach and the client.

- A coach might prepare for each session by searching for that experience of Inner Love. His own life would be immeasurably enriched by this repeated, nearly constant awareness of love.

- When a coach is aware of love, she is much less tempted to advise, teach, or say too much about herself. Awareness of love makes full listening the most natural of processes.

- When a coach is aware of her own Inner Love, her intuition flows more strongly, clearly, and easily into awareness. This might manifest as knowing the best process in any moment or the best timing for a particular coaching process.

- Once we are in touch with Inner Love, it can be directed—toward people, toward work, toward visions and goals, toward the Divine— anywhere we choose to direct it.

- Even if the client is not aware of this loving *soup* in which he is soaking, there will be movement and an opening. It cannot be otherwise, since awareness of our own Inner Love is the most creative force that exists.

There are many ways of becoming aware of Inner Love. You may already know and practice methods that keep you aware of love. You also may want to experiment with the following:

- Take a few minutes to still yourself. Focus on your chest, in your heart. Just hold your attention there until your mind slows down a bit. Be aware of inner movement. Watch. Love can arise as a subtle thread or a full-flowing river. Let it be. When you notice it, let your attention rest there and watch it increase in power. Enjoy it for as long as you can.

- Sit comfortably and take a few deep breaths. Recall an experience during which you felt great love, or a person for whom you felt great love. Allow yourself to get in touch with that situation again as fully as you can. Now, ever so gently, shift your attention to the love you felt and let the "object" of your love or the trigger for the experience fade from your awareness. Focus on the love alone. There it is, in your own heart. Stay with it if you wish. Return gently when you are ready.

- Again, while relaxed and quiet, simply request inside to experience the love that is there. Wait. It will appear.
- Practice "acting as if" love is the root of your being, your anchor, your constant nourishment from within, and is always accessible. While doing this, you may wish to pause often to "check in" with your own heart.

Once we have practiced becoming aware of our own Inner Love and have discovered that it is not so hard to access whenever we are willing to be attentive, we can direct this experience of love wherever we want. If we are with our favorite person, we can become aware of love inside and then direct it to him or her. If we are coaching, the client becomes our direction. If we are dealing with a difficult person, we can direct Inner Love to him or her. The possibilities are as infinite as love itself.

As we finish this chapter, we also complete this book. We hope that you have enjoyed the journey and will continue to revisit the skills, strategies, and techniques for launching or improving your coaching business. We chose to end this book with the Inside Out work and conclude with a focus on love because truthfully, that is at the heart of life coaching. Life coaching is a service that comes from a deep caring for clients' fulfillment now and in the future as total human beings. Working from the inside out and caring deeply for our clients as well as ourselves, we have the makings of becoming masterful coaches as well as masterful human beings. Better coaching brings better living.

APPENDIX A:
REFLECTIONS ON COACHING AND POST-PANDEMIC GLOBAL STRESS

Demand for mental health services and for personal coaching have all increased in our current post-pandemic life. I observe that other stressors such as natural disasters due to climate change, political upheaval, social media hysteria, economic crises, and the changing ways in which we work will all be part of the "new normal" for some time to come. Adam Grant (2021) wrote a great piece in the *New York Times* (and presented a corresponding TED Talk) about how most of us are languishing; a term meaning we may not be depressed, but we are also not highly energized and flourishing. There is a heaviness that most are experiencing at some level. Even the most optimistic, healthy, and secure are at risk of slipping into grief or isolation. Thus, the demand for coaching in companies, in relationships, and even grief- and trauma-informed coaching has recently increased. Mental health counseling has also increased, but, for many, the partnership of a well-trained coach and the ability to engage in honest, whole-life perspective-taking is a prevailing trend.

Challenges that were always part of coaching conversations have become magnified with the mass shift to a virtual workplace—which, for many, has become a permanent situation—as well as with limitations on social interaction, travel, in-person meetings etc., which have not yet returned to what they were before pandemic repercussions. Some of these challenges include work-life balance, energy for work, family, and fun. All of these have had both positive outcomes—as more people work virtually—and also challenges, including time management, doorbells ringing, and young children as well as pets needing attention. This list is, of course, not comprehensive.

THE RAPID SHIFT TO VIRTUAL COACHING

As my (Dr. Pat's) clientele has grown globally over my four decades of coaching, my coaching and the classes taught at the school I created (the Institute for Life Coach Training) have shifted from in-person to telephone connections in group format or individual coaching. Thus, the pandemic effects of the COVID-19 crisis fortunately did not derail this work. I have observed, however, that the pandemic-induced rise in popularity of virtual meeting platforms (such as Zoom or Microsoft Teams) has had both beneficial and harmful effects on the coaching community and profession.

Coaching schools and institutions who relied on in-person, experiential training had to quickly shift to virtual, video-enhanced learning; even schools who were already using phone-connected classes upgraded to virtual meeting platforms where possible. While this has been enjoyable and made coaching more accessible to many, I have observed that the workplace and coach training institutions have lacked the in-person opportunity of conferences, retreats, and the unplanned and insightful sharing that may take place in a hallway conversation or over a meal.

My (Dr. Pat's) corporate clients relate that while much work can get done efficiently remotely, the spontaneous conversations that take place in the halls, lunchrooms, or cafes and bistros nearby are missing. They feel that all meetings are now "official" and no longer spontaneous, like knocking on a colleague's door and popping in with a question or comment. Many of us have returned or will return to a hybrid work environment, mixing work from a home office (or kitchen table, or basement) and an office location. Many feel it is beneficial that colleagues have gotten to know one another's family, pets, and children, and for many the work-from-home environment can still be professional while also being transparent and authentic.

APPENDIX B:
EMOTIONS IN COACHING

Our understanding of emotions comes from a long history of humanistic psychology. It is crucial that we understand the power of unresolved, unexpressed, or misunderstood emotions. Advances in neuroscience now offer useful and powerful information on why, and how, people should not deny their emotions but, rather, express them in the right place and time, and with the right person. E-motion is indeed *energy in motion*.

It is important to understand that working with emotions in coaching is less about knowing and utilizing certain tools and techniques than it is about the capacity of the coach to demonstrate in the coaching relationship that emotions can be acknowledged. Suppressed emotions inevitably surface in unintended ways—a process that psychologists call emotional leakage. This gives one awareness that our emotions are messengers, or harbingers of new awareness, and call for emotional flexibility and resilience.

A groundbreaking book written by Harvard psychologist and coach Susan David, PhD, called *Emotional Agility* has proven to be valuable and practical research for coaches and clients. *Permission to Feel* by Yale University psychologist and researcher Marc Brackett, PhD, was inspired by the desire to bring emotional intelligence to education systems, and elementary schools in particular. The Yale Center for Emotional Intelligence developed the system of RULER, an acronym for the five skills of emotional intelligence *(recognizing, understanding, labeling, expressing, and regulating)*. What does this mean for coaching? Both coach and client can begin to understand that emotions are all good; some just don't feel good in the moment (sadness, grief, anger, despair, frustration). But when expressed and clarified with a committed listener as a coach, the energy then shifts (and different parts of the brain are engaged), often leading to a creative insight or newfound availability of other emotions such as enthusiasm and hope.

UK researchers Elaine Cox and Tatiana Bachkirova collected data from thirty-nine UK coaches using a stem-sentence questionnaire approach. Their results: "Findings suggest that coaches can have very different viewpoints in relation to dealing with difficult emotional situations that arise when working with clients, dealing with them in one of four ways: Using self-reflection or supervision, Avoiding tackling the emotion considering it to belong to the client, Actively exploring with the client, or Referral of the client/termination. They also see control of their own emotions as important and recognized some gender issues" (Cox & Bachkirova, 2007). Cox and Bachkirova recommend that a greater understanding of emotions be included in the education and training of coaches. They also emphasized that strong supervision or mentoring is important in the development of masterful coaches. (Please read the entire paper for a more detailed and valuable knowledge of this key research.)

In the early days of the coaching movement in the 1990s, emotions were a delicately handled aspect of coaching, as many did not want to step on the territory of psychotherapy. Now we know that coaching is not mental health treatment, "fixing," or doing a deep dive into one's unresolved pain. Instead, coaching clients are generally mentally healthy, but may have an unhealthy understanding of emotional intelligence. There is much to be gained from the integration of emotions into coaching, for both the client and the coach. The more accepting and aware we are of emotions in our own life, the more present we can be with our clients. As coaches, we are faced with the challenge to become masters in the ability to open our hearts. "But it requires an open heart to really feel how another feels. An open heart gives us empathic energy to connect directly with another person from within" (Scharmer, 2013).

Masterful coaches are not afraid of their own emotional reactions, and they *normalize rather than pathologize* their clients' challenging emotions. These coaches bring new awareness to the message of their client's emotion in a non-judgmental fashion; this often leads to a shift in the energy of the client (or in you as the coach). Carol Dweck's work on the Growth Mindset is important here as well:

The Fixed Mindset: "In a fixed mindset, people believe their basic qualities, like their intelligence or talent, are simply fixed traits. They spend their time documenting their intelligence or talent instead of developing them. They also believe that talent alone creates success—without effort." (Dweck, 2015)

The Growth Mindset: "In a growth mindset, people believe that their most basic abilities can be developed through dedication and hard work—brains and talent are just the starting point. This view creates a love of learning and a resilience that is essential for great accomplishment." (Dweck, 2015)

There is also a growing subset of health and wellness coaching called trauma-informed or grief coaching. This involves carefully maintaining a coaching approach to a client who has worked through an event of trauma or loss, but for whom the effects of this trauma are sometimes triggered unconsciously. Transformational coaching, be it with leaders or those wanting personal development life coaching, will and must include unconscious thoughts and triggers that need to be brought to the surface. Many have used the metaphor of the iceberg and speak of the 90% of awareness—or unknown triggers, or opportunities—beneath the tip of the iceberg For me, what's under an iceberg is cold and dark; I much prefer the metaphor of snorkeling in the Caribbean or Great Barrier Reef. Putting on mask and fins and seeing the beauty (with, for some, fearful reactions) is not a deep dive, but rather a peek just under the surface at the beauty and mystery that is right there. The lesson is this: look for and notice your clients' emotions and energy shifts (their tone of voice, deep breath, heavy sigh, or new excitement and lit up face). And if you ever want to add some tools or techniques for when challenging emotions arise in your coaching, there are meditations, guided imagery, and heart brain resonance exercises that can be a helpful addition to a coaching relationship. Sometimes in the sharing of a client story, you (the coach) may have emotions that arise. Be real, be authentic, and then, if you need to, debrief with your coach mentor. That is a skill of the *self-reflective practice*.

Emotional intelligence has long been an important aspect to include and teach in coach training and in coaching. But one cannot express their emotions and relationship triggers at work without *psychological safety*. This term was first coined in 1999 by Harvard business school professor Amy Edmondson, and refers to "an environment of protected vulnerability, a condition in which you feel (1) included, (2) safe to learn, (3) safe to contribute, and (4) safe to challenge the status quo . . . all without fear of being embarrassed, marginalized, or punished in some way" (Clark, 2020). The term was repopularized in a famous research study of effective teams by Google (the Aristotle Project) in 2012. To their surprise, the data showed that psychological safety was the best indicator for a successful team. This finding can and should be applied to the coaching relationship as well, and reveals the importance of being aware of the emotions of both client and coach.

I came across this blog on the International Coaching Federations website and thought it was quite relevant to current research on emotions, neuroscience and how that informs the coaching we may provide.

Irena is an ICF certified coach and the founder of The Neuroscience School (https://neuroscienceschool.com/).

CONSTRUCTED EMOTIONS:
BLOG BY IRENA O'BRIEN | JULY 13, 2020

Reprinted with permission
© Irena O'Brien and The Neuroscience School

When things go wrong, my client, Mark, always blames his staff. He walks around the office with a sour face and is often angry. And his staff has learned to walk on eggshells to avoid his next angry outburst.

We used to think that these outbursts were an example of the "amygdala hijack," a term coined by Daniel Goleman, in his 1995 book *Emotional Intelligence: Why It Can Matter More Than IQ*, to explain immediate, uncontrollable responses that are out of proportion to the circumstances.

But, Dr. Lisa Feldman Barrett's 30 years of research has shown us that we're not at the mercy of our amygdala. Rather, we construct our emotions on the spot from the incoming stimuli.

The New Theory of Constructed Emotion
In her book, *How Emotions Are Made*, Dr. Feldman Barrett defines an emotion as your brain's creation of what your bodily sensations mean in relation to what is going on around you in the world.

Under this new theory, we construct our emotions on the spot from incoming sensations from both outside, such as the event itself, and inside the body (e.g., our heart rate, our breath). These sensations are filtered through our brain, which makes a prediction as to what they mean, resulting in our own emotional experience and our interpretation of the emotions of others. This happens in an instant, outside of conscious awareness.

Our brain has evolved over our lifetime and from our past experience, making each brain unique. Given the same incoming sensations, our emotional experience and interpretation of the emotions of others will be unique. And because the culture we were brought up in is part of our past experience, emotions are culturally specific.

We're Not at the Mercy of Our Amygdala

What this new theory means for us is that we have more control over our emotions than we think. Although our incoming sensations are filtered through our past experience via our unique brain, we can reinterpret them to mean something more resourceful.

While it's true that our brain creates our emotional experience or interpretation in an instant, we can catch ourselves and reinterpret the incoming sensations, even after the fact. And every time we do that, we're changing our past experience, and consequently our brain, through something called neuroplasticity. The more we reinterpret our sensations in this new way, the easier and quicker the new response becomes because our brain has been rewired. What we need is not a blind faith in an emotion determined by our brain, but an awareness of our physical sensations so we can interpret them to mean something more resourceful.

EMOTIONS ARE NOT UNIVERSAL

The new theory also means that emotions are not universal, and they don't come with predetermined facial expressions or body language. Facial expressions and body language are only a clue to the emotion. In fact, we can never be certain of what someone else is feeling unless we ask them. Otherwise, it's just a guess, based on our own experience, not theirs. A well-known example is that of the nervous smile by some cultures. If we interpreted the smile as defiance rather than saving face, we would be incorrect.

Dr. Feldman Barrett stresses the importance of our body budget for good emotional intelligence. Emotions are also shaped by our mood, which is simply the sum of our body budget, or how our brain budgets the energy in our body to keep us alive and well. The most important thing we can do to keep our body budget in good shape is to make sure that we eat a healthy diet, exercise, and get adequate sleep.

Let's go back to my client, Mark. His brain took a triggering event (perhaps a staff member was late with a report), mixed it together with his inner sensations (racing heart, shallow breath, blood pumping, for example), ran them through his past experience via his unique brain, and called the combination of sensations "anger." That's because, many times in the past, beginning in childhood, this combination of sensations meant anger and have now formed part of his past experience. But, if he reinterpreted this combination of sensations as simply annoyance, disappointment or frustration, he'd respond differently.

HOW TO NAVIGATE EMOTIONS UNDER THIS NEW THEORY

We can help our clients deal with a negative emotion by bringing it down to its component sensations: the triggering event and the bodily sensations. We can then help them interpret this combination of sensations in a new way to mean something more resourceful. Over time, this will become easier and quicker.

We can encourage them to use different, more specific words to label an emotion. We could use words such as annoyed, disappointed or frustrated, rather than angry. This will change our emotional experience.

And we can encourage them to keep a healthy lifestyle.

APPENDIX C:
THE IMPORTANCE OF PROFESSIONAL COACHING COMPETENCIES

Working with mentors and learning and practicing coaching skills in a structured program can help you gain competence and confidence in your life coaching abilities.

The International Coaching Federation is the 'gold standard' in the profession as both a membership organization and an accrediting body. Other such organizations include the Association for Coaching in Europe, the International Association of Coaching, the Center for Credentialing and Education (creator of the Board-Certified Coach, BCC), and the European Mentoring and Coaching Council (EMCC Global). Training and educational entities will embrace one or all of these, creating a robust and thorough training program that helps develop skilled life coaches who coach professionally, not just in title but in practice.

Below are the main coaching organization websites for you to learn more about which best fits your unique circumstances. Here you will find coaching skills and competencies as well as professional ethics.

International Coaching Federation: www.CoachingFederation.org
European Mentoring and Coaching Council: www.EMCCGlobal.org
Association for Coaching: www.AssociationforCoaching.com
International Association of Coaching: https://certifiedcoach.org
Center for Credentialing & Education (Board Certified Coach): www.CCE-Global.org

REFERENCES

Adams, M. (2009). *Change your questions, change your life: 10 powerful tools for life and work.* San Francisco: Berrett-Koehler.

Adler, A. (1998). *Understanding human nature.* C. Brett, (Trans.). Center City, MN: Hazelden. (Original work published 1927)

Adrienne, C. (1998). *The purpose of your life: Finding your place in the world using synchronicity, intuition, and uncommon sense.* New York: Eagle Brook.

Albom, M. (1997). *Tuesdays with Morrie: An old man, a young man, and life's greatest lesson.* New York: Doubleday.

Anderson, G. (1997*). Living life on purpose.* San Francisco: Harper.

The Arbinger Institute. (2010*). Leadership and self-deception: Getting out of the box.* San Francisco: Berrett-Koehler.

Arloski, M. (2021). *Masterful health & wellness coaching: Deepening your craft.* Duluth, Minnesota: Whole Person Associates.

Armour, J. A. (2007). The little brain on the heart. *Cleveland Clinic Journal of Medicine, 74*(1), S48–51.

Assagioli, R. (1965). *Psychosynthesis: A collection of basic writings.* New York: Penguin.

Bachkirova, T. (2009). Cognitive developmental approach to coaching: An interview with Robert Kegan. *Coaching: An International Journal of Theory, Research, and Practice, 2*(1), 10–22.

Barner, R., & Ideus, K. (2017). *Working deeply: Transforming lives through transformational coaching.* Bingley, UK: Emerald Publishing.

Bar-On, R. (1997). *Bar-On emotional quotient inventory technical manual.* New York: Multi-health Systems.

Barrows, S. B. (2006). Retrieved October 2006, from www.quotationspage.com/subjects/integrity/

Belf, T. & Ward, C. (1997). *Simply live it up: Brief solutions.* Bethesda, MD: Purposeful Press.

Berg, I. K., & Szabó, P. (2005). *Brief coaching for lasting solutions.* New York: W. W. Norton.

Berger, J. G. (2012). *Changing on the job: Developing leaders for a complex world.*

Stanford: Stanford University Press.

Berger, J. G., & Atkins, P. W. B. (2009) Mapping complexity of mind: Using the subject-object interview in coaching. *Coaching: An International Journal of Theory, Research, and Practice, 2*(1), 23–36.

Berman Fortgang, L. (1998). *Take yourself to the top.* New York: Warner.

Berrigan, F., & Berrigan, K. (2003). Fearless and full of hope. *Sojourners Magazine*, March–April, pp. 37–46.

Blanchard, K., & Peale, N. (1988) *The power of ethical management.* New York: William Morrow.

Block, P. (1999). *Flawless consulting: A guide to getting your expertise used.* New York: Jossey-Bass.

Bohm, D. (1996). *On dialogue.* New York: Routledge.

Boroson, M. (2009). *One moment meditation: Stillness for people on the go.* Winter Road Publishing.

Borysenko, J. (1994). *Pocketful of miracles.* New York: Warner Books.

Boyatzis, R., Smith, M., & Van Oosten, E. (2019). *Helping people change.* Harvard Business Review Press

Brackett, M. (2019). *Permission to feel.* New York: Celadon Books.

Braham, B. (1991). *Finding your purpose: A guide to personal fulfillment.* Los Altos, CA: Crisp Publications.

Braig, N., & Snook, S. (2014). From purpose to impact. *Harvard Business Review, 92*(5), 104–111.

Bregman, P. (2018). *Leading with emotional courage.* New Jersey: Wiley.

Brehony, K.A. (1997). *Awakening at midlife.* Riverhead Trade.

Brock, V. (2014). *Sourcebook of coaching history* (2nd Ed.).

Brown, S. (2009). *Play: How it shapes the brain, opens the imagination and invigorates the soul.* New York: Penguin.

Budd, M., & Rothstein, L. (2000). *You are what you say: The proven program that uses the power of language to combat stress, anger, and depression.* New York: Three Rivers Press.

Cameron, J. (2003). *Walking in this world.* New York: Jeremy P. Tarcher.

Campbell, J. (Ed.) (1971). *The portable Jung.* New York: Viking.

Carlson, R. (2003). *Taming your gremlin: A surprisingly simple method for getting out of your own way.* Fort Mill, SC: Quill.

Cashman, K. (1998). *Leadership from the inside out*. Provo, UT: Executive Excellence Publishers.

Chopra, D. (2005). *The seven laws of spiritual success*. Nashville, TN: Broadman & Holman Publishers.

Christy, M. (1986, September 10). Mayflower Madam tells all. *Boston Globe*, p. 27.

Clark, T. R. (2020). *The 4 stages of psychological safety*. San Francisco: Berrett-Koehler.

Cook-Greuter, S. R. (2004). Making the case for a developmental perspective. Industrial and Commercial Training, *36*(7), 1–10.

Courcy, C. (2012). *Save your inner tortoise!: Learn to cross the finish line joyful and satisfied*. Balboa Press.

Covey, S. R. (1989). *The 7 habits of highly effective people: Powerful lessons in personal change*. New York: Simon and Schuster.

Cox, E., & Bachkirova, T. (2007). Coaching: A process of personal and social meaning making. *Coaching Psychology Review, 2*(2), 191-201.

Csikszentmihalyi, M. (2008). *Flow: The psychology of optimal experience*. New York: HarperCollins.

Dalai Lama. (2002). *How to practice the way to a meaningful life*. New York: Pocket Books.

David, S., & Congleton, C. (2013, November). Emotional agility. *Harvard Business Review*.

David, S. (2016). *Emotional agility*. New York: Penguin Random House

de Mello, A. (1992). *Awareness*. New York: Doubleday.

de Shazer, S., & Lipchik, E. (1984). Frames and reframing. *Family Therapy Collections, 11*, 88–97.

Dossey, L. (2006). *The extraordinary healing power of ordinary things: Fourteen natural steps to health and happiness*. New York: Harmony Books.

Drucker, P. (2003). *The essential Drucker: The best of sixty years of Peter Drucker's essential writings on management*. New York: Harper Business.

Ellis, D. (1998). *Life coaching: A manual for helping professionals*. Rapid City, SD: Breakthrough Enterprises.

Ellis, D. (2002). *Falling awake: Creating the life of your dreams*. Rapid City, SC: Breakthrough Enterprises.

Ellis, D. (2006). *Life coaching: A new career for helping professionals*. Norwalk, CT: Crown House Publishing.

Ellis, D., & Lankowitz, S. (1995). *Human being: A manual for health, wealth, love, and happiness*. Rapid City, SD: Breakthrough Enterprises.

Erhard, W. (2000). Werner Erhard. Retrieved Oct. 7, 2002, from www.working-minds.com/werner.htm

Flaherty, J. (1998). *Coaching: Evoking excellence in others*. Burlington, MA: Butterworth-Heinemann.

Frankl, V. (2006). *Man's search for meaning*. Boston: Beacon Press. (Original work published 1946)

Fredrickson, B. (2009). *Positivity: Top-notch research reveals the 3 to 1 ratio that will change your life*. New York: Harmony.

Fredrickson, B. (2013). *Love 2.0*. Hudson Street Press.

Gallwey, W. T. (2000). *The inner game of work: Focus, learning, pleasure, and mobility in the workplace*. New York: Random House.

Gawain, S. (1997). *Meditations* (Audio CD). Novato, CA: New World Publishers.

Gladwell, M. (2005). *Blink: The power of thinking without thinking*. New York: Little, Brown and Company.

Goldstein, A. (2000, July 3). Paging all parents. *Time, 3*(47), 1.

Goleman, D. (1995). *Emotional intelligence*. New York: Bantam Books.

Goleman, D. (2002). *Primal leadership: Realizing the power of emotional intelligence*. Boston: Harvard Business School Press.

Goodier, S. (2002, September 27). The Friday morning story. [E-newsletter].

Google. (2012). The Aristotle project. https://rework.withgoogle.com/print/guides/5721312655835136/

Graham, E., & Crossen, C. (1996, March 8). The overloaded American: Too many things to do, too little time to do them. *Wall Street Journal, 8*, R1.

Grant, A. (2021, December 3). Feeling blah during the pandemic? It's called languishing. *The New York Times*. https://www.nytimes.com/2021/04/19/well/mind/covid-mental-health-languishing.html

Graves, C. W. (n.d.). Retrieved August 6, 2006, from www.clarewgraves.com/theory_content/quotes.html

Greenstreet, K. (2004). Retrieved March 1, 2022 from https://www.thesuccessalliance.com/webinar/start-a-mastermind-group/

Haley, J. (1986). *Uncommon therapy: The psychiatric techniques of Milton H. Erickson*. New York: W. W. Norton.

Halpern, B.L., & Lubar, K. (2003) *Leadership presence: Dramatic techniques to reach out, motivate and inspire*. New York: Gotham.

Hargrove, R. (1995). *Masterful coaching*. San Francisco: Pfeiffer.

Hayes, S. C., Strosahl, K. D., & Wilson, K. G. (2012). *Acceptance and commitment therapy: The process and practice of mindful change*. (2nd ed.). New York: Guilford Press.

Helgeland, B. (2013). *42*. Warner Bros. Pictures.

Heller, S., & Surrenda, D. (1995). *Retooling on the run*. Berkeley, CA: North Atlantic Books.

Hill, N. (1966). *Think and grow rich*. (New and revised edition.). New York: Hawthorn Books. (Original work published 1937)

Hill, H. (1976). *From goo to you by way of the zoo*. Plainfield, NJ: Logos International.

Hirshberg, J. (1998). *The creative priority: Driving innovative business in the real world*. New York: HarperBusiness.

Hoffer, E. (1951). *True believer: Thoughts on the nature of mass movements*. New York: Harper & Row.

Hudson, F. M. (1999). *The adult years: Mastering the art of self-renewal*. San Francisco: Jossey-Bass.

Hudson, F. M. (2002). *Planning on purpose: Discovery guide*. Santa Barbara, CA: The Hudson Institute. (Pamphlet available from www.hudsoninstitute.com).

Hudson, F. M., & McLean, P. D. (2000). *Life launch: A passionate guide to the rest of your life*. Santa Barbara, CA: Hudson Press.

Humbert, P. E. (2001). The innovative professional (TIPS) newsletter. Retrieved December 6, 2001, from www.philiphumbert.com

James, W. (1983). *The principles of psychology*. (New edition.) Cambridge, MA: Harvard.

University Press. (Original work published 1890)

James, W. (1994). *The varieties of religious experience: A study in human nature*. (Modern Library reprint edition.) New York: Random House. (Original work published 1902)

Johnson, B. (1992). *Polarity management: Identifying and managing unsolvable problems*. Amherst, MA: HRD Press.

Johnson, S. (2002). *The one-minute salesperson*. New York: William Morrow.

Johnston, R. K., & Smith, J. (2001). *Life is not work, work is not life: Simple reminders for finding balance in a 24/7 world*. Berkeley, CA: Wildcat Canyon Press.

Joiner, B., & Josephs, S. (2006). *Leadership agility*. San Francisco: Jossey-Bass.

Jones, L. B. (1996). *The path: Creating your mission statement for work and for life*. New York: Hyperion.

Jung, C. G. (1969a). *Man and his symbols*. Garden City, NY: Doubleday.

Jung, C. G (1969b). *Collected works*, Vol. 9, Part 2. Princeton University Press.

Kaufman, S. B. (2020). *Transcend: The new science of self-actualization*. New York: Tarcher Perigree.

Kegan, R. (1994). *In over our heads: The mental demands of modern life*. Cambridge, MA: Harvard University Press.

Kegan, R. (1982). *The evolving self: Problem and process in human development*. Cambridge, MA: Harvard University Press.

Kegan, R. & Lahey, L. (2009) *Immunity to change: How to overcome it and unlock the potential in yourself and your organization*. Boston: Harvard Business Press.

Kimsey-House, H., Kimsey-House K., Sandahl, P., & Whitworth, W. (2011) *Co-active coaching: Changing business, transforming lives*. Boston: Nicholas Brealey.

Kunzig, R. (2000, August). Antigravity in Pisa. *Discover, 21*(8).

Laing, R. D. (1983). *Politics of experience*. New York: Pantheon.

Lakoff, G., & Johnson, M. (2003). *Metaphors we live by*. (Updated edition with an afterword by the authors.) Chicago: University of Chicago Press. (Original work published 1980)

Laske, O. (2003). An integrated model of developmental coaching: Researching new ways of coaching and coach education. In Stein, I. & Belsten, L. (Eds.), *Proceedings of the First ICF Coaching Research Symposium* (pp. 52–61).

Leider, R. J. (2005). *The power of purpose*. San Francisco: Berrett-Koehler.

Levinson, D. (1986). *Seasons of a man's life*. New York: Ballantine.

Levoy, G. (1997). *Callings: Finding and following an authentic life*. New York: Random House.

Loevinger, J. (Ed.). (1998). *Technical foundations for measuring ego development*. Mahwah, NJ: Erlbaum.

Lowry, S. & Menendez, D. (1997) *Discovering your best self: Through the art of coaching*. Belmont Books.

Lynch, D., & Kordis, P. (1988). *Strategy of the dolphin*. New York: William Morrow.

Marshall, J. (n.d.). Five Types of Affirmations for Personal Development. http://www.empowering-personal-development.com/types-of-affirmations.html

Maslow, A. H. (1971) *The farther reaches of human nature.* New York: Penguin.

Maslow, A. H. (1998). *Toward a psychology of being.* (3rd ed.). New York: John Wiley & Sons.

May, R. (1983). *The discovery of being.* New York: W. W. Norton.

McCraty, R., & Childre, D. (2006). *The appreciative heart: The psychophysiology of positive emotions and optimal functioning.* [E-book]. Boulder Creek, CA: The Institute of HeartMath. https://www.heartmath.org/assets/uploads/2015/01/appreciative-heart.pdf

McWilliams, J. R., & McWilliams, P. (1992). *Wealth 101: Getting what you want—enjoying what you've got.* Los Angeles: Prelude Press.

Monk, G., Winslade, J., Crocket, K., & Epston, D. (Eds.) (1997). *Narrative therapy in practice: The archaeology of hope.* San Francisco: John Wiley & Sons.

Moore, M., Drake, D., Tschannen-Moran, B., Campone, F., & Kauffman, C. (2006). Relational flow: A theoretical model for the intuitive dance. In F. Campone & J. Bennett (Eds.), *Proceedings of the Third International Coach Research Symposium,* ICF, Lexington, Kentucky.

Mountain Dreamer, O. (1999). *The invitation.* New York: HarperCollins.

Nadler, G., & Hibino, S. (1998). *Breakthrough thinking: The seven principles of creative problem solving.* Roseville, CA: Prima Lifestyles.

National Institute of Business Management (2006, March). 8 keys to leadership genius. *Executive Leadership,* p. 1.

Nelson, P. (1993). *There's a hole in my sidewalk: The romance of self-discovery.* Hillsboro, OR: Beyond Words Publishing.

O'Connor, J., & Seymour, J. (2000). *Introducing neuro-linguistic programming: Psychological skills for understanding and influencing people.* London: Thorsons Publishers.

O'Hanlon, B., & Hudson, P. (1995). *Stop blaming, start loving: A solution-oriented approach to improving your relationship.* New York: W. W. Norton.

O'Hanlon, B. (1998). *A guide to possibility land.* New York: W. W. Norton.

Oliver, M. (1986). *Dream work.* New York: Atlantic Monthly Press.

Ortony, A. (2001). Why metaphors are necessary and not just nice. *Educational Theory,* 25, 45–53. Reprinted in M. J. Gannon (Ed.), *Cultural metaphors:Readings, research translation, and commentary* (pp. 9–21). Thousand Oaks, CA: Sage Publications.

Palmer, H. (1997). *Resurfacing: Techniques for exploring consciousness.* Los Angeles: Stars End Creations.

Palmer, H. (2014). The forgiveness option. Retrieved March 2, 2022, http://www.whomi.org/adobe/forgiveness(eng).pdf

Patterson, K., Grenny, J., McMillan, R., & Switzler, A. (2011). *Crucial conversations: Tools for talking when stakes are high*. (2nd ed.). New York: McGraw Hill.

Perls, F. S. (1969). *Gestalt therapy verbatim*. Lafayette, CA: Real People Press.

Piercy, M. (2003). To be of use. In C. Mauro (Ed.), *Prairie of fertile land*. Seattle, WA: Whit Press.

Prochaska, J. O., Norcross, J. C., & DiClemente, C. C. (2007). *Changing for good: A revolutionary six-stage program for overcoming bad habits and moving your life forward*. New York: Harper Collins.

Proctor, B. (1997). *You were born rich: Now you can discover and develop those riches*. Phoenix, AZ: LifeSuccess Productions.

Quinn, R. E. (1996). *Deep change: Discovering the leader within*. San Francisco: Jossey-Bass.

Remen, R. N. (2000). *My grandfather's blessings: Stories of strength, refuge, and belonging*. New York: Riverhead Books.

Reynolds, M. (2020). *Coach the person, not the problem*. San Francisco: Berrett-Koehler.

Richardson, C. (1998). *Take time for your life: A personal coach's seven-step program for creating the life you want*. New York: Broadway Books.

Rilke, R. M. (1992). *Letters to a young poet*. (J. M. Burnham, Trans.) San Rafael, CA: New World Library. (Original work published 1929)

Rogers, C. (1951). *Client-centered therapy: Its current practice, implications, and theory*. Boston: Houghton Mifflin.

Rooke, D. & Torbert, W. R., (2005, April 4). Seven transformations of leadership. *Harvard Business Review*.

Rotary International. (n.d.). Four-way test. https://my.rotary.org/en/guiding-principles

Ruiz, D. M. (1997). *The four agreements: A practical guide to personal freedom, a Toltec wisdom book*. San Rafael, CA: Amber-Allen Publishing.

Scharmer, O. (2013). Uncovering the blind spot of leadership. [Blog post]. Retrieved on March 23, 2020 from www.dailygood.org/story/450/uncovering-the-blind-spot-of-leadership-c-otto-scharmer/.

Searle, J. R. (1997). *The mystery of consciousness*. New York: The New York Review of Books.

Seligman, M. E. (2002). *Authentic happiness: Using the new positive psychology to realize your potential for lasting fulfillment.* New York: Free Press.

Seligman, M. E. (2003). Using the new positive psychology to realize your potential for lasting fulfillment. [Online class].

Senge, P. M. (1990). *The fifth discipline: The art and practice of the learning organization.* New York: Doubleday/Currency

Sholl, J. (2011) *How to overcome immunity to change.* Experience Life. https://experiencelife.lifetime.life/article/how-to-overcome-immunity-to-change

Siegel, D. (2011). *Mindsight: The new science of transformation.* New York. Random House.

Silsbee, D. (2008). *Presence-based coaching: Cultivating self-generative leaders through mind, body, and spirit.* San Francisco: Jossey Bass.

Simon, S. B. (1972). *Values clarification: A handbook of practical strategies for teachers and students.* New York: Hart Publishing Co.

Snyder, C. R., & Lopez, S. J. (Eds.) (2002b). *Handbook of positive psychology.* Oxford, U.K.: Oxford University Press.

Solomon, R. C., & Flores, F. (2001). *Building trust: In business, politics, relationships, and life.* New York: Oxford University Press.

Spinosa, C., Flores, F., & Dreyfus, H. L. (1997). *Disclosing new worlds: Entrepreneurship, democratic action, and the cultivation of solidarity.* Cambridge, MA: MIT Press.

Spring, J. A. (2004). *How can I forgive you? The courage to forgive, the freedom not to.* New York: HarperCollins.

Strozzi-Heckler, R. (1993). *The anatomy of change: A way to move through life's transitions.* North Atlantic Books.

Strozzi-Heckler, R. (2007). *The leadership dojo: Build your foundation as an exemplary leader.* Berkeley, CA: Frog Books.

Strozzi-Heckler, R. (2014). *The art of somatic coaching: Embodying skillful action, wisdom and compassion.* Berkeley, CA: North Atlantic Books.

Terry, R. (1993) *Authentic leadership.* San Francisco: Jossey-Bass.

Tolle, E. (1999). *The power of now: A guide to spiritual enlightenment.* Novato, CA: New World Library.

Tompkins, P. & Lawley, J. (1997). Less is more: The art of clean language. Retrieved March 2, 2022, from https://www.cleanlanguage.co.uk/articles/articles/109/1/Less-Is-More-The-Art-of-Clean-Language/Page1.html (An introduction to David Grove's questioning technique called Clean Language)

Torbert, W., Cook-Greuter, S., Fisher, D., Foldy, E., Gauthier, A., Keely, J., et al. (2004). *Action inquiry: The secret of timely and transforming leadership.* San Francisco: Berrett-Koehler.

Vanderpool, L. (2019). *A shift in being.* Imaginal Light Publishing

Warren, R. (2002). *The purpose-driven life.* New York: Zondervan.

Weir, P. (1989). *Dead Poets Society.* Touchstone Pictures.

Wells, S. (1998). Choosing the future. Burlington, MA: Butterworth-Heinemann.

Wheatley, M. J. (2009). *Turning to one another: Simple conversations to restore hope to the future.* San Francisco: Berrett-Koehler.

White, G. (1998, December 13). Consumed by consumerism. *Atlanta Journal-Constitution,* p. RI.

Whitworth, L., Kimsey-House, H., Sandahl, P., & Whitmore, J. (1998). *Co-active coaching: New skills for coaching people toward success in work and life.* Palo Alto, CA: Davies-Black Publishing.

Wilber, K. (2000). *Integral psychology: Consciousness, spirit, psychology, therapy.* Boston: Shambhala Publications.

Williams, P., & Davis, D. (2007). *Therapist as life coach.* New York: W. W. Norton.

Williams, P. & Thomas, L. (2005). *Total life coaching: 50+ life lessons, skills, and techniques to enhance your practice . . . and your life.* New York: W. W. Norton.

Wind, Y., & Crook, C. (2004). *The power of impossible thinking: Transform the business of your life and the life of your business.* Upper Saddle River, NJ: Wharton School Publishing.

INDEX

Note: Italicized page locators refer to figures.

A

ABC framework, 336–37
abundance, 313–15, 325
abundance thinking, scarcity thinking *vs.*, 314, 318
Acceptance and Commitment Therapy, 202
accountability
  for change, 166
  creating, 26–28
  ensuring, 27–28
  forwarding action within coaching sessions and, 170–71
  questions, 65–66
achiever conscientious self stage, 97–101, 113
Achilles heel issues, 53
acknowledging and endorsing clients, 138–39
acting as if, forwarding action within coaching sessions and, 170, 172
action inquiry, 88
Action Inquiry (Torbert), 94, 112
action(s)
  aligning values with habits and, 262–67
  forwarding, 165–66
  identifying, 27
  purposeful, requesting, 26–28
  results-oriented, 167, 168
  see also forwarding action within coaching sessions, skills for
action stage, in Prochaska's six stages, 77
active listening, 5
Adams, M., 65
ADD. *see* attention deficit disorder (ADD)
Adler, A., xviii, 18
adolescence, egocentric self and, 90–91
Adrienne, C., 225
adult development and consciousness
  levels of, 85–91
  post-conventional stages of, 108–11
  principles common to theories about, 88
  sequential and hierarchical developmental stages and, 90
  three conventional stages of, 91–101
  transformations in, 86, 87, 89
  why it matters, 113–19
aesthetic needs, *249,* 250
affirmations, 338–42
  acting/claiming, 341
  being/intending, 341
  integrating/embodying, 341–42
  as lifestyle, 342
  popular, 339–40
  receiving/accepting, 340–41
  releasing/cleansing, 340
Alcoholics Anonymous, 292
Alderman, R., 47
alignment integrity, 278. *see also* personal integrity
alliance, definition of, 40
"All You Need Is Love" (Lennon & McCartney), 349
Alpert, R. (Baba Ram Dass), xviii
alternative actions and choices, creating, 170, 173–74
amends, making, 292
American Psychological Association (APA), xxi
amusement, 201, 203
amygdala, 195
"amygdala highjack," 202
analogies, using metaphors and, 154–60. *see also* metaphors
APA. *see* American Psychological Association (APA)
"Appreciative Heart, The" (McCraty & Childre), 317
Arby's, 282
Argyris, C., 101
Arloski, M., 4
Armour, J. A., 8
Arrien, A., 281
Aspinwall, L., xxiii
Assagioli, R., xviii, 18
assessments
  assertions *vs.,* 331–32
  of developmental stage of client, 95
Association for Coaching, 373
assumptions
  developmental perspective and, 80–81
  in immunity to change map, 115
  ladder of inference activity and, 101–5, *103*
  sharing directly, 69
Atkins, P. W. B., 93
attention deficit disorder (ADD), 138
attraction principle, 315–16
Aurobindo, xxi
Austin, J. L., xx

Authentic Happiness (Seligman), xxiii, 211n20
Authentic Happiness Inventory, xxiii, 203
authenticity
    achievers and, 98–99
    in coaching, 58
    self-disclosure and, 9
"Autobiography in Five Short Chapters, An" (Nelson),
    326
avoiding form of silence, 198, 199
awareness
    choice-driven change and, 63
    conversation for, 19, 20
    creating, 39, 52–53
Awareness (de Mello), 359
awareness-based coaching, solution-focused coach-
    ing *vs.*, 16
awe, 201, 203

B
Baba Ram Dass. *see* Alpert, R. (Baba Ram Dass)
Baby Boomers, mind-sets or worldviews of, 84
Bachkirova, T., 369, 370
Bandler, R., xix
Bandura, A., xxi
barometer questions, 52
Bar-On, R., 336
Bateson, G., xix
BBC, xiv
beginner's mind, 202, 344
behavioral junkyard, 141
behavioral self-assessments, 42
behaviorism, xvii
being, values drawn from, 268
being at choice, 294–95, 298–99
being needs, deficit needs *vs.*, xix
Belf, T., 225, 298
beliefs
    disputing, 336–38
    ladder of inference activity and, 101–5, *103*
    matrix, *345*
belly breathing, 186, 190
Berg, I. K., xx
Berger, J. G., 93, 94
Berrigan, F., 350
Berrigan, K., 350
Berrigan, P., 350
bias, 102, 104–5
"Big Five." *see* listening for the "Big Five"
big requests, making, 160–62
Blink (Gladwell), 65
Block, P., 294, 300
body, moods, emotions, and, 342–43
body language, listening to and, 5
body-mind state, habitual, 179
body scan, 181–82, 185, 190, 197
Bohm, D., 19, 135
Boroson, M., 110

Borysenko, J., 281, 338
boundaries
    definition of, 298–99
    exercises on, 302–6
    freedom and, 301, 311
    personal issues with, discovering, 49
    reworking, 311
    safety and protection with, 299
    tight, keeping, 300–301, 305–6
Brackett, M., 369
Braham, B., 112, 225
brainstorming, 147
breakdowns, renegotiations and, 292
breathing exercises and techniques, 197, 344–45
Brehony, K. A., 115
Brief Coaching for Lasting Solutions (Szabó & Berg),
    xx
"Broaden and Build" theory of positivity, 199, 200
Brock, V., xv
Brown, S., 295
Budd, M., 331
Buffett, W., 282
burnout (or rust out), 118

C
CAC. *see* Center for Action and Contemplation (CAC)
Caillet, A., 183
Cameron, J., 129
Cardinal Suenens, L. J., 229
Casals, P., 175, 176
Cashman, K., 362
catalyst stage, 108–10
"centered presence" exercise, 188–89
Center for Action and Contemplation (CAC),
    110–11
Center for Credentialing and Education, 373
centering, 186–90
challenge(s)
    common ways to make, 151–52
    definition of, 145
    meeting, stretching clients to, 150–51
change
    choice-driven, 63
    deep, life purpose work and, 221–22
    emotions of, 231
    Ken Wilber's Four Quadrants of, 81–85, *82*
    see also developmental change process, coach-
        ing as
change theory, xviii
Change Your Questions, Change Your Life (Adams),
    65
*Changing on the Job: Developing Leaders for a Com-
    plex World* (Berger), 94
Childre, D., 317
choice(s)
    conversation for, 19–20
    creating alternative actions and, 170, 173–74

exercising your power of, 294
identifying, 27
obligations *vs.,* 320–21
small, big results and, 290
Chopra, D., 321
Christian mysticism, 111
cingulate gyrus, 195
Clean Language questioning model, 66
Clean Space, 66
clearing form of conversation, 134–35
client preparation, coach/client partnership and, 56
clients
    assessing developmental stage of, 93–95
    building long-term capacity of, 79
    contracting with, 170, 171
    see also empowering the client; momentum with
      the client, creating; stretching the client
closing the gap worksheet, *240*
closure, solid, 59
clutter, eliminating, 284
CNBC, xiv
coaches
    certified, around the globe, xiv
    different styles of, 145
    forwarding the action, 165–66
    "in the inquiry," 65
    learner mind-set of, 65
    questions for reflection, 113
    referring to therapists, xxvii
    specialized, xxvii
    as truth tellers, 24
    when empowering skills are used by, 129–30
    see also listening as a coach
coaching
    authenticity in, 58
    cross-cultural, 84
    definition of, xiii, 1
    differences between positive psychology and,
      xxiv–xxvi
    eclectic approach in, 79
    educating clients about, 53
    emotions, rise of positive psychology, and,
      193–98
    emotions in, 198–204, 369–72
    evolving profession of, xiii, xiv
    the expansion of consciousness, 114
    future of, xxvi–xxviii
    grief, 371
    holistic view of, 176
    inter-developmental aspect of, 41, 208
    Ken Wilber's Four Quadrants and, 81–85, *82*
    to the large life, goals and, 43
    learning and, 88–89, 165
    masterful, 128, 150
    need for, xiii
    as a possibilities *vs.* guarantees conversation, 327
    post-pandemic global stress and, 367

    professional distinctions between therapy, consult-
      ing, mentoring, and, *42*
    shadow, 144
    somatic, 175
    by telephone, 31, 35, 37, 58
    therapists transitioning to, 121–23
    transformational, 371
    transformational *vs.* transactional, xviii
    unique paradigm of, xv
    virtual, 368
    what listening is not in, 16
    see also language of coaching; life coaching
coaching alliances
    breakdown in, signs of, 43–44
    co-creation of, 40–41
    designing, 44, 46
    renegotiating, 43–44
    therapeutic relationship alliances *vs.,* 40–41
coaching competencies, importance of, 373
coaching continuum, 145–50
    add your input to clients' lists of possibilities, 147
    ask clients to generate a few new possibilities, 146
    ask clients to generate many possibilities, 146
    give advice or give the answer, 150
    listen fully and affirm, 145–46
    listen fully and feed back the problem, 146
    offer an option, 149
    present at least 10 possibilities, 147–48
    present at least three possibilities, 148–49
    teach a new technique, 149
coaching conversations, 137
    beginning, middle, and end in, 18, 19
    preparing sacred space for, 35
    special quality of, 19
    three levels in, 19–20
    transcript of a coaching session, 28–39
    utilizing metaphors in, 69–71
    whole-person approach to, 19
coaching conversations, flow of, 20–28
    coaching model and, 22–27
    fulfillment goals and, 21
    learning goals and, 21
    performance goals and, 20–21
Coaching Mandala, 229. *see also* Life Balance Wheel
coaching model
    basic, 18–20
    honest feedback and observation (step 3), 24–25
    listen and clarify (step 2), 23–24
    request purposeful action (step 5), 26–28
    return to focused listening (step 4), 25
    the situation and the desire (step 1), 22–23
coaching session preparation worksheet, 55, 56
Coach the Person, not the Problem (Reynolds), 16
coach to the gap, 23, 144
cocooning phase, in Hudson's cycle of renewal, *117,*
    118–19
codes of ethics, therapeutic alliances and, 40

cognitive–behavioral psychology, xvi
Columbo series, 63
commitment, examining, 27
compassion, universal, 111
compassionate edge, using, 163–64
Compassionate Love Scale, xxiii, 204
compassion exercise, 353–54
competencies of coaching, 38–39
    creating awareness through evocative questions and
        inquiry, 39
    curiosity, 38
    presence, 38
    silence, 39
complimenting, acknowledging and endorsing *vs.*,
    139
confidence, 130
conflict styles, diplomat stage and, 93
Congleton, C., 202
consistency, in coaching relationship, 55
constructive development, techniques for fostering,
    114
consulting, professional distinctions between therapy,
    mentoring, coaching, and, *42*
contact, effective, 180
contemplation stage, in Prochaska's six stages, 76
contemplative prayer, 110
contracting with clients, forwarding action within
    coaching sessions and, 170, 171
contradictions, identifying and naming, 162–63
conversation for exploration and discovery, 47–54
    ask "ouch" questions, 49–50
    clarify issues, 54
    coach's goal during, 48
    create awareness, 52–53
    discover personal boundary issues, 49
    discover what is working, 53
    discuss mutual commitment, 50–51
    educate about coaching, 53
    focus client's attention on values, 51–52
    get to important issues, 49
    get to the financials, 51
    make a declaration, 53–54
    make an offer, 54
    plant the seed of self-care, 50
    powerful questions for, 56–57
    process check, 52
    reassessing outcome of, 48
    start with an ice breaker, 49
    testing, 52
conversations, six types of, 131–37
    clearing, 134–35
    coaching conversation, 137
    debriefing, 133–34
    discussion and debate, 135–36
    sharing, 132–33
    teaching, 136
Cook-Greuter, S., 88, 89, 112

Cooper, C., 279
Core Competencies, of the International Coaching
    Federation, xxvi, 38
core values
    aligning life and work goals with, exercises for,
        272–73
    definition of, 266
    exercises for identifying, 268–70
    exploring, case example, 271
    identifying, 267–68
    personal standards and, 288
countertransference, 9
courageous conversations, 287, 292, 306
Courcy, C., 202
Covey, S. R., 225, 307
COVID-19 pandemic, virtual coaching and, 368
Cox, E., 369, 370
creating, values drawn from, 268
Crook, C., 104
cross-cultural coaching, 84
*Crucial Conversations: Tools for Talking When the
    Stakes Are High* (Patterson), 195, 198
Csikszentmihalyi, M., xxii, xxiii, 200n17, 216
cultural conditioning, diplomat stage and, 92
curiosity, 38
Cycle of Renewal, 232
Cycle of the Promise, 292

D
Dalai Lama, 214, 219, 295
David, S., 202, 369
Dead Poets Society (film), 141, 143
debriefing, 133–34
defensive mechanisms, 178
deficit needs, being needs *vs.*, xix
de Mello, A., 359, 360
depression, in teenagers, 334
Descartes, R., 175
de Shazer, S., xx, 62
design, definitions for, 228
Desktop Yoga, 146
developmental change process, coaching as, 72–123
    case study: George the chiropractor, 73–75
    importance of adult development, 113–19
    ladder of inference activity, 101–5, *103*
    levels of development of the adult consciousness,
        85–91
    making the shift, 119–23
    post-conventional adult development, 108–11
    preparing for a meeting exercise, 106–8
    Prochaska's six stages, 75–78
    reflective questions for clients based on the ladder
        of inference, 108
    three conventional stages of development, 91–101
    transitioning stages: George the chiropractor,
        112–13
    views on human life and change, 78–81

Wilber's Four Quadrants of change, 81–85, *82*
dialogue, discussion *vs.*, 135
Diener, E., xxiii
diplomat or conformist stage, 91–95, 113
directive actions, 148
DISC assessment, 42, 97
discernment, Big Five and importance of, 26
discussion and debate, 135–36
disease model, moving beyond, 250
disidentification journal exercise, 303
distinctions, using, 152–54
distractions strategy, 197
doldrums phase, in Hudson's cycle of renewal, *117,*
    117–18
Dossey, L., 350
Drucker, P., 326
Dweck, C., 370

E
eclectic approach, in coaching, 79
Edmondson, A., 371
egocentric self, 90–91
Eight Flows Practice, 191
Einstein, A., 80
Ellis, A., 336
Ellis, D., 16, 19, 23, 131, 232
embodied life, living, 177–81
Emergent Knowledge, 66
Emotional Agility (David), 369
emotional agility, developing, 202–4
"Emotional Agility" (David & Congleton), 202
emotional audit, 198, 203
emotional charges, probing questions for, *97*
Emotional Competence Inventory, 279
emotional intelligence, 194, 250, 336, 369, 371
Emotional Intelligence (Goleman), 316
emotional inventory, using, 198
Emotional Quotient Inventory (EQ-I), 336
emotions
    of change, 231
    coaching, rise of positive psychology, and, 193–98
    in coaching, 198–204, 369–72
    information communicated by, 37
    moods, the body, and, 342–43
    negative, 200
    positive, 199, 200, 201, 203
    root word for, 193
    shifting patterns of, 202
empathic listening, xviii
empathy, 113, 114, 145
empowering the client, 127–44
    case of the dentist seeking career change, 131, 133,
        134, 135, 136, 137, 142
    selecting the right type of conversation and the right
        skills for, 130–44
    when do coaches use empowering skills?, 129–30
empowering the client, seven skills for, 137–44

acknowledging and endorsing, 138–39
focusing on strengths, 137–38
meta-view or perspective taking, 141–43
never make the client wrong, 143–44
possibility thinking, 144
reframing, 140–41
standing for, 139–40
Energy, listening for, 10, 15
energy drainers, 242–48
    big or chronic complaints--life's sufferings, 243
    clutter, 284
    definition of, 59
    eliminating or reducing, 58
    little annoyances--life's gnats, 242, 244–48
    working with, 59–61
Energy Drainer Worksheet, *247–48*
Energy Gainers, 248
Enneagram, 42, 111, 333
enrollment conversation, 47
Enron scandal, 279, 280
Erhard, W., xx, 285
Erhard Seminars Training (est), xx
Erickson, M., xix, xxi, 63, 226
European Mentoring and Coaching Council, 373
events, mediated responses to, 326
evidence-based best practices, in health care, 287
evocative questions, 38, 39
Evolving Self, The (Kegan), 90
excellence, sustaining, 166
expansion of consciousness, coaching, 114
expectations, 54, 57
experiencing, values drawn from, 268
expert level, self-determination and, 113
experts, coaching, 96, 97
eye contact, 180, 190

F
facts, stories *vs.*, 22
Falk, P., 63
family therapy, xix
Family Therapy Networker, The, 79
fear
    replacing with love and trust, 346–47
    trust *vs., 345,* 345–46
feedback, in coaching conversation, 24–25
fees, conversation about, 51
fieldwork, focusing on "right action" through, 166–
    70
Fifth Discipline, The (Senge), 101
fight-or-flight-or-freeze response, 20, 178
figure, in Gestalt psychology, 79
figure-ground of the situation, working with, 68
Finding Your Purpose (Braham), 225
FIRO-B psychometric instrument, 348
first coaching conversation, 39–54
    initial contact call, 45–46
    living brochure and, 46–54

first coaching conversation (*continued*)
  therapeutic relationship alliances *vs.* coaching alliances and, 40–45
  welcome packet and, 41
first coaching session
  beginning work on client's goals, 58
  clarifying expectations in, 57
  coaching the client's being and life, 58
  discovering intentions and desires in, 58
  model how it is to be an authentic human being, 58
  time needed for, 57
first contacts with clients, varieties of, 44–45
first paying session, coach's intention for, 55
first-person perspective, 328
first sessions, powerful questions for, 56–57
"Five Rings of Nonverbal Movement," 191–92
"Five Types of Affirmations for Empowerment" (Marshall), 339
fixed mindset, 370
Flaherty, J., 79, 170
Flores, F., xx, 18, 160, 292, 331
flow state, 173, 216
focused listening, in coaching conversation, 25
force, power *vs.,* 128
forgiveness, power of, 356–59
"form of mind," probes or questions and, 94–95
Fortgang, L. B., 308
42 (film), 127
forwarding action within coaching sessions, skills for, 170–74
  accountability, 170–71
  acting "as if," 170, 172
  contracting with clients, 170, 171–72
  creating alternative actions and choices, 170, 173–74
  stepping into the future, 170, 172–73
Four Horsemen, working with, 198–99
Fowler, R. D., xxi
Fox, T., 212
Francis, Pope, 111
Frankl, V., xix, 334
Fredrickson, B., xxiii, xxiv, 199, 200, 201, 203
Freud, S., xvii, xviii, xxi, 348
"From Purpose to Impact" (*Harvard Business Review*), 206
Frost, R., 279
fulfillment, 21, 226–29
  creating more, 242
  definition of, 228
  helpful habits and, 275
  three basic findings on achieving, xxiii, 211n20
  value-based life and, 264
  values, life purpose, and, 228–29, 240
full-circle feedback assessments, 75
fun, 28–38, 36

G
Gallwey, T., 19
Gandhi, Mahatma, 200, 276
gap, identifying, 236, 239
Gawain, S., 129
General Happiness Scale, xxiii, 203
generational mind-sets, 84
Generation X, mind-sets or worldviews of, 84
George the chiropractor
  adult development stages, 86–87, 89
  case study and discussion questions, 73–75
  Ken Wilber's Four Quadrant model and, 81–85, *82, 332–34, 333, 342–43*
  midlife changes and, 115–19, *117*
  mind-set transformational shift, 330, 331
  transitioning stages for, 112–13
Georgetown Leadership Coaching Program, 183
Gestalt Institute of Cleveland, Gestalt Body Work at, 177n9
Gestalt therapy, xviii
getting ready phase, in Hudson's cycle of renewal, *117,* 119
Gilligan, C., xx, xxi
Gladwell, M., 65
gnats, 258
  counting the cost of, 244
  eliminating, 244–45
  identifying, 244
  setting a termination date for, 246
goals
  aligning with core values, exercises for, 272–73
  beginning work on, 58
  coaching to the large life and, 43
  creating momentum toward, 28
  fulfillment, 21
  in immunity to change map, 115
  initial contact call and, 45–46
  learning, 21
  performance, 20–21
"go for it" phase, in Hudson's cycle of renewal, 116–17, *117*
Goleman, D., 193, 195, 202, 316, 336
Good Morning America, xiv
Gottmann, J., 199
Grant, A., 367
gratitude, 192, 201, 203, 245, 347, 352
gratitude journal, 203
Graves, C., 87
grief (or trauma-informed) coaching, 371
Griffith-Haney, M., 279
Grinder, J., xix
Grit Survey, xxiii, 204
Grof, S., xviii
Grove, D., 66, 67
growth, lateral or horizontal, 89

growth mindset, 370, 371
Gustin, M., 360
"gut feeling," 8, 180

H
habits
  aligning values with actions and, 262–67
  changing, time frame for, 120
  helpful, 275
  mind-set and, 326, 329
  new, practices for creating, 167
Habits and Behaviors, listening for, 10, 14–15
hallucinogens, xviii
Halpern, B. L., 179n10, 190
Handbook of Positive Psychology (Snyder & Lopez),
  xxiv
happiness assessments, 203
Hargrove, R., 128
Harvard Business Review, 202, 206
"heart brain," 8
Heart Breathing, 192–93
HeartMath Institute, 192, 193, 317
Heller, S., 177n9, 178, 188, 190, 191, 192, 192n13
Helping People Change (Boyatzis), 19
Hibino, S., 226
hierarchy of needs (Maslow), xix, *249,* 249–50,
  251–52, 313
Hill, N., 272
hippocampus, 195
Hirshberg, J., 62
hoarding, saving *vs.,* 321
Hoffer, E., 208
Homo Mechanicus, xvii
hope, 201, 203
Horney, K., xviii
Hudson, F. M., 115, 116, 118, 225
Human Being (Ellis & Lankowitz), 220, 290, 323
human development, as a never-ending quest, 87
humanistic psychology, xvi, xvii, xix
Humbert, P., 59
hypnosis, 227
hypothalamus, 195

I
ice breaker, starting with, 49
ICF. *see* International Coaching Federation (ICF)
"I Have a Dream" speech (King, Jr.), 172
"I" interior domain (Quadrant 1), in Ken Wilber's
  Four Quadrants, 81–82, *82*
ILCT. *see* Institute for Life Coach Training (ILCT)
Immunity to Change (Kegan & Lahey), 115
immunity to change map, 115, 115n6, *116*
important issues, getting to, 49
impulsive or opportunist stage, 90
incompletions, addressing, 286
inconsistencies, identifying and naming, 162–63

independent self or expert/technician stage, 95–97
"Influence Coming into Play, The: The Seven of Pentacles" (Piercy), 158
informational learning, 89
initial contact call, purposes of and recommended
  length of, 45–46
Inner Balance program (HeartMath Institute), 193
inner critic, 129
inner directedness, 252
Inner Love, coaches and awareness of, 363–65
In Over Our Heads (Kegan), 90
inquiry, 144, 145
  creating awareness through, 39
  Socratic, 64
  as special kind of provocative question, 64–65
  two main purposes of, 64–65
"inside out" concept, uniqueness of, 205
insight, 25, 47, 129
  choice-driven change and, 63
  coaching conversation and, 61
  generating, questions for, 64
  learning and, 165
  metaphors and, 70–71
  provocative questions and, 62
inspiration, 201, 203
Institute for Life Coach Training (ILCT), xiv, xv, xviii,
  39, 40, 81, 120, 207, 209, 220, 230, 336, 368
Institute of Professional Coaching (Harvard University), 113
integrity. *see* personal integrity
Intention and Attention, listening for, 10–12, 137
inter-developmental aspect of coaching, 41, 208
interest, 201, 203
inter-individual stage, 108–10
International Association of Coaching, 373
International Coaching Federation (ICF), 373
  coaching as defined by, 1
  coach referral location, 49
  Core Competencies of, xxvi, 38
  founding of, xiv
intervention, definitions of, xxv
introspection, whole person approach to coaching
  and, xvi
intuition, 8, 179–80
"Invitation, The" (Mountain Dreamer), 227, 228
"it" behavioral domain (Quadrant 2), in Ken Wilber's
  Four Quadrants, *82,* 82–83
"its" social domain (Quadrant 4), in Ken Wilber's
  Four Quadrants, *82,* 84–85

J
James, W., xvi–xvii
Johnson, B., 76
Johnson, M., 69
Joiner, W., 88, 112
Jones, L. B., 225

journaling, 64, 119, 134, 203, 221, 283–84, 287, 303

joy, 201, 203

judger mind-set, 65

judging mind, working with, 343–44

Jung, C., xviii, xxi, 18, 69, 70, 128, 177, 318

K

Kafka, F., 3, 4

Kegan, R., xx, xxi, 86, 88, 90, 91, 92, 95, 97, 100, 108, 110, 113, 114, 115, 276, 330

Kennedy, J. F., 73, 84

Ketchum, P., 281

Kimsey-House, H., 141

Kimsey-House, K., 141

King, M. L., Jr., 84, 172, 276, 349

Knight, B., 150

"know in order to grow" principle, 165–66

Kohlberg, L., xxi

L

ladder of inference

examining assumptions and beliefs with, 101–5, *103*

preparing for a meeting and, 107

reflective questions for clients based on, 108

Lahey, L., 115

Laing, R. D., 85

Lakoff, G., 69

Landmark Education, xx

language of coaching, 18–71

accountability questions and, 65–66

basic coaching model, 18–20

coaching session transcript, 28–39

first coaching conversations: setting the stage, 39–54

flow of coaching conversations, 20–28

inquiries and, 64–69

metaphors and, 69–71

powerful and evocative questions, 61, 62–64

purposeful inquiry and, 61, 63

staying close to the client's language, 66–69

transparent language, 61

using structures, 55–64

lateral or horizontal growth, 89

law of attraction, 315–16

Leadership Agility (Joiner & Josephs), 88

"Leadership Agility" workshops (Joiner), 112

Leadership and Self-Deception (Arbinger Institute), 44

Leadership from the Inside Out (Cashman), 205, 362

leadership log, 99

Leadership Presence (Halpern & Lubar), 179n10, 190

leadership presence, description of, 190

leadership timeline, 96, 99–100

Leaning Tower of Pisa, integrity of, 280, 281

learner mind-set, 65

learning, 129, 135

in adulthood, two kinds of, 89

coaching and, 88–89, 165

goals, 21

Seligman's research on, 334–36

unconscious blocks to, 208–10

Leary, T., xviii

Lennon, J., 349

Leonard, G., 10n1

Leonard, T., xx, 253–54

Less Is More: The Art of Clean Language (Grove), 66

Levinson, D., xx

Levoy, G., 212

Lewin, K., xviii

Life Balance Wheel, 42, 100, 142, 206, 229, 233, 298

contemporary, using with clients, 232–36

fun in area on, 28, 36

instructions for the client, 229–33

money and, 324–25

"life chapters," midlife changes and, 115–19, *117*

life coaching

all coaching as, xiii

as an operating system, xiii–xv, 1–2

as applied positive psychology, xx

love at heart of, 363–65

popularity and prevalence of, xiv

positive psychology's influence on, xxi–xxiv

powerful questioning and, 23

psychology's contributions to, xvi

psychology's major theorists and, xvi–xxi

roots of, xv–xxvi

whole-person, client-centered approach to, xiii–xiv, 12

see also coaching

life design exercises, 229

life design process

are you thriving or surviving?, 233–36

closing the gap worksheet, *240*

conscious choices in, 228

frequently asked questions about, 240–41

sample exercise, 235, *237*

worksheet, *238–39*

life design work, as trance-formational, 226–27

Life Launch (Hudson & McLean), 225

life purpose, 212–25

being purpose-full, working with, 219–20

as a calling, 213, 215, 219

clients' visions as context for, 214–15

deep change and working on, 221–22

definition of, 213

discovering, 211

examining past experiences relative to, 215–19

knowing, importance of, 214

quotations relevant to issue of, 213

resources on, 225

using as a guide, 224

using with clients, 221

life purpose work, example of, 222–24
life span developmental psychology, xx
limbic storm, weathering, 195–98
limbic system, 195
Lincoln, A., 357, 358
Linley, A., xxvi
listening, xviii, 5, 145–46, 152. *see also* listening as a coach
listening and clarifying, in coaching conversation, 23–24
listening as a coach, 3–17
  clarifying the client's desires and, 17
  intentional focus of, 3
  lapses in, forms of, 3–4
  listening for (level two listening), 4, 5–7
  listening for the "Big Five" template, 10–15
  listening to (level one listening), 4, 5
  listening with (level three listening), 4, 8–9
  what listening is not, 16
listening for a solution, as a block to coaching process, 6–7
listening for the "Big Five," 10–15, 26
  Energy, 10, 15
  Habits and Behaviors, 10, 14–15
  Intention and Attention, 10–12, 137
  Mind-set, 10, 12–13
  Skills and Capabilities, 10, 13–14
"listening for the large life," 5
listening templates, 10
living brochure, 46–47
living from a deep place, 211–12, 221–22
Loevinger, J., 88
logotherapy, xix
loose ends
  impact of, 285–86
  tying up, 284–85
love, 201, 203
  choosing to, 352–56
  for the coach, reflections on, 360–65
  connectedness and, 348–49
  expressions of, 349–51
  for ourselves, 351–52
  replacing fear with, 346–47
Love 2.0 (Fredrickson), 203
Loving Kindness Meditation, 203
Lowry, S., 47, 48
loyalty, diplomat stage and, 91, 92
LSD, xviii
Lubar, K., 179n10, 190
Lyubomirsky, S., xxiii

M
magician stage of development, 111
maintenance stage, in Prochaska's six stages, 77–78
mammillary bodies, 195
Man and His Symbols (Jung), 69
Mandela, N., 111

Man's Search for Meaning (Frankl), xix
MAP. *see* Maturity Assessment Profile (MAP)
Marshall, J., 339
masking, 198–99
Maslow, A., xvii, xix, 18, 249, 250, 251, 252, 260, 313
masterful coaching, 128, 150
Masterful Health and Wellness Coaching (Arloski), 4
mastermind groups, 272
mastery, therapist-client relationship and, xxvi
Maturity Assessment Profile (MAP), 93, 112
McCartney, P., 349
McIntyre, R., 357, 358
McLean, P. D., 118, 225
Meaning in Life Questionnaire, xxiii, 204
meaning-making capacities, development of, 86
meditation, 110, 119, 203, 221, 317, 363
Meditations (Gawain), 129
meeting preparation, exercise for coaches, 106–8
Meinke, L., xxvi, 195n15
mental models
  challenging biases and, 104–5
  stereotypes and, 104n5
  uncovering, 102
  updating, 104
mentoring, professional distinctions between therapy, consulting, coaching, and, *42*
metaphors
  in coaching conversations, use of, 69–71
  in corporate coaching, 157
  effective, requirements for, 157
  of a game, 156
  of a garden, 155, 158
  generating, questions for, 158–59
  of a journey, 156, 158
  from students expressing how they learn, 159
  using analogies and, 154–60
Metaphors We Live By (Lakoff & Johnson), 69
meta-view (or perspective taking), 141–43
"me too" listening, avoiding, 8
Midler, B., 297
midlife changes, phases in
  cocooning (Phase 3), *117,* 118–19
  doldrums (Phase 2), *117,* 117–18
  getting ready (Phase 4), *117,* 119
  go for it (Phase 1), 116–17, *117*
  mini transition, 118
midlife crisis, 118
mind–body connection, bringing new awareness to, 180–81
mindfulness, 228
mind-heart alignment, 192–93
Mindset, listening for, 10, 12–13
mind-set(s)
  abundance and, 314
  affirmations and, 338–42
  causative nature of, 327

mind-set(s) (*continued*)
   changing, 327–28
   definition of, 326
   generational, 84
   how it is sourced, 329–32
   judger, 65
   learner, 65
   self-care and, 331–32
   work with, coaching methods for, 336–47
mini transition, 118
Miracle Question, 62, 63, 80
mirroring, 5, 152
mission, life purpose and, 219
momentum with the client, creating, 165–74
   focusing on "right action" through fieldwork and, 166–70
   "know in order to grow" principle and, 165–66
   skills for forwarding action within coaching sessions, 170–74
   for stressed attorney, 167–70
   three factors essential to, 167
money
   early beliefs about, 322–23
   health habits about, 322
   Life Balance Wheel and, 324–25
   matching values and, 324
   meaning of, 321–22
   in reserve, 312–13
   shifting beliefs about, 315
   taking a first step about, 323–24
moods, emotions, the body, and, 342–43
Moore, M., 19
Mother Teresa, 349
motivation, 128, 130
Mountain Dreamer, O., 227
multitasking, achievers and, 98
Murray, S., xxiii
mutual commitment, discussing, 50–51
Myers-Briggs Type Indicator, 42, 97
My Grandfather's Blessings (Remen), 363

N
Nadler, G., 226
naming, power of, 153
narrative therapy, 18
National Longitudinal Study of Adolescent to Adult Health, 349
needs
   acknowledging, 253, 254–56
   case study of, 259–60
   choices and possibilities driven by, 253
   coaching view of, 250–59
   four major categories of, 256
   fulfilling, as critical to clients, 260
   how they are met, analyzing, 257–58
   identifying, 248–49, 255, 256, 260–61
   listing top 10 for you, 257
   making friends with, 253, 254
   Maslow's hierarchy: a classic view of, *249,* 249–50
   meeting, in satisfying and healthy ways, 258–59
   situational, 252–53
   unmet, 255
   values aligned with, 261, 264, 266
negative emotions, 200
Nelson, P., 326
neuro-linguistic programming (NLP), xix, 227, 328
neuropsychology, coaching profession and, 195n15
Newcomb, D., 177n9
Newfield Network, 177n9
NLP. *see* neuro-linguistic programming (NLP)
"no"
   good boundaries and, 299
   New York-style, how to say, 309–10
   saying gracefully, 306–11
   tight boundaries and, 300–301
nonbinding agreements, 54
nonverbal coaching goals, 180–81

O
obligations, choices *vs.,* 320–21
O'Brien, M., 7, 246
observation, in coaching conversation, 24–25
observing, Wilber's Four Quadrant model used for, 332–34, *333*
   "I" interior domain (Quadrant 1), 332, 333, *333*
   "it" behavioral domain (Quadrant 2), *333*
   "its" social domain (Quadrant 3), *333*
   "we" cultural domain (Quadrant 4), 332, *333*
observing self, 328–29, 330
offers, making, 54
O'Hanlon, B., xix, 22, 226, 338
Oliver, M., 72
One Moment Meditation (Boroson), 110
optimism, learned, 334–36
Optimism Test, xxiii, 204
Ortony, A., 69, 154
"ouch" questions, asking, 49–50
overfocusing, 11

P
Palmer, H., 349, 353
Palmer, W., 177n9, 189
Papez circuit, 195, 196, 197
paradoxes of our time, finding life purpose within, 214
Path, The (Jones), 225
Patterson, K., 195
perceptions, ladder of inference activity and, 103
Perennial Tradition, 111
performance goals, 20–21
Perls, F., xviii, 285
Permission to Feel (Brackett), 369
personal and professional coaching, as powerful and personalized career, xiii–xv

Personal Eco-System, working with energy drainers, 59–61

personal integrity
creating, simple rules for, 281–82
details of daily life and, 290–91
extraction, replacement, and restraints approach to, 280–81
lack of, 278–79
living up to, 279–80
making and keeping promises, 291–93
personal journal questions, 283–84, 287

personal operating program (POP), 275

personal power, claiming, 128

personal reserve, 312–13

personal standards
setting: workable system for, 286–93
values and, 288–90

Personal Support System, environment and, 60

perspective taking, 140, 141–43

pessimism, learned, 334–36

Peterson, C., xxiii

physicians, benevolence as guiding principle for, 264

Piaget, J., xxi

Piercy, M., 158

placater role, in family, xix

play
good boundaries and, 298–99
the story of Rose, 296–97

play at work (plurk), 295–96, 298

Play: How It Shapes the Brain, Opens the Imagination and Invigorates the Soul (Brown), 295

playing full out
exercise for, 302–3
meaning of, 295, 302

"Play Is More than Fun" (TED video), 295

pluralist/strategist stage, of adult development, 108–10, 115

plurking, definition of, 298

Pocketful of Miracles (Borysenko), 338

polarity management model, 76

POP. *see* personal operating program (POP)

positive emotions, 200
developing, 203
power of, xxiv
set point for, 201
studying, 199

positive psychology, xvi, xx, 18, 228
aim of, xxii, xxiv
coaching, emotions, and rise of, 193–98
differences between coaching and, xxiv–xxvi
major theorists in, xvi–xxi
three pillars of, xxiii

positivity, 201–2

Positivity (Fredrickson), 201, 203

Positivity Self Test, 203

possibility thinking, 144

post-conventional adult development, 108–11
inter-individual, catalyst, pluralist/strategist, 108–10
meditation and, 110
the sacred self and the magician, 110–11
self-transformation and, 113

post-pandemic global stress, coaching and, 367

power, force *vs.*, 128

powerful questions, 23, 56, 57, 61, 62–64, 66

Power of Purpose, The (Leider), 225

practices, building, 169–70

prayer, 317

pre-contemplation stage, in Prochaska's six stages, 75–76

preparation stage, in Prochaska's six stages, 76–77

preparing for coaching sessions, 58–59

presence, as coaching skill, 38

Presence-Based Coaching, 185–86

Presence-Based Coaching (Silsbee), 185

present in the moment, learning to be, 4

PRES model of presence, 179n10

pride, 201, 203

Primal Leadership (Goleman), 194, 316

priorities, based on values, 309

probing questions
for emotional charges, 97
"form of mind" and, 94–95

process checks, 52

Prochaska, J., 74

Prochaska's six stages, 75–78
action (stage 4), 77
contemplation (stage 2), 76
maintenance (stage 5), 77–78
pre-contemplation (stage 1), 75–76
preparation (stage 3), 76–77
termination (stage 6), 78

Proctor, B., 316

professional coaching, 1

promises, making and keeping, 291–93

provocative questions, 62. *see also* inquiry

psychoanalysis, xvii

psychological safety, 371–72

psychology
coaching and contributions from, xvi
definition of, xvi

psychosynthesis, xviii

purpose-driven leadership, 206

Purpose-Driven Life, The (Warren), 213, 225

purposeful action, requesting, 26–28

purposeful inquiry, 61, 63

purposeful pausing, 39

Purpose of Your Life, The (Adrienne), 225

purpose statements, creating, 216–19

purpose to impact plan, setting, 206

Q
questions, purposes of, in coaching, 63
Quinn, R. E., 222

R

rapid body scan, 185

rational-emotive behavioral therapy (REBT), ABC framework, 336–37

re-creation, as touchstone in coaching session, 34, 38

Reese, P. W., 127

referrals, 48, 50

reflection, 99, 101–5, *103*

reframing, xix, 140–41, 149

Remen, R. N., 363

reminding strategy, 197–98

repeated words strategy, 197

requests. big, 160–62

rescuer role. in family, xix

reserve

    examining, 319–20

    of time, creating, 320

resilience. positivity and, 200

resistance to learning, recognizing, 209–10

results-oriented actions, 167, 168

Retooling on the Run (Heller & Surrenda), 188, 191

Reynolds, M., 16

Rickey, B., 127

"right action," focusing on, through fieldwork, 166–70

Rilke, R. M., 64, 86, 211

risk taking, costs and benefits of, 303–4

Robbins, T., xix

Roberts, L., 282

Robinson, J., 127

Rogers, C., xvii, xviii, 3, 18, 143, 145

Rohr, R., 110–11

Roosevelt, E., 229

"Rose, The" (Midler), 297

Rotary International, four-way test of the things we say and do, 282

Ruiz, D. M., 281

RULER system, 369

S

sabbaticals, 119

sacred self stage of development, 110–11

safety, boundaries and, 299

sailboat metaphor, determining the destination and, 11

Sandahl, P., 141

SAT. *see* style, approach, and tone (SAT)

Satir, V., xix

Save Your Inner Tortoise! (Courcy), 202

saving, hoarding *vs.*, 321

schedules, taking charge of, 275

Schroeder, A., 282

Schwarzenegger, A., 246

screening, initial, 45–46

Searle, J., xx, 18

second-person perspective, 328–29

security needs, 255, 256, 260

Self, B., 150

self-acceptance, 202

self-actualization, xix, *249*, 250, 252

self-authorizing mind, 97, 98

self-awareness, 65, 68, 194

self-awareness observations, 167, 168–69

self-care, 50, 331–32

self-coaching, returning to, 44

self-deception, 44

self-disclosure, two purposes of, 8–9

self-esteem, 130, 251, 260

self-esteem movement, 334

self-love, 351–52, 356, 358–59

self-observation, clean language and, 66

self-reflection, 221

    inquiry and, 64

    language of coaching and, 61

    welcome packet and, 55

self-reflective practice, 371

Seligman, M. E. P., xx, xxi, xxii, xxiv, 130, 199, 200n17, 203, 211n20, 334, 335

Senge, P., 101, 102

September 11, 2001 terrorist attacks, rapidly updated mental models and, 104

serenity, 201, 203

7 Habits of Highly Effective People, The (Covey), 225

SFT. *see* solution-focused therapy (SFT)

shadow archetype of our personality, positive aspect of, 128

shadow coaching, 144

shadow self, 177

shadow work, 34, 38

Shakespeare, W., xvii

sharing, 132–33

Sholl, J., 115

Shoney's, 282

Siegel, D., 179

signature strengths, knowing and using, 130

silence, 35, 39

    in context of the coaching moment, 25

    as the "fertile void," 58

    three common forms of, 198–99

silent retreats, 64, 119

Silsbee, D., 185, 188, 188n11

Simply Live It Up (Belf & Ward), 225

situation and desire, in coaching conversation, 22–23

Six Simple Resilience Practices, 186

Skills and Capabilities, listening for, 10, 13–14

Skinner, B. F., xvii

small talk, 43

Snowball, The: Warren Buffet and the Business of Life (Schroeder), 282

Socrates, xv, 64

Socratic method, xxv, 135

SOI. *see* Subject Object Interview (SOI)

solution-focused coaching, awareness-based coaching *vs.,* 16
solution-focused therapy (SFT), 80
somatic coaching, 175
Sopranos, The (television series), 91n2
soulful listening, 145–46
Sourcebook of Coaching History (Brock), xv
Spiral Dynamics, 87
sports psychology, 10n1
Spring, J. A., 356, 357
standards, defining and setting, 286–87
standing for clients, 139–40, 145
stepping into the future, forwarding action within coaching sessions and, 170, 172–73
stereotypes, mental models and, 104n5
stories, facts *vs.,* 22
strategic thinking, 62
strengths, focusing on, 137–38
stressed attorney
    accountability for, 171
    acting "as if" with, 172
    coaching, 167–70
    contracting with, 171
    creating alternative actions and choices with, 174
    practices for, 169–70
    self-awareness observations for, 168–69
    stepping into the future with, 173
stretching the client, 145–64
    choosing many ways to challenge clients, 151–52
    coaching the continuum and, 145–50
    compassionate edge and, 163–64
    identifying/naming contradictions and inconsistencies, 162–63
    making big requests, 160–62
    to meet challenges, 150–51
    metaphors and analogies for, 154–60
    using distinctions and, 152–54
Strozzi-Heckler, R., 175n7, 177n9, 179, 181
style, approach, and tone (SAT), 44
Subject Object Interview (SOI), 93
subject-object theory, 113
sufferings, 243, 258
    counting the cost of, 244
    eliminating, 244–45
    identifying, 244
    setting a termination date for, 246
Surrenda, D., 188
synchronicity, 318
synergistic partnership, building, 48
systems thinking, achievers in tune with, 109
Szabó, P., xx

T
Taming Your Gremlin (Carlson), 143
Tandy Corp, 282
teaching, 136, 149

telephone, coaching by, 31, 35, 37, 58, 176
termination stage, in Prochaska's six stages, 78
Terry, R., 9
thalamus, 195
therapeutic relationship alliances, coaching alliances *vs.,* 40–41
Therapist as Life Coach (Williams & Davis), 55, 229
therapist-client relationship, mastery and, xxvi
therapists
    referring to coaches, xxvii
    transitioning to coaching, 121–23
therapy, professional distinctions between mentoring, consulting, coaching, and, *42*
Think and Grow Rich (Hill), 272
Thinking Path, 183–85, 198
third-person perspective, 328
Thomas, L., 301
Thoreau, H. D., 314
360-degree feedback assessments, 75, 88, 99, 279
time, reserve of, 320
time-competence, 252
time management, 14
Titchener, E., xvi
Today show, xiv
tolerations, 60
Tolle, E., 228
Toltec practices for personal integrity, 281
top-of-mind awareness (TOMA), 15
Torbert, W., 88, 94, 112
Total Life Coaching (Williams & Thomas), 301
transactional coaching, transformational coaching *vs.,* xviii
transcendence, in Maslow's hierarchy of needs, 249, *249,* 250
transcript of a coaching session, 28–38
    comments on, 35–38
    evocative questions in, 35
transference, 9
transformational coaching, 371
    essence of, 79
    transactional coaching *vs.,* xviii
transformational learning, 89
transparency, self-disclosure and, 9
transparent language, 61, 67–68
transparent questions, 66
transpersonal psychology, xvii–xviii, xix
treatment protocols, therapeutic alliance and, 40
True Believer (Hoffer), 208
trust
    conversation for, 20
    fear *vs., 345,* 345–46
    replacing fear with, 346–47
Tuesdays with Morrie (Albom), 295
Turning to One Another (Wheatley), 18
Twain, M., 295

U
unconditional positive regard, 143
unconscious mind, metaphors and, 69–70
Underhill, xxi
Unitive consciousness, 111
universal compassion, 111

V
Vaillant, G., xxiii
value(s)
    aligning with actions and habits, 262–67
    chosen, 263
    clarity about, 265
    compass points and function of, 262
    core, definition of, 263
    core, identifying, 266–70
    creating, 47
    definition of, 262
    driven by pleasure vs. pain, 274–75
    focusing client's attention on, 51–52
    great coaching and working with, 264–65
    knowing and articulating, 267
    living your own, exercises for, 270–71
    matching money and, 324
    needs and, 261
    new, developing, 276–77
    new opportunities for living from, 271–72
    personal standards and, 288–90
    priorities based on, 309
    superficial shoulds and, 263
Values in Action (VIA) Survey of Character Strengths, xxiii, 204
Varieties of Religious Experience, The (James), xvii
venting, 134
vertical or transformational learning, 89
victimology, 334–35
victim role, in family, xix
video conferencing, 176
virtual coaching, 368
vision, 214–15, 220
visualization, as mind-set work, 327
von Braun, W., 315

W
Ward, C., 225, 298
Warren, R., 225
Washburn, M. F., xxi

water bearer story, 358–59
Watkins, S., 279
Watson, J., xvii
"Ways to Know Yourself" (Ellis), 232
wealth
    abundance and, 325
    definition of, 312
    shifting beliefs about, 315
"we" cultural domain (Quadrant 3), in Ken Wilber's Four Quadrants, 82, 83–84
welcome packet, 41, 55–57, 60–61
Wells, S., 62
Wheatley, M. J., 18
Wheel of Life, 231–32
Whitworth, L., 5, 141
whole-person approach to coaching, xvi, 12, 19
Wilber, K., xx, xxi
Wilber, K., Four Quadrants model of, 81–85, 82
    depression in teenagers and disturbance in, 334
    "I" interior domain (Quadrant 1), 81–82, 82
    "it" behavioral domain (Quadrant 2), 82, 82–83
    "its" social domain (Quadrant 4), 82, 84–85
    moods, emotions, the body, and, 342–43
    "we" cultural domain (Quadrant 3), 82, 83–84
"Wild Geese" (Oliver), 72
Williams, R., 141, 143
Williamson, M., 220
Wilson, W., 219
Wind, Y., 104
withdrawing form of silence, 198, 199
work-life balance, achievers and, 99
Work-Life Questionnaire, xxiii, 204
Work Triangle, performance, learning, and satisfaction in, 7, 7
WorldCom, 279
Wundt, W., xvi

Y
Yale Center for Emotional Intelligence, 369
"yes"
    graceful "no" vs., 306
    groundedness and, 300
yoga, 110
You Were Born Rich (Proctor), 316

Z
Zeig, J., xix